RALPH T. FISHER JR.

for rev. ly 1 Dec 90

in Nationalities Papers

WITHDRAWN
University of
Illinois Library
at Urbana-Champaign

NATIONALITIES PAPERS
Monograph Series "Studies in Issues" No 6

Editor: *Henry R. Huttenbach*

Soviet Nationality Policies

Ruling Ethnic Groups in the USSR

Edited by Henry R. Huttenbach

MANSELL

First published 1990 by **Mansell Publishing Limited**
A Cassell imprint
Villiers House, 41/47 Strand, London WC2N 5JE, England
125 East 23rd Street, Suite 300, New York 10010, USA

© The Association for the Study of the Nationalities (USSR and East Europe) Incorporated 1990

All rights reserved. No part of this publication may be reproduced or transmitted in any form or by any means, electronic or mechanical including photocopying, recording or any information storage or retrieval system, without prior permission in writing from the publishers.

British Library Cataloguing in Publication Data
Soviet nationality policies: ruling ethnic groups in the
  USSR—(Nationalities papers)—(Studies in issues; no. 6).
  1. Soviet Union. Ethnic minorities. Policies of government
  I. Huttenbach, Henry R.   II. Series   III. Series
  323.1'47

ISBN 0-7201-2055-1

Library of Congress Cataloging-in-Publication Data
Soviet nationality policies: ruling ethnic groups in the USSR /
  edited by Henry R. Huttenbach.
       pp.   cm.—(Nationalities papers. Monograph series "Studies in issues"; no. 6)
    ISBN 0-7201-2055-1
    1. Minorities—Soviet Union—Congresses. 2. Soviet Union—Politics and government—1917—Congresses. 3. Nationalism—Soviet Union—Congresses. 4. Soviet Union—Ethnic relations—Congresses.
  I. Huttenbach, Henry R.   II. Series.
  JN6520.M5S654 1990
  323.1'47—dc20   89-29070
                                                                  CIP

Typeset by Colset Pte. Ltd., Singapore
Printed and bound in Great Britain by Biddles Ltd.,
Guildford and King's Lynn.

In memory of my father
And in dedication to my mother
Who showed me to respect all peoples

Contents

ix   List of Contributors

xiii   Foreword   *Edward Allworth*

xv   Preface   *Henry R. Huttenbach*

1   1. Introduction: Towards a Unitary Soviet State: Managing a Multinational Society, 1917–1985   *Henry R. Huttenbach*

9   **Part I: Determining the Character of Soviet Nationality Policy**

9   2. Leninist Nationality Policy: Its Source and Style   *Gregory Gleason*

24   3. A Theory of Soviet Nationality Policies   *Edward Allworth*

47   4. Codification of Soviet Nationality Policies   *John N. Hazard*

62   5. Searching for Soviet Nationalities Policy   *Michael Rywkin*

73   **Part II: Striving for a *Homo sovieticus***

73   6. Making Soviet Citizens: Patriotic and Internationalist Education in the Formation of a Soviet State Identity   *Karen A. Collias*

94   7. New Soviet Rituals and National Integration in the USSR   *Natalia Sadomskaya*

Contents

121	8. Regional Population Redistribution and National Homelands in the USSR *Lee Schwartz*
163	**Part III: Observing Soviet Nationality Policies in Action**
163	9. Territorial Units as Nationality Policy *Allan Kagedan*
177	10. The Famine of 1932–1933: A Watershed in the History of Soviet Nationality Policy *James E. Mace*
206	11. Baltic Nationalism and Soviet Language Policy: From Russification to Constitutional Amendment *Romuald J. Misiunas*
221	12. Islam and Nationality in Tsarist Russia and the Soviet Union *Tadeusz Swietochowski*
235	13. Soviet Emigration Policies toward Germans and Armenians *Sidney Heitman*
260	14. Soviet-Jewish Emigration Policy: Anti-Zionism and Philo-Semitism *Zachary Irwin*
286	15. Conclusion: Towards a Multiethnic Soviet State: Managing a Multinational Society since 1985 *Henry R. Huttenbach*
293	Index

The Editor and Contributors

Edward Allworth is Professor of Turco-Soviet Studies, Department of Middle East Languages, Columbia University; head of the Center for the Study of Central Asia; Chairman, University Seminar on Soviet Nationality Problems; editor, Central Asia Book Series; author of articles in *Central and Inner Asian Studies, Central Asian Survey* and *Nationalities Papers*; editor and coauthor of *Central Asia: 120 Years of Russian Rule* (1989) and *Tatars of the Crimea; Their Struggle for Survival* (1988); and author of *The Modern Uzbeks* (1990).

Karen A. Collias is an international affairs analyst and writer specializing in Soviet affairs at Evidence Based Research, Inc., a Washington, D.C., consulting firm. She holds a Ph.D. from Columbia University and has served as a policy analyst in the Office of the Historian, United States Department of State. Her articles have appeared in national magazines and newspapers. She is currently writing a book entitled *News from the Front: Soviet Public Diplomacy in the United States*.

Gregory Gleason is a member of the faculty of Political Science at the University of New Mexico, where he also serves as coordinator of the International Conflict and Cooperation Project. A specialist in Soviet domestic politics, Dr. Gleason has held research appointments at the Kennan Institute for Advanced Russian Studies and the Hoover Institution at Stanford University. He is the author of *Federalism and Nationalism: The Struggle for Republican Rights in the USSR*. His current research concerns federal relations in the USSR.

John N. Hazard, a student of Soviet law, Moscow Juridical Institute (1935–1938), is Nash Professor of Law Emeritus, Columbia University, and a fellow of the American Academy of Arts and Sciences. From 1941 to 1945 he served as Deputy Director, Lend Lease Program to the USSR, and from 1945 to 1946 as Adviser on State

Trading, Department of State. His articles have appeared in the *American Journal of International Law*, *Columbia Law Review* and *Slavic Review*. He is author of *Managing Change in the USSR* (1983).

Sidney Heitman is Professor of History at Colorado State University. His research has been published in *Nationalities Papers, Soviet Geography, Soviet Jewish Affairs, Problems of Communism*, and *The Social Science Journal*. The Bundesinstitut für Ostwissenschaftliche und Internationale Studien (Cologne, West Germany), published his studies *The Third Soviet Emigration* (1987) and *Soviet Emigration Since Gorbachev* (1989). He is preparing a full-length study of Jewish, German, and Armenian emigration from the USSR since World War II.

Henry R. Huttenbach is Professor of Russian History at The City College of New York and editor-in-chief of the journal *Nationalities Papers*. His articles have appeared in *Canadian and American Slavic Review* and *Slavonic Review*, as well as in journals and publications in England, Germany, Israel and Poland. He was a contributing author in *Russian Imperialism* (1974) and *Russian Colonial Expansion to 1917* (1988). In conjunction with the Program for Nationalities and Siberian Studies, the Harriman Institute for Advanced Soviet Studies, Columbia University, he has coedited a special issue of *Nationalities Papers*, "The Soviet Nationalities and Gorbachev" (1989). For the past 20 years he has also written, reviewed and lectured extensively on the Holocaust and genocide.

Zachary Irwin holds degrees from Hamilton College, Johns Hopkins, and the Pennsylvania State University. He is Associate Professor of Political Science at Penn State Erie, The Behrend College. He has published in *East European Quarterly*, *Commonwealth* and *Problems of Communism* on Yugoslav and Soviet politics.

Allan Kagedan holds a Ph.D. from Columbia University and is presently Adjunct Professor, Institute of Soviet and European Studies, Carleton University, Ottawa. He has coedited *The Status of Soviet Minorities under International Law* (1988).

James E. Mace is Staff Director of the US Commission on the Ukraine Famine and was principal researcher and writer of its *Report to Congress* (GPO, 1988). After June 1990 he will be a senior fellow of the Harriman Institute for Advanced Soviet Studies, Columbia University. He is the author of *Communism and the Dilemmas of National Liberation: National Communism in Soviet Ukraine, 1918–1933* (1983), and numerous articles in *Soviet Studies, Nationalities Papers, Holocaust and Genocide Studies* and elsewhere.

Romuald J. Misiunas received his Ph.D. from York University. He has taught at the University of Nebraska and Williams College, and was a researcher at the Center for International Studies, Yale University. Since 1982, he has been an independent consultant and researcher in New York City. He is co-author of *The Baltic States' Years of Dependence, 1940–1980*.

Michael Rywkin, born in eastern Poland, spent his youth in France and in the USSR. He attended higher educational institutions in Samarkand, Lodz, Paris and New York. He completed a doctorate in political science at Columbia University. Currently Professor of Russian Area Studies at The City College of the City University of New York, he is also Chairman of the Association for the Study of Nationalities (USSR and Eastern Europe). He is the author of *Moscow's Muslim Challenge: Soviet Central Asia* (1982), and *Soviet Society Today* (1989), and editor of *Russian Colonial Expansion to 1917* (1988).

Natalia Sadomskaya was trained in anthropology at Moscow State University. She received her Ph.D. from Micklukho-Maclai Institute of Ethnography of the USSR Academy of Science, where she later worked as a senior research fellow. At present she teaches anthropology at Queens College of the City University of New York and at the Harriman Institute for Advanced Soviet Studies, Columbia University. She is editor of "Studies of the North Caucasus," a special issue of *Soviet Anthropology and Archeology* (1987) and has an article in *Cahiers du Monde russe et soviétique*.

Lee Schwartz is an Assistant Professor of Geography at The American University's School of International Service. He has worked extensively on Soviet census materials. His publications include "The History of Russian and Soviet Censuses" in Ralph S. Clem (ed.), *Research Guide to the Russian and Soviet Censuses* (1986), and "The Political Geography of Soviet Central Asia" in Robert A. Lewis (ed.), *The Geography of Soviet Central Asia* (1990).

Tadeusz Swietochowski is Professor of Soviet and Middle East Studies at Monmouth College, New Jersey. He was a fellow at the Kennan Institute, Washington, D.C., and at the Harriman Institute, Columbia University. His articles have appeared in *Cahiers du Monde russe et soviétique* and he is author of *Russian Azerbaijan, 1905–1920* (1985).

Foreword

News of events taking place in the Soviet Union in the late 1980s might make the publication of *Soviet Nationality Policies* seem opportunistic because it is so timely. But this timing belies the real history of the book's origin. In 1971 the Seminar on Soviet Nationality Problems issued its first volume under the title *Soviet Nationality Problems*. In that book, the group aimed to focus attention beyond numbers and traits of nationality identity among the many Soviet nationalities. It examined the general problems that they experience in common and the broad dilemmas they create for the political authorities of the USSR. That first study looked at anthropological, demographic, historical, political and other factors connected with problems shared throughout many of the Soviet ethnic subdivisions. In fact, dozens of meetings of the Seminar, established in 1968 in Columbia University, preceded the academic season that generated the present volume. In important part, the University Seminar's activity underlay coordinated inquiries that resulted in publication of several related academic studies, each prepared by a number of authors: *The Nationality Question in Soviet Central Asia* (1971), *Nationality Group Survival in Multiethnic States* (1977), *Ethnic Russia in the USSR: The Dilemma of Dominance* (1980), and, most recent, *Tatars of the Crimea: Their Struggle for Survival* (1988).

The newest in the series, *Soviet Nationality Policies: Ruling Ethnic Groups in the USSR*, reflects the University Seminar's concentration on large ethnic matters. It worked to give participants, and ultimately readers, insights into the specific range of policies adopted and applied especially to the non-Russian population by Communist Party and government officials in the USSR. Usually, Seminar members undertook to debate policies and supply illustrative examples of them, rather than to offer microscopic detail and research. A few sessions concentrated more narrowly on individual nationalities in order to test the general propositions implicit or explicit in the work. As intended, therefore, the discussions upon which this book is based generalize whenever they can and avoid presenting a catalogue of nationalities, their characteristics, or their problems. The group effort also offers a contribution to the further development of theory about the Soviet nationality question in the hope that it may enable informed inquiry regarding both the history of nationality affairs in the USSR and the developments unfolding in the period after 1986–1989.

The core of this new book comes from sessions of the University Seminar on Soviet Nationality Problems held during the academic year 1986–1987. The following members of the University Seminar wrote chapters for the volume: Edward Allworth, John N. Hazard, Allan Kagedan, Romuald Misiunas, Michael Rywkin, Natalia Sadomskaya and one of Professor Allworth's advanced students, now Dr. Karen A. Collias. Other participants who contributed observations and comments to the discussions during that year included Gregory Massell, Daniel C. Matuszewski, Alexander Motyl, George Shevelov and Mark van Hagen.

At the request of University Seminar members, Professor Henry R. Huttenbach has brought together and edited those seven chapters, supplemented them with six additional essays, as well as with his own Introduction and Conclusion, and prepared this edition for the benefit of the Seminar and the academic community.

Edward Allworth
Seminar Chairman

Preface

As a multinational entity, the Soviet Union clearly stands at a turning-point. Once governed almost unquestionably from a center which took it for granted that a diverse population was rapidly evolving into a single citizenry, dozens of national minorities are beginning to voice and openly struggle for their own individual agendas. With Communist Party First Secretary Mikhail S. Gorbachev's call for *glasnost'*—for open discussion, indeed debate, of critical national, regional, and local issues—President Mikhail S. Gorbachev now faces the task of harmonizing the dissonant chorus of demands and counter demands emanating from virtually every Soviet republic and ethnically autonomous unit. Pent-up frustrations of national minorities, many of them antedating the 1917 Bolshevik Revolution, have surfaced, forcing the Soviet leadership based in Moscow and stationed throughout the USSR to re-examine past policies towards these increasingly restless peoples and the homeland territories that make up the multicultural totality of Soviet society and its internal organization along ethnic lines. What had been generally accepted guidelines for Soviet nationality policy now seem obsolescent and may have to be discarded in whole or in part if relative domestic stability is to be maintained in the foreseeable future. Past assumptions and attitudes will have to be abandoned or, at least, critically re-examined. A new nationality policy, more in tune with the prevailing realities, will have to be put in place if the preconditions (social equilibrium) of *perestroika* (economic recovery) are to be achieved. Much of the Soviet future hinges on the success or failure to govern (to find an acceptable nationalities policy for) the heterogeneous population of the Soviet Union.

The overall purpose of this volume is to provide an overview of Soviet nationality policies since 1917. It is, as it must be (given the complexity of the subject), a collective effort. Both the chronological (over seven decades) and the geographic (Eurasian) spans, as well as the cultural breadth and depth of the topic, necessitate a multi-disciplinary approach. Anthropologists, demographers, historians, legal and literary scholars, as well as linguists and political scientists, have contributed to this investigation of Soviet nationality policies. Obviously, no attempt at any kind of completeness was ever intended; all one can hope for, especially in the light of fast-moving contemporary events, is an introduction to the many dimensions of Soviet nationality policy, here presented under three rubrics: the ideological underpinnings of nationality policy; the strategic goal of this policy; and some individual case studies of applied nationality policy from 1917 to 1988.

As editor, I must express my gratitude to all the authors who agreed to contribute to this volume. My first thanks go to those seven scholars whose work came out of Columbia University's Seminar on Soviet Nationality Problems—Allworth, Collias, Hazard, Kagedan, Misiunas, Rywkin and Sadomskaya—for having waited so patiently for the fruits of their labor to appear in print. My even deeper appreciation as editor goes to those six other contributors—Gleason, Heitman, Irwin, Mace, Schwartz and Swietochowski—for having faithfully met a very tight and rigidly imposed deadline so that this volume could appear without further delay. My gratitude also goes out to those who worked so expeditiously to hasten the preparation of the manuscript: to Professor Edward Allworth for allowing me to consult him so often; to Dr Tanya Mairs for her style-editing; to Ms Dallas Arnold, the editorial assistant of *Nationalities Papers*, for performing many crucial chores, from proofreading to retyping; and to Colin Hutchens, the book's editor at Mansell Publishing Limited, for constant patient encouragement. Finally, I would like to acknowledge the financial support to cover many editorial costs from the Simon H. Rifkind Center for the Humanities, made possible by Professor Paul Sherwin, Dean of the Division of Humanities of the City College of New York, a man who never hesitates to affirm the primacy of scholarship.

Henry R. Huttenbach

Chapter 1

Introduction: Towards a Unitary Soviet State: Managing a Multinational Society, 1917–1985

Henry R. Huttenbach

Recognizing the significance of the Soviet Union and its predecessor, the Russian Empire, as primarily a conglomerate of many nationalities and cultures—beyond the simple fact of taking cognizance of the obvious phenomenon of multinationalism—has been painfully and almost inexplicably slow. On the academic level, those publications that do focus on some aspect of this central reality stand out by their exceptionality[1] if measured against the magnitude of all publications on the pre- and post-1917 eras. Only isolated case studies of multinationalism (in contrast to specific studies of individual minorities such as Georgians or Ukrainians) spring to mind, whether for the Tsarist period[2] or the Soviet period.[3] What concerns itself specifically with nationality policy, namely with the ideology, politics and administration of a multinational entity, is even slimmer for *both* periods,[4] even though enormous amounts of thought, talent, personnel and resources were and are *constantly* invested to deal with the chronic problems associated with governing a multinational population.

In retrospect, while the victory of the Bolsheviks over the bulk of the peoples once subjects of the Romanovs comes less of a surprise today, their reconstitution of most of the far-flung Tsarist territorium and their subsequent successful dominion over its vast array of peoples still strikes one, as it did originally, as an outcome less than predictable. A more modest triumph over political rivals in the primarily Russian (Tsarist) heartland might have seemed, at the time, more likely. The re-emergence anywhere after World War I of a viable multinational political entity of great geographic expanse seemed improbable and, certainly, unrealistic, given the trends embodied in dramatic contemporary events; the disintegration of the multinational Habsburg and Ottoman Empires and the continued rise of ethnically driven nationalism strongly dictated against the wisdom of pursuing a more imperial—some would have argued, indeed,

Utopian—dream of believing in the possibility of ruling over diverse and mutually antagonistic peoples within the same borders.

Not even Lenin, the chief architect of the Bolshevik rise to power, foresaw the grandiose geographic (Eurasian) outcome of his Party's struggle for control over a territorial base upon which to consolidate revolutionary power. In March 1919, as the full weight of the Civil War and Allied intervention pressed upon the Bolsheviks, Lenin harbored deep doubts as to whether even a modest victory was within his grasp, at least according to the experience of William C. Bullitt, who briefly visited him that month.[5] Bullitt had been sent to speak informally with Lenin on behalf of Colonel Edward House, private advisor to US President Woodrow Wilson. During a conversation held purely for informational purposes, Bullitt posed Lenin a crucial question. Though not authorized to conduct any form of negotiation, Bullitt nevertheless asked Lenin what the Bolsheviks were willing to offer as an inducement to the Allies to withdraw their troops. Lenin's surprise answer contained a totally unexpected offer. In return for the Allies' ending their intervention in the Civil War, Lenin was ready to retract any territorial claims in the Baltic, in Belorussia, in Finland, and even in the western and central Ukraine, as well as in Transcaucasia and anywhere east of the Urals. In effect, Lenin was ready to accept peace in return for land populated largely by Russians.

Had this off-the-record offer become fact, Soviet history would have been restricted, at least for many years thereafter, to the core lands of the former empire (Greater Muscovy) and limited to one ethnic nationality enjoying an overwhelming majority over a few much smaller minority groups. Such a Soviet government would not have had to contend with the theoretical and practical challenges of multinationalism and multiculturalism, an ideological and administrative challenge that is one of the major constants in Soviet history linking it integrally to the Tsarist past.

Unfortunately, the multinational and hence multicultural character of the Soviet Union and the obvious difficulties of governing a heterogeneous population has not been the central concern of most scholars of the Soviet Union, perhaps, in part, because the Bolsheviks themselves and their heirs also did not stress the highly visible fact of the multifariousness and potential divisiveness of the composition of their citizenry. (From the outset, an optimistic emphasis was placed upon the singleness rather than the plurality of the post-Revolution Soviet population.) Even the more recent publications place little or no emphasis on the Soviet Union as a multinational entity.[6] For example, in Gordon Smith's *Soviet*

Politics: Continuity and Contradiction[7] fewer than ten pages (out of 388) deal with national and ethnic diversity in general and ethnic issues in particular; similarly, Donald R. Kelley in his *Soviet Politics from Brezhnev to Gorbachev*[8] analyzes the internal crisis exclusively in economic terms and makes virtually no reference to minority nationalisms which are partly at the heart of the Brezhnev era's "stagnation" and now stand in the way of many *perestroika*-inspired reforms; even a shrewd observer such as Michel Tartu—in *Gorbatchev: L'URSS va-t-elle changer*?[9]—looks mostly at Party structure and rivalries and environmental issues rather than at accumulating ethnic tensions; as for the venerable historian, the late Cyril E. Black, in his last publication, *Understanding Soviet Politics: The Perspective of Russian History*,[10] he, too (though eloquently stressing his long-held thesis of continuity from Tsarist to Soviet times), found no room for a new and last article devoted exclusively to the continuing governmental problems inherent in population diversity—a problem the Bolshevik founders, despite Lenin's tactically inspired remarks to Bullitt, walked into with covetous open eyes as victory after victory opened up more and more opportunities to bring the Revolution to peoples and places further and further away from Petrograd and Moscow. Indeed, Black's myopia to multi-nationalism is demonstrated by his subtitle: "*Russian* History." That is more than a slip of the pen; it is the same trap the Bolsheviks, especially the Stalinist cohort, fell into as they began to manage a Eurasian territorium populated by peoples of European, Asian and other backgrounds, at once recognizing diversity, but automatically assessing it as a *temporary* condition, assuming, at the same time, that the future outcome of Soviet rule would be a basically Russified Soviet citizenry. Commitment to a unitary state with a homogeneous citizenry lies at the heart of all Soviet nationality policies since Lenin, the belief that the hodgepodge of Eurasian peoples could be fused by shrewd government management into a single, essentially Russian-oriented, people.

Indeed, in contrast to the Lenin–Bullitt anecdote and all it implies, the Bolsheviks—which is to say, Lenin—perceived themselves from the outset as the legitimate heirs to the entire Tsarist Empire. When the political vacuum developed in 1917, they looked upon themselves as the only true successors to the Romanov regime. Once in power, and with the last of the Civil War behind them, they lost little time in affirming this claim in order to legitimize their rule beyond the traditional Russian lands. By the mid-1920s Soviet historiography made this claim the crux of the underpinnings of authority to govern non-Russian territories and their native populations. Aside from resorting to Marxist-Leninist and, increasingly, Stalinist ideological syllogisms to prove Moscow's revolutionary right to sovereignty over non-Russian peoples, the first generation of Soviet leaders also promoted the more traditional argument of "replacement": that, regardless of their ideological pre-eminence over other claimants, they, the Bolsheviks, were justified to rule *in loco* not just by virtue of their military successes but precisely because of the indivisibility of the Tsarist Empire. Ever since 1922 and the formation of the federation of the USSR, the Communist leadership portrayed the Soviet state as the direct heir of the tsarist Empire,[11] a theoretical framework employed by Stalin in 1939–1941 to justify in part his invasion, seizure, occupation and annexation (in his word, "reintegration") of eastern Poland, the Baltic countries and northern Romania.

Indeed, the earliest pronouncements of the Bolsheviks, even before the totally unexpected gains made during the course of the Civil War and while their influence was restricted to a dozen major cities, betrayed their ambitions to win over as many of the peoples of the former Tsarist domain as possible. On the very eve of the Bolshevik seizure of power on October 25, 1917, during the meeting of the second All-Russian Congress of Soviets of Workers' and Soldiers' Deputies, the official line, authorized by Lenin himself, called for guaranteeing autonomy (self-determination) to all nations that found themselves under Soviet (read Bolshevik, and most of them were Russians) rule.[12] A few days later, on November 2, flushed with their initial victory, the Bolsheviks issued the "Declaration of Rights of the Peoples of Russia," in which they offered a full range of options to the non-Russian nationalities in order to induce those already under Bolshevik rule to accept the new status quo of Bolshevik rule from Petrograd and to lure others still beyond their control to join them in a grand union of all the former subjects of the tsar, this time under the aegis of a Soviet (supposedly ethnically neutral and not Russian-dominated) government.[13] Evidently, all indications of Bolshevik strategy—short of the tactical impossibility indicated by the Lenin "offer" to Bullitt—pointed in the direction of a multinational population. This meant facing the immediate consequences of a diverse population, among them dealing with polarizing centrifugal tendencies fueled by a combination of anti-Bolshevism, anti-Russianism, interethnic conflicts, and the positive demands of local nationalisms. From the outset, therefore, the Bolshevik's maximal territorial goal as contemplated by Lenin was to preside over a Soviet state with a multinational population, a fact that necessitated at least an interim nationalities policy until all people had been sufficiently Sovietized (i.e. made loyal to the central government).

In preparation for devising nationality policy there was never any question about its end purpose, namely, the fusing (*sliianie*) of all nationalities, no matter what their cultures, into a single Soviet people. Nor was there any question as to its practicability. Marxist ideology left no room for doubt over the historical nature of nationalism as a bourgeois condition, a product of a class society, fated to obsolescence in a Socialist context.[14] Lenin himself added to the optimism about an eventual post-Revolution resolution of multinationalism by insisting on the maxim that "workers know no fatherland," until recently an indisputable truism in Soviet parlance. In the context of a Soviet state and a Soviet society forged by a supranational Party, Lenin foresaw the creation of a classless (denationalized) proletariat as the logical conclusion of Soviet rule. His commissar of nationalities, Stalin, fortified this vision of union (*edinstvo*).

Where there was a division of minds, largely between Lenin and Stalin, it stemmed from disagreement over how best to achieve *sliianie*. To begin with, whereas Stalin preferred a Soviet state essentially composed of one large unit—a Russian Federation—with subordinate segments to accommodate national minority units, Lenin, forever the pragmatist, insisted on a less Russian-dominated and Russian-centered arrangement in order to overcome strong resistance from Ukrainians, the Central Asian peoples and Transcaucasians, who had already demonstrated powerful separatist tendencies. To appease, in part, their political ambitions for independence and ethnoterritoriality, and to assuage their real fears of Russian primacy, Lenin opted for a union of separate republics (reflecting national differences) as a compromise stage prior to the attainment of mass Soviet consciousness (*sliianie*). The Leninist administrative structure would be the context within which the process of merging (*sblizhenie*) the different nationalities would take place. Initially, the immediate goal was to neutralize their mutual antagonisms and bring about a common friendship of nations (*druzhba narodov*) by making them all beneficiaries of the advantages of being members of the Soviet Union. The state instrument for this task would be the Communist Party, a suprarepublic institution, which, in theory, was to be ethnic-neutral, though in fact its membership was heavily Russian. Though Stalin initially promoted the Leninist policy of *sblizhenie* by relying mostly on cadres drawn from the indigenous minority populations (a policy known as *korenizatsiia*), by the late 1930s he embarked on an open course of blatant Russification as a way to Sovietization and denationalization, thereby running counter to Lenin's original course which sought to steer clear of the shoals of overt Russification, a danger he had condemned with one of his more famous aphorisms: "Scratch a Russian Communist and you will find a Russian chauvinist." Before his death, Lenin had harbored a genuine fear of a resurgence of pre-1917 Russo-centric imperialism which, he knew, would delay and even render impossible the fusing of all the Soviet peoples into one.[15]

Eventually, instead of enjoying a pre-*sliianie* stage of relatively equal development (*rastsvet*), the many national republics and autonomous ethnic regions within them suffered glaring economic disparities. This, over the decades, nurtured among the peripheral, non-Russian national republics a deep sense of alienation toward the center (Moscow in particular and the RSFSR in general), a profound discontent that is an integral part of the crisis that confronted Mikhail Gorbachev in 1985. Nearly 70 years—more than two generations—of nationality policy have *not* brought about population homogenization. Sixty years after Lenin's death, after six decades of Party machinations and state-promoted social "engineering," the Soviet Union remains more multinational than ever—ironically, in part precisely because of Lenin's original administrative structural accommodation of ethnic territorialism, which proved to be a convenient container and preserver of national consciousness and separatism. The conglomerate of peoples of 1985—the year of Gorbachev's assumption of the post of General Secretary—is no less a multiplicity of ethnic groups than it was in the days of its grandparents in 1922. Like the Tsarist administrators before them in the nineteenth century, their twentieth-century Communist Party counterparts are frustrated by the tenacious continuity of multinationalism. The demographic tapestry now is as colorful and vibrant as it was then, and Gorbachev has no choice but to face the challenge of ruling over a permanently disparate and sometimes rancorous population.

Nevertheless, his predecessors can take heart, if only posthumously. Despite extraordinary, critical moments, the Soviet Union had not been torn asunder by internal nationalisms by the time Gorbachev assumed power. Neither the stresses of the Civil War, nor of mass collectivization, nor the apocalyptic shocks of World War II brought on sufficient minority-inspired centrifugal forces to trigger off the dismemberment of the USSR. On the other hand, the multinational population scattered over the transcontinental expanse of Soviet territory has retained its own identities confounding Marxist ideological assumptions and expectations. Localized loyalty has blocked the path to a unitary state and society and continues to weaken Soviet patriotism. *Homo sovieticus* has yet to emancipate himself from strong national ties. Marxist-Leninist ideology notwithstanding, national minority consciousness retains strong roots, defying all efforts to expunge it. Twentieth-century Soviet rulers have been no more nor less successful in metamorphosing the dozens of national and ethnic minorities into one patriotic cultural entity than their nineteenth-century predecessors. Neither carrots nor sticks proffered by tsars or commissars—neither generous economic inducements nor violent assaults, ranging from mass deportation to mass starvation—have fundamentally altered the multinational, multicultural demographic reality of the Soviet Union. The Party ruling elite has spent as much energy administering an entrenched multinational population as it has executing a nationality policy designed to promote an ideological vision of a culturally harmonized Soviet citizenry. The chapters that follow investigate this dilemma of the Party leadership—of coping with an intractable multinational reality while pursuing the seeming mirage of a compliant Soviet populace.

Notes

1. For a general survey of the historical literature dealing with multinationalism in Tsarist Russia and the Soviet Union, see Andreas Kappeler, "Historische Voraussetzungen des Nationalitätenproblems im Russischen Vielvölkerreich," *Geschichte und Gesellschaft*, 8 (1982), pp. 159-83.

2. For example: E. Drabkina, *Natsional'nyi i kolonial'nyi vopros v tsarskoi Rossii* (Moscow, 1930); Taras Hunczak, *Russian Imperialism from Ivan the Great to the Revolution* (New Brunswick, 1974). H. Nolte, *Religiöse Toleranz in Russland 1600-1725* (Göttingen, 1969); B. Nolde, *La formation de l'empire russe*, 2 vols. (Paris, 1952); B. E. Nol'de, *Ocherki Russkago gosudarstvennago prava* (St. Petersburg, 1911); M. Slavinskij, "Natsional'naia struktura Rossii i velikorossy" in A. I. Kastelianskii (ed.), *Formy natsional'nago dvizheniia v sovremennykh gosudarstvakh* (St. Petersburg, 1910), pp. 277-303; Georg von Rauch, *Russland: Staatliche Einheit und nationale Vielfalt, föderalistische Kräfte und Ideen in der russischen Geschichte* (Munich, 1953); Ia. E. Vodarskii, *Naselenie Rossii v kontse XVII-nachale XVIII veka* (Moscow, 1977) and *Naselenie Rossii za 400 let* (Moscow, 1973).

3. For example: Edward Allworth (ed.), *Soviet Nationality Problems* (New York, 1971); Razma Karklins, *Ethnic Relations in the USSR* (Boston, 1986); Ivan Dzyuba, *Internationalism or Russification? A Study in the Soviet Nationalities Problem* (London, 1968); Richard Pipes, *The Formation of the Soviet Union: Communism and Nationalism* (Cambridge, 1970). See also Alexander J. Motyl, *Will the Non-Russians Rebel? State, Ethnicity, and Stability in the USSR* (Ithaca, 1987); and, by the same author, "The Sobering of Gorbachev: Nationality, Restructuring, and the West" in Seweryn Bialer (ed.), *Politics, Society, and Nationality inside Gorbachev's Russia* (Boulder, Co., 1989).

4. N. G. Appollova, "K voprosu o politike absoliutizma v natsional'nykh

raionakh Rossii v XVIII v.," *Absoliutizm v Rossii* (Moscow, 1964), pp. 355–88; Edward Allworth (ed.), *Ethnic Russia in the USSR. The Dilemma of Dominance* (New York, 1980); J. R. Azrael (ed.), *Soviet Nationality Policies and Practices* (New York, 1978); P. G. Galuzo, "Das Kolonialsystem des russischen Imperialismus am Vorabend der Oktoberrevolution," *Zeitschrift für Geschichtswissenschaft*, 15 (1967), pp. 997–1,014; W. Kolarz, *Russia and her Colonies* (New York, 1952); Marc Raeff, "Patterns of Russian Imperial Policy toward the Nationalities" in Allworth, *Soviet Nationality Problems*, pp. 22–42; S. F. Starr, "Tsarist Government: The Imperial Dimension" in Azrael, *Soviet Nationality Policies and Practices*, pp. 3–38; L. I. Strakhovsky, "Constitutional Aspects of the Imperial Russian Government's Policy toward National Minorities," *Journal of Modern History*, 13 (1941), pp. 467–92; Edward C. Thaden, "Nationality Policy in the Western Borderlands of the Russian Empire, 1881–1914" in A. Cienciala (ed.), *American Contributions to the Seventh International Congress of Slavists, Warsaw, 1973*, 3: *History* (The Hague, 1973), pp. 69–78.

5. Bullitt's report is in Arno J. Mayer, *Politics of Peacemaking: Containment and Revolution at Versailles, 1918–1919* (New York, 1967), pp. 65–6.

6. For a short but highly critical review of the state of Sovietology and its failure to give credence to the centrality of multinationalism in the Soviet Union, see Alexander J. Motyl, " 'Sovietology in One Country' or Comparative Nationality Studies," *Slavic Review*, vol. 48, no. 1 (Spring 1989), pp. 83–8.

7. New York, 1987.

8. New York, 1987.

9. Paris, 1987.

10. Boulder, 1986.

11. For example, in M. Bochacher, *Moldavia* (Moscow-Leningrad, 1926), p. 11—part of a multi-volume series on all the republics and provinces of the USSR—this theme was repeated as a common denominator for all segments and their populations.

12. V. I. Lenin, *Polnoe sobranie sochinenii* (Moscow, 1950) vol. 35, p. 11.

13. *Ocherkii istorii kommunisticheskoi partii Moldavii* (Kishinev, 1968), pp. 64–6.

14. Walker Connor, *The National Question in Marxist-Leninist Theory and Strategy* (Princeton, 1984).

15. On the Lenin and Stalin approaches to *sblizhenie*, see Alex de Jonge, *Stalin and the Shaping of the Soviet Union* (New York, 1986), pp. 81–2; Adam B. Ulam, *Stalin: The Man and His Era* (Boston, 1973), p. 178 and p. 182; John B. Dunlop, *The Faces of Contemporary Russian Nationalism* (Princeton, 1984); and Robert Conquest (ed.), *The Last Empire: Nationality and the Soviet Future* (Stanford, 1986).

PART I

Determining the Character of Soviet Nationality Policy

Chapter 2

Leninist Nationality Policy: Its Source and Style

Gregory Gleason

The Communist Party of the Soviet Union (CPSU) Party Program adopted in 1986 reflects the deep-seated ambivalence of the Soviet leadership regarding the problems of contemporary national relations in the USSR.[1] The Program asserts that "the nationality question, *as it has been inherited from the past*, has been successfully solved."[2] By relying on this subtle formulation, the Program's drafters could offer symbolic concessions to two powerful and competing constituencies. On the one hand, the formula appears to address the concerns of those who believe that the national question is "solved" and thus no longer requires special compensatory provisions by the Soviet state to "accelerate" the development of minority populations. On the other hand, the Program's language also appears to conform to the view of those who maintain that national relations reflect deeply rooted historical problems which will continue to present challenges for Soviet internal political integration.

The basic philosophical division reflected in the formula can be viewed in terms of extreme, polar positions on the political spectrum. Although both sides would disavow these labels, the ideological orientations toward the national question range from the "integrationists," who favor a strong, centralized, even unitary state, to the "segregationists," who favor the implementation of the principle of national autonomy in the republics in accordance with the federal guarantees of successive Soviet Constitutions. The ambivalence of the Party's position on the nationalism issue follows from the fact that, as Soviet sources endlessly repeat, the Party reflects "the whole people." The USSR's cultural heterogeneity makes undisguised "unionist" policies impossible. At the same time, even many "nationalists" recognize that, because of the resilience of politicized ethnicity in the USSR, the granting of many of the nationalists' demands would soon lead to devolution, if not to secession.

After 70 years of Soviet power, the traditional argument that nationalist manifestations are "remnants" of the presocialist past has lost much of its credibility. It has been replaced by a more nuanced interpretation, which views national enmity and ethnic antagonisms as partially derived from previously influential traditions, mores, values and habits, and partially the result of lingering "antagonisms" within Soviet society. It is often noted that Lenin predicted that even though "contradictions" would attenuate with the coming of socialism, "antagonisms" could be expected to endure.[3] The persistence of interpersonal discrimination, occasional outbursts of violence, and the cautious but determined defense of nationalist traditions in the borderlands are often attributed to the "dialectics" of historical progress. Thus, it is often naturally observed that this "*Zhguchii vopros*" (burning question) of contemporary Soviet affairs requires a dialectical solution. Mikhail Gorbachev made this point to the 27th CPSU Congress delegates in 1986, noting: "Our achievements should not create the impression that there are no complications in nationality processes. The contradictions characteristic of all development are unavoidable in this sphere as well."[4]

The dialectical solution to the nationality problem is called the "Leninist nationality policy." Successive Soviet leaders following Lenin have referred to this policy or set of principles as the guiding force which has steered the Soviet multinational state toward a very difficult if not Utopian goal, namely, heterogeneous unity. Abstract definitions of Leninist nationality policy abound. For instance, Gorbachev recently noted that "the goal of the Leninist nationality policy is to achieve a situation in which every person and every nation can develop freely and every people can satisfy its requirements in all spheres of sociopolitical life, in its native language and culture, and in its customs and religious beliefs.[5] Similarly, a leading commentator on nationality affairs, Eduard Bagramov, summarized Leninist nationality policy as "the continual strengthening of the free and voluntary union of peoples based on the fullest trust and a clear consciousness of fraternal unity.[6] Such formulations as these are meant to be instrumental statements. They are designed as and function as propaganda, that is, for the purposes of socialist "consciousness raising." These statements and many others like them that appear regularly in the popular media are part of the Soviet rhetoric of political motives.

Comparative research on nationalism and minority group relations has raised a number of questions concerning Soviet nationality policies. What is the real, as opposed to rhetorical, definition of Soviet nationality policy? Do different nationalities in the USSR fare appreciably better or worse than their neighboring groups? If so, does this provide evidence of differential policies on the part of the center? How does overall Soviet nationality policy differ from minority group policies pursued in other multinational states? Can "Leninist nationality policies" be replicated in other multinational states that are in a stage of national consolidation? Soviet scholars and many Western scholars and analysts often disagree on the specific answers to these questions; by and large, however, they do agree that these questions form the core of the theoretically and practically important cluster of questions surrounding Soviet nationality policy.

The purpose of this essay is to suggest a reconceptualization of Leninist nationality policy, to argue that it is not a set of principles on how to decide such questions as language policy or economic redistribution: rather, it is a set of goals for social change which are based upon Marxist assumptions regarding the socioeconomic transition from capitalism to socialism. Given these assumptions, any analytical definition of Leninist nationality policy should stress two factors. The first pertains to the source of Leninist nationality policy. As a strategy for political consolidation in a multinational empire, nationality policy imposed an initial compromise on the Bolshevik leaders. The Bolsheviks granted political recognition to ethnoterritorial groups in the form of "national-statehood" in exchange for political support. As the Azeri–Armenian clashes of 1988 demonstrate, the Soviet Union is still living with the legacy of that compromise. The second factor pertains to the style of bureaucratic politics that is fostered by the Leninist tradition and the nature of the Soviet bureaucratic apparatus. It is important, I maintain, to view Soviet nationality policy not as a set of specific programs, but as a teleological program with a specific source and style.

The Source of Soviet Nationality Policy and Lenin's Design for a State

In their theoretical pronouncements on the subject, both Marx and Engels held to a simple, straightforward interpretation of nationalism. In theory, neither thinker attached much enduring importance to national sentiment. Since Marx and Engels both saw sociopolitical change as a function of economic forces, the collective sentiments which supported national movements were regarded by these thinkers as epiphenomenal in nature and ephemeral in significance. They were part of the ideational "superstructure." Thus, their influence was derived from fundamental economic conditions and processes. The nation—identified by Marx and Engels as a collective united on the basis of common language and "sympathies"—was destined to transubstantiate as economic reality changed.

If both Marx and Engels dismissed nationalism in theory, their attitude toward national sentiment and national movements in practice was quite different. The year 1848, which saw publication of the antinationalist tract, *The Communist Manifesto*, was also a year of nationalist fervor throughout Europe. One is inspired with a sense of historical irony recalling that the antinationalist doctrine of "proletarian internationalism"—with its slogan, "the worker has no country"—was formulated amid the politically charged atmosphere of competing European nationalisms. Yet Marx and Engels eventually gave their assent to a number of nationalist causes, such as the Irish independence movement, perhaps seeing in them less the ineluctable movement of history than the advisability of showing solidarity with the oppressed. The basic incompatibility between classical Marxist assumptions and the realities of nationalism explains why Marx and Engels could operate on two tracks, dismissing nationalism in theory while acknowledging it as a real force in practice.

Lenin, in contrast, appropriated the Marxist teleology but superimposed upon it an activist attitude toward politics. His early writings in an abstract vein are critical of nationalism. Only later, during the dramatic and dizzying events of 1917, did he reverse his position and come to embrace the concept of national self-determination within a federal framework. He adopted it not as a principle of political theory, but as a maxim of political power. His position on the national question derived from political expediency rather than logical inference.

Like Marx, Lenin viewed national sentiment as ephemeral and thus malleable. And, like Marx, Lenin differed from his contemporaries and rivals in being at once less willing to accept nationalism as a legitimate force and more willing to use national sentiments as a means to promote his own political agenda. For Lenin, nations became assimilated to the role of social classes. The discontent and the appeals for autonomy voiced by nationalists were viewed by Lenin as symptoms of real injustices, but also as signals of the availability of constituencies to be mobilized in the socialist cause.

For the theoretical Lenin, it was precisely the institution of capitalist private property and the capitalists' control of the means of production which were the principal causes of antagonism and enmity among nations. The harnessing of national sentiment was a temporary expedient. In language destined to become charged with political significance decades later, Lenin explained:

> Socialism organizes production without class antagonism, and thus supports the well-being of all citizens. In so doing it gives full scope to the "sympathies" of the population. It therefore facilitates and greatly speeds the rapprochement (*sblizhenie*) and fusion (*sliianie*) of nations.[7]

Lenin's reasoning led him to a form of integrationism. He did not dwell on the issue of assimilation, because integration was inevitable in his view. Moreover, he could feel confident that concessions would not be permanent, since nationalism would disappear as the vestiges of capitalism atrophied.

In the struggle for ascendancy after the Revolution, the Bolsheviks, with promises of peace, land, food and power to the Soviets, won popular support in the Russian heartland. Yet their initial bids for popular support in the borderlands of the Baltics, the Western provinces and Ukraine, Transcaucasia and the Central Asian regions were not successful. In these areas political support naturally swung behind the national intelligentsia. The political organizations of the borderlands were internally divided, poorly organized, and not driven by the millennial zeal of a revolutionary ideology. The Bolsheviks, in contrast, were ready to exploit these cleavages by making alliances with even the most reactionary groups in order to maintain their dominant central position. As though out of a false pride and a lingering Great Russian chauvinism, the White Army generals were unwilling to forge political alliances with local political actors.

During the process of political consolidation, the issue of the political incorporation of the borderlands into the central governmental structure brought forth a debate over the appropriate framework within which participation would take place. The debate resolved itself into a competition between those who, along with Lenin's Commissar of Nationalities, Stalin, favored a principle of "national-territorial" autonomy; and those, including the Mensheviks, Budnovtsy and the Austro-Marxists, who championed "cultural-national" autonomy. The national-territorial principle won the day.[8]

The national-territorial principle was implemented with the establishment of a federal structure granting "independent" national-statehood to some of the most numerous and historically important ethnic collectivities. The federal structure of the Soviet state provided a sense of self-determination, a promise of autonomy, and a feeling of natural representation to the national minorities. At the same time it integrated them into the central institutional framework in such a way that their legal rights would not be institutionally defended through an institutionalized pluralism.

It is against this background that Leninist nationality policy emerged. Its distinguishing feature was its tactical manipulation of local national sentiment in the interests of ideology. Its principal organizational feature was the "Leninist solution" to the national problem, that is, a political formula which involved the division of the USSR along pseudo-federal lines while maintaining a rigidly centralized government–party organization.

The Evolution of Leninist Nationality Policy

Policy with respect to the borderlands during Stalinism was characterized by dualism. The Utopian aims of policy were used to rationalize the great pressures and injustices placed upon the national minorities of the USSR. The plight of specific national minority groups—the Crimean Tatars, the peoples of the Baltic countries, the Jews and so on—have been detailed elsewhere. Here I am interested in noting that the fearful instruments of Soviet political consolidation—and we must remember that Draconian measures were not an invention of Stalin—were also directed toward eliminating the injustices of the past. Such indeed was the public rationale for their existence. As Stalin told the Tenth Party Congress in 1921:

> The essence of the national question in the Soviet [Union] is to liquidate the economic, political and cultural backwardness of the nationalities. We inherited this backwardness from the past. We do this in order to give the backward peoples the opportunity to catch up with central Russia both in governmental, cultural and economic respects.[9]

When these instruments failed to achieve their goals, as they so dramatically did with the collectivization campaign, the instruments were redirected toward convincing the citizenry that they were a success. "Battles" that had been lost in the fields and the factories, Stalin discovered, could still be won in the minds of a credulous populace and a naive outside world. It was from failure that the totalitarian impulse sprang.

While the national minorities were not in the same situation throughout the USSR in terms of their ability to protect themselves, most were economically weak, with dependent political elites. Most minority regions had a populace that was no longer dominated by the peasantry, but was not yet a working class; no longer widely illiterate, but not yet universally educated; no longer entirely docile, but far from self-confident. In these circumstances Stalin could expand the command economy in accordance with a military model, a development which no doubt appeared, from the perspective of the Kremlin, to put control over events into the hands of Moscow officials.

A measure of the extent to which Stalin's policies were resented can be gained from the swiftness of the changes following his death. New life was breathed into the national republics. The reasons for this are several. First, there was the effect of events in Eastern Europe, especially in Hungary and Poland. Second, there were generational changes within the republics themselves. Third, there was a shifting political balance in the borderland regions. For instance, in a rather sudden fashion, Soviet Central Asia became an asset to central leaders as Soviet foreign policy shifted southward in an effort to embrace national liberation movements in Asia, Africa and the Middle East.

Khrushchev's style of nationality policy, like his style in other policy areas, was exceptionally volatile. In theoretical pronouncements he expressed a buoyant optimism. He told the delegates to the 22nd Party Congress in 1961 that "the Party has solved one of the most complex of problems, which has plagued mankind for ages and remains acute in the world of capitalism to this day—the problem of relations between nations."[10] Khrushchev spoke of *sliianie* (fusion) of nations. This gave currency to the arguments of those who felt that, since the federal structure had been adopted as a temporary solution to the national question, and the national question had now been solved, the rationale for the existence of the federal republics had evaporated.[11] Thus, some scholars suggested that the federal division into union republics had outlived its usefulness and might be dispensed with in the foreseeable future. Indeed, the version of the new Party Program adopted by the 22nd Party Congress in October 1961 included the rather ominous proposition that "the borders between the union republics within the USSR are increasingly losing their former significance" and that the nations in the USSR are "all united into one family by common vital interests and are advancing together toward a single goal—Communism."[12] Even while propounding centrist, integrationist views himself, Khrushchev found many of the surrogates of central authority in the regions to be intractable. His disagreements with regional officials precipitated a wave of personnel and organizational changes aimed principally at denationalizing the republican branches of the ministries and Party.

The Brezhnev regime moved swiftly in the areas of economic "reform" and foreign policy but was hesitant to announce a formal nationality policy during its first years in power. By 1972 events had proceeded to such a point that the center was called upon, as a matter of policy, to state plainly its preferences on the nationality question. Brezhnev took the occasion of the 50th anniversary of the USSR to publicize the facile formula which became the hallmark of the Brezhnev period. The main lines can be found in the CPSU's Central Committee's resolution "On the Preparation for the 50th Anniversary of the Formation of the USSR."[13] Brezhnev adopted a "dialectical" solution to the national question.[14] It was announced that "a new historical community, the Soviet people" had emerged. Brezhnev's compromise formula did not deny the importance of nationhood. Brezhnev averred that Soviet nationality policy called, at once, for the *rastsvet* (development) of nations and the *sblizhenie* (rapprochement) of nations. Repeatedly pronouncing himself against "artificially forcing" the *sblizhenie* process, Brezhnev maintained that the "best" national traditions, values and tendencies would be promoted in the Soviet multinational state. Like parallel lines converging on the horizon, the nations were seen as developing along a course which would bring them, eventually, to convergence in an indefinite Soviet future.

The agenda of the short-lived Andropov reign was clearly activist in the nationality realm. Although it was not stated publicly, one suspects that Andropov and his advisors, no doubt because of his close ties with the security police, had grounds for the belief that causes of the economic stagnation of the Brezhnev period were not always central mismanagement but regional—read "national"—attempts to either subvert unpopular policies or to enrich the regions at central expense. Andropov reportedly sought discreetly to eliminate the expression "national republic," in favor of "union republic," in an effort to diminish the ethnoterritorial meaning and significance of the republics.[15] Andropov was surely not a "Russite nationalist,"[16] but he did feel that economic decentralization was an urgent necessity. Decentralization of the economy, however, could only take place in the context of other policies which would entail greater cultural uniformity. Naturally, then, Andropov's integrationism was seen as assimilationism by those who championed minority rights. Economic decentralization would mean delegating authority by breaking down the central bureaucratic apparatus. In the borderlands, this would mean turning power over economic decision-making to the local "national" bureaucracies. Upon Andropov's death, the issue of nationality policy returned to a holding pattern, awaiting new direction. Similarly, Chernenko's reign was too brief to affect the situation.

A Leninist Style and the Policy Process

In these general and necessarily brief characterizations of policies regarding the borderlands, I have stressed the points of historical continuity. But in terms of the changes that have taken place under successive leaders, it is clear that the main structural influence on policy is exerted by the nature of the bureaucracy. As Rigby has noted, "In an authoritarian system, the politics of policy implementation [assumes] at least equal importance with the politics of policy formation."[17] Gail Warshofsky Lapidus underscores this point in noting how effectively regional actors have bargained in the forum of bureaucratic politics to "modify centrally imposed policies in the course of implementation."[18] To understand how nationality policy is implemented in the Soviet case, it is important to understand two things. The first of these is the particular political style that Lenin imparted to the system. This is not a matter of "atmospherics" but a specific set of "rules of the game." Second, it is important to understand how the bureaucracy works in the context of a minority borderland.

Leninism as a style of practicing politics proceeds from three premises. First, Communist construction is logically correct, humanistically oriented, and the sole justifiable basis for sociopolitical organization. Second, ends justify means in politics. Third, politics is struggle. In practice, the Leninist is a political realist, action-oriented, tactical, conflictual. Lenin himself never defined the term "nation." The definition was unimportant for him. The granting of "independence" and "autonomy" to the national groups was partial, provisional and conditional. While normative principles loom large in Leninism, the political style is sensitive to a calculus of competing interests. These same features of Leninism are expressed in the style of Leninist national policy that characterizes the regional responses to central policy. Leninist nationality policy is a forum for competition wherein confrontation takes place over critical values. Soviet sources are not reticent about this; Lenin is often lauded for his nononsense style and his use of "political audacity" in achieving aims.

How does this Leninist style interact with the administrative apparatus in the USSR? The most salient feature of the Soviet policy process is that it takes place within a vast "mobilizational" bureaucracy. Some of the tendencies within this bureaucracy are fairly common ones. We can note the following general patterns of bureaucracies.

Organizations tend to become highly stratified internally. A lack of communication between strata in these organizations encourages the adoption of abstract "standard operation procedures." The frequent lack of fit between the rules of the organization and the tasks that are handed down from above encourage line personnel to resort to informal "understandings" to circumvent the rules in order to achieve the organization's goals. The informal understandings periodically prove insufficient, precipitating a crisis. Thereupon, the high strata intervene, reimposing new operating procedures, and the cycle begins anew.[19]

These tendencies also characterize what Sidney Tarrow has called a "territorial bureaucracy."[20] As Tarrow notes, in a territorial bureaucracy the gap between horizontal strata is compounded by the distance between the place where rules are formulated and the place where they are implemented. The lack of communication between strata is exacerbated by the partial independence that territorial agents enjoy because the bulk of their actions are hidden from their superiors. And the resentment of lower-level bureaucrats at the irrelevance of the impersonal rules they administer is intensified by their social and personal affinity with the local population. Thus, Tarrow says, "the sharp edge of central policies is softened by the peripheral agent of the state in his contacts with grassroots publics."[21]

The phenomenon of a territorial bureaucracy results in a very pronounced psychology of "enclaving" in the ethnoregional territorial bureaucracy. The Uzbeks begin to think of the Uzbek SSR Ministry of Fishing as "their" ministry; the Azeri begin to think of the Azerbaijan SSR Ministry of Education (and its subordinate facilities in Nagorno-Karabakh) as "their" ministry; and so on. It is this phenomenon of bureaucratic enclaving that Rasma Karklins refers to in noting that in the non-Russian regions the rank-and-file members of officialdom "feel that within 'their' republics they should be the decisive group."[22] The final result of this process is the development of a climate of national protectiveness. In this context, the policies that are adopted by Moscow, be they in the realm of bilingualism, treatment of historical figures, or financial allocations, are policies which are indelibly imprinted with a national stamp.

Unavoidably, then, since all nationality regions are heterogeneous and all are at odds with the center, the promotion of national rights and privileges boils down to a competition. There are two arenas in which the competition takes place. One is the bureaucratic arena which, for a variety of reasons, is generally hidden from the view of both the West and the Soviet citizenry. Leninist nationality policies are not a set of Marxist principles regarding "proportional development," "regional equalization," "fraternal assistance," "skipped stages of capitalist development," "internationalist rapprochement" or any of the other hackneyed phrases of the standard Soviet political lexicon. The arena of Soviet nationality policies is an arena of social competition in which region is pitted against center and, collectively, the regions are pitted against the center. As Karklins has observed, whatever the topic of discussion—allocations, education, industrial siting policies, language policy—eventually this "has to be related to the distribution of power between the center and the periphery, and between the Russians and the non-Russians."[23]

The other area of competition over goals is the arena of symbolic definitions. Much of the discussion of nationality problems is marked, as the Chairman of the Soviet Government Publishing Committee remarked by "ritual recitation, generalization, circumlocution and conventional wisdoms."[24] The debates over these seeming abstractions are proxy debates. Abstract definitions of, for instance, *narodnost* ("nationality" or national group) or *sblizhenie* are important because they are symbolic of underlying political and economic values which form the basis of Soviet nationality conflict.[25]

Perhaps one of the most telling pieces of evidence of the resilience and flexibility of the Leninist political style in nationality relations is the recent reliance of segregationist groups upon the language and concepts of Leninist nationality policy to defend their positions.[26] While it has long been a standard practice of defenders of minority rights to use Leninist quotations to "buttress every argument for national rights," it is relatively new that these same tactics should be used by the defenders of Russian predominance.[27]

Conclusion

Glasnost' has given rise to an unprecedented level of debate. As the *perestroika* activists frequently point out, *perestroika* is a creative process. Gorbachev has sought to move away from the orthodoxy of Brezhnevism by calling for a "socialist pluralism."[28] Buoyed by this development, some nationality theorists have echoed this with a call for recognition of "ethnic pluralism."[29] Yet more sensationalistic expressions have recently found their way into print. For instance, see the discussion of opponents of *perestroika* who refer to "counterrevolutionary nations."[30] What does this new candor hold in store for Leninist nationality policy?

If the foregoing observations are accurate, the essence of Soviet nationality policy flows from the two factors I have outlined. These are, first, the the USSR's federal structure and, second, the way in which policy is made in the USSR. Regarding the *source* of Leninist nationality policy, three significant phases may be identified: (1) the federal structure was adopted as a strategic compromise; (2) this move gave legitimacy to the national-territorial groups in terms of formal recognition in the form of national-statehood; and (3) these structures then became the poles around which national sentiment was able to sustain itself. Regarding the *style* of Leninist nationality policy, three significant aspects may be identified: (1) it is aggressive, result-oriented; (2) the result of Stalin's imprint has been to fashion a mobilizational system which is contemptuous of individual rights and legalization; and (3) a gradual increase in the resources and resourcefulness of minority groups has come about as a natural, generational phenomenon. The federal structure has offered major Soviet minority groups a form of national-statehood which has provided a sense of psychological satisfaction in the search for identity and belonging in the ascriptionless world of proletarian uniformity. The mobilizational aspect of the system has actually accelerated national cohesion by encouraging institution-building, education, urbanization, and, ultimately, a sense of pride in national accomplishment.

It should not seem surprising that Gorbachev has been so reluctant to articulate a formal nationality policy. Chernenko's was an unannounced non-policy. Andropov had a specific program agenda ready for implementation but no time to carry it out. Brezhnev waited almost eight years before clearly formulating his "two tendencies" dialectical theory. Khrushchev's pronouncements on nationality were not made until after his consolidation of power. From a certain perspective, even Stalin and Lenin can be said to have re-evaluated and stated their approaches to nationality policy only significantly after their tenures began. Gorbachev's reluctance is thus understandable: he has little to gain and much to lose from a formal announcement. It was only after events such as the Alma-Ata riots and the growing conflicts over administrative jurisdiction in Transcaucasia that he was willing to recognize publicly that the national question was an "extremely important, vital question of our society."[31]

Perestroika lies at the center of the policy toward the regions because so much of the economic malaise of the *zastoi*—universally attributed in the USSR to the faceless bureaucrats—is actually the product of various strategies of self-protection and self-assertion on the part of entrepreneurial officials in the regions. Nationality theorist Eduard Bagramov rightly observed in *Pravda* that restructuring "calls for deep changes in nationality affairs."[32] What this means for the national minorities is going to be decided in a struggle. The smaller groups will not fare well in this struggle unless there is a turn toward regulatory mechanisms such as proportional representation, legal guarantees and a measure of regional self-determination through the political process. So far, Leninist nationality policy has not provided these things. The analysis of the source and style of Leninist nationality policy presented here suggests that it is not apt to.

Notes

Note: I am grateful to Alexander Motyl for his criticism of an earlier version of this essay.

1. The ambiguity in the use of the English expression does not occur in Russian. "National" in the sense used in this paper refers to any of the nations, peoples or nationalities that make up the Soviet general populace, and not to the central or federal government.

2. Literally, the phrase reads: *natsional'nyi vopros, ostavshiisia ot proshlogo, v Sovetskom Soiuze uspeshno reshen*. See *Kommunist*, no. 4 (1986), p. 127. I have added the italics.

3. For a recent discussion, see Ianis Peters, "Podlinnyi internatsionalizm predpolagaet," *Literaturnaia gazeta*, no. 47 (November 18, 1987).

4. As quoted on p. 80 in Iuri Bromlei, "Sovershenstvovanie natsional'nykh otnoshenii v SSSR," *Kommunist* no. 8 (1986), pp. 78-86. Also see Iu. Bromlei, *Oktiabr' i razvitie natsional'nykh otnoshenii v SSR* (Moscow: Znanie, 1987).

5. See Gorbachev's address to the people of Azerbaijan and Armenia which appeared in *Bakinskii rabochii* (February 27, 1988), reprinted in *Current Digest of the Soviet Press*, vol. 40, no. 8 (1988), p. 6.

6. Eduard Bagramov, "Zhivoi vopros zhivoi zhizni," *Agitator*, no. 23 (December 1987), p. 9.

7. V. I. Lenin, *Polnoe sobranie sochinenii*, vol. 30 (Moscow: Politizdat, 1967), p. 21.

8. "Territorial" was actually called "provincial" by Stalin at this point, i.e. *oblastnoi* was used instead of territorial.

9. J. V. Stalin, *Marksizm i natsional'no-kolonial'nyi vopros* (Moscow, 1937).

10. *Pravda*, October 18, 1961.

11. See Gregory Gleason, *Federalism and Nationalism: The Struggle for Republican Rights in the USSR* (Boulder, Co.: Westview, 1990).

12. "Programma Kommunisticheskoi Partii Sovetskogo Soiuza," *Kommunist*, no. 16, (1961), p. 84.

13. "O podgotovke k 50-letiiu obrazovaniia Soiuza Sovetskikh Sotsialisticheskikh Respublik," February 21, 1972.

14. See Teresa Rakowska-Harmstone, "The Dialectics of Nationalism in the USSR," *Problems of Communism* (May-June 1974), pp. 1-22.

15. Ilya Zemtsov claims that Andropov was seeking to eliminate the republican status altogether. See Ilya Zemtsov, "Andropov and the Non-Russian Nationalities: Attitudes and Policies," *Nationalities Papers*, vol. 8, no. 5 (Spring 1985), pp. 5-23. Discussion of the "defederalization" of the USSR emerged in the early 1960s and even found a place in the 1961 version of the Party Program which spoke of the republican boundaries losing their significance. However, the debate over Soviet federalism lost much of its momentum in the 1970s. See A. I. Lepeshkin, *Sovetskii federalizm* (Moscow, 1977).

16. For a definition of this term in the Soviet context, see Alexander Yanov, "The New Russian Right: Right-Wing Ideologies in the USSR," University of California, Berkeley Institute of International Studies, Research Series, no. 35 (1978).

17. T. H. Rigby, "Was Stalin a Disloyal Patron?" *Soviet Studies*, vol. 38, no. 3 (July 1986), p. 315.

18. Gail Warshofsky Lapidus, "Ethnonationalism and Political Stability: The Soviet Case," *World Politics*, vol. 36, no. 4 (July 1984), p. 576.

19. This argument is adapted from Michael Crozier, *The Bureaucratic Phenomenon* (Chicago: University of Chicago Press, 1966).

20. Sidney Tarrow, *Between Moscow and Tashkent* (New Haven: Yale University Press, 1977), p. 29.

21. Sidney Tarrow, *Between Center and Periphery* (New Haven: Yale University Press, 1977), p. 29.

22. Rasma Karklins, *Ethnic Relations in the USSR* (Boston: Allen and Unwin, 1986), p. 8.

23. Karklins, *Ethnic Relations in the USSR*, p. 77.

24. M. Nenashev, *Pravda*, November 24, 1987.

25. On this debate, see P. M. Shmorgun, "Voprosy dal'neishego rastsveta i sblizheniia sotsialisticheskikh natsii i narodnostei SSR i v dokumentakh XXVII s"ezda KPSS," *Voprosy obshchestvennykh nauk*, no. 70 (1987), pp. 32-40.

26. See, for instance, Vadim Kozhinov, "Uroki istorii," *Moskva* no. 11 (1986), pp. 183-98; Also see S. Kaltakhchian's response in *Sovetskaia kul'tura*, March 17, 1987, p. 6. See, as well, S. Andreev, *Pravda*, March 19, 1987.

27. See James Critchlow, "Signs of Emerging Nationalism in Central Asia" in Norton T. Dodge (ed.), *The Soviets in Asia* (Mechanicsville, Maryland: Cremona Foundation, 1972), p. 26.

28. This expression has been used with growing frequency by Gorbachev. For a discussion see Archie Brown, "The Soviet Leadership and the Struggle for Political Reform," *The Harriman Institute Forum*, vol. 1, no. 4 (April 14, 1987), p. 7.

29. In a round-table discussion of the national question sponsored by the journal *Istoriia SSSR*, Sergei A. Arutiunov noted that "the concept of ethnic pluralism should have its Communist variant." Sergei A. Arutiunov, "Natsional'nye protsessy v SSR: itogi, tendentsii, problemy: Beseda za kruglum stolom," *Istoriia SSSR*, no. 6 (1987), pp. 50–120.

30. See "Printsipy perestroika: Revoliutsionnost' myshleniia i deistvii," *Pravda*, April 5, 1988.

31. *Pravda*, February 19, 1988.

32. Eduard Bagramov, *Pravda*, August 14, 1987.

Chapter 3

A Theory of Soviet Nationality Policies[1]

Edward Allworth

This inquiry considers several mutually exclusive arguments concerning the nature and purview of official policies relating to Soviet nationality affairs. These propositions range from the claim that the USSR always sustains a comprehensive set of stable nationality policies to the hypothesis that the authorities carry out no long-term policies at all in this sphere. An investigation of this issue must consider the possibility that nationality affairs in the USSR function through the momentum of custom at least as much as by contemporary design. Pure prejudice or unthinking imitation may add their force.

Numbers of intelligent persons focus upon this subject, but imperfect communication both inside and outside the USSR confuses the study of Soviet nationality affairs. Politicians and ideologists engage in endless discussion, published in reams of pages, about what they often call "Soviet nationality policy." With regard to that policy, analysts and scholars of and beyond the Soviet Union express opinions and make many judgments, but often seriously misunderstand one another. Besides the stalemates that arise owing to ideological disagreement, pointless exchanges frequently occur because analysts lack common assumptions and an accepted vocabulary of colloquy in the field. As a result, in both political and academic debate, the subject of Soviet administration of nationality affairs evades sharp focus or clarity.

Many analyses proceed through studying supposed changes in Soviet nationality policies or identifying the ethnic attitudes expressed by various politicians in the USSR to answering broader questions about the country—measuring the blood pressure of the entire Soviet body politic or detecting the political motives behind overall Soviet actions. The present undertaking aims at a narrower target. It looks into the nature and scope of reputed nationality policies themselves, rather than attempting to use them as guides to the general health of the Soviet government or indicators of a Communist Party line.

Soviet officials usually speak in an obscure tongue when they refer to the topic of nationality policies. Students of the subject have no choice but to infer and isolate its semantics and stabilize terminology in order to understand the true nature of what are termed Soviet nationality policies. The choice of words usually prefigures an approach taken in the field. Consider the first of two main aspects of this large subject: policies that broadly relate to creating or resolving ethnic tension in the Soviet Union. For a consideration of this aspect one must embrace the matter as a whole, employing an appropriate generalizing term, "nationality policy," counterpart to its logical object, "the nationality question." In this conception the quantity or array of nationalities, whether two or two hundred, holds only relative importance, for the terminology engages comprehensively the problems of all at the highest common level of inquiry. The term "nationality policy" suggests the idea of systematic investigation into an overriding concern, and it links discussion to the essence of ethnic/nationality designation and its consequences rather than to the plural possessors of ethnic identity.

In this chapter the term "nationality" distinguishes only non-Russians; the phrase "ethnic group" includes nationalities and Russians. No hierarchic standing attaches to either term. To avoid terminological ambiguity in West and East, this analysis avoids using the word "nation" (*natsiia*).

Another form, "nationalities' policy," and its partner, "the nationalities' question," emphasize the atoms comprising ethnic multiplicity, rather than pointing toward the general subject. Using this terminology directs attention to the second major aspect of nationality study: compiling and interpreting data about the circumstances, background and characteristics of the many separate nationalities in the state. Using the words nationalities' policy and nationalities' question stresses detailed descriptions of demographic and ethnographic differences, trends in geographic dispersion, administrative arrangements, social regulation, and the like. But it specifically skirts the basic question of policy overlying them all.

Semantic imprecision spreads because Soviet spokesmen utter the set expression "Soviet nationality policy" as if everyone knows its content and form, yet Soviet users fail to convey its true meaning. And its singular, not plural, number implicitly lays claim to a doubtful political condition. Evidence drawn from the short life-history of the Soviet Union establishes no certainty that a single nationality policy exists or has existed in that country. Inquiries probably should speak not about nationality policy, but about different policies. Insight may come from looking into their disparities, rather than from attempting to see in them even ephemeral order beyond their one obvious purpose of exerting political control.

Despite the likelihood that Soviet authorities may have conducted more than one policy regarding the nationality question, Mikhail S. Gorbachev, General Secretary of the Communist Party of the Soviet Union (CPSU), in his political report to the 27th Congress of the CPSU in February 1986, spoke in this way:

> Our Party's tradition as handed down from Lenin has a special sensitivity and discretion toward everything respecting nationality policy (*natsional'naia politika*); it [policy] affects the interests of each nationality and sub-nationality (*natsiia i narodnost'*), and the national (*natsional'nye*) feelings of individuals; and at the same time it touches on the fundamental battle against manifestations of nationality (*natsional'nyi*) narrowness and self-importance, nationalism and chauvinism, no matter what guise they may take."[2]

In this passage Gorbachev refers to the volatility of the subject to which putative nationality policies relate. He speaks only broadly, without citing concretely any policy adopted during his or earlier regimes. Policy exerts an impact upon groups, individuals and ideological conflict, he says, but, through the deliberate vagueness and lack of particulars in the speech, he seems intentionally to avoid issues pertinent to his country's nationality problems. He couples a remark about the need for politicians to show sensitivity to the nationality issue with the admonition that they oppose the more robust expressions of nationality strivings for satisfaction. Three times during the same brief passage devoted to the nationality question in his long political report, Gorbachev warned Party members about the dangers of provincialism, excessive self-importance, nationalism, and the like. In this way, without contributing to a concrete understanding of fundamental policies beyond their function of defending the regime, he revealed the grave concern of his leadership over the possibilities of ethnic opposition to his rule through the people's exercise of lively ethnic feeling within various nationalities of the USSR. He evidently worries about the instability inherent in the force of group expression among dissatisfied nationalities.

In the March 1986 version of the *Third Program of the CPSU*, a similar vagueness, possibly an intentional evasion of the issues, characterized the treatment of the nationality question. In this text of the *Program* the statements seemed significant because they conveyed the official attitude, because of their ritual quality, and because they entirely avoided specifying or defining any examples of nationality policies. At the same time, a passage referred explicitly to the principles (*printsipy*) underlying nationality "policy" and to the principles of socialist federalism (*printsipy sotsialisticheskogo federalizma*).[3] The CPSU Program leaves unclear the origin of the term "principles" or the range of meaning intended by it in the context. Principles will come under scrutiny later in this chapter, but this inquiry does not aim to examine the nationality policies of Gorbachev because, at the time of writing, he had not yet definitely enunciated them. These references simply demonstrate that ambiguity in terminology continued to plague scholars seeking enlightenment in this field throughout, and following, the period considered.

Identifying and Responding to the Nationality Question

Serious debate over the existence or non-existence of Soviet nationality policies and their presumed nature can perhaps side-step the pitfall of vagueness in the description of these policies. However, compromise on an understanding of the nationality question poses a much greater hazard to the exchange of ideas in this field. The nationality question of the Soviet Union, its ideologists say, consists essentially of the difficulties in interethnic relations arising largely from physical and cultural differences between ethnic groups. The second, revised edition of the *Third Program of the CPSU*, issued in final form in 1986, confirmed by implication this conception of the nationality question. In a brief passage from that long document, devoted to "The Party's Social Policy," its authors categorized as two of "the fundamental tasks of social policy": "to refine nationalities' (*natsional'nye*) relations and strengthen fraternal friendship among the nationalities (*natsii*) and sub-nationalities (*narodnosti*) of the country."[4]

For non-Soviet and Soviet scholars, such an equation (interethnic relations = the nationality question) confines the subject to a limited area of communication. It closes off consideration of the nationality's sense of its own situation and of what causes its discomfort or comfort. It substitutes a perspective that is above and outside the groups which are, generally speaking, hardly interacting in a way observed among sovereign states. Moreover, a further restriction occurs in some discussions when the expression "nationality relations" refers simply to the interactions between the Russians and non-Russians of the Soviet Union. Focusing upon that single type of linkage further limits the discussion unnecessarily.

For these and related reasons, this investigation will define the nationality question as a disequilibrium that occurs when dissatisfaction overwhelms the satisfaction of Soviet nationalities collectively and, at certain times, individually, in their immediate as well as extended environment throughout the state. Given this understanding, ethnic group interrelations combine with all other significant aspects of group life to make up the satisfactions and dissatisfactions experienced, anticipated or expressed by a single nationality or by several nationalities.⁵ This conception also allows for consideration of the interests and efforts of the state's political leadership in its dealings with the nationality question. It is important to examine the charge often repeated among the Soviet nationalities that the Russian leadership in the USSR in fact creates the nationality question. Accommodating that two-way process seems to offer a more promising approach than one that views developments only from Moscow or Baku, but not both.

When an ethnic group's dissatisfaction outweighs satisfaction, the imbalance evidences one or more nationality problems. Nationality problems as a whole, whether viewed from inside or outside the nationality, comprise the sole nationality question. Without nationality problems, there is no nationality question. In terms of function, scholars can expect the USSR's nationality policies to authorize measures taken for the purpose of resolving the nationality question by dealing successfully with nationality problems.

But some customs or policies may produce a contrary effect. They can work to create and prolong some nationality problems. Measure-takers or managers might accomplish this by contributing to the satisfaction of one nationality at the expense of another. In the Soviet Union the authorities preserve a number of territorial arrangements that leave concentrations of people from one nationality within the region designated for another. In several cases, the government maintains special administrative units to protect the outsiders from absorption. And it is not extraordinary to find small islands of territory officially assigned to one constituent republic, but isolated within another. These arrangements almost always lead to ethnic friction. The Shahimardan [Hamzaabad] district of the Uzbekistan Soviet Socialist Republic (SSR), in fact located within the Kirgizistan SSR, offers a typical example. Again, the policy of allocating the Karabakh region of Transcaucasia to one SSR rather than another has for decades focused conflict on a territory that each desires to possess.

Dissatisfaction among nationalities has increased sharply over the decades of the Soviet Union's existence. As late as 1977, in discussions about the revised Soviet Constitution, certain ideologists urged the dissolution of ethnonymic administrative units in the USSR. The proposal provoked great apprehension among leaders of the Union and of the autonomous republics. In their minds lingered fresh memories of drastic actions taken in the 1940s to dissolve a number of ethnically named territorial-administrative units and expel their eponymous inhabitants. Local leaders in particular recalled that the Soviet authorities scattered the Crimean Tatars and Volga Germans beyond the Urals and in Central Asia after disbanding their Autonomous Soviet Socialist Republics (ASSRs) in 1941 and 1944: they were never reconstituted. At least seven other nationalities experienced similar punitive handling to a lesser or greater degree in the same period. Even earlier, large parts of certain other groups, such as Estonians, Gypsies and Jews—especially their educated leadership in culture and society—had undergone physical destruction in the political purges and state forced-labor camps that functioned under the auspices of the CPSU and the United State Political Administration (OGPU), and subsequently the Peoples' Commissariat for Internal Affairs (NKVD), in the 1920s and 1930s. From 1946 the Ministry of the Interior (MVD), and from 1953 the Committee of State Security (KGB), assumed similar duties in overseeing camps for political prisoners, in which numerous members of nationality groups were incarcerated.

Managers can also indirectly create dissatisfaction in certain nationalities through applying cultural or economic pressure. Such was the result when central planners mandated the siting of heavy industry in the Latvian SSR despite the obvious shortage of indigenous manpower. By compelling Latvia to accept a large in-migration of non-Latvians, this resulted in the dilution of compact settlements of local ethnic groups by ethnic Russians, who populated certain Baltic areas.

The Soviet Union has witnessed certain nationality problems whose satisfactory solution defied the abilities of leaders. A widespread problem stems from the tension that persists between the prevalence of ethnic inequality in the country on the one hand, and ideological and policy requirements for its eradication on the other. Despite the fact that a long-standing precept of the Soviet state calls for equality among nationalities, after seven decades central administrators in the USSR tacitly accept something less. This dilemma so frustrated leaders in the post-Stalin era that theoreticians endeavored to find an interpretation of conditions that would mask the failure of the regime to remove ethnic group inequality from the country. Though CPSU General Secretary Leonid I. Brezhnev in 1972 once again called for ending inequality among nationalities both legally and practically, it could not be accomplished.

To rid policy-makers of this ambivalence and logical citizens of their grounds for complaint, theoreticians separated the concept of real equality from the equalization of levels of economic and cultural development. True equality means, they said, that the Communist Party abolished non-socialist economic systems, established the socialist mode of production and production relationships among all ethnic groups of the country, and thus put an end to the backwardness of all those groups formerly oppressed. They asserted that such equality also derives from the fact that all nationalities have the same type of social structure and that the principle of equal rights and equality of nationalities has been established in all areas of society. They called the alleged national statehood of the Soviet nationalities an intrinsic feature of the single multiethnic socialist (Soviet) state. In cultural affairs evidence for the true equality of nationalities, according to the theoreticians, came from the nationalities' overcoming cultural backwardness and creating, adopting and developing a culture that was socialist in content and national in form. Further proof cited for Soviet achievement of this equality included a claim that a unified Soviet people had taken root as "a new historical community."[6]

Quantitative differences among nationalities in economic and cultural development did not matter now, the theory proposed, for those differences would eventually disappear. Ideologists warned ethnic groups against measuring, enumerating and comparing their tangible disadvantages. Later on, the argument against applying the principle of numerical proportion in ethnic affairs was echoed in the statements of CPSU leaders about political inequities. In his report commemorating the 60th anniversary of the USSR in December 1982, General Secretary Yuri V. Andropov emphasized that "an arithmetical approach to the solution of . . . problems [of representation for citizens in the Communist Party and government] would be irrelevant," and he rejected any idea of applying formal quotas.[7] In part, this casuistry was meant to explain away the disproportionate share of memberships held by Russians and Belorussians in the sole Soviet political party. The ideologists thus claim that the policies of officials have achieved among the nationalities what the theoreticians call "qualitative parity." The nationalities might regard this as mere hypothetical equivalence.

Because this opinion about the attainment of ideological parity implies uniformity among nationalities, it leads doctrinally to the further declaration that ethnic groups are naturally converging more than diverging. According to that theory, the identifying traits and separate ethnic characteristics of nationalities tend to diminish and become replaced by general, international factors. By assuming these positions the CPSU comes out openly on the side of allowing, even encouraging, ethnic groups to dissolve into one another.[8] Andropov expressed the Communist Party vision of a finite existence for Soviet nationalities once again when he voiced the Party's ultimate ideological aim: complete integration of all ethnic groups in the USSR.

Government and party policies by their nature contrast with political platform statements in two important particulars. Official policies imply a responsibility for action to be taken and a high degree of probability that the aim will be accomplished. Both policies and platforms entail a process of conscious decision-making that rules out inadvertence in adoption or intent (though not necessarily in effect), but policies call for specific action or inaction and authorize means for accomplishing it. Platforms usually spell out idealized opinions.

The measures that ideologists have openly put forward in the USSR combine some elements of both policies and platforms. Like most politicians guided mainly by ideological aims, Soviet leaders often issue statements in a declarative wording that obscures policy. This results, perhaps intentionally, in puzzling the citizenry, as well as outside observers, about the specific identity and nature of policies in nationality affairs. It also creates doubts among some analysts about the positive, as opposed to the negative, political importance of ethnic phenomena in the USSR.[9] At the same time, such lack of clarity hints at uncertainty among the decision-makers about what measures to take or how much to discuss them publicly. This tendency toward equivocation in enunciating policy inevitably draws attention to the assumptions or prejudices behind the political belief system.[10] The reluctance of officials to propose and describe concretely any nationality policies suggests that Soviet executives now prefer to let nationality affairs evolve through the impetus of habits based upon those ingrained assumptions, rather than by engaging in specific decision-making. Their behavior adds to doubts about the existence of contemporary policies in the field.

The Guidance System

Officials can manage nationality problems in the manner outlined above because a dense system of prior beliefs or tenets lies behind their opinions. This dogma, not questioned by adherents, has been laid down authoritatively by Marxism and elaborated by its disciples. Karl Marx's idea of a leading social class, the belief of Marx and Friedrich Engels in a link between class and ethnic oppression, their thoughts about historic and progressive nationalities, and other postulates, offer convinced ideologists a general social value system within which to function. Some of the doctrine formulated upon that base relates particularly to nationality affairs. Vladimir I. Lenin's conception of two contending nations present within one nation, Joseph V. Stalin's notions about the changeable nature of the nationality question, and other positions adopted by them and their comrades, reflect a strong background in Marxist dogma. Their doctrine probably incorporates prejudices that originated in Russia outside Marxism: intolerance of nonconformity, suspicion of foreigners, and contempt for migrant or scattered groups such as nomads, traders, and the like.

Principles built upon such premises express accepted, established rules. Principles set a standard for measuring and regulating practice: therefore, they guide conduct or choice. In 1972 Brezhnev proclaimed that old nationality problems stemming from legal discrimination and economic inequality had been removed forever. Thus, he established a principle that countered in advance anyone who challenged as unfair the heritage of inequities preserved in the arrangements for nationalities in the USSR.

Theory, as such, offered a third layer of guidance in nationality affairs. Marxism-Leninism-Stalinism elaborated on the opinion that the rights and status of nationality groups depend not upon ideals of equality or democracy, but upon an order of preference dictated by factors such as location, size, stability and the dominance in its area by the nationality group. Following similar reasoning, Communist Party First Secretary Joseph V. Stalin arranged the numerous Soviet nationalities according to a hierarchy of recognition. Many factors contributed to the standing of an ethnic group and the kinds of recognition accorded to it. That sort of thinking produced certain hypothetical prerogatives for those placed on the highest level—union republics (SSRs)—such as the right to a separate flag, to a republic anthem, to a written constitution, later to an encyclopedia in its own tongue, and, most of all, to self-determination through secession from the USSR.

These rich strata of assumptions, plus dogma, doctrine and principle, combined with numerous theoretical elaborations and commentaries to lay a complex foundation to steer leaders at any level of society in nationality affairs. So well did the managers throughout the Soviet Union absorb this political belief system for ethnic matters that they hardly required prompting from explicit nationality policies. This may supply one reason why Soviet ideologists seldom, if ever, list their policies in nationality affairs, and it explains the origin of difficulties that outside analysts have in identifying specific Soviet nationality policies.

The inquiry can approach the analysis of potential nationality policies as a whole in several productive ways—through focusing upon categories of human targets, by taking account of function, or in terms of the impact such measures have upon nationality groups and their leaders. If the analysis defines policies with reference to their intent to affect certain categories (groups) of human beings, then (A) *Soviet nationality policies* consist of:

(1) courses of action or inaction, and methods of accomplishing them, which are consciously decided upon and adopted

(2) by central authorities who hold the power to execute them,

(3) and have the specific, long-range goal or purpose

(4) of changing effectively or sustaining unaltered the Soviet nationality question in general,

(5) and thus affect in certain ways to a noticeable extent at least a major category or number, if not all, Soviet nationality groups,

(6) but probably operate without touching the Russian group in the same manner or degree as they touch the nationalities.

(*Comment*: Accident or inadvertence that might result from undertaking mistaken economic measures, for example, may negatively affect single ethnic groups, perhaps whole categories of them, and resemble nationality policies. But unintended actions lack the consciously adopted purpose and probably sufficient effect upon the nationality question to qualify them as nationality policies.)

In contrast to those official measures directed specifically toward nationalities in general, come actions that lack the aim of altering the equilibrium between satisfaction and dissatisfaction felt by one or more nationality groups as a whole. Unlike nationality policies, certain measures exert an influence more narrowly upon group life and identity. In this category, (B) *Policies affecting nationalities* may include:

(1) decisions or measures designed and/or neglect planned

(2) by Soviet authorities, at one of various administrative levels,

(3) but as temporary measures they do not address themselves explicitly and specifically to nationality affairs in general,

(4) nor do they mean to cause appreciable alteration in the Soviet nationality question as a whole,

(5) for they are, in fact, measures that do not single out major categories and large numbers of nationalities but mean directly to affect one, or very few, nationalities,

(6) and they may on occasion also influence the Russians.

(*Comment*: When the authorities direct pointed attention temporarily at one nationality or another, no matter how drastic the step taken, such a measure does not necessarily qualify as one of the Soviet nationality policies defined in paragraph (A) above. This second kind of measure usually lacks an intent to influence the Soviet nationality question broadly or to affect major categories and numbers of ethnic groups generally and substantially. One exception to the rule may arise if policy-makers wish to make such a narrowly focused action exemplary, delivering a powerful message with potential application to other nationalities.)

In addition to deciding upon those two sorts of policies in nationality affairs, administrators of the USSR high and low take innumerable actions that inescapably touch the lives of individual members of nationality groups. Because such actions may indirectly condition the attitudes and contentment of persons in all nationalities, these measures play a part in maintaining or undermining group awareness and intergroup harmony.

(C) *Actions reaching personal nationality* consist of measures making their main impact directly upon individual Soviet citizens, and are

(1) measures that relate to traits significant for ethnic awareness,

(2) though these policies take effect very widely without specific focus upon nationality groups, as such,

(3) and are only tangentially relevant to the nationality question as a whole, neither rising to the level of intentionally influencing the corporate satisfaction or dissatisfaction of nationalities regarding their group status, nor focusing upon single or small numbers of nationality groups,

(4) but the cumulative impact of these measures upon separate members of groups affects some nationalities differently from other groups, depending upon regional circumstances or cultural patterns.

(*Comment*: In addition to these policies, an even broader category relates to Soviet society as a whole, and cannot avoid touching many members of the nationality groups. The importance of such measures in the present consideration lies in the fact that in a society such as the USSR, where everyone is ethnically labeled, individuals habitually generalize and interpret personal experience to include others of their group. That broadest category of measures, though falling outside the range of the policies described above, also has the potential to affect various nationalities unequally. Universal draft laws, for example, draw less heavily upon older populations than on nationalities that have a large proportion of young people. Younger generations predominate in parts of the Soviet East, but not in the Soviet West.)

The Range of Policies

Evidence for the existence of the multilayered guidance system outlined above reveals itself not only through the nature and identity of its targets but in the degree of effect or impact it exerts upon them. To ascertain whether or not an investigation can usefully infer the existence of and identify policies through measuring their strength, analysts may consider a scale of strength. The extremes and median point on a curve illustrate the extent of force felt by nationality groups from actions taken or neglected by the authorities.

At one extreme of the curve (see the upper tip on the illustration in Figure 3.1) start the ostensibly affirmative actions taken in the nationality field. These include *establishing* or *reviving* nationality groups, and, from the standpoint of the Soviet leadership, *annexing* nearby nationalities in order to give them the benefit of living in the ideologically, economically and culturally preferable society of the USSR. Establishment of the Karakalpak nationality in Central Asia and the Belorussian nationality, and the annexation of the groups in the Baltic region in the Soviet West, as well as the Tuvans now in South Siberia, exemplify this category.

At the other extreme appear disintegrative actions. *Ethnocide* of groups and *genocide* of their members severely threaten their revival or further existence as corporate entities. Actions taken against Crimean Tatars, Kalmyks, Karachays, Kazakhs, Ukrainians and others in the USSR between the early 1930s and mid-1940s constituted genocide, and almost ethnocide, according to standard definitions of those crimes against humanity.

Expulsion abroad in the form of forced emigration or obligatory repatriation from Soviet home territory comes close to ethnocide, for the action destroys the vitality of a nationality or a compact community. Russian authorities in either or both the Tsarist and Soviet periods employed mass expulsions of Circassians, Chinese, Crimean Tatars, Koreans, Japanese and others to rid the motherland of nationalities that occupied land Russians wanted to possess.

On the opposite position in the spectrum comes *encouragement*. This takes material and ideological forms aimed at bolstering the vitality of a group that has undergone foreign peril or for other reasons may serve Soviet purposes in international affairs by fostering irredentist urges. Examples are the Armenians of

36 *Edward Allworth*

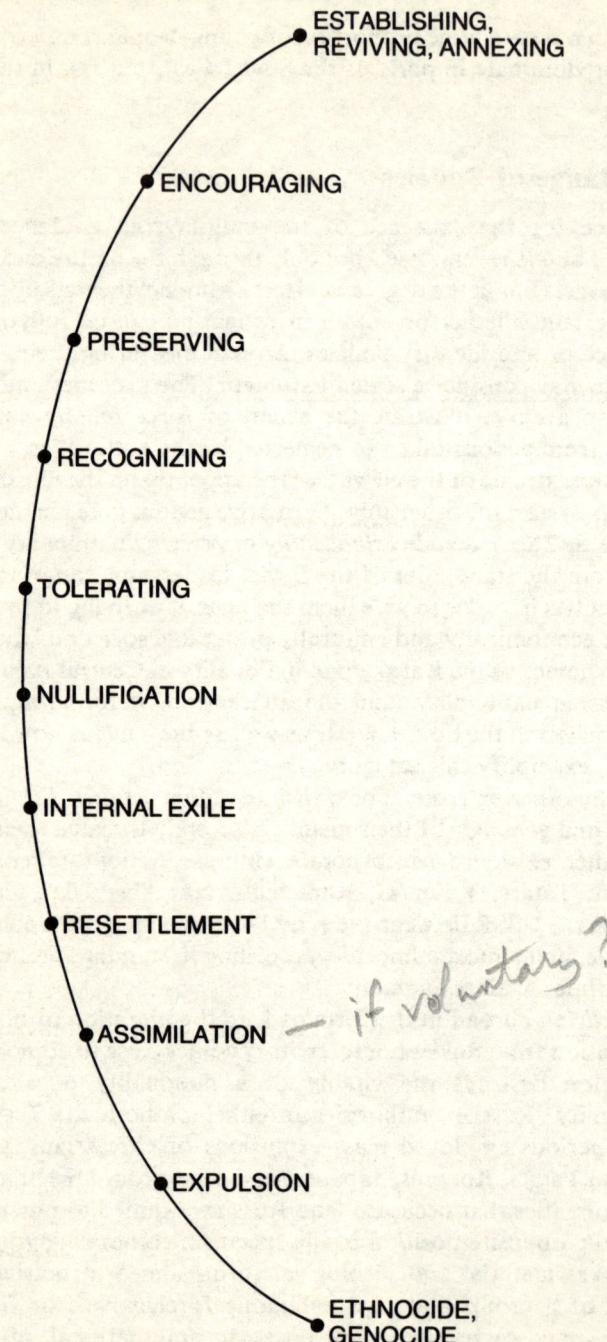

Figure 3.1 Scale of measures affecting Soviet nationalities.

Transcaucasia, as well as the Moldavians of the Soviet West. In each case, the internal group constitutes a fraction of a nationality known in larger numbers outside the USSR and existing widely fragmented or under the heavy domination of others.

Assimilation ranks third in the scale of disintegrative measures, for it results in the shrinking of the nationality, and perhaps ultimately its absorption by others. Techniques of assimilation include imposition of outside languages and institutions, denial of indigenous names and observances, and pressure to integrate physically into another ethnic group. Ajars, Karaims, Karelians, Talysh and others struggled to remain alive under these circumstances.

Counterbalancing assimilation is purposeful *preservation* of groups, such as the Kurds of Transcaucasia, as well as the Uyghurs and Baluch in Central Asia. Such groups are unlikely to perform highly important tasks in domestic or international affairs, but their symbolic value lies in demonstrating the treatment—allegedly superior to that experienced by kinsmen elsewhere—received by nationalities of the Soviet Union.

Resettlement follows assimilation as an action strongly affecting target groups, for it not only uproots from native soil but purposely settles nationalities or fragments of nationalities. They are removed to inhospitable places, perhaps close to stronger groups and often amidst ethnically unrelated ones. Resettlement implies no possibility of returning to the homeland. The Volga Germans and Soviet Koreans experienced such resettlement.

On the other pole across the curve come those groups that administrators might have forgotten but have instead awarded official *recognition* or *tolerance*. Chukchis, Evenks, Itelmans, Nenets and other very small groups located primarily in Siberia and the Far East enjoy recognition irrespective of their minor economic contribution and numbers, possibly as a painless, inexpensive ideological demonstration of state benevolence. The numerically insignificant Arabic and Bukharan Jewish communities in Central Asia remain under such tolerance.

The last segment of the disintegrative spectrum carries a measure that, at first sight, seems hardly less forceful in its impact than the preceding actions. Inner *exile*, notwithstanding the trauma induced by removing a group from the homeland area, gives a potential advantage to the people deported. It leaves the surviving nationality intact and hypothetically able to reconstitute itself elsewhere. In this respect and in the possibility of collective return, it contrasts strikingly with resettlement. The nationalities that the Soviet authorities exiled during World War II—Balkars, Chechens, Crimean Tatars,

Ingush, Kalmyks, Karachays, Karapapakhs, Meskhetian Turks and others—underwent the experience of group exile while suffering great loss of life. Even so, technically, they retained the right to return.

Finally, somewhat gentler tendencies converge from both disintegrative and neutralizing halves of the arc at the center of the scale. Together, they constitute a relatively passive class of measures that collectively amount to ethnic *nullification*. In it are grouped those measures consisting essentially of minimizing or omitting positive actions. These include employing gradualism and tokenism in cultural advancement and self-expression; withholding completely or granting only very low-level official group recognition; diluting the community with members of other ethnic groups; misidentifying or renaming the group; dispersing and fragmenting the group through economic development; withholding religious protection; reducing intragroup communications—especially forbidding full-scale employment of the native tongue and repeatedly changing the alphabets; encouraging supranationality linkage and integration; and avoiding drastic, inflammatory actions that stimulate or unify active ethnic awareness. A common technique of nullification is a measure that drains away the meaning in names and institutions by denigrating any genuine, positive importance of separate identity, and by denying authority and responsibility to the ethnic or administrative leadership of eponymous territorial units. This occurs, for example, when the authorities put Russians in charge of Kazakhstan or make Uzbeks dominant in Karakalpakistan. Many nationalities feel the effects of nullification in the USSR, but the more vulnerable ones, such as Chinese, Gagauz, Jews and Karelians, have experienced it most strongly.

Nullification, in the long run, may remain the most effective measure used by Soviet authorities to forward their aims in nationality affairs if those goals continue to include substantial denationalization or full integration of distinct groups. Through persistent attrition, nullification undermines vitality while it discourages group cohesion.

The Functions of the Supposed Policies

Despite or because of its complexity, the multilayered guidance system (including assumptions, dogma, doctrine, principle, theory, nationality policies, policies affecting nationalities, policies reaching individuals) discriminates between nationalities and among their members. The system does not, perhaps cannot, function even-handedly in Soviet nationality affairs. The persisting inequity suggests that politicians take a functional approach to managing the nationalities: in other words, that their emphases, sketched in Figure 3.1, relate mainly to the goals envisioned by political leaders, not to the aspirations of most nationality groups.

An entirely different side of this investigation might examine the degree of energy, percentage of resources, or amount of manpower put into the execution of certain policies by the USSR's leadership. That should give grounds for confirming the priorities and revealing the thinking of the authorities in Soviet nationality affairs. Even without findings to be gained from such a worthwhile fact-finding mission, the motives of politicians become clearer when an inquiry turns to the functions of measures advocated or adopted.

Broadly speaking, the leadership exhibits, but seldom acknowledges directly in so many words, three aims in nationality affairs: to classify groups ideologically and administratively for convenient management; to prohibit effective growth or expression of ethnic feeling; and to prescribe acceptable forms and channels for developments in the Soviet nationality question.

In this discussion, moving beyond a concentration upon the human targets of policy to penetrate the function of policies may help reveal not merely how and to what degree, but to some extent why, the system treats various nationalities differently. A sensitivity to the population's ethnic composition colors every public reflex rooted in tradition and surely informs each action considered in Soviet decision-making. A great many responses and measures inevitably distinguish between individuals and between ethnic groups through procedures of *classification*.

Classification—historical, qualitative or quantitative—can embody or determine status, limitations, recognition and disabilities for members of different groups. The very act of defining nationality becomes a major aspect of classification. For most of its years, the USSR's ideologists defined nationality mainly with reference to externally perceptible traits: economic, territorial, linguistic and cultural (inferring psychological) community. Some political leaders arbitrarily selected this combination of what they called objective characteristics required for qualification as a nationality in the USSR. The definition delineates most groups on the basis of notions preconceived by the definers rather than according to the choices of nationalities. Consequently, throughout the USSR, almost every nationality must jealously defend its existence on the basis of terms set by others. It clings to administrative name and, perhaps, territory. The politicians assign these partly according to the nationality's concentration, numbers, cultural level, and the like, rather than by reference to the group's wishes. The authorities do not conduct plebiscites within individual Soviet nationalities in order to determine their ethnic preferences.

Through methods entailing classification the executives set about nullifying the potential for self-assertion and survival among nationalities. These measures diminish the potency of ethnic identity and, through fundamentally discriminating between groups, manipulate the nationalities' access to benefits or means of self-expression. Classification obviously roots itself partly in deep-seated beliefs of the decision-makers and especially in the Marxist dogma declaring that there are worthless ethnic groups which deserve to die out or to live in inequality. That dogma generates an attitude of contempt toward certain groups, and therefore puts them at a disadvantage under the Soviet system. Designating certain ethnic groups as proletarian (and therefore preferred) and others as agrarian, for example, ideologically relegates half or more of the Soviet nationalities to second-class status. In this respect, the echoes of ideology continue to resonate through nationality affairs in the late twentieth century.

Classification confines itself narrowly to the fairly pacific measures of nullification. But the authorities' inclination to control, intimidate or eradicate troublesome groups expresses itself generally in the *prohibition* of activity that nationalities might consider crucial, especially in other states where greater equality prevails.

Prohibition characterizes the drastic measures shown along the lower half of the curve in Figure 3.1, from the extreme of ethnocide to the somewhat less destructive group exile. Standing between them, assimilation, slow and gradual in contrast to other measures in that half of the scale, produces an equally definitive effect.

Sufficient evidence may sustain an argument that the seemingly less forceful measures of formation and annexation, encouragement, preservation, recognition and tolerance—shown along the upper arc of the curve—in their own way also exert a powerful influence upon each nationality. To a significant extent, they prescribe the lifestyle, location, timing and limits of expression of the nationality. Virtually no major initiative remains open to the groups in the larger arena of ethnic self-determination.

Prescription, as much as nullification and prohibition, typifies Soviet treatment of nationalities by Soviet managers. Prescription follows Soviet assumptions, doctrines and principles in setting the rules by which ethnic groups live. One such prescription with many ramifications arises from an assumption that monoethnicity must form the only natural arrangement of society in modern times. That view has validated the practice of partitioning supraethnic complexes, especially in the Soviet East. The establishment of special eponymous administrative units for even very small groups, such as Uyghurs and other nationalities, grew out of that prescription.

Measures of prescription also convert into guidelines for nearly all thinking about nationality affairs in the USSR the three foremost slogans/principles of Soviet ideology in the field: socialist internationalism, Soviet patriotism and friendship among ethnic groups. These principles prevent the occurrence of intra-group alignments resting upon the assertion of common ethnic group interests and feelings in the USSR. They function by prescribing multiethnic working-class solidarity in place of general monoethnic, linguistic or regional cohesion. Likewise, they prescribe fealty to the state and a single Soviet people, rather than to locality or nationality, and call for obligatory deference to the Russian group coupled with required estrangement from other ethnic groups or complexes. Ideologists use these three principles to shape nearly every argument or critique delivered in the field of nationality affairs. Prescriptions based on these principles obviously militate against alternative ecumenical forms, such as the ideologically unacceptable cosmopolitan outlook, which is regarded in the USSR as pernicious, non-class internationalism.

Attention to these ideological aspects of nationality affairs rises and falls in accordance with some fluctuation in political gravitation. Analysts sometimes remark that crisis conditions inside the USSR result in an easing of strict attitudes toward the wishes and aspirations of the nationalities. Political and economic confidence within and confusion without the country, the thinking goes, lead to heavy-handed treatment of nationalities. A combination of both internal and external chaos might mix both harsh and moderate handling of Soviet nationalities. Detailed study can test those propositions, but in general terms they appear to have some validity. They may help to account for the fairly distinct, successive stages that characterize nationality affairs in the USSR.

Periodization of Nationality Problems

The extraordinary events that shook the Russian Empire and the world between the collapse of the Tsarist government in March 1917 and the first de-Stalinization of the Soviet regime in February 1956 left their imprint upon developments in nationality affairs. The disruption continuing outside Russia during the final 12 months of World War I enabled Soviet Russian leaders to initiate a mixture of changes in response to the nationality question in their country. Some of those measures increased the satisfaction of certain nationalities, others provoked some nationalities and supraethnic complexes to active dissatisfaction, even secession. By the time the CPSU exercised strong control over the USSR in the early 1930s, the Western world was floundering in the morass of the Great Depression. That condition of general crisis abroad evidently permitted Soviet politicians to exert heavy pressure upon their nationalities for ideological conformity.

The ensuing war affected both external and internal ethnic affairs tremendously. Mass deportations carried out during that time culturally and physically devastated many nationalities. At the same time, the authorities made conciliatory gestures toward religious observance and added a constitutional provision for military units composed of men from single nationalities. Nevertheless, drastic, unstable, arbitrary actions in nationality affairs characterized the period 1917-1956 as a whole. Therefore, measures taken during those years belong to the categories of both prescription and prohibition.

After 1956 the times seemed less perilous for the groups, but dogmatism among the ideologists threatened to erase internal borders and dismantle the structures that nationalities had come to regard as shields against ethnic annihilation. Simultaneously, new pressure to generalize the use of the Russian language for every purpose among all groups frightened large and small nationalities alike. The government took measures to reinstate Balkars, Chechens and some other deported nationalities approximately to their former positions. In spite of the steps taken toward removing some excesses of the Stalin era, ideological rigor and renewed Russian chauvinism unexpectedly made the period 1956-1964—the tenure of CPSU General Secretary Nikita S. Khrushchev—a time of apprehension for the survival of nationalities and religious denominations in the USSR.

Those fears subsided during the long incumbency of Khrushchev's successor, Brezhnev (1965-1982). During that period no important structural changes occurred in the outlines of eponymous ethnic administrative units. In 1972 Brezhnev, evidently for the first time during his tenure as General Secretary, formally and publicly acknowledged the permanent nature of the nationality question. After decades of assertions that the question had been resolved, by facing reality he usefully widened public consideration of nationality affairs in the USSR; however, the quiet working of nullification proceeded throughout these years, steadily removing obligatory links between nationalities and administrative units, draining ethnic content from under the namesake structures, and the like.

In the years following Brezhnev's acknowledgement that the nationality question still existed in his homeland, Soviet ideologists made a little progress in confronting the actual situation that prevailed in nationality affairs. But the Soviet pretence in the late 1970s that true equalization existed among nationalities demonstrated that spokesmen lean toward obfuscation rather than real solution. This conclusion raises two possibilities: either genuine nationality policies, defined above, do not exist in this field, or they remain ineffectual. How do we know which possibility is correct?

Identifying True Nationality Policies

In the mid-1960s a history teacher from the Ukraine, Ivan Dzyuba, uttered the unacceptable when he questioned the honesty of Soviet measures in nationality affairs: "... this policy does not wish to appear publicly as it really is.... Its basic principle is at all costs to avoid calling things by their proper names."[11] Why should nationality policies remain secret? Because in regard to the nationality question the leadership in the USSR follows a hidden agenda, he thought. Through inference Dzyuba had determined that unpublicized Soviet policies were aimed at denationalizing, centralizing, homogenizing and amalgamating the nationalities, while Russifying all Soviet culture and history. His pessimistic thinking emerged in the severe ideological weather prevailing toward the end of Khrushchev's sway.

Dr Andrei D. Sakharov corroborated Dzyuba's assessment of Soviet nationality policies with additional authoritative dissent. In a memorandum directed to Brezhnev in June 1972, he too, verified the existence of what he called "an increasingly acute nationality question." In his analysis it stemmed from illegal and legal policies and actions in nationality affairs. In other words, the nationality question emanated from initiatives, measures and the inaction of Soviet political authorities.[12]

By placing the onus upon political managers of the USSR for persistent, troubling nationality problems, these analyses disagree fundamentally with the Communist Party assessment expressed openly in late 1972. From then until the mid-1980s, various Soviet leaders have declared that the contemporary nationality question essentially consists of intractable problems intrinsic to the life of multiethnic states and that its full resolution will not come until the millennium, if ever.

Both intellectual leaders and large numbers among the nationalities disagreed with the leadership. As a sort of popular referendum, members of various groups (including Estonians, Kazakhs and Volga Germans) repeatedly demonstrated dissatisfaction with the authorities' handling of Soviet nationality affairs. Between 1922 and 1986 dozens of nationalities experienced the effects of various practices shown in Figure 3.1 on p. 36. Probably never in those decades did Soviet life exhibit the working of free positive choice among the nationalities. Reviewing the patterns of management, it is difficult to discover recent actions other than measures meant to right previous wrongs that showed affirmative intent. Thus, the responsibility for the nationality problems evident in Soviet affairs cannot fall on the shoulders of the nationalities themselves. Nor, as the experience in other heterogeneous countries has shown, does the circumstance that many ethnic groups coexist in the USSR sufficiently explain the persistence of the nationality question in the Soviet Union. A more likely explanation arises from the exercise of rigid opinions and arbitrary behavior rather than thoughtful, purposeful decisions made in high places.

In light of all these contradictory indications, the investigator may sum up the operation of the mechanism known as Soviet nationality policies in several arguments:

1. The leadership of the USSR apparently maintains no constant nationality policies; instead, it adheres to general dogmatic positions and ideological principles that guide actions taken by managers working at lower levels in the sphere of nationality affairs.

2. Whatever measures the political leadership of the USSR authorizes in nationality affairs, dogma and principle pertinent to this field allow for applying such policies or measures inequitably to various nationalities.

3. As a result of the flexibility/adaptability provided by the lack of explicit nationality policies [argument 1.], as well as the inequity permitted in taking actions affecting nationalities [argument 2.], some groups—for example, the Crimean Tatars, Jews and Lithuanians—undergo discriminatory treatment in this sphere. The system provides not only for mistreatment but for unequal treatment of nationalities.

4. Since 1922 Russian habits and Soviet ideology have thwarted any serious, comprehensive attempt to satisfy the aspirations or remove the dissatisfaction of nationalities.

5. Up to the mid-1980s Soviet authorities believed that they could not comfortably resolve the nationality question and that they could absorb the costs of leaving it unresolved.

6. Voices heard and signs appearing at the end of this period suggest that Soviet leaders have begun to take cognizance of the need to reconsider their theories and practices in order to deal with widespread expressions of dissatisfaction among the nationalities.

In the domestic situation the USSR presently faces, as long as the

State retains its present configuration and form of government, Soviet leaders appear to find themselves ideologically incapable of adopting an effective program of nationality policies. Without such policies, they cannot resolve the nationality question. If they abdicate responsibility for removing the nationality problems apparent nearly everywhere in the country, the nationalities will accomplish what they regard as desirable changes within their territories. The initiative in nationality affairs and perhaps other matters may then pass out of the hands of the central leadership and its ideologists.

Notes

1. This chapter presents the author's most recent as well as some earlier thinking regarding Soviet nationality policies. Preliminary discussions about them appeared in *Minority Problems in Eastern Europe between the World Wars*, ed. Avraham Greenbaum (Jerusalem: The Institute for Advanced Studies, The Hebrew University of Jerusalem, 1988) and in *Tatars of the Crimea*, ed. Edward Allworth (Durham, N. C.: Central Asia Book Series, Duke University Press, 1988). Writing of the present essay began in 1987 at the Institute for Advanced Studies, Hebrew University of Jerusalem, Givat Ram, Jerusalem. Development of the theory benefited from both the congenial environment and the thoughtful comments of participants in the Institute's Seminar, led by Professor Mordechai Altshuler, devoted to problems of Jews and other nationalities in Eastern Europe and the Soviet Union.

2. "Politicheskii doklad Tsentral'nogo Komiteta KPSS XXVII S"ezdu Kommunisticheskoi Partii Sovetskogo Soiuza. Doklad General'nogo Sekretaria TsK KPSS Tovarishcha Gorbacheva M. S. 25 fevralia 1986 goda," *Pravda*, February 26, 1986, p. 6.

3. "Programma Kommunisticheskoi Partii Sovetskogo Soiuza. Novaia redaktsiia. Priniata XXVII s"ezdom KPSS," *Vodnyi transport*, March 7, 1986, p. 6.

4. "Programma Kommunisticheskoi Partii Sovetskogo Soiuza. Novaia redaktsiia. Priniata XXVII s"ezdom KPSS," *Vodnyi transport*, March 7, 1986, p. 5.

5. Edward Allworth (ed.), *Nationality Group Survival in Multiethnic States* (New York: Praeger Publishers, 1977), p. 2.

6. I. P. Tsamerian, "Certain Theoretical Problems in the Leninist Nationality Policy of the CPSU," *Voprosy istorii KPSS*, no. 8 (1973), trans. in *Soviet Law and Government*, no. 4 (Spring 1974), pp. 8-9.

7. Yuri V. Andropov, "The USSR: Sixty Years. Report on the Occasion of the 60th Anniversary of the USSR," *Speeches and Writings* (New York: Pergamon Press, 1983), p. 28.

8. Tsamerian, p. 17. Andropov, p. 25.

9. Paul A. Goble, "Managing the Multinational USSR," *Problems of Communism*, no. 4 (July–August 1985), p. 83.

10. Peter H. Juviler and Henry W. Morton (eds.), *Soviet Policy-Making* (New York: Frederick R. Praeger, 1967), pp. 6–16; Geoffrey K. Roberts, *A Dictionary of Political Analysis* (London: Longman Group, Ltd., 1971), p. 152.

11. Ivan Dzyuba, *Internationalism or Russification. A Study in the Soviet Nationalities Problem*, 2nd ed. (London: Weidenfeld and Nicolson, 1968), pp. 211, 208–10.

12. Andrei D. Sakharov, "Memorandum [to Gen. Sec. Brezhnev]," *Survey*, no. 3 (Summer 1972), pp. 223–4, 231.

Chapter 4

Codification of Soviet Nationality Policies

John N. Hazard

Soviet laws have carried statements of nationality policy ever since the founding of the Soviet state in 1917, but, as with law in any land, its meaning is obscure unless interpreted. Soviet jurists, like many others, look to three sources for guidance on interpretation: the intention of the parties at the time of establishing a rule; analysis of the text; and the purposes which the rule was intended to serve.[1] Anglo-American common lawyers use the same methods, most notably when interpreting an ancient document like the United States constitution, whose meaning is sought through examination of what the Founding Fathers had in mind when they drafted the text.

The non-Soviet analyst searching for statements of Soviet nationality policies in statutes, codes and constitutions senses the need for study of interpretation with reference to supporting literature, because political and legal cultures are so different in the United States and the USSR that one cannot assume that words mean the same thing in both cultures. The American has to try to step into Lenin's shoes as he sat down with his colleagues to draft a formal blueprint in law for a revolutionary society: Jeffersonian principles are no guide to an understanding of the probable stimulation to Marxist-oriented draftsmen.

The historical record of what the Russian revolutionaries read is no mystery. Both Marx and Engels were prolific authors, and Lenin wrote the blueprint for his colleagues in his *State and Revolution*.[2] There is no dearth of historians on each side of what Marxists often call "barricades" to speculate on what politicians were thinking in 1917–1918 and why they thought that way. Lenin made clear his motives for revolution well before 1917, when he called together a small band of persons in the village of Zimmerwald, Switzerland, in 1915.[3] He grieved with them over what they took to be the betrayal of the socialist cause by deputies elected to the parliaments of the belligerent powers by the various Social Democratic Parties of 1914.

In the eyes of the Zimmerwald plotters the parliamentarians had abandoned the first rule of their creed, the rule established by Marx and Engels in the *Communist Manifesto* of 1848.[4] They had set aside their duty to take a common working-class position and had voted in their several parliaments to support national armies. They ignored the *Manifesto*'s declaration that "workers know no fatherland."[5] To Marx a socialist can have only one loyalty, namely to the working-class. Frenchmen, Germans, Englishmen and Austrians had no right in light of their creed to support a war conducted by national states. Socialists were expected by Lenin to adhere to the *Manifesto*'s additional admonition that "National differences and antagonisms between peoples are daily more and more vanishing," and "the supremacy of the proletariat will cause them to vanish still faster."[6]

Stalin's writing on the subject of nationality policy must be prominent among the papers studied as bases for interpreting Soviet laws on nationality. It was he whom Lenin chose to formulate in print the Party's thoughts on the topic. In his pamphlet entitled "Marxism and the National and Colonial Question," published in 1913 on the eve of World War I, he stated the Social Democratic vision when he wrote that "if national autonomy is unsuitable now, it will be still more unsuitable in the future society, a socialist society."[7]

With such a creed Lenin presents to an outsider a basis for doubt as to his policy by his support during the early months following the Russian Revolution for a policy of partial dismemberment of what had been the Russian Empire. A glance at the history of the time provides a clue to his tactics. It was a time when US President Woodrow Wilson was proclaiming a heady doctrine to nationalists in support of the efforts of the Allied Powers to break up their principal enemies, the German and Austro-Hungarian Empires. His slogan was "self-determination" for all peoples. The Wilsonian slogan suited Lenin equally well in his effort to weaken the Russian Empire. His Russian Social Democratic Labor Party had long been calling the Russian Empire a "prison of peoples," and there were attentive listeners in the Ukraine, the Baltic and Transcaucasia.[8] Lenin would have had difficulty in holding these restless minority peoples to the socialist faith had he preached the rule of socialist solidarity and abandonment of the long-cherished dream of national independence.

Lenin often proved himself a wily tactician when he thought his cause could benefit. He was prepared to take what he called a "step backward" in order later to take "two steps forward." On the national issue he took a tactical line. He consented to secession from the unitary structures of the collapsed Russian Empire by the Finns, the Ukrainians, the Belorussians, and the Baltic peoples of Latvia, Lithuania and Estonia.[9]

What had been units of the Russian Empire became a group of legally proclaimed independent states, ready to take their places in a "concert of Europe" if permitted by the victorious Allied Powers to do so. One cannot but wonder whether the prompt acceptance of these states by Western European statesmen as partners in recreating Europe on the ashes of the Austro-Hungarian, German and Russian Empires might have changed the course of history in Eastern Europe.

Western Europe paid no need to the Eastern possibilities until Lloyd George, Prime Minister of Great Britain, called together in 1922 the Genoa Conference to recreate a concert of Europe. By that time Lenin's plans for reuniting his peoples had matured: most of the liberated former regions of the Russian Empire were prepared to rejoin the Great Russians in a single delegation under the terms of a treaty which indicated that formal union in some form was to follow.[10]

Lenin held some powerful and unfamiliar cards in his hand when he began to reconstitute a state within the confines of what had been the Russian Empire. His ace was his Social Democratic Party, now renamed the Communist Party. Since its beginning at the turn of the century, the Party had been structured in accordance with the principles of the *Communist Manifesto*. In spite of a desire on the part of some national groups, notably the Jewish Bund, that they be permitted to form their own nationally oriented unit, cooperating with other nationally oriented units in a federal party structure, Lenin resisted the pressure, Lenin argued that although members of the Party might be Jews, Ukrainians, Lithuanians and others, they must first of all see themselves as proletarians. The Party must not be federalized in structure. Although he had been willing to grant independence to a "state" in order to weaken fears of Russification even in a socialistically organized "state," it was to be noted that he was selective in his choice of peoples for release from the Russian core. He released only the borderlands of what had been the Empire.

For the non-Russian minorities in the heartland of the country—surrounded as they were by Russians, or living in Central Asia far from the influence of national liberation ideas and subject to the pressures of Russian arms—there was to be no release. The boundaries of the old Empire were to be retained for these regions, but with a rhetorical concession. Lenin named his new state a Russian Federation. He also established one structure to indicate his understanding that these peoples of the interior feared Russification as much as the peoples of the borderlands.[11] This structure was a People's

Commissariat of Nationalities, whose mission was to develop a policy of cultural advancement as proof that the Russian majority was no longer to attempt Russification.[12] At the head of the agency Lenin placed Stalin, presumably because of his well-established role within the Party as its specialist on minority aspirations.

There is evidence that Lenin expected his Communist Party members to be mindful of their rigid training in class unity as the ultimate goal. With this training as inspiration they were expected to lead the new states back into association with the Russians in their Russian Federation. The Russian Republic's statutes were in several instances copied by the Ukrainian and Belorussian draftsmen.[13] Not only were statutes copied, but, more importantly, administrative agencies for the railroads and armed forces in the Ukrainian and Belorussian Republics were united with those of the Russian Republic. The goal was made clear in a new postrevolutionary Program of the Communist Party, published in 1919, in which Article 9 declared the principal aim to be the bringing together of proletarians.[14]

Evidently, the time was not yet ripe for class-oriented union, for the 1919 Program stated two principles which appear to be concessions to a lingering fear of Russification. The Program read:

1. In order to remove mistrust . . . it is necessary to abolish all privileges of any national group; to proclaim the fullest equality of all nationalities.
2. For the same purpose, as a temporary measure toward achieving the unity of nations, the Party suggests a federative combination of all states organized on a Soviet basis.[15]

To interpret what Lenin conceived to be an appropriate national policy at the time, the word "temporary" is a guide. It suggests that unity remained the goal, but that it would be counterproductive to rush toward that goal. Perhaps this attitude was supported in Communist minds by their training in the Hegelian dialectics which sees progress toward synthesis only after moving from thesis to antithesis. If this be so, it is conceivable that Communists expected to achieve unity after developing diversity so as to quiet fears of Russification.

An event in 1922 suggests that by then Lenin altered his 1917–1918 thinking. Prior to 1922 he was building a federation under the banner of the Great Russians. In early 1922 he was proposing something looser than the Russian Federation. This change became clear in a letter he wrote to his colleague Kamenev on September 26, 1922. He proposed that the new union be one in which Ukrainians and the other minority peoples join in a USSR where all would share equally with the Russians in exercising power.[16]

Lenin's new tactics took institutional form within three months in a proposal for a new federal structure to be placed before a Constitutional Convention in Moscow at the very end of December. To prepare for the Convention, Lenin first took the three republics of Azerbaijan, Georgia and Armenia—which had been created by the Communists in 1921-1922 to oust the Allied Armies of occupation—and grouped them together in one federal republic. Thus the Transcaucasian Federated Soviet Socialist Republic was brought into being on March 12, 1922. In this federation each of the three constituent republics maintained its parliamentary and administrative structures, though they were subordinate to the structures of the federation.

Stalin explained this new federation on the basis of the history of centuries of strife between the three peoples involved. He expected that federation would teach them the advantages of living in peace.[17] There may, of course, have been other unexpressed reasons, but it may be surmised that the power-conscious Communist Party members thought that a major advantage of federation would be its influence upon peoples to abandon their long-held nationalist sentiments, stimulated over centuries by differing religions, languages, cultures and alphabets.

Once the Transcaucasian federation was in place the Communists hastened to create the new USSR, and by the end of December 1922 plans were complete. Historians in the West have since concluded that the new federation of Russians, Ukrainians, Belorussians and Transcaucasians was designed to achieve two aims: first, the calming of fears that a Russification policy might emerge again; and second, the attraction to the Soviet fold of other peoples farther away. Proof of the latter aim is found in the joyous cry of the observer from the Third (Communist) International at the Constitutional Convention, which was heard after the four delegations had agreed upon union: the protocol to the Convention records his shout of "Long Live the USSR of the World."

The new USSR differed in structure from the federal structure Lenin had devised for the Russian Federation. While the Russian Federation's symbol of class sovereignty was recreated at the apex of the USSR's hierarchy of state institutions in the form of a Congress of Soviets, representing the electorate on a federation-wide basis, a new institution was established to serve as an interim parliament between the infrequent meetings of the Congress.[18]

The new interim parliament was created as a bicameral body, one chamber of which was to represent the various minority peoples within the federation; the other chamber represented the population on the basis of numbers. Although this system may at first glance look like the two-chamber legislature in the United States, there was a difference: the Chamber of Nationalities included not only blocks of equal size from each of the four founding republics, but also an equal number of deputies from other large national minorities. The most noted of these were the Bashkirs and the Tatars, but they were not the sole outsiders. Together with them were to sit, albeit in lesser numbers, delegations from the less numerous national groups who lived within the Russian Republic. In practice, since the Congress met rarely, this bicameral legislature became the principal formal mouthpiece of policy formulated for legislative promulgation by the Communist Party's Central Committee and its Politburo.

A second apparent concession to lingering national sentiments was a constitutional provision granting the four republics that had constituted the union the right to secede from it.[19] This constitutional provision, perhaps more than any other, requires a study of history before it can be interpreted meaningfully, for much was written by Communist leaders before and after it was adopted. In 1923, soon after promulgation of the principle, Stalin wrote, "This must be said bluntly—the right of self-determination cannot and must not serve as an obstacle to the exercise by the working-class of its right to dictatorship."[20] He continued to state his position subsequently, for in 1927 he hailed the "blossoming of cultures nationalist in form and socialist in content under proletarian dictatorship in one country."[21] On another occasion he wrote that the Communist Party would not favor secession.

Finally, and less dramatically, the administrative structure of the new federation was established with three types of Commissariat: All-Union, Federated and Republic:[22] the first (All-Union) was a unitary administrative structure with only a single line of command from the USSR capital to the operating bodies situated in the republics; the second (Federated) passed the line of command through the republics on the way to the operating enterprises; the third (Republic) was self-contained within the republic and had direct command of its operating units without need to receive instructions from the federal level of administration, except about broad policy matters related to economic planning.

Examination of the division into three types suggests a concern that activities closely related to national minority cultures be freed from any hint of central direction, lest the minority peoples think that they were being Russified under administrative procedures. Thus, the fields of education, justice (law courts and Bar), and agriculture were all free from formal central direction. On the other hand, in the industrial departments of the Supreme Council of National Economy, which were thought to be in need of close relationship to planning and where there was no ethnic sensibility involved, structures were designed solely to foster efficiency. The biggest industrial establishments were administered through All-Union Commissariats; the lesser ones, where consumer preferences might be a matter of concern, were placed in the Federated category; and the smallest ones, using locally obtained resources and designed to cater to local needs, as with musical instruments, hotel-keeping and local transport, were placed in the Republic category.

If ethnicity can conceivably be given as the reason for distinguishing between administrative structures in 1922–1923, changes were to come in subsequent years as the Communists moved toward an ever-closed union. Both justice and agriculture were soon moved out of the Republic category to the Federated category as centralization proceeded, and even education—in the universities, although not in the schools—was brought under centralized direction in the Federated category.

Students of Soviet constitutional history know that among Communists there has never been a reluctance to change constitutional structures. There is no sentiment like that in the United States that constitutions are eternal. For the Marxist, law is a reflection of the correlation of forces as it exists at any given time. As those change, so also must the constitution. The first federal Constitution was drafted in implementation of the 1922 Treaty of Union, and adopted provisionally in 1923 and finally in January 1924: since it was drafted during a period of mixed economy, when private and state enterprise existed side by side, it was by definition outdated when Lenin's New Economic Policy of a mixed economy was terminated in 1928. It was unsuited to a wholly state-owned enterprise system subject to state economic planning. While it took some time to replace the Constitution, the process began on June 11, 1936, when a draft was circulated by the Central Committee of the Party and the Presidium of the state legislature to the public for comment. By December of that year the new text was ready for adoption, and on December 5, 1936, the Congress of Soviets ratified it.[23]

This second federal Constitution for the USSR introduced changes in the federal structure, the most notable being an increase in the number of constituent units. The Transcaucasian Federation was dissolved and its three constituent units were given status equal to that of the Russians, Ukrainians and Belorussians. Further, some of the former Central Asian, autonomous republics, which under the 1923 constitution had been subdivisions of the Russian Republic, were placed on a par with the original founders. This raised the total number of republics on the constituent level to 12.

The Congress of Soviets, which had stood at the apex of the state's institutional legislative pyramid, was abolished, and the former interim legislature with its bicameral structure was elevated to the top. In a sense, this change suggested that the need to maintain a class-structured rather than an ethnic-structured legislature, as a symbol of the *Manifesto*'s continuing emphasis upon class unity, had passed with the achievement of the Communist Party's unquestioned domination over national aspirations.

In spite of the prominence given to the Chamber of Nationalities in the revised state structure, no one expected surprises in the form of block-voting by the minority peoples against the Russians. In some measure these minorities were reduced in political power, for those that were not elevated to constituent status lost their equal representation with the founders in the chamber. While in 1923 the Bashkirs and Tatars, with their populations of more than one million, had the same number of seats in the interim parliament's national chamber, they were now to send fewer deputies to Moscow. Stalin thought it necessary to explain, perhaps to quiet claims for equality based on pride, that no people, even if their numbers exceeded one million, could be granted the right to secede. That was a right limited to the constituent members of the federation, who had to be situated on a frontier of the USSR.[24] They had to remain as autonomous republics within the Russian Republic. In light of what Stalin had written earlier about his expectation that no secessions would be countenanced by the Communist Party, the explanation seemed contrived to foster further adhesions to the USSR rather than to encourage expectations of secession among Ukrainians, Belorussians and peoples south of the Caucasus and in Central Asia.

The expectation of further adhesions must have seemed more realistic to Stalin than outsiders might have supposed, for when the 1939 Pact with Hitler had stabilized the USSR's frontier with Germany, Stalin entered into a war with Finland which began under circumstances evidently designed to attract Finns to the Soviet federation. As soon as the Soviet armies crossed the Finnish frontier near Leningrad, the government of a Soviet Finland was proclaimed. The Finnish people were invited to rally to it. The world knows that on the contrary the Finns resisted stiffly; and although they were finally defeated and required to cede Viborg and its environs as well as the northern seacoast near Murmansk to the USSR, there was no move among the people to unite with the USSR.[25]

Stalin seems not to have given up hope of regaining Finland, however: following the occupation of the three Baltic states in 1940 under color of treaties of defense and their entry into the USSR as constituent republics, he established a Karelo-Finnish Republic of constituent status, presumably with the expectation that eventually the defeated Finnish Republic would join it. When it became evident that no such union of Finns was to be anticipated, the Karelo-Finnish Republic was demoted in 1956 from its constituent status, on a par with the Russian Republic, and restored to the inferior status of autonomous republic within the Russian Republic. This surprising move was explained as a step designed to further economic development of a region which was in reality linked economically to the Russian Republic.[26] Now the USSR, which in 1940 had incorporated 16 constituent members termed union republics, became a federation of 15 constituent members with full constitutional equality with the Great Russians. Since that time the number of union republics has remained constant.

Another structural manifestation of the 1936 Constitution's attitude toward republic autonomy is to be found in its provision that codes of law, which up to that time had been promulgated by each republic separately, albeit on a general pattern set by the federal legislature's adoption of general lines of commonality, were to be federal codes.[27] Although this provision would have led, if applied, to considerable centralization of legislative authority, it had no such result because it was not put into effect, probably because World War II occupied the full attention of Stalin. Even after the end of the war there was no move to implement the provision, and in 1957 an amendment removed it from the Constitution.[28] This meant that the system of law codes remained the same as it had been under the first federal Constitution, namely a set of republic-adopted codes conforming to federally adopted "general principles."

Throughout the history of the Soviet federation, the state economic planners have sensed that they could improve the level of production if they could subdivide the geographical territory occupied by the Soviet state along lines that would be more rational for economic administration than are the current boundaries established for the republics on the basis of linguistic criteria resulting from the migration of peoples over a millennia. Each time that the planners have presented proposals, beginning in the 1920s, they have been rejected by the Communist Party Politburo.[29] It is evident that the Party still senses the need to adhere to traditional national policies in order to reduce fears that national cultures will be obliterated and homogenized in a new all-union "Soviet" culture, probably having more in common with the Russian culture than with that of any of the minority peoples.

There is some reason to anticipate that although obliteration of national boundaries and homogenization of cultures has been resisted to the present, a reversion to the principles of the *Communist Manifesto* may occur. This would take the form of reasserting the rule that "workers know no fatherland." The Communist Party's 1961 Program, which was adopted to replace the 1919 Program, contained the hint of a move in this direction. One sentence read, "The development of nations does not proceed along the lines of strengthening national barriers, national narrow-mindedness and egoism, as it does under capitalism, but along lines of their association, fraternal mutual assistance and friendship."[30]

Another pair of sentences pointed in the same direction: "The boundaries between constituent republics of the USSR are increasingly losing their former significance since all nations are equal." The second sentence reads, "Full-scale Communist construction constitutes a new stage in the development of national relations in the USSR in which the nations will draw still closer together until complete unity is achieved."

This last sentence has given rise to the sharpest controversy among Western specialists on the Soviet system. What can it mean for a federation? It will be remembered that Nikita Khrushchev, while continuing to recognize the need for a federation structured along national lines, established an administrative pattern built around economic regions. While each of the small republics was treated as an economic region with its own economic council, some were grouped together for economic planning purposes. The Party Program covered this amalgamation with the phrase, "inter-republic organs may be set up in some zones (notably for such matters as irrigation, power grids, transport, etc.)."[31]

Cultural unification was, however, also anticipated, for the Program said, "An international culture common to all Soviet nations is developing," and "the Party will promote the formation of the future worldwide culture of Communist society."[32] Evidently to make clear that this did not entail the suppression of languages, a sentence was added in which the Party promised to "continue to promote the free development of languages of the peoples of the USSR."

After Khrushchev's ouster in 1964 there followed a quiet period of a decade during which there was no revision of the Program or the Constitution, although scholars suggested the desirability of drafting a new Constitution to replace that of 1936. Krushchev formed a committee to prepare a draft, but none appeared. The world began to wonder whether Leonid Brezhnev, Khrushchev's successor, would activate the draftsmen. Fortunately for Western scholars, one of the many Soviet emigrant lawyers to enter the United States claims knowledge of what occurred on the drafting committee. Konstantin Simis has told the West that there was indecision within the committee as to the role to be assigned to the republics in a new constitution.[33] This was one issue that caused delay in drafting, but finally, in December 1976, Brezhnev called for speedy completion of the document, and the draft was published for discussion on June 4, 1977, and promulgated on October 7, 1977.[34]

To the surprise of many, in light of reports of indecision as to the status of the republics and the homogenization of cultures, no change was made in the number of union republics. This meant that the practice of 1936 of elevating some of the autonomous republics to the highest level was not continued. The Bashkirs and Tatars, in spite of their large populations, remained within the boundaries of the Russian Republic, even though one of the conditions for elevation given by Stalin had changed. With the spread of socialism to China and to Poland and Romania, the Soviet frontiers no longer bordered on capitalist states. It was hard to argue that only frontier people could be union republics with the constitutional right to secede because only they could by secession change their social and economic systems. The border criterion had become pointless, and some other rationalization of the argument against secession had to be found. Some hint as to what that had become was given by a lecturer from the USSR, speaking in Australia soon after the new Constitution was promulgated. Asked why the Bashkirs and Tatars could not now be union republics, since their position was now no different geographically from the Uzbeks, the Kirghiz and the Kazakhs, who had union republic status, he replied simply that there was no need for change; indeed, it would be a step backward.[35]

The bicameral feature of the Supreme Soviet was maintained as were the republic codes of law subject to "fundamentals" enacted by the federal legislature.

The anniversary of the 1922 Treaty of Union presented CPSU General Secretary Yuri Andropov with an opportunity to restate nationality policy. At the jubilee session of December 22, 1983, he said:

> What did Lenin indicate as the essence of the path of socialist federalism? It can be summarized as follows: the completely voluntary union of free peoples . . .; the complete equality of all nations . . .; and a consistent line of policy designed to eliminate not

only their legal but also their actual inequality; the free development of each republic and nationality within the framework of the fraternal union of all; the continuous cultivation of an internationalist consciousness, and a steady course aimed at the convergence of all our country's nations and nationalities . . .[36]

Here again was a restatement of the convergence goal for the future, a goal which has aroused the fears of many emigrants from the national groups that their fatherlands were on the eve of homogenization, not as subordinates to the Russian Republic, but as elements of a new Soviet-type culture in which the Russian culture would be blended with the best of the others.

When the Communist Party published in 1986 a revision of its 1961 Program, declaring it to be no more than a revision and not a new text, it contained only a short section on the nationality policy.[37] In Part III, "The Social Policy of the Party," there was a subsection entitled "A Further Flourishing and Drawing Closer Together of Socialist Peoples and Nationalities." Its most notable paragraph read: "Characteristic of the national relations of Soviet society are both the continued flourishing of the various peoples and nationalities and their steady coming closer together voluntarily, on the basis of equality and fraternal cooperation."

The Program then listed the tasks considered to be the prime tasks: (1) strengthening the integral multinational state and struggle against manifestations of parochialism and national narrow-mindedness, while simultaneously showing constant concern for further increasing the role of the republics . . .; (2) blending the initiative of the union and autonomous republics with central control at the countryside level in the rational use of resources . . .; (3) advancement of the Soviet people's integral culture . . . free development and use of national languages . . . at the same time learning the Russian language.

From this record, now capped by the Party Program, adopted in final form at the 27th Congress in February 1986, one cannot but conclude that the policy on national groups has become stabilized. It comprises four elements: (1) central economic planning and administration of resources, utilizing, however, the concept of delegation of powers to republics when this is thought to facilitate the administration of those sectors of the economy of primary concern to customers; (2) continuation of the federal structure with its division into union and autonomous republics and "national provinces" and "districts" for less numerous peoples; (3) preservation of national cultures with emphasis upon encouragement of language and art in the local idiom, although all must learn Russian; and (4) the ultimate blending of national cultures into a common Soviet culture with, perhaps, a language which is spoken in common, if not homogenized into a sort of Russian-oriented "esperanto."

This latter step of homogenization seems still to remain remote as an active policy. One cannot forget that Stalin envisioned a society of his dreams only when Communism had spread throughout the world. Since such an eventuality now appears to both Westerners and Easterners to be remote indeed, it is visionary to speculate on the form homogenization may take, but in the interest of completeness of presentation of a long-term nationality policy, this ultimate goal cannot be ignored.

Notes

1. This point has been made with regard to treaties by O. I. Lukashuk in his "Tasks and Principles of Interpretation of Contemporary International Law Rules" in *Soviet Yearbook of International Law 1984* (Moscow, 1986), p. 158. Although the author is speaking of international treaties, his remarks are equally valid for Soviet statutory law.

2. As there are many editions of this text, none will be cited here. One or another is available almost universally.

3. The Zimmerwald Conference of the autumn of 1915 is chronicled by a Soviet historian. See P. Kerzhentsev, *Life of Lenin* (Moscow, 1937), p. 157. Lenin's report on a meeting of revolutionaries in Berne is available in English translation as "Conference of the Sections of the RSDLP Abroad" in V. I. Lenin, *Selected Works*, vol. 5 (Moscow, 1943), pp. 131-7.

4. K. Marx and F. Engels, *Manifesto of the Communist Party* (authorized English translation, New York, 1933) (1st ed., London, 1848).

5. *Communist Manifesto*, ch. 2, par. 54.

6. *Communist Manifesto*, ch. 2, par. 55.

7. For English translation see 1935 edition, "Marxism and the National Question," published in Moscow and Leningrad. The quotation is from ch. 4, par. 59, p. 33.

8. Lenin expressed his view of self-determination in an article published in 1914. For an English translation, see "On the Right of Nations to Self-determination" in V. I. Lenin, *Selected Works*, vol. 4 (Moscow, 1943), pp. 249-93.

9. Some of the decrees recognizing the independence of states formerly integral parts of the Russian Empire are printed in Akademiia Nauk SSSR, Institut Sovetskoi Stroitel'stva i Prava, *Istoriia Sovetskoi Konstitutsii v*

Dekretakh i Postanovleniiakh Sovetskogo Pravitelstva 1917–1938 (Moscow, 1936), pp. 46, 51, 87, 108.

10. Protocol between the RSFSR and the Azerbaijan, Armenian, Belorussian, Bukhara, Georgian, Far Eastern, Ukrainian and Khorezm Republics, February 22, 1922. Ibid., p. 202.

11. See Constitution of the RSFSR, July 10, 1918. For English translation see A. L. Unger *Constitutional Development in the USSR: A Guide to the Soviet Constitutions* (New York, 1982), p. 25.

12. Ibid, Art. 43 (j).

13. For an indication of this process, see J. N. Hazard, *Settling Disputes in Soviet Society* (New York, 1960), pp. 85, 204–9.

14. For English translation of the text, see J. F. Triska (ed.), *Soviet Communism: Program and Rules. Official Texts of 1919, 1952 (1956), 1961.* (San Francisco, 1962), p. 138.

15. 1919 Program, Art. 9.

16. For text, see Document no. 101 in *Obrazovania Soiuza Sovetskikh Sotsialisticheskikh Respublik: Sbornik Dokumentov* (Moscow, 1972), p. 297; also op. cit. (note 9), p. 223.

17. See Stalin, op. cit. (note 7), p. 159 (Report to 12th Congress of Russian Communist Party, April 23, 1923, Part II).

18. Arts. 13–28 of the Constitution.

19. Art. 4 of the Constitution.

20. See Stalin, op. cit. (note 7), p. 168 (Report to 12th Congress, Reply to Discussion).

21. Ibid., p. 261 (Report to 16th Congress of CPSU, June 27, 1930).

22. Arts. 50–4, 67–8 of the Constitution.

23. For an English translation, see Unger, Op. cit. (note 11), p. 140.

24. Stalin put this requirement in his speech of November 25, 1936, on the draft constitution at ch. 5, par. 3. For English translation, see *Leninism: Selected Writings* (New York, 1942), p. 400. For Unger's comments on the right of secession, see Unger, op. cit., p. 86.

25. See Unger, op. cit., p. 88 for the legislative history of the transition in Karelo-Finnish Republic status.

26. Ibid, p. 88.

27. Art. 14 (u) of the Constitution.

28. Amendment of February 11, 1957, limiting federal jurisdiction to the establishment of "fundamentals" of legislation to the various branches of law. See footnote 17 to Art. 14 (u) in Unger, op. cit., p. 160.

29. I am unable to find the original reference for this fact which I incorporated into my class notes decades ago.

30. See Triska, op. cit., (note 14), p. 107.

31. Ibid, p. 108.

32. Ibid, p. 109.

33. Dr Simis did not include this statement when he reconstructed his remarks at the conference for publication as "The Making of the New Constitution," published in *Soviet Union/Union Soviétique*, vol. 6, pt. 2 (1979), p. 203. The chair at the session, Professor Louise Shelley, has confirmed at my request with Dr Simis that delay was caused by discussion of the federal structure.

34. For an English translation of the text, see Unger, op. cit., p. 140.

35. In keeping with the general rule established by Soviet scholars that they are to be quoted only from published sources, I must omit the speaker's name.

36. See Y. V. Andropov, "Sixty Years of the USSR," *Pravda*, December 22, 1983, p. 1.

37. The Program in draft form was published in English translation in *Current Digest of the Soviet Press*, vol. 37, no. 44 (November 27, 1985), Special Supplement.

Since completion of this chapter momentous events have occurred. Several republics have rebelled against centralized controls; the federal state structure has been restored to Lenin's model (with a Congress of Deputies of 2,250 persons at the top, electing a bicameral full-time Supreme Soviet as legislature); a Constitutional Supervision Committee with representation of all 15 union republics has been established to provide advisory opinions on the constitutionality of laws; the competence of republics is being reviewed by a constitutional drafting committee; the three Baltic republics have been given a measure of economic autonomy, and a law on procedures for secession has been enacted requiring a waiting period after the submission of a demand and ultimate acceptance of the demand by the Congress. In light of these developments it can no longer be said that policy calls for a convergence of peoples eventually.

Chapter 5

Searching for Soviet Nationalities Policy

Michael Rywkin

A great deal has been written about the nationalities policies of each new successor to Stalin. The hope of detecting major changes, discovering new trends and tracing radical departures from old methods has kept interest alive. But changes have most often been superficial, new trends of limited impact, and radical departures from established patterns isolated instances.

True, Moscow has on several occasions toyed with some radical ideas: dismembering the majority Slavic Kazakh republic, creating an all-Turkestani Party leadership (Khrushchev's short-lived Turkestan Party "Bureau"), even getting rid of national republics altogether (see some of the debates around the 1977 Constitution). Curiously enough, all the aborted projects were aimed at diminishing, not increasing, the national autonomy of non-Russian nationalities. But aside from Stalin's abolition of the autonomous republics of the "punished nations" and the purely foreign-policy-related appearance (and demise) of the Karelo-Finnish SSR, no discarding of basic principles of Soviet nationalities policies has ever taken place. Otherwise, minor aberrations notwithstanding, Stalin's old structure remains largely untouched, its elements so interlocked as to make radical changes not only difficult, but risky as well.

In this essay I will attempt to pinpoint several permanent components of Soviet nationalities policy, linked together by what Moscow describes as a "dialectical" policy of "simultaneous enlargement of both federal and republican powers." In our translation from "dialectics" into plain language, it sounds rather like an act of balancing the need for interethnic peace with reluctance to relax Russian control.

I. Four principles of political governance

1. The overriding principle of national-territorial autonomy.

2. A governmental structure dividing spheres of competence between federal and republic (state) jurisdiction, but clearly in favor of the former.

3. A consistent cadres policy, opening the bulk of local positions to natives, while reserving specific key power jobs within the republics for Russians and other Slavs (during Stalin's times for Georgians and Armenians as well), and limiting non-Slavic role in the federal apparatus.

4. A wide gap between the constitutional rights of a union republic within the federal system and the freedom to exercise those rights in reality (a phenomenon familiar from other domains of Soviet life as well).

II. Three principles of national-cultural development

5. The requirement that the culture of nationalities enjoying the "national in form" autonomy becomes and remains "socialist in content," alleviating the danger of centrifugal development.

6. A mythical vocabulary consisting of formulas and code-words defining the route for developing the component nationalities into "the Soviet people—a new community of nations."

7. The egalitarian principle of nondiscrimination, either against individuals or against their national republics, inherited from the revolutionary past, and carried on as long as Moscow's domination is not being contested (or rather, is not perceived as being contested).

Each of these principles is organically connected with one or more of the others. One cannot possibly conceive, for example, of allowing the union republics to exercise all their written constitutional rights without altering the established cadres policies or reviewing the "socialist in content" principle; it is equally impossible to abolish the national-territorial principle without upsetting the traditional division of spheres of competence and the constitutional rights of the republics, and so on.

Let us survey the seven principles listed above in more detail.

1. The first principle, dealing with territorial autonomy, has its origin in the prerevolutionary dispute between the Jewish Bund and the Russian Social Democrats. The 5th Congress of the Bund (April 1901) espoused the principle of extraterritorial cultural autonomy for Jewish workers by arguing that Jews are "people of one nationality spread out throughout the country." This point of view was rebuffed by Stalin as early as 1913 (in his *Marxism and Nationalities*) when he defined the four conditions for nationhood: community of language, economic cohesion, similarity of psychological make-up, all tied to a

specific territory (an overriding condition). After the Revolution, the dispute between the idea of national extraterritorial autonomy and the idea of national-territorial autonomy was clearly settled in favor of the latter. The whole history of the Soviet federal state points to the importance of a designated territory as the key factor in the relative status of a given nationality. Thus, during World War II, "punished nationalities" were first of all deprived of their territories. Khrushchev's full "forgiveness" came with the restoration of territory, as with the Kalmyk Autonomous Soviet Socialist Republic (ASSR); limited "forgiveness," such as in the case of Crimean Tatars, brought no territorial restitution.

The position of the Jews is most curiously related to the wholly fictitious existence of the Jewish Autonomous Region (Birobidjan), where roughly 10,000 Jews constitute about 5 per cent of the population. Another oddity was the 300th anniversary "wedding gift" from Russia to the Ukraine of the defunct Crimean-Tatar ASSR, whose not fully forgiven natives are still kept in exile in Central Asia. The idea of ethnic rights unconnected to specific territory is still basically foreign to the Soviet way of thinking, despite the fact that Stalin's definition of nationhood has by now been discarded. We know that the American Communist Party was directed in the 1930s to seek territorial autonomy for American Blacks by advocating that five southern states be put aside as a Black homeland. Curiously enough, in his 1987 mention of the Black problems in the United States, Gorbachev repeated this long-forgotten stand.

2. The three levels of people's commissariats (later ministries)—those of all-union or federal status; those of mixed status, present at both federal and republic level; and those of republic status, confined to the lower level—were established by the 1924 Constitution of the USSR.

During the 60 years that followed, some ministries moved from one level to another, but the three-level division remained unchanged. However, the domain under exclusive jurisdiction of a union republic has consistently shrunk. It is true that during the Brezhnev years the purely federal domain also lost some ground, while the area of mixed competence, dominated by the federal side, extended its scope. But under Gorbachev, and despite decentralization measures implemented below ministerial level, several areas are being moved from mixed status back to federal.

3. The traditional cadres policy in non-Slavic republics, and especially in the Muslim ones, based on the specific role assigned to the Russian ethnic *nomenklatura*, has never been substantially altered. The method of controlling top offices in those republics by position-

ing Russian second party secretaries behind native first party secretaries, and providing Russian vice-ministers to native ministers, has remained in force since at least the 1930s, if not earlier. The same pattern applies to regional (and even to some *raion*) Party Committees. Russians are directly in command in KGB headquarters, army garrisons and military districts, and in enterprises of "all-Union importance." "Reserved" positions are numerically few, but politically essential for effective control of the national republics.

Certainly, some minor changes did take place from time to time. After Stalin's death, not only Georgians and Armenians lost their special status, but their own republics were provided with Russian second secretaries. On the positive side, district Party Committees in the Central Asian republics, if in charge of economically nonessential areas, were often left without Russian Party secretaries (whether second or "third"). No similar relaxation was observed for regional Party Committees.

Despite the growing number of qualified native cadres, the very principle of Russian staffing (*obsadka*) in non-slavic republics remains in force. The most recent developments, such as the appointment of an ethnic Russian, Genadii L. Kolbin, as a First Secretary of the Central Committee of the Communist Party of the Kazakh Republic, and the parachuting of Russian first secretaries into two regions of Uzbekistan and into the capital city of Tashkent (with similar cases in the neighboring republics), show a tightening of the old cadres policy. It has been a long-established tradition dating from Stalin's time to forget about ethnic niceties and appoint reliable Russians to do the job the right way whenever serious economic difficulties arise. This was the case during World War II, and it is the case now with Gorbachev, who, in order to enforce his much-needed economic reforms, feels at times obliged to disregard national sensitivities in the republics. This first of all results in a freeze (permanent or temporary) of affirmative action especially in promoting marginally qualified natives, and greatly reduced tolerance of local nepotism.

At the 26th Party Congress in 1982, Andropov objected to "mathematical formulas" in cadre promotion[1] (translated into American terms, he opposed ethnic quotas). Speaking four years later at the 27th Party Congress, Ligachev went even further. He argued that *mestnichestvo* prevents the promotion of "representatives of all the nationalities," as well as of "interregional exchange of cadres" in the national republics: "It is necessary to select and assign cadres two ways—from among local comrades and by moving cadres from the center and from other areas of the country."[2] The subsequent parachuting of cadres into Central Asia shows that Ligachev's directives were well followed.

At the federal level, natives of Muslim and Baltic republics have been increasingly under-represented within the real seats of power, such as the Politburo, the Secretariat or even the Council of Ministers in Moscow, but not in ceremonial bodies such as the Supreme Soviet. Again, Georgians and Armenians lost at Stalin's death: the old *khoziain* trusted his Caucasian brethren more than his successors.

4. The constitutional rights of the union republics were established between 1917 and 1936. Central among the rights was the one allowing a union republic to secede from the USSR, something a state of the United States cannot do. This right originated in the November 2, 1917, Declaration of the Rights of the Peoples of Russia. But in a *Pravda* article of October 10, 1920, Stalin was already branding any attempt to exercise this right as "counter-revolutionary."[3] Still in 1935, explaining the reason why the Bashkir or the Tatar autonomous republics could not be granted union republic status, Stalin underlined their technical inability to exercise the key right of withdrawal precluded by their enclosed geographic location within the RSFSR.

The "Supreme Soviets" of the union republics, supposedly embodying the sovereignty of their respective republics, were granted wide rights as long as they remained "rubber-stamp" bodies. When some took the opportunity from Gorbachev's *glasnost'* to exercise those rights, federal authorities lost no time finding legal restrictions limiting their initiatives. Another constitutional aspect, namely the largely ceremonial federal bicameral system, with one chamber being the Council of Nationalities, dates back to the 1924 Constitution. The delegates to that Council are elected from each national territorial unit, with an equal number of delegates assigned per unit of the same level (union republic, autonomous republic, autonomous region, national district). The impact of constitutional reforms in late 1988 remains unclear, but they appear to be aimed at diminishing, not enlarging, the role of national representations.

The 1944 establishment of Ministries of Defense and of Foreign Affairs in the union republics was a public relations gesture aimed at strengthening Soviet claims for larger representation in the United Nations and at creating a public image of genuine sovereignty of component republics of the USSR. Since the outset, these Ministries played only a very limited role as state tourist offices and draft boards, and little else.

5. Turning to national-cultural issues, we can distinguish three basic principles. The first among them, Stalin's formula of culture "national in form and socialist in content," can itself be divided into

three components: that of national versus all-union culture; that of native versus Russian language; and finally that of the survival of national contradictions under socialist conditions.

The idea of culture "national in form, socialist in content" was devised by Stalin while Lenin was still alive, with the word "proletarian" instead of "socialist." It attracted wider attention after Stalin's May 18, 1925, address to the Communist University of the Toilers of the East, about a year after Lenin's death. Its present formulation can be found in Stalin's early-1930s *Foundations of Leninism*:

> The flourishing of culture national in form and socialist in content under the conditions of the dictatorship of the proletariat in one country . . . [will lead] to a merger [fusion] into one common socialist (in form and content) culture with one common language, when the proletariat will win in the whole world and socialism will penetrate the lifestyle [*byt*].[4]

This formula, half a century old, has never been officially discarded, neither in its form/content correlation, nor in its long-term implications. The wording of the second part has been altered by dropping the term "fusion," but even this without open official rejection.

The second problem, that of Soviet language policies, is not fully covered by Stalin's formula despite the "content" role assigned to the Russian language as the "socialist" language of future "fusion," while national languages are meant to remain of "formal" local usage. First of all, Soviet language policies have been shifting between *korenizatsiia*-inspired cultivation of national languages (*korenizatsiia* being a program of "indigenization") and the promotion of Russian as *lingua franca* for interethnic intercourse, with sometimes both policies carried out simultaneously. Linguistic Russification, whenever it takes place, presents important regional variations, In Slavic Ukraine and Belorussia, there is a mixture of the traditional Great Russian policy of linguistic assimilation aimed at consolidating the Slavic components in the country as a whole, with the natural attraction of the easily understandable Russian language. In the Turkic-speaking regions of the country, Russian is promoted as the indispensable tool for technological advancement and career success. In the Baltic republics, Russian appears mostly as the language of the filing cabinet: useful, but not very attractive.

Only those nationalities which remain without territory of their own—such as Germans, Jews (the fiction of Birobidjan notwithstanding), Crimean Tatars, and finally those Ukrainians and

Belorussians who live among the Russians outside their own republics, succumb to linguistic Russification. Those non-Russians who live in their own republics do not lose their native language in favor of Russian, and their bilingualism, whenever it occurs, carries no assimilative features.

The third problem, that of alleged disappearance of ethnic conflicts under socialism, underwent some realistic reappraisal even prior to the events in Nagorno-Karabakh. While the principle of "socialist content" remains in force, an inquiry about the survival of nationalities problems in the Soviet Union no longer receives the proverbial response of Ostap Bender (from Ilf and Petrov's novel *The Little Golden Calf*), "Yes, we have Jews, but no, there is no Jewish question." Instead, the permanency of nationality problems, even under "developed socialism," was publicly acknowledged by Andropov in his 1982 speech on the occasion of the 60th anniversary of the formation of the USSR: "Life shows that economic and cultural progress of all nations and nationalities unavoidably leads to increased self-consciousness."[5] The fact that modernization increases rather than decreases nationalism is a well-known fact, but it goes against the classical Marxist dogma predicting exactly the contrary. Andropov's admission showed a propensity to acknowledge reality. But in order to justify past claims of having already solved the national question, the 1986 Party Congress rephrased Andropov's formula in the following manner: "The national question *as inherited from the past* [my emphasis] has been successfully solved."[6] Thus the issue acquired a new "dialectical" dimension, and still awaits solution, but at a higher stage of historical development.

In his February 1986 speech to the 27th Party Congress, Gorbachev goes one step further on the road to a more realistic view of the situation. He acknowledges not only the existence of a problem, but of "contradictions" as well, a term formerly taboo as far as social and national relations under socialism are concerned. According to Gorbachev, "Contradictions are characteristic of any development; they are inevitable in [the nationalities] sphere as well."[7]

6. The specific vocabulary of interethnic relations has undergone changes over the years, but still favors myths over reality. Among more visible shifts is the change in code-words defining the unreachable final stage of national development. In his time Stalin spoke of "fusion" taking place in the remote future after the socialist stage of development has been reached, the socialist way of life has triumphed, and world revolution has taken place (it is necessary to bear in mind that Stalin used the term "socialist" to denote the Communist

future, not present-day socialism, whether "developed" or not). Brezhnev prudently avoided the use of "fusion" and replaced it by a series of less dramatic code-words such as "unity," "full unity," "unification," etc. Kulichenko, a leading Soviet commentator in this field, wrote in 1984 that "general fusion or even her elements are totally absent from the life of the Soviet people."

The 1985 Party Program goes even further: Brezhnev's "full unity" is in turn relegated to "remote historical perspective."[8] In his February 1986 speech Gorbachev lowers the goals still further, speaking only of "unity of economic, ideologic and political aims," not of unity between collective bodies of various nationalities.[9] We are thus witnessing an obvious return to more realistic projections, which can be classified in the following descending order:

fusion of nationalities
fusion in remote historical perspective
full unity
unity
full unity in remote historical perspective
unity in remote historical perspective
unification
unity of aims among the nationalities

Moving from the fusion of nationalities into one nation to a unity of aims among nationalities is a salutory descent from the world of dreams to real life. Together with the admission of the survival of ethnic problems in the USSR, it reflects not only a more realistic vision of the future, but a deliberate decision to put some restraint on the use of mythical semiotics in the vocabulary of Soviet nationalities affairs.

Nevertheless, the usage of such phraseology, implanted by Stalin, survives around the issue of *sblizhenie* (rapprochement). *Sblizhenie* is supposed to take place during the unending intermediate stage which corresponds to the socialist stage on the road to Communism. Since socialism has supposedly been achieved already under Stalin, the present stage of development in the USSR had to receive a higher-sounding label in order to underline the progress supposedly achieved on the road to Communism. Similarly, the endless *sblizhenie* was adorned by "higher-level" adjectives, ranging from "close" to "steadfast" to "ever-increasing," to name just a few. *Sblizhenie* has even been given a kind of minimum/maximum speed limit, defined as "not to push, not to hold back," an old Brezhnev-era concept still retained by Gorbachev in 1986.

Another code-word, "flourishing," traditionally signified the flourishing of various national cultures within the USSR, a symbol of the achievement of Soviet nationalities policy. But now, when used by non-Russians, "flourishing" expresses opposition to further *sblizhenie*, rather than acknowledging achievement, supposedly taken for granted.

Finally, the very expression "Soviet people—a new community of nations" is by no means a Brezhnev-era invention, as some Western scholars think, but a formula dating from the 1930s and used at that time in such varied media as Molotov's speeches and patriotic songs.

7. The equalitarian principle of the Soviet regime, which emerged from the Marxist doctrine itself, was embedded in the abovementioned 1917 Declaration of the Rights of the Peoples of Russia, but failed to affect the principle of Russia's political domination over its former colonial possessions. Speaking before the Petrograd Soviet on September 17, 1920, Zinoviev asserted: "We cannot do without the petroleum of Azerbaijan or the cotton of Turkestan. We take those products which are necessary for us not as former exploiters, but as older brothers bearing the torch of civilization."[10]

Zinoviev's cynicism has never been openly matched, even by Stalin, and it resulted in Lenin's rebuke in 1922. But the term "elder brother" survived, in Zinoviev's original meaning, long after Lenin, Stalin and Zinoviev were gone. Only after Brezhnev's death did Moscow leaders finally abandon this expression, leaving it to those first secretaries of national republics who feel a sudden urge to restate their love for the "elder brother."

Still, Russian political domination over non-Russian republics has not been translated into personal privileges for individual Russian settlers residing in those republics. On the contrary, before *perestroika* natives of national republics were favored by Soviet-style affirmative actions carried out in their own homelands, except for the already mentioned specific positions reserved for Russians. Only "punished people" or Jews remained outside both merit and affirmative action systems. Otherwise, the principle of individual equality of opportunities enjoyed by the great majority of Soviet citizens regardless of nationality has remained the key achievement of Soviet nationalities policy.

The seven premises of Soviet nationalities policies we have discussed remain in effect in 1988, some alterations notwithstanding. No significant shifts can take place unless some of these premises are effectively discarded. Such would be the case, for example, if the constitutional rights of national republics were either made operational, as Estonia demands, or, on the contrary, formally downgraded, as

Estonia fears, to reflect the real limits of their sovereignty; or if the division of spheres of responsibility between the federal, the mixed, and the republic ministries shifted seriously in favor of the republics; if the territorial integrity of a union republic were seriously violated through major border changes (here the difficulty of satisfying Armenian demands is clear), or by the amalgamation of the republics into new territorial units no longer based on historical or ethnic criteria, but on economic or other considerations. These are just a few possibilities.

Will Gorbachev's preoccupation with socioeconomic matters continue to override nationalities policy considerations? As it was already mentioned, in the Muslim republics "affirmative action" is, at least for the time being, frozen. "Mature" Russian cadres are moving in.[11] Moreover, subsidies to Asian republics (mostly in the form of the return of turnover taxes) are down, with investments redirected into established industrial regions.

But in the Baltic republics the reverse is true. Symbols of nationalism—from flags to national anthems—are being legalized, non-Communist organizations (but not parties) are allowed to function. National histories are no longer shamelessly distorted. Thus, while under *glasnost'* national problems and even conflicts are widely reported in the press, different regions of the country do not benefit equally from the new openness. At the same time Moscow seems increasingly lenient toward Russian nationalists, who share the anti-*sblizhenie* feelings of the *natsmeny* ("national minorities"), albeit for different reasons. Russian nationalists resent all concessions to other ethnic groups, even if granted in payment for acquiescence to Russian rule, viewing it as "reverse discrimination."

Despite the increased self-affirmation in the Baltic republics and the collapse of *druzhba narodov* in Transcaucasia, no departure from the functional principles of Stalin's nationality policy has been implemented by Moscow. Established principles have, by now, grown into the body politic of the Soviet state. They are as much parts of the Soviet whole as central planning or a one-party system. But as with economic reforms, every partial alteration of traditional policies may endanger established practices, forcing the overhaul of the system in its entirety. Economic *perestroika* and political relaxation are obviously shaking the bureaucratic apparatus, but it is the non-Slavic elites who are most affected. Thus the Estonian *nomenklatura* has largely allied itself with its own people. The Latvian and Lithuanian followed, albeit to a lesser degree. In Armenia and in Azerbaijan the national *nomenklatura* have espoused their respective national causes to the extent of challenging federal authority. In Georgia nationalist feelings among local officials are increasing, especially on the personal level. In Central Asia local cadres are not yet able to shake the trauma of endless corruption purges, and remain, at least for the time being, obedient. Ukrainian and Belorussian *nomenklatura* has yet to be moved by other than language issues.

Perestroika is, however, in its early stages, and the nationalist genie is already out of the bottle, testing the established Stalinist bases governing interethnic relations within the Soviet family of nations.

Notes

1. Iurii Andropov, "Shestdesiat let SSSR," *Kommunist*, no. 1 (1983).

2. Yegor Ligachev, Speech at the 27th Party Congress, *Izvestiia*, February 28, 1986.

3. Iosif Stalin, *Sochineniia*, vol. 4 (1948–52), pp. 351–63, quoted by E. H. Carr, *The Bolshevik Revolution, 1917–1923*, vol. 1 (New York: The Macmillan Co., 1951), p. 383.

4. Quoted from Iosif Stalin, *Foundations of Leninism*, in *Sochineniia*.

5. Iurii Andropov, Speech on the occasion of the 60th anniversary of the formation of the USSR. *Shestdesiat let SSSR* (Moscow: Izd Politicheskoi Literatury, 1983).

6. Andropov, Speech at the 26th Party Congress. Also 1985 Party Program, *Pravda*, pt. 3, October 26, 1985.

7. Milhail Gorbachev, Speech at the 27th Party Congress, February 1986.

8. 1985 Party Program, loc. cit.

9. Gorbachev, loc. cit.

10. Albert Cobban, *National Self-Determination* (Chicago University Press, 1947), pp. 107–8, quoting Zinoviev.

11. Speech by I. B. Usmankhodzhaev at the 27th Party Congress, *Izvestiia*, February 1986; also Timur Alilov, "Sozidatel'naia sila bratstva. Obmen kadrami mezhdu respublikami uskoriaet sotsial'no-ekonomicheskoe razvitie strany," *Izvestiia*, January 2, 1987.

PART II

Striving for a *Homo sovieticus*

Chapter 6

Making Soviet Citizens: Patriotic and Internationalist Education in the Formation of a Soviet State Identity

Karen A. Collias

The ethnic crises in several Soviet republics, including Armenia, Azerbaidzhan, Kazakhstan, Tadzhikistan and the Baltic states, illustrate vividly the perils faced by Soviet authorities in their management of ethnic relations. Despite Mikhail Gorbachev's over-optimistic proclamation that the "nationalities question . . . has been successfully resolved,"[1] his own policy of *glasnost'* begins a qualitatively new chapter in the unfolding story of the Soviet nationality question. While some ethnic upheavals are separatist and unmistakably represent a threat to the integrity of the Soviet system, others indicate a new intra-system ethnic assertiveness that will influence the evolving ethnic dynamics in Gorbachev's Soviet Union.

Indeed, Gorbachev's political and economic policies assume a change in the status quo of ethnic communities as enunciated in the "little deal" of the Brezhnev era, which allowed more local corruption and less accountability than Gorbachev and his lieutenants would like.[2] But Gorbachev also inherited from Brezhnev a scheme of ethnic relations designed to balance local, regional and state identities as the Party leadership strove to create a population of citizen-patriots.

Creating these Soviet patriots, loyal sons and daughters of the Communist cause, from the human raw material of more than 100 ethnic groups preoccupied Soviet leaders throughout the Brezhnev era. The Communist Party, realizing that Russian nationalism alone could not provide the glue to hold the multiethnic state together, eschewed an exclusive focus on the Russian nationality in building a state identity. Instead, Party leaders, supported by massive bureaucracies in the military and educational institutions, as well as youth organizations, fashioned an ideal supra-ethnic Soviet identity. They then presented and popularized this identity in an extensive socialization program called patriotic and internationalist upbringing (*patrioticheskoe i internatsional'noe vospitanie*), or simply patriotic education.

Soviet Party and government officials paid particular attention to developing the union-wide patriotic and internationalist upbringing program for young people of all ethnic groups. The evolution of that youth program during the Brezhnev era and its legacy in building a Soviet state identity among a multiethnic population during the Gorbachev years form the subject of this essay.

Presenting State Values to Young Citizens

What were the official values Soviet elites in the Brezhnev era wished to transmit to youth through *vospitanie*? The Communist Party neatly laid out Soviet socialist values in the "Moral Code of the Builder of Communism" found in the Party Program. Major Soviet values include: collectivism, discipline, love of work, patriotism, internationalism—among all peoples of the Soviet Union and peoples of socialist countries—and atheism.[3] According to Marxist theory, love of work should be the most important attribute of the young Communist. But in Soviet society under Brezhnev, values were ranked somewhat differently: the core of the ethical system was patriotism, contained in an interpretation of Marxist-Leninist ideology designed to transform Russian, Georgian or Uzbek into Soviet man.

Communist Party officials define Soviet patriotism as "love for, fidelity to, a single multinational Soviet homeland, and its common traditions, achievements and ideals."[4] The message of Soviet patriotism during the Brezhnev era was directed toward all Soviet citizens, not just Russians. Soviet patriotism denoted a vertical relationship between citizen and state, manifested in public support for official policies, and included a military dimension of loyalty to the Soviet state. The concept could best be understood as a dialectical relationship between love of homeland and hatred of enemies.

> Hatred for class enemies and love for the socialist homeland are two externally opposite feelings that form a unitary and dialectical relationship. They are two aspects of socialist patriotism. Fervent love for the socialist fatherland is inconceivable without irreconcilable class hatred for its enemies.[5]

Fervent love of homeland alone, however, does not a socialist patriot make. Soviet patriotism is international in character, ideally expressing the interests and aspirations of all ethnic groups in the Soviet Union. At its most fundamental level, this internationalism comes directly from the writings of Marx and Engels. The proletariat of the world unites against the bourgeoisie of all countries, surmounting antagonisms between nationalities in favor of international worker solidarity.

That early Marxist notion of internationalism has been replaced in Soviet practice by an internationalist solidarity of the citizens of socialist states throughout the world. Afghanistan, for example, became a nominal member of the family of socialist states with an April 1978 Communist coup d'état led by the late Nur Mohammed Taraki. And, from the Soviet invasion in December 1979 to the Soviet army exodus some ten years later, soldiers have fulfilled their "internationalist duty" by accepting the Afghan "invitation" to help a socialist brother.

In addition to this feeling of solidarity with workers of the world and with populations of socialist states, Soviet citizens are supposed to feel a special solidarity with members of other ethnic groups in their own socialist state. To encourage this citizen-to-citizen horizontal relationship of socialist internationalism among the Soviet people, Party policy advocated the internationalization of certain aspects of public life to promote common patterns of behavior. In practice, socialist internationalism within the Soviet Union was promoted by policies such as mandatory service in the Soviet Armed Forces, referred to by Brezhnev's Chief of the Soviet Army and Navy Main Political Directorate, the late A. A. Yepishev, as "a living embodiment of socialist internationalism."

Patriotism and internationalism were introduced and implemented in various educational settings throughout the Soviet Union in a type of multiethnic cultural management. Whether a youth was in school, or working in a factory or collective farm, his interaction with the Soviet system revolved around official socialization in which the process of building a state identity permeated all institutional structures. Operationally, the Party particularly called upon the Communist Youth League (Komsomol), the Volunteer Society of the Army and Navy (DOSAAF) and Soviet schools to organize the in-school and extracurricular activities through which official patriotic education took place.

These organizations coordinated the presentation of patriotism to young people. Beginning in the first grade, teachers emphasized the local (village or city) identity, progressing to ethnic, to regional, to republic, to state identity by the time the students graduated from secondary school. Outside the school setting, youth and paramilitary organizations sponsored activities to inculcate patriotic values, including interethnic sporting competitions, youth meetings, unionwide excursions, and ceremonial rituals and rites.

The Universal Importance of Building a State Identity

The notion of building a state identity, of creating true patriots loyal to the state out of substate building blocks, is not a new nor a uniquely Soviet concept. Indeed, the state has traditionally relied upon its educational system to produce good citizens out of its youthful population. For Plato, an education that highlighted heroism by encouraging discipline, virtue and courage was the key component in producing the good citizen who could be depended upon to serve the Athenian city-state.[6]

In the modern state, educators traditionally have had the job of inculcating patriotism into their young charges. They have often done so on the basis of a scheme of concentric circles, extending from the family outward through the village or locality, to the region, and finally to the state level itself. In forging a French identity, for example, nineteenth-century French leaders implemented a universal secular educational system about which their revolutionary predecessors only dreamed. The curriculum highlighted moral and civic training to inculcate into children from Normandy to Provence love and respect for a unified French homeland. Teachers encouraged children to abandon the regional *patois* and become acquainted with the heroes and patriots of France.[7] The leaders of republican France advocated an exclusive *French* political culture at the expense of inclusive regional cultural expressions.

A hierarchy of substate loyalties, however, need not be destroyed in the process of creating a state identity. Some contemporary studies have shown that loyalties progressing from the family, to the tribe, through the ethnic group, to the nation, to the state can coexist peacefully. A British study of Scottish children, for example, illustrated that young people were socialized to a progressive awareness of themselves as, say, members of the Duncan clan *and* Glaswegians *and* Scots *and* British subjects. Moreover, they could express these various identities in different contexts while still identifying themselves as loyal British subjects.[8] Brezhnev-era leaders encouraged an analogous process in the Soviet Union through which the state socialized its young citizens by presenting a hierarchy of identities leading to an overarching Soviet state identity. If a young person can be a Duncan,

Glaswegian, Scot, and a British subject, why cannot the same be true for, say, a Bukharan, Uzbek, Central Asian, and Soviet citizen?

Patriotic Ritual as Education

To implement a socialization program building a hierarchy of loyalties with the ideological tools of patriotism and internationalism, Brezhnev officials developed a vast network of heroes to personify desired values and role models for youth. Heroes act as symbols and as directing spirits—ideally the motive power in the life of the multitude. They are bound up with the rationalization of society as a means of maintaining consensus. In the Brezhnev era, heroes embodied the patriotic and internationalist ideals that Soviet officials felt crucial to building the state identity that, in turn, was intended to contribute to the maintenance of the existing sociopolitical order by legitimating the Communist party. The presentation of heroes whose attributes officials wished the young to emulate was bound up in a complex series of rites and rituals, in many of which the dead hero was connected to the living patriot—that is, the young person taking part in patriotic and internationalist activities.

In Brezhnev's Soviet Union, officials asserted that the use of ritual in socialization was essential to maintaining the socialist status quo. If heroes were idealizations representing the values and norms of Soviet socialism—models of the desired end product of Soviet education—then rituals were a key means by which these values and norms were introduced and reinforced, overcoming, if necessary, preexisting moral orientations fixed by habit, custom or older forms of (often religious) ritual.

Soviet officials since Aleksandr Bogdanov in the 1920s have advocated ritual as a means of inculcating Soviet values to override pre-existing traditions. But until the early 1960s, ritual as a tool of multiethnic socialization had been used only selectively. Nikita Khrushchev introduced and Brezhnev co-opted and vastly extended a *system of ritual* to express the values and norms of Soviet socialism. Though rituals can be performed in nearly every aspect of life from birth to death, those directed toward young people in particular formed an integral part of Soviet patriotic education during the Brezhnev era.

The systematic use of ritual in patriotic education evolved into a full-fledged socialization program during the Brezhnev years. But the end result of the ritual was not necessarily true belief or a comprehensive internalization of the Marxist-Leninist ideology. Rather, complexes of symbols embedded in ritual and lying outside the individual in "the intersubjective world of common understanding" shaped the world by inducing in the individual a certain distinctive set of dispositions that resulted in actions.[9] The merit of this sort of view of what are usually called mental traits or psychological forces is that it gets them out of the "dim and inaccessible realm of private sensation into the same well-lit world of observables where investigation is possible."[10] In short, active, measurable participation—not necessarily internalized belief—is the primary goal of ritual.

Thus, during the Brezhnev era young people were constantly exposed to the messages of Soviet patriotism and socialist internationalism through ritual. But a society filled with true believers, while desirable, was not the normative goal of Soviet socialization. Rather, Brezhnev-era officials were more concerned about levels of participation as an indication of the success of the patriotic and internationalist program. To ensure maximum participation, officials set up a program of patriotic education that permeated every aspect of school life—academic subjects as well as extracurricular activities—and was filled with ritual.

Soviet Patriotic and Internationalist Ideology

The vital role patriotic and internationalist ideology plays in Soviet nationality policy is often underrated. Most Western observers prefer to view Soviet ethnic groups as locked in a struggle that pits their loyalty to the Soviet state—Soviet patriotism—against their individual ethnic identity. To sum up this view, the multiethnic make-up of the Soviet Union presents the Soviet leadership with a challenge to state stability in that the loyalties of various nationalities, and of the Russian majority itself, give a direction to their political aspirations counter to that desired by the Soviet leadership.

Having assumed that any loyalty to the ethnic group or substate territory is at the expense of loyalty to the state, many Western analysts treat the ethnic identities of Soviet citizens as an objective fact cast in stone, rather than as a subjective condition in which identity can be molded in various manners depending upon a particular situation. For a growing number of Soviet citizens of various ethnic groups, the real question is which combinations of several possible identities, or levels of identity, are perceived as a core identity, and in what contexts. "To assume that national affiliation is the single most salient identity of the Soviet citizen," one analyst scolds Western scholars, "is to ignore the degree to which national identities overlap with other social identities and the degree to which their salience varies not only among individuals but with specific situations."[11]

Most scholars rely on a model of Soviet nationalities based on theories of nationalism applied to the development of the Western European "nation-states," the breakdown of their colonial empires, and the replacement of these empires with new nation-states. There is an underlying assumption of "one state—one culture." Citing studies where nationalism is used as an explanation for the evils of war and genocide, students of Soviet matters assume the Soviet Union will follow a similar path to destruction. One scholar, for example, argues that ethnic subcultures "may conflict with or altogether supersede" patriotic loyalty to the Soviet Union, implicitly ruling out the possibility that these two phenomena might actually coexist in Soviet reality.[12]

The widespread tendency to assume that Soviet nationality policy during the Brezhnev era was devoted to Russification ignores the evolution of Soviet views about the relationship between nationalism and socialism: in particular, the growing recognition among the Soviet leadership that ethnic identity is ubiquitous and durable and that efforts must be made to integrate these identities into an overarching loyalty to the state. And that is where the patriotic and internationalist socialization program enters the Soviet multiethnic equation.

To be sure, Brezhnev-style Soviet patriotism did ascribe a leading role to Russians in the development of the Soviet social system; Russian is the *lingua franca* of the Soviet Union; and elements of Russian traditions in music, literature, art and folklore are expressed in the Soviet popular culture to a larger extent than those of any other ethnic group in the Soviet Union. The Soviet patriotism presented by the leadership, however, was designed to include the non-Russians of the Soviet Union, and was based primarily on Soviet achievements rather than those of prerevolutionary Russia.

Multiethnic Military Heroes and Patriots

The formal educational system was the primary vehicle by which Soviet patriotism and socialist internationalism were presented to youth during the Brezhnev era. The content of education, which was permeated with ritual, presented young people with the preferred behavior patterns of the young patriot and internationalist in a personalized manner, emphasizing the importance of a young person's local, ethnic, regional and republic identities as building blocks toward the desired goal of Soviet patriotism. Thus, patriotic and internationalist socialization did not preclude the properly channeled expression of different ethnic identities within the framework of the Soviet identity it aimed to create.

Military heroes, feats and experiences—first and foremost, of course, World War II, or the Great Patriotic War in Soviet parlance—served as essential unifying symbols for all ethnic groups in the Soviet Union. Some see this emphasis on the military as primarily reflecting Soviet "militarism." But it is more useful to view the Great Patriotic War during the Brezhnev era as a symbol of patriotism and internationalism, and thus of integration. The war as myth had three vital functions: a source of heroes for youth to emulate, a past model of interethnic cooperation useful to values encouraged in present-day youth, and the event that consolidated the Soviet Union, made it a great power, and buttressed its contemporary successes.

Brezhnev-era officials tried to present these ideas in differentiated ways throughout the Soviet Union, setting forth the heroic deeds of local people who served the state during the Great Patriotic War as suitable role models for young people. In this process of socialization, the regime legitimized the existence of substate identities—both territorial and ethnic—within prescribed parameters. Indeed, officials even encouraged pride in these substate identities if this served the greater glory of the Soviet Union.

A typical hero of the Great Patriotic War was the composite Ivan Tsuba, characterized as a "glorious son of the Belorussian people," who fought as a partisan during the war and was killed in the defense of the Soviet Union. This is an example of a legitimate expression of pride in an ethnic group as long as it is presented in a Soviet context: in this case defending the homeland.[13] Or take the Uzbek, Aziz Burnashev, a member of the Uzbek Academy of Sciences, who fought in Latvia during the war and returned to Uzbekistan to enjoy a successful career in scientific research. Burnashev represents an expression of ethnic pride in defending the homeland, but also territorial pride as manifested in a successful career in a Soviet republic, a career made possible by Soviet power.

In another part of the Soviet Union, students in the Batyrevo village school in the Chuvash ASSR created a room of military glory to Chuvash heroes of the Great Patriotic War, gathering information through interviews with local veterans and the remaining families of those heroes who had perished during the war. The young people requested and received materials from Volgograd, including "sacred" battlefield soil. The themes of their exhibit emphasized the roles of ethnic Chuvash people in the war: "Heroes of the Soviet

Union—Chuvashi" and "Warriors of the Native Land (*voiny-zemliaki*)." Again, the goal was to present patriotism in an intimate and personalized manner to young people, emphasizing that all Soviet people contributed to the wartime victory.

Teachers and youth workers used these examples of local heroes as building blocks of patriotism, as a means of making patriotism personal and immediately relevant to young people. Much effort went into discovering local heroes, bringing them to life for the students, canonizing their heroic deeds in the dedication of museums, setting up rooms of glory in schools, and visiting local monuments. Indeed, during the Brezhnev years, hundreds of thousands of museums and monuments were dedicated to these heroes, serving as gathering places where rituals were performed.

Personalizing heroes by taking students to the sites of their heroic deeds such as battlefields and cemeteries was a relatively easy task in areas of the Soviet Union where battles had been fought. Visits to the sites of the Siege of Leningrad, ending with a solemn ceremony at the Piskarevsk Cemetery and followed by placing wreaths on the graves of the fallen, cannot help but be emotionally meaningful to young people in the area, most of whom had lost family members during the siege.

Young people residing in ethnic areas removed from the actual fighting offered more of a challenge to Soviet officials. In Central Asia this challenge was met by selecting local heroes who had fought in battles outside the local republic (which, as will be discussed below, also underlines socialist internationalism as the basis of Soviet patriotism), and by creating "heroes of the rear," who glorified labor during the war while simultaneously presenting contemporary occupational role models to young people. In Uzbekistan, for example, students read poems at the foot of newly created monuments praising the "ordinary Uzbek, Tadzhik and Karakalpak Komsomolites who had passed into legend and immortality" or "noble sons of the Fergana Valley," who had served the Soviet motherland at the front or in the rear during the Great Patriotic War.

The stormy period of the initial consolidation of various regions into the Soviet state was employed as another source of heroes and patriots for young people in parts of the country that had not directly experienced wartime battles. The Basmachi Wars in Central Asia ("Basmachi" referring to those who opposed Soviet power and fought the Red Army in the 1920s and 1930s) illustrate the point. Heroes of both Central Asian and Slavic ethnicity who fought with the Red Army or who generally supported the incorporation of Central Asia into the Soviet Union were lauded as suitable heroes and role models for young people. Indeed, during the 1970s, the regime spent much time and money building monuments and memorials in Central Asia where youth might ritually honor these heroes of mythologized history.

In other patriotic rituals, officials underlined the superior situation of ethnic groups living within the Soviet borders as opposed to their ethnic counterparts residing outside the USSR. Young Central Asians bemoaned the fate of their non-Soviet co-ethnics who were not in the homeland of Soviet Uzbekistan—thus legitimizing an attachment to their territory, the republic. In one poem, an Uzbek who had ended up in Saudi Arabia wrote of his longing for Uzbekistan: "Are there only a few who speak of the Fatherland, who look homesick for its enchanting greetings and salutations, who listen to its voice and echo?" he asked. "No," he wrote, "they are very numerous."[14]

No matter which ethnic heroes were presented to Soviet young people, or where they were presented, teachers and youth workers emphasized that the noblest of Soviet heroes possessed both native and Russian characteristics. Famous Russian heroes such as the folk-hero of the seventeenth century, Ivan Susanin, the hero of a Glinka opera—or the World War II hero, Aleksandr Matrosov—were frequently connected to non-Russian heroes, giving them a sort of hyphenated identity. In ritualized dedications to non-Russian local heroes teachers characterized them as, for example, a Belorussian Susanin, or an Uzbek Matrosov.

The sort of ethnic pride that was officially accepted, then, was one in which a non-Russian's special and valuable characteristics were acknowledged in themselves, but took on even greater value the more closely they could be identified with Russian characteristics. It was laudable to be a proud resident of the Uzbek SSR; it was even better to be an heroic Uzbek who fought in the war; but it was best to be an Uzbek hero whose heroism could be attributed, in part, to what appeared to be ethnic Russian characteristics—an Uzbek Matrosov. Hence, the hybrid Soviet man—fully capable of assuming his place as a member of the multiethnic socialist internationalist community—is created.

Internationalism as a Key Component of Soviet Patriotism

The Great Patriotic War also served as a symbol of interethnic cooperation. Local heroes were coupled with heroes of other ethnic groups to underline the critical ideal that Soviet patriotism was based not on a narrow nationalism, but on socialist internationalism. The

Tadzhik Saidkul Turdyev, for example, was a "glorious son of the Tadzhik people" who had monuments, schools and factories dedicated to him throughout Tadzhikistan and was the subject of children's folk-songs, but he was also a hero who understood the force of internationalism. At a ceremony commemorating his birth, officials stressed the ideal of the Soviet Union as a "friendly family of peoples." Saidkul had given his life for his country and had the heart of a patriot because he "knew the house of the Russian, the house of the Ukrainian, and the house of the Belorussian had to be defended, like his own house."[15]

A more dramatic illustration of interethnic bravery in the face of adversity was found in an account of an Uzbek and a Ukrainian who became sworn comrades during the war. In the heat of a battle, the two comrades literally tied themselves together with grenades and threw themselves under a Nazi tank to save their brigade. This story does not mean, of course, that successful interethnic cooperation could take place only beneath the treads of a Fascist tank. There were more prosaic examples, such as Uzbeks who sheltered Russian families in Central Asian villages during the war. There were also contemporary examples, such as interethnic brigades working together harmoniously in the oil fields of the Tyumen *oblast'* and the hydroelectric plants of Lake Baikal.

Teachers and youth leaders used war stories to encourage interethnic ties among Soviet students. A group at a school in a village in the Mary *oblast'* of Turkmenistan, the home of a local hero who had been killed in the war, for example, wrote to their counterparts in the Smolensk *oblast'* in the Ukraine to find the exact battlefield where the Turkmen had been killed. Not only did the students in the Smolensk *oblast'* respond to the letter, they also gathered up a shell casing of earth from the battlefield where he had fallen and sent it to their young comrades in Turkmenistan. At the end of the school year, the class from Turkmenistan joined the class from Smolensk to dedicate a monument to the war dead.

Interethnic cooperation also had a regional aspect, emphasizing a grouping of republics in the Soviet Union, such as Central Asia and Kazakhstan or the Baltics, as a means of bringing the wartime model of internationalism up to date. Young people gathered at the physical borders dividing the republics to participate in rituals denoting interethnic friendship among youth. These ceremonies often celebrated the richness of the local cultures or underlined the importance of fulfilling regional economic goals. In many of these regional gatherings, the Russian identity was inserted, sometimes in an almost defensive manner, as if Party officials feared what might happen in its absence. A cultural festival held simultaneously in Tashkent and Alma-Ata, for example, celebrated the contributions of Uzbek and Kazakh cultures to Central Asian civilization. The organizers of the festival, however, were obliged to emphasize the fact that the "great" Uzbek and Kazakh cultures had been nurtured by the same root—"the wise folklore of the ancient east and the high Russian culture."[16]

State Identity: The Soviet Union as Superpower

Finally, the Great Patriotic War was a symbol of consolidation of the Soviet Union as a great power. This notion was concretized in unionwide patriotic rituals in which young people from all over the Soviet Union participated. Sports events were often the source of these rituals. The *Zarnitsa* (Summer Lightning) games for 10–15 year olds and the *Orlenok* (Eaglet) games for youth 15 years and older were events at which young people of all Soviet ethnic groups participated in simulated war games, collectively defeating foreign "imperialists." After their victory, the young people marched in interethnic regiments in ceremonial victory parades. Indeed, officials strove to achieve a successful simulation of what they hoped real military service in the Soviet Armed Forces would mean to Soviet youth.

Young people also participated in union-wide meetings in particular republics, often Belorussia, where pageants were held depicting Soviet international accomplishments, such as space flights. Again these pageants endorsed a multiethnic vision of a Soviet people marching collectively toward world accomplishments worthy of a superpower. In a sense, the glorification of these accomplishments illustrated the culmination of the patriotic socialization program—the concept of the great potential of the joint efforts of Soviet ethnic groups.

The Success of the Brezhnev Program in the Inculcation of Substate Identities

Brezhnev-era leaders claimed that the purpose of the patriotic program was to inculcate loyalty to the Soviet state, not by destroying substate identities but by using them as building blocks toward the ultimate goal of creating Soviet man. As already mentioned, the Brezhnev regime asked not for a deep feeling of "Sovietness," but for proper behavior as Soviet citizens that could be acted out in various forms of ritual. Many different identities were allowed to exist, ranging from local to ethnic to republic to state. Among non-

Russians particularly, these identities could fall into a variety of fluid combinations that served the best interests of the individual or group in a specific situation.

Socialist internationalism played a mediating role in this all-inclusive patriotism by emphasizing the friendship of peoples as the backbone of Soviet patriotism and by permitting and channeling into approved modes some expression of individual ethnic pride. Thus was the Stalinist theory of "national in form and socialist in content" put into practice during the Brezhnev era.

In legitimizing the expression of circumscribed ethnic pride within the confines of socialist internationalism, however, the Soviet leadership walked a narrow path full of political dangers, as already witnessed in the resurgence of Russian nationalism in the 1960s. In theory, political chauvinism and exclusivity were to be completely ousted from this officially sanctioned "cultural nationalism." But the distinctions possible in theory are not necessarily as clear in practice.

Indeed, the dividing line between a depoliticized cultural ethnicity and a politically nationalistic orientation is far from rigid. That is why the Party and its representatives tried to keep close control over the development of local heroes and local monuments at which rituals took place throughout the Soviet Union. Socialist internationalism could be an effective basis of Soviet patriotism. But there was the risk that the expression of an exclusive, politicized ethnic pride (nationalism) could take place outside the context of socialist internationalism, as did occur in a variety of contexts, most notably in the Baltic republics.[17]

Cognizant of such dangers, Soviet officials underlined their notion of Soviet patriotism and its corollary, socialist internationalism, by increasing celebrations and rituals encompassing several ethnic groups living in contiguous areas, stressing the theme of friendship of ethnic groups. The activities reported in *Soviet Patriot* exemplify this trend, featuring meetings of young people who were members of ethnic groups of various regions—for example, Central Asia or the Baltic—to honor regional heroes, often at rituals acted out in the shadow of monuments on the borders between their administrative units.

Despite the numerous shortcomings in patriotic and internationalist education during the Brezhnev era, the program enjoyed large-scale, albeit pro forma, participation among large numbers of young people, especially in the Slavic union republics and urban portions of the USSR.[18] Patriotic education was concentrated in the predominantly urbanized RSFSR (69 per cent urban according to the

1979 census), notably in Leningrad, Moscow, Volgograd, Rostov-on-Don—located in the European portions of the Federation. The smaller administrative units in more remote areas of the RSFSR barely received notice as part of the patriotic program.[19]

The other two Slavic union republics also had high participation levels. The Ukraine (61 per cent urban) recorded the most participation in its urbanized eastern portions. Belorussia had the highest participation levels of the two republics, even though it is only 55 per cent urban. This was due, in part, to the republic's special role as a union-wide example of the successes of patriotic and internationalist activities.

The urban portions of the Baltic republics of Latvia (68 per cent) and Estonia (70 per cent) also saw a high proportion of youth participation in patriotic and internationalist activities, but primarily among the Slavic populations living in the cities. Lithuania (61 per cent urban) had lower levels of participation and was plagued with allegations of incompetence on the part of youth leaders throughout most of the 1970s. In Moldavia (39 per cent urban) participation in patriotic and internationalist activities took place almost exclusively in the capital city of Kishinev.

Participation rates were generally lower in the Caucasian republics of Armenia and Georgia, though here they fluctuated widely throughout the Brezhnev era. Although more than half of their populations live in urban areas (66 per cent in Armenia and 52 per cent in Georgia), the strong local traditions in both republics, officially tolerated to some extent by local Party officials, may have contributed to lower participation in patriotic and internationalist activities.

In the nominally Muslim republics of Central Asia, Kazakhstan, and Azerbaidzhan, low levels of urbanization, and, more importantly, the relative strength of Islam as a cultural system contributed to lower rates of participation. The number of young people participating in patriotic and internationalist activities did, however, reportedly increase significantly during the 18 years of the Brezhnev period, although mainly in urban areas heavily populated with Slavs. (Of course, given the extent of corruption in these republics—Uzbekistan, for example—during the Brezhnev period, one recognizes the greater probability that the increase of participation in patriotic and internationalist activities reported by officials was exaggerated.)

Soviet officials correlated the success of the patriotic program in these areas (as indicated by increased participation) directly with the status of religion. They wanted Soviet youth leaders to replace the mullahs as the agents of influence among young people. But they realized that such a transference would be a long and slow process. Recognizing that performance of Islamic rituals was not necessarily an indication of militant Islamic belief, Soviet authorities relied upon a highly ritualized socialization regimen that might, they believed, over time, contribute to acceptance of the Soviet state identity represented in Soviet patriotism and socialist internationalism.[20]

Most tellingly, after nearly 20 years of experience with the program, Soviet authorities were promoting it more intensively than ever as the Brezhnev era came to a close. Evidently in their view it had paid good dividends in terms of fostering a state identity built upon substate identities through Soviet patriotism and socialist internationalism, and continued to show potential for improvement and development.

Ethnic Expression in Sociological Studies

Sociological studies released under the aegis of Mikhail Gorbachev reveal the extent to which notions of substate identity became a part of Soviet reality during the Brezhnev years.[21] In a five-republic study (RSFSR, Uzbek SSR, Moldavian SSR, Georgian SSR, Estonian SSR), conducted at the end of the Brezhnev era, pollsters asked Soviet citizens about their attachment to the Soviet Union, to their home republic, and to their native ethnic group: "What do you consider your motherland (*rodina*)—the country as a whole, the republic in which you live, the republic of your own nationality . . . ?" The overwhelming majority of the people surveyed listed as their motherland "the USSR and the republics of their own nationality." In the RSFSR and Uzbekistan, for example, "77–80 per cent" of the representatives of the population sampled listed the USSR and the republics of their own nationality as their motherland. In the republic of Moldavia, which had been a part of Romania until World War II, more than three-quarters of those sampled listed the Soviet Union as their motherland.

Among ethnic groups living outside their own republic, or among other minorities lacking a republic of their own, the responses change little. For example, 60 per cent of the Armenians, Azerbaidzhanis and Ossetians living in Georgia named the Soviet Union as their motherland; 25 per cent of them named Georgia, and about 15 per cent named their home ethnic territory.

The authors of the study readily admitted that these various levels of Soviet identity remained fluid, depending on the particular situation of an individual or group. Indeed, a Soviet citizen may emphasize a specific ethnic identity on occasion to provide advantages in competition for a particular job or entry into an institution of higher education. In other situations, for instance a military setting, such an emphasis might be less desirable. Indeed, the authors of the study concluded that identity changes from city to region to republic to country as a whole, "depending on the time and the situation."[22]

While the data are far from complete, they do suggest some important conclusions about the Brezhnev legacy. Most importantly, the vast majority of those questioned—Russians and non-Russians—in effect identify themselves as Soviet citizens. Secondly, most of the respondents also report a strong attachment to the republics of their own nationality, pointing to the relative strength of substate identities in the Soviet Union. The responses of these Soviet citizens suggest the existence of multiple identities that are not necessarily system-threatening. Moreover, the responses indicate that a type of hyphenated identity—that of the USSR plus the republic of one's own nationality—is beginning to take root among the peoples of the Soviet Union.

The existence of ethnic and republic identities suggests that Brezhnev's formula of using substate identities as building blocks of a state identity has made considerable headway in Soviet society. Hence, post-Brezhnev outbursts among certain Soviet ethnic groups do not necessarily suggest a failure in the Brezhnev policy, but may even indicate its success. The building-block approach, in other words, has worked, but is at various stages of development in various situations.

Moreover, as already discussed, different identities can exist simultaneously, depending on the situation in which an individual is involved. For educational purposes, a person may find an ethnic identity advantageous; in other contexts, a republican or union-wide identity might offer substantial benefits. The organization and content of the Brezhnev program did not exclude any of these possibilities, though, of course, the adoption of a dominant Soviet state identity was the preferred goal of the program.

It is necessary to consider the perspectives of young people now coming of age who were socialized under the Brezhnev program and are currently concerned with prospects for jobs and career advancement as young adults. As more non-Russians become qualified for jobs held by Russians, competition and its product, increased ethnic sensitivity, can be expected to be more common. The state, which encouraged local, ethnic and territorial pride among its young charges, cannot avoid the logical conclusion of its educational campaign—enhanced ethnic assertiveness. A similar phenomenon is experienced in a variety of sociopolitical contexts in multiethnic states throughout the world, often manifesting itself as a framework for the enunciation of communal demands, especially in competing for the distribution of sociocultural and economic goods within society.

Thus, most expressions of ethnic assertiveness cannot be labeled simply as deviant, even in the Soviet context. The Brezhnev socialization policies, after all, encouraged the strengthening of local, republic and regional identities. In other words, the patriotic program succeeded in legitimizing ethnoterritorial pride, assuming this to be non-system-threatening, but was not as successful in its planned next stage, which was the integration of these substate identities into an international union of Soviet citizens professing exclusive loyalty to the Soviet state.

Viewing National Disturbances During the Gorbachev Era

The years since Gorbachev's accession to power have seen some of the most spectacular national disturbances in the Soviet Union in decades. Due to the scope of his agenda for economic and social reform in the Soviet Union, Mikhail Gorbachev faces different and more dynamic nationality issues than any of his recent predecessors.[23] Gorbachev has demanded efficiency and accountability in the Soviet system, which may entail greater political centralization but at the same time demand greater economic initiative from below. These demands run counter to the notion of local Party autonomy. Indeed, during the Brezhnev era some republics developed a quasi-feudal Party leadership distant from Moscow. These comfortable arrangements are threatened by Gorbachev's calls for increased economic efficiency through strengthened economic accountability.

One might argue that the very existence of these widespread ethnic disturbances illustrates the failure of the Brezhnev policies and suggests that the patriotic program served no purpose. But closer examination of these uprisings illustrates that the majority of the young people who participated in them—the university students and young adults of the 1980s who as schoolchildren were inculcated in the patriotic program during the 1970s—were expressing ethnic desires *within* the Soviet system rather than *against* it.[24]

During the December 1987 riots in Alma-Ata, for example, young people were expressing dissatisfaction about their career prospects within the republic, not advocating secession from the Soviet Union. The demonstrations in Soviet Armenia throughout 1988 saw the Armenians calling for the transfer of a subrepublic administrative unit (Nagorno-Karabakh, presently in the Azerbaidzhanian SSR) to the Armenian SSR as their primary demand. Indeed, troops had to be called into Armenia and neighboring Azerbaidzhan not to quell a revolt against the Soviet system, but to maintain order in the face of interethnic tensions rooted in centuries-old disputes, but acted out very much within a Soviet framework. In other words, the socialization program of the Brezhnev era could well have planted the seeds of an enhanced ethnic confidence and assertiveness in the youngsters of the time that is being acted out today in terms of demands for increased cultural and political benefits within—not separate from—the Soviet system.

When Gorbachev came to power in 1985, he showed little interest in the nationality question, focusing his energies primarily on the economy. Only after unprecedented upheaval in several republics has he begun to recognize the importance of the nationality question in the Soviet Union. And he has responded with a formula that echoes the calls of the Brezhnev era. To remedy the ethnic frictions between Armenia and Azerbaidzhan, for example, Gorbachev demanded that "Communist parties of Azerbaidzhan and Armenia work out a set of long-term measures to improve the internationalist education of working people and to solve in a coordinated manner topical questions" on various aspects of mutual relations between the two republics, including language and culture.[25]

In a major speech on education before his demotion, Politburo member Yegor Ligachev underlined the importance of patriotic and internationalist education to yet another generation of Soviet youth.

> Comrades! Young Soviet people are growing up in a multinational country. They are also growing up in a world of closely interwoven human interests, but one that is also torn by contradictions. Two indivisible educational tasks arise in these conditions: training *both patriots and internationalists.*[26]
>
> In the school classroom itself, at Pioneer gatherings, and later, in training workshops and student auditoriums, the younger generation learns to feel involvement with the traditions and values of the Soviet homeland, the spiritual make-up and culture of the peoples, the activities and preoccupations of the country, and its prestige in the modern world. It is the duty of school and institute to instill in a graduate the qualities of a genuine—that is, active—patriot and internationalist.[27]

In his speech Ligachev precisely echoed the Brezhnev formula of the creation of the Soviet patriot and internationalist as the duty of the Soviet educational system, down to the detail of defining a "genuine" Soviet patriot as one who is "active," that is, one whose participation is concretely measurable. True, the demotion of Ligachev, in concert with efforts to erase Brezhnev from the landscape of Soviet history, calls into question the extent to which the Gorbachev regime will adhere to the patriotic formula. But for the time being, Gorbachev and his lieutenants offer Soviet youth no alternative to increased international education in Soviet schools.

Gorbachev's *perestroika*, however, has the side effect of challenging the legitimacy of the Brezhnev-era patriotic and internationalist upbringing program, which offered a hierarchy of identities through the use of a ritualized explanation of Soviet ethnic relations transposed onto a system of youth socialization. In saying that the rationalization of society under Brezhnev was really irrational, in suggesting that some of Brezhnev's heroes might really be scoundrels, and in challenging the Brezhnev vision of societal integration achieved not through a belief in the system but through overt participation in its patriotic and internationalist ritual, Gorbachev may pay a high price for upsetting the painstakingly maintained ethnic balance he inherited from Brezhnev. The ensuing reactions from the periphery may ultimately push the Gorbachev regime further in the direction of granting some forms of territorial and cultural autonomy to Soviet ethnic groups as an outlet for ethnic grievances—a solution that Brezhnev-era officials by and large avoided through an insistent and tenacious system of patriotic and internationalist ritual.

Notes

1. *The Communist Party Program and Party Statutes: Final Versions*, translated in *Current Digest of the Soviet Press*, Special Supplement, December 1986, p 14.

2. James Millar, "The Little Deal: Brezhnev's Contribution to Acquisitive Socialism," *Slavic Review*, 44 (Winter 1985), p. 697. Under Brezhnev's "deal," petty private economic practices were tolerated, thereby reallocating "by private means . . . a significant fraction of the Soviet national income according to private preferences," giving people "increased freedom to wheel and deal at the microlevel of Soviet society, while at the macrolevel managerial discretion was restrained. . . ." The "little deal" had an effect on the nationalities of the Soviet Union insofar as local autonomy was tolerated, creating a stake in the system for many non-Russians who profited from the local economic practices tolerated by Moscow.

3. *Program of the Communist Party of the Soviet Union* (New York: International Publishers, 1963), p. 122.

4. Maxim Kim, *The Soviet People: A New Historical Community* (Moscow: Progress Press, 1977), p. 201.

5. B. Demin, "Nenavist' k vragu—neot'emlemaia storona patriotizma sovetskikh voinov," *Kommunist vooruzhennikh sil* (July 1969), p. 26.

6. For a discussion of Plato's educational philosophy, see *The Republic* (New York: Penguin Books, 1972), pp. 113-55.

7. For a history of patriotism and its inculcation into the population during the French Third Republic, see Carlton J. H. Hayes, *France: A Nation of Patriots* (New York: Columbia University Press, 1930).

8. G. Jahoda, "The Development of Children's Ideas about Country and Nationality, Part I: The Conceptual Framework," *The British Journal of Educational Psychology*, 33 (February 1963), pp. 47-60; and "The Development of Children's Ideas about Country and Nationality, Part II: National Symbols and Themes," ibid., 33 (June 1963), pp. 150-1.

9. Clifford Geertz, "Ideology as a Cultural System" in David Apter (ed.), *Ideology and Discontent* (London: Free Press of Glencoe, 1964), pp. 47-76.

10. Simon R. F. Price, *Rituals and Power: The Roman Imperial Cult in Asia Minor* (Cambridge: Cambridge University Press, 1984), p. 8.

11. Gail Warshofsky Lapidus, "Ethnonationalism and Political Stability: The Soviet Case," *World Politics*, 36 (July 1984), p. 560.

12. Stephen White, *Political Culture and Soviet Politics* (London: Macmillan Co., 1979), p. 144.

13. The characteristics of the heroes from the republics and *oblasts* mentioned in the following examples are composites of the numerous examples given in the newspaper *Sovetskii Patriot* during the years 1965-1982. More than 18,000 articles were read and categorized using the *oblasts* of the Soviet Union as the operational administrative unit of analysis. For a quantitative and qualitative analysis of these articles, see Karen A. Collias, "Heroes and Patriots: The Ethnic Integration of Soviet Youth during the Brezhnev Era, 1965-1982," Ph.D. Dissertation, Columbia University, 1987.

14. See Collias, "Heroes and Patriots," chapter 5.

15. Ibid.

16. Ibid.

17. There are many instances in which circumscribed Soviet holidays designed to be celebrated by mass mobilization events, such as parades, turned into displays of Estonian, Latvian or Lithuanian nationalism. Indeed, some turned into events in which young Balts called for independence by protesting their forced incorporation into the Soviet Union during World War II. Such calls for independence have greatly increased since Gorbachev came to power in 1985.

18. The following analysis is based on the research and conclusions in Collias, "Heroes and Patriots."

19. One notable exception was the Bashkir ASSR, whose high activity figures were partially due to the plethora of indigenous military heroes of the Great Patriotic War.

20. For a discussion of the notion of ritualized participation, without belief, see Nursakhat Bairamsakhatov, *Novyi byt i islam* (Moscow: Biblioteka ateista, 1979), p. 30.

21. See *Sotsial'no-kulturnyy oblik sovetskikh natsiy* (Moscow: Nauka, 1986).

22. Ibid., p. 243.

23. For a general discussion of the nationality problem faced by Mikhail Gorbachev, which includes a section on ethnic attitudes toward substate and state identity, see Paul A. Goble, "Gorbachev and the Soviet Nationality Problem," in Maurice Friedberg and Heyward Isham (eds.), *Soviet Society Under Gorbachev* (New York: M. E. Sharpe, 1987), pp. 76-100.

24. The situation in the Baltic republics is generally an exception. In the 1987-1989 demonstrations in Estonia, Latvia and Lithuania, most of the participants specifically demanded secession from the Soviet Union.

25. *Washington Post*, March 10, 1988, p. a37.

26. Emphasis in source text.

27. *Pravda*, February 18, 1988, p. 3.

Chapter 7

New Soviet Rituals and National Integration in the USSR

Natalia Sadomskaya

It has been almost 30 years since the government of the USSR began to introduce "new socialist, nonreligious rituals." Beginning in the 1960s, there appeared a great deal of patriotic,[1] scholarly and propagandistic literature, books and articles by Western sociologists and anthropologists.[2] Until now, however, little attention has been paid to experiments involving the use of holidays and ceremonies as tools in the policy of national integration.[3] The policy of the new rituals set for itself not so much an ideological as a pragmatic goal—to promote the blending of folk cultures of various nationalities. Although the policy had one aim, its application to different ethnic groups with different cultural traditions met with varied reactions. Thus the policy became differentiated and changed its tactics in the various regions. Introduced in the course of this campaign was the use of a "secondary folklore,"[4] which appealed to local pre-ecclesiastic cults (pre-Christian, pre-Muslim) and legitimized the antireligious tendency of the policy.

The idea of "new rituals" and, linked to it, theories of the nonreligious origin of ritual forms in popular life were not new. Leon Trotsky (in 1925) was the first person in the USSR after the Revolution to express the thought of actually designing new socialist family and calendar ceremonies.[5] In 1930 the writer Vikentii Veresaev[6] initiated a discussion of the question in the journal *Krasnaya nov'*. In the 1920s much was written and a lot of experimentation was carried out in connection with the "new way of life," but, as with many revolutionary undertakings of the time, this idea disappeared in the 1930s, along with the dreamers who had given birth to it.

The idea was revived in a new guise at the end of the 1950s in the form of a state campaign that followed an organized pattern. It began with articles in the press, discussions, followed by resolutions and conferences, and meetings in various Party and Soviet institutions to draft concrete measures and directives. Parallel activities went on at the Institute of Ethnography, Philosophy, Religion and Atheism of the Academy of Sciences of the USSR, at institutes of the Academies of Science of the Union Republics and at the Ministry of Culture and similar places.

Numerous descriptions of new festivities appeared in scholarly and in propagandistic literature: Farewell to Winter, Welcome Spring, Russian Birch Tree, and Ivan Kupala quaintly merged into Soviet Youth Day, Name-Giving Day, Coming of Age, Komsomol Wedding, Solemn Funerals and many others. More than 50 new holidays and solemn ceremonies were invented, according to the claim of N. A. Belyk, who was Moscow's representative at a 1966 All-Union Conference on the struggle against holdovers from the past.[7]

Anthropological and propagandistic literature, as I have already said, explain the necessity of introducing new rituals as a task in the fight against holdovers of religious faiths. This is true, of course, but not the whole truth. It is worth noting that this was a decision made 40 years after the October Revolution, when, it would seem, the traditions of the new society had become a matter of habit to two generations, and a rhythm of life had been worked out to which everyone was accustomed. If it had occurred immediately after the Revolution or during the Civil War, it would have been understandable. History knows of antireligious outbursts when, in the rush of negative emotions, places of worship are destroyed. At the time of the French Revolution they attempted to invent new cults. At the time of the Spanish Civil War in 1936 there was a period of anti-Catholic pogroms. In Russia itself the atheistic temper of the 1920s and efforts to organize nonreligious rituals were similarly roused by the staying power of the rebellion.

However, we are encountering here a wholly new phenomenon in which the logic of the fight against old institutions explains very little about the introduction of new civic rituals. A study of the material available indicates that the creators of new rituals are concerned not only that traditional rites be replaced with nonreligious ones, but also that the new rites are, as far as possible, standardized among the different peoples that inhabit the Soviet Union. And, if the negative spirit of the campaign is atheism, then its positive program is unity—unity through denial and extermination of anything that detracts from the idea of a collective homeland, denial of religions of whatever persuasion, and denial of national customs that create the threat of separatism.

At first glance it seems that, in creating new rituals, the government wanted to overcome the conflict between tradition and ideology. We will discover, however, that this campaign is, to an extreme degree, itself full of contradictions. Those who wish to see Russian nationalism in it will be astounded by the profanation of Russian folklore traditions. Those who wish to call it internationalistic will be amazed at the violence done to the local traditions of non-Russian peoples. It will be worse still for the logical atheist, who couldn't possibly understand why Christian holidays are automatically bad and pagan holidays good.

These rituals were introduced in the late 1950s when Khrushchev, after the death of Stalin, had already strengthened his power and had begun to re-examine the religious policies of his predecessor. During World War II religious ceremonial practices had been revived among the Soviet population. As is well known, in 1941 Stalin concluded a series of compromises with the Orthodox church and Muslim representatives, allowing freedom of religious practice in exchange for aid from their sides. Having been annexed on the eve of the war, the Baltics, Moldavia and Western Ukraine continued their ritualistic practice more or less freely after the war in sharp contrast to the situation in other republics (it is not coincidental that the first experiments began in Latvia and the Ukraine).

After the death of Stalin and the dethroning of the "cult of personality" at the 20th Party Congress in 1956, the powerful figure of "father and teacher," which had symbolized the unification of all nationalities and had served as psychological compensation for the religious emotion of the population, disappeared. The sharp withdrawal of the symbol from everyday ideological circulation gave rise to some confusion, as is evidenced by the crowds at Stalin's grave. The initiative from the center was quickly colored in local tones. Decentralization became a threat. This gave rise to the idea that the vacuum had to be filled with something and thus the people would return to their various national traditional cults and rituals.

Khrushchev himself was rather nostalgic about the pre-Stalinist period when he began his political career. Everyone was young and full of enthusiasm, and many interesting things were devised which were later rejected by Stalin. Whoever first proposed the revival of ritual creation from the 1920s is unknown, but the idea appealed to Khrushchev. Of course, the name Trotsky was not recalled. In the literature, the writer Veresaev figured as the initiator of the discourse.

Under Khrushchev the tendency of the rituals was more antireligious; later, under Brezhnev, the struggle against separatist tendencies assumed primary importance. In a report to the 24th Party Congress in 1971, Brezhnev announced the birth of a "new historical community of the people—the Soviet nation."[8] Soviet anthropological literature began to discuss in earnest the problems of creating an integrated culture founded on the basis of a "synthesis of the elements of the old progressive culture of a given nation and the new international forms that occur in the socialist era."[9] And already, by 1979, P. K. Kurochkin, director of the Institute of Scientific Atheism, appearing before the Central Committee of the Communist Party, was saying:

> Socialist rituals were not conceived to force out religious ones . . . the antireligious essence of the rituals will extend even more in the latest plan. . . . Socialist rituals, imbued with Communist ideals, will assist in the unification of people, *regardless of their world view and national affiliation.*[10]

In this article I will deal particularly with how the new system of rituals serves to overcome conflicts between nationalities and, in general, serves the integration policy of the state. This policy can be traced best of all in the new calendar holidays which are bound together today by the new title of "folk festivals."

These festivals are supposed to supplant the older, traditional ones, which are bound to the religious calendar. New holidays had previously been introduced by the Soviet government. But now, something truly without precedent appeared. The authorities decided to displace the old holidays by scheduling new holidays according to the dates of the old. They openly justify this procedure in the Soviet literature with references to the practice of early Christian substitutions for pagan festivals. They recall, for example, that the origin of the date of Christmas was timed to the holiday of the sun god Mithra.

I. S. Remizov proposed, for example, the following substitution of the most revered Orthodox holidays in the Voronezh oblast:

> Schedule the Russian Winter Holiday on the days when Christmas and Epiphany are celebrated; set the Holiday of Spring Sowing and First Furrow according to the Day of Annunciation; the Spring Holiday to Easter; Green Friend Day to the Day of Trinity; the Day of Mass Planting of Trees to Palm Sunday; the Harvest Holiday to the Day of the Three Saviours and the Protection of the Virgin.[11]

Difficulties arise in construing the components of a new holiday which are not supposed to remind one of religion and, at the same time, are supposed to represent to the populace something quite familiar and appealing. They seek these components in the life of nature, in the change of the seasons, and in the agricultural tasks that are cyclically tied to them. However, these phenomena must be symbolically represented in the specific language of culture in order to become the structural framework for a holiday. As symbols, they use ceremonies that are "even more ancient, and even more traditional, than Christian ones."

Hence the paradoxical situation arises in which new substitute holidays invoke old pagan mythology. A variety of symbols of national traits, which have been linked with ancient pagan beliefs in Russian literature since the age of Romanticism, are involved. They are called upon to awaken patriotism through love for nature in one's native land and for ancient legends.

This appeal to national feelings is especially intensive in Russian territory, where efforts have been made to resurrect ancient folk holidays and fetes. V. A. Rudnev gives us a description of the new Russian Winter Holiday in Leningrad:

> Thousands of Leningraders gather in the Kirov Central Park of Culture and Rest for a traditional folk fete, "Welcome Dearest Wintry Winter." A *skomorokh* (minstrel-buffoon) at the park entrance tells where and when the holiday events will take place. Meanwhile, other *skomorokhi* blow trumpets calling for everyone to come to the outdoor folk festivities. Guests arrive through wooden plank gates hewn in peasant fashion and ornaments of olden times and find themselves in a snow-covered park. A dashing troika with bells has just set off from the "Coachman's Settlement," a brief stand by a crossroad. The passengers are children whose faces are lit with happy smiles. And in the Magic Meadow and the Field of Fun, the merrymaking is already under way.
>
> A lane of Dymkov and Vyatsk toys leads to Carnival Meadow where a booth towers overhead—a spacious *izba* (peasant hut) for *skomorokh* funning. In old Russia such extraordinary shows were put on, at one time, on fair days and at outdoor folk festivities. Nearby many peddlers trade in hot tea, cakes and fancy breads.
>
> At two in the afternoon, a comedy show begins.
>
> *Skomorokhi* and their retinue, merry fellows all, dash in like a noisy gang with laughter and jokes. A canon fires a burst of pyrotechnics. An old fairy-tale wizard begins prophetic tales about the seasons and tells intriguing riddles and fortunes to the listeners around him.
>
> The indispensable participants in the festivities— Magpie, Fox and Hare—solemnly announce the arrival of Mother Winter, the long-awaited guest of honour. She is welcomed with bread and salt, according to the ancient tradition of hospitality. The *skomorokh* at the gate greets the Snow Tsarina with noisemakers. A troika harnessed to horses with bells is brought up and, accompanied by the *skomorokhi*, Winter sets off in the sled on a trip through her domain, the alleys and lanes of the park.[12]

To create a feeling of ancient Rus, they have lumped into one heap jester-*skomorokhi*, troikas with bells, fairy-tale foxes and hares, cakes and sugar candies and the special turns of speech of folklore ("dearest wintry winter," "hewn wooden plank gates," "field of fun," etc.).

In the European part of Russia it was recommended that, instead of the Feast of Trinity, there now be a Russian Birch Tree holiday in the first half of June when the spring work on the field ceases:

> The white birch tree has become a poetic personification of our Motherland. No matter where a Russian may be, no matter how far fate may cast him from his native soil, when recalling the Motherland he will always resurrect in his memory a slender, beautiful birch tree rustling in the wind, bathed in sunlight, or powdered with hoarfrost.
>
> A beautiful young girl usually portrays the Birch Tree. Grandfather-Heat-Wave and Old-Lady-Drought (direct parallels with Grandfather-Frost and Snow-Maiden) take part in the pantomime. They make a retreat as the story proceeds, conquered by Spring-Song and Rain-Drop, who are also played by young girls. The spring and summer months—March, April, May, June, July, and August, dressed in costumes—are also on hand for the holiday. The principal personae are surrounded by a retinue dressed in elegant costumes based on motifs from fairy tales and heroic poems.
>
> The holiday begins at midday with a procession through the streets of the town or village. A band goes in front followed by the months. They carry Birch-Tree on a palanquin. Behind the palanquin come Spring-Song and Rain-Drop, and following them a variety of gymnasts, dancers and singers who are to take part in the holiday.
>
> The negative personae—Drought, Hail, Tumbleweed, Indolence, Parasite, Drunkard, Scrounger, and Eye-wash—are hauled in on a squeaking cart at the end of the procession.[13]

Birch Tree gets down from the palanquin, ascends a tribune and presents bread and salt to the leaders of the local Soviet. Then she makes a brief speech about the results of the spring work in the fields, the achievements of production collectives, and the best worker-winners in socialist competition. She crowns them with wreathes of flowers from the field.

I have had occasion to see the Russian Winter Holiday in different cities of the Moscow oblast and in the Lenin Hills Park in Moscow. It is usually organized like a fair or an amusement park, with rides for sale on horse-drawn troikas, a huge snowman and balalaika music on a loudspeaker turned up to a deafening volume. People took their children for rides on the troikas and, from time to time, had a nip of vodka at the stalls. But they never took part, never sang, never danced. The holiday for them was only a show.

These holidays are not in any way comparable to the old

Maslenitsa (Shrovetide) or Easter which were celebrated by practically the entire population and were truly national holidays. The new spectacles cannot be marked down in the diaries even of those who attend, and they do not correspond with the way they look at the world.

The snatches of old rituals which are incorporated in the new holidays are used apart from their functional essence, and apart from their mythological foundation. Holiday rituals were formerly tied to fertility magic and to cosmogonic cults. While rejecting any recollection of these things, clumsy rituals are difficult to justify in the eyes of the population. The lack of content in the rituals allows them to be combined with rather casual elements—from reworked versions of Russian folklore for children to a variety of folklore stylizations similar to those of the opera *Snow Maiden*, all in the lost style of "Rus" of the days of the Emperor Aleksandr III.

In the Ukraine, particularly in the countryside where the old holidays are loved and still not forgotten, the efforts of reformers create a scene that is indistinguishable from Russian territory. I include here a rather lengthy description of an experiment that in the Ukraine was considered a success: the holiday of Soviet Youth, which was organized on the basis of the traditional Ivan Kupala.

In many parts of the Ukraine, especially in the western regions, Ivan Kupala (or Midsummer Night, which also became Saint John the Baptist Day) was celebrated on the night of June 24, the summer solstice widely celebrated throughout all Europe. Popular beliefs linked this night with revelry of the Evil Spirit and all sorts of wonders. Young people would search for the red flower of a fern that bloomed once a year. This flower granted the power to find a treasure if you fulfilled the terms of the Evil Spirit.[14] On this night they burned bonfires and leapt through them. They rolled flaming wheels that symbolized the sun. A Madder Doll was made and burned or set afloat on a raft with blazing candles. Symbolism of fertility magic and sun worship were interwoven. In the Christian epoch, legends began to detail the temptations of the Evil Spirit on this holiday. This is what Gogol was writing about in his story, "The Eve of Ivan Kupala."

The renovated Ivan Kupala appears as follows:

> The holiday begins with a traditional election of a Master and Mistress of the Holiday—a Prince and Princess. These were most respected persons: Marija Mazur, Deputy of the Supreme Soviet of the USSR, and Vladimir Grishchuk, the finest tractor driver of the Mikhajlovskij Kolkhoz named for the 22nd Communist Party Congress. To applause and ceremonial marches by several bands,

the Prince and Princess are crowned and dressed in brightly decorated robes. Then they parade about with an honoured retinue made up of Wheat, Pea, Beet and Corn. Afterwards the Prince and Princess sit down on their Royal Thrones beneath willow trees that have been decorated with flowers, ribbons and multicolored flags. From that moment on, they direct the holiday: they solemnly declare its beginning and announce the order of events. A huge balloon rises in the sky with a red pennant on which is written in golden letters: "Happy Holiday of Kupala, Dear Friends!"

And when twilight darkens above the old part that once belonged to a Polish landowner and now to a Collective Farm, a traditional scene is played out in the middle of the lake. A large raft floats out with a stuffed figure pierced with arrows. Around it are Death with a Scythe, Atomic War, and all sorts of evil spirits (Drunkards, Idleness, Bureaucracy, Youth-Slobs, etc.).

Dozens of young people with blazing torches jump into the water and soon the stuffed figure with its "escort" is in flames. An enormous red flag with golden letters, "Long Live Communism!" soars high in the sky above.[15]

Thus we have a pagan return to nature without faith in its spirituality, and an incantation without faith in its magic powers. Obviously we are talking, not about the rebirth of a pre-Christian ritual and the popular reaction to the life of nature, but about a rationalized attempt at the creation of new ideological holidays that make use of folklore images.

In the Western regions of the Ukraine, adjacent to Moldavia and annexed to the USSR just before World War II, Ivan Kupala was celebrated in the villages in the traditional manner until the 1960s. After several unsuccessful attempts at reformation, it was decided that this holiday was harmless and in the 1970s it was included as an element of *rapprochement* with Moldavia. However, the anthropologist A. V. Kurochkin writes that none of the ethnic groups (Moldavians, Bulgarians and Gagauzy—Orthodox Turks in Bessarabia) of this Orthodox population accepted the foreign pagan holiday, even with socialist additions.[16]

A somewhat different picture can be observed in those national republics where traditional holidays are still alive in the consciousness of the population.

In Latvia, for example, Ligo or Yanov's Day (the Latvian version of Ivan Kupala) was the most popular holiday in the period of the independent Republic. Latvia was annexed to the USSR in 1940. In an effort to win over the Latvians, the government announced in May 1941 that Yanov's Day was an official holiday, with June 24 as a day off.

At the beginning of the 1960s, however, just at the time when the campaign for new rituals was inititated, the persecution of the celebration of Ligo in Latvia began. In 1965 Lev Kopelev, a Moscow writer and literary scholar, and Dzidra Kalnyn, a Latvian professor, published an article that made an effort to defend Ligo. They wrote:

> In the national holiday is seen not only a waste of worker's time, but also the miasma of bourgeois nationalism. There were those who, at the very least, out of naiveté supposed that it was possible just to remove Ligo from the national way of life, from the language, and from the literature. To that end a kind of surgery was performed in several publishing houses on new editions of the classics, on anthologies, textbooks, etc. In October 1960 the publishing of the second volume of *Contemporary Latvian Grammar* was delayed in order to replace all literary examples which in any way referred to Yanov's Day or Ligo or to customs and concepts related to them. Complete paragraphs, whole segments of prose, and stanzas of classical poetry were removed; folk-songs, proverbs, and aphorisms that in any way mentioned Yanov's Day or Ligo were distorted or completely eliminated. Everything connected with this word was renamed: a record factory, kolkhozes, movie theaters. Corrections were inserted even in cookbooks; the mention of Yanov cheese and Yanov beer was excised. There were demands to review dictionaries and replace several words in popular usage, for example, currant in Latvian is Yanov berry, fire-fly is Yanov beetle, and so on. Production was halted on A. Kalnynsha's opera, *Banjuta*, and M. Zarinysha's heroic oratorio, *Val'mijerskije geroi*, etc., etc.
>
> A plan for introducing a "happy and interesting holiday" to be called Fisherman's Day was developed with the aim of supplanting Ligo.[17]

The reasons for the state's conflict with the holiday of Ligo in Latvia were obvious. They have little in common with educational intentions to eradicate religious holdovers. Ligo had to disappear from popular memory and from the language and literature, first and foremost, because it had become a national holiday of the Latvian people, a symbol of their consolidation. Fisherman's Day, on the other hand, was innocuous, even if individual elements of Latvian folklore were included in it.

The experiments with Fisherman's Day were perceived in the Latvian Republic as an insult to their national feelings. In 1972, 17 Latvian Communists sent an appeal to Communist parties around the world in which they enumerated infringements of the national rights of Latvians. They wrote:

> The Latvian people have a remarkable holiday, Ligo, which

they have celebrated freely for centuries, even in the time of the German-Fascist occupation. This holiday has been categorically forbidden up until last year; this year, although not officially forbidden, Ligo was once again not recognized as a holiday.[18]

The Latvian intelligentsia tried to defend their holiday using arguments that, from the government's viewpoint, should have been convincing. They contended, first, that Ligo is not a Christian, but a pagan holiday, and, second, that not only Latvians but also many Slavic peoples celebrate it, and so there is in no danger of it being nationalistic. The well-known poet, Jan Sudrabkaln, wrote:

> In its essence, the Latvian Yanov Day has always been an anti-Christian, anti-church, peasant and plebeian holiday ... it has always expressed with special vividness the deep bond which exists between Latvians, Russians, and other peoples of the Soviet Union.[19]

This circumstance, where efforts to nullify local nationalism are made under the guise of supplanting religious beliefs, gives unexpected arguments to the national intelligentsia. They often proved that this or that holiday did not have Christian (or Muslim or Buddhist, etc.), but pagan origins and, hence, had a right to exist. The theoretical slipshodness of official theory, in this way, leaves an opportunity to protect what remains of local traditional culture.

Using such a method, the Latvians managed to defend Ligo and it is now celebrated, though not on such a scale as before.

In Central Asia in 1960 the conflict surrounding the first holiday of the spring New Year, Navruz ("new day") in Tadzhik, developed. Until the 1920s Navruz was celebrated by all the agricultural peoples in Central Asia and by the Azerbaijani in the Caucasus. The holiday preceded spring sowing and, since spring begins early in these hot areas, the date of Navruz was March 21. The holiday differed in the cities and the *kishlaki* (villages). In Khiva, Bukhara, Samarkand and Tashkent, magnificent parties were thrown with contests in poetry-reading, tournaments and feasts. Peasants from the villages came to bazaars in the cities, and bachelors looked for brides. Navruz was accompanied by the holiday of the first spring flowers, when children went to the mountains to gather snowdrops, and the Holiday of Roses, when young men gave red roses to the young women. Since ancient times the red rose has been surrounded by many symbolic legends connected with love, the death of the beloved and his rebirth in the form of roses growing on the grave.

In the *kishlaki* this was primarily a women's holiday. The old women of the community gathered to cook a special *kasha*, called *sumaliak*, the entire night before Navruz. It was prepared from sprouted grains mixed with flour. All the women sat around the *sumaliak* for the entire night and, toward morning, they each received a portion, which they ate while performing various rituals. The ceremony was intended to guarantee both a bountiful harvest and the fertility of each woman. Thus, infertile women and newlyweds particularly awaited Navruz.

Before sowing the oldest, most respected man in each *kishlak* performed an ancient ritual of plowing the first furrow around the field. Despite the fact that the dates of the Muslim New Year (calculated by the lunar calendar) and Navruz (calculated by the solar calendar) did not coincide, there was no conflict in their celebrations since the function of Navruz was the greeting of spring. It was precisely this peaceful coexistence of two New Years that destroyed Navruz. It was included in the Islamic calendar and prohibited in the cities at the beginning of the 1930s.

In the *kishlaki*, both Tadzhik and Uzbek, Navruz continued to be observed every spring, but not as openly as before. Lobacheva observed the celebration of Navruz in the 1950s among the Uzbeks of the Khorezm oblast (in Priaril').[20] In 1987 Ustaev published a most interesting description of the holiday in two *kishlaki* in the Surkhardar'in oblast of Uzbekistan, one Tadzhik and one Uzbek. He stressed that Navruz was celebrated there in its traditional form up until the mid-1960s.[21]

Judging from this, persecution of the holiday in the villages coincided with the campaign for new rituals. But this same campaign by the national intelligentsia gave arguments for the preservation of the holiday. In scholarly journals in Tadzhikistan and Uzbekistan, the publications of anthropologists in the 1960s and 1970s demonstrated that Navruz was not a Muslim holiday—not a religious holiday at all—but rather an agricultural and seasonal holiday of Zoroastrian origin. Rakhimov of Tadzhikistan, for instance, wrote:

> Navruz is really a pre-Islamic holiday of the Sogdijans, Khorezmijans, Tokhar and several other ancient peoples of the East. However, in time it absorbed some elements of Zoroastrianism and Islam.
>
> Purifying it of religious elements (both Zoroastrian and Islamic) and celebrating it in new ways as a holiday of Spring and the start of agricultural labor, would serve the cause of displacing a whole series of religious ceremonies and rituals from the daily life of the workers of our Republic.[22]

Ethnographers (O. A. Sukhareva[23] and G. P. Snesarev[24]) have traced ties between this holiday and cults of dead and resurrected vegetation, which were brought to Central Asia from Mesopotamia and the Middle East long before Islam. Navruz remained. Recently, Leokadija Drobizheva, deputy director of the Miklukho Maklai Institute of Ethnography, wrote with satisfaction that "in Uzbekistan, it is remembered how an attempt was made to prohibit the traditional spring holiday Navruz on the grounds that it had religious roots. The community intervened—fortunately, scholars in Moscow and Uzbekistan were united and brought back life and rights to Navruz."[25]

In 1967 a special resolution on the celebration of Navruz was published and in the same year it was celebrated in Baku and Urgench. In what form did this ancient holiday return? First, it lost its name. In the cities it was renamed Holiday of Spring and in some mountainous areas it became Day of the Shepherd.[26] Later, the name was returned.

Navruz subsequently lost its status as New Year, which was moved to winter, as in Europe. Beginning in the 1960s, fir trees were flown into the cities from Russia, and in the villages people began to give out kapron trees and toys and to teach children how to decorate the tree. For two weeks after New Year morning shows were held in the schools with characters from Russian folklore such as Father Frost and the Snow Maiden. In special lectures it was explained that the whole country celebrates New Year in the winter and that it is "uncultured" to celebrate it at another time.

The celebration date of Navruz itself was also changed. In Leninabad it is observed on March 7 and in Dushanbe on March 21.[27] In Tashkent, at one time, it was celebrated in December.

In the cities the ritual of the holiday repeated the structure of the May 1 and November 7 ceremonies: a meeting, a report on labor achievements, occasionally a procession with flags (Baku, 1967), and sometimes a concert and various games (Urgench, 1967).

The next stage was to develop a new scenario for the farmers. The scientific atheism sector of the Tadzhik Academy of Sciences worked out systematic recommendations for Tadzhikistan. The holiday was held in the Kurgan-Tiubin oblast on March 21, 1980, according to the scenario of Dr M. Mirrakhimov.[28]

The task was to encourage the spread of the holiday from the borders of one *kishlak* and to make it an oblast-wide holiday. In the Komsomol *obkom* (Regional Committee), a sub-committee—including *kolkhoz* leaders, the directors of cultural houses and Komsomol secretaries—was formed in order to implement Navruz.

In mid-March a contest of beauty and skill was held among young girls in the oblast. The most beautiful and industrious girl would play the role of Spring. March 21 was the holiday of the first furrow, which took place only in the progressive Gorky *kolkhoz* in the Kommunisticheski region. Everyone had to travel there to see the ritual. In addition, a motorcade, decorated with slogans and posters, made its way through the region. In one of the cars rode Spring, a high-school teacher. The young mechanics of the *kolkhoz*, dressed in national costume, greeted Spring with bread and salt (according to Russian custom) and with dishes made from sprouted wheat (a Tadzhik custom). The beauty queen/Spring wished everyone a "Happy Spring" and explained the symbolic meaning of a ritualistic tray bearing seven types of food. Afterward, there was a lively party with modern dances.

Meanwhile, in the *kishlaki*, women continued to cook *sumaliak*, to go into the mountains to collect flowers and to perform all the ritualistic customs.

Another type of experiment was made when a traditional holiday of one nationality was adapted for international use. Sabantui was and still is one of the favorite holidays of the Kazan Tatars. It was celebrated in ancient times by their predecessors, the Volga Bulgarians. However, the Crimean Tatars do not observe it. The holiday is pre-Muslim, but was long ago added to the calendar of these Islamic peoples. The Tatars observe it in spring before the beginning of sowing.[29] As with all agricultural holidays, it includes many ceremonies linked with fertility magic.

Preparation for Sabantui sometimes began more than two weeks in advance. During this period separate adolescent groups were brought together and assigned duties. As soon as the snow melted, boys would go around the farmsteads collecting groats, milk, butter and eggs to make a special *kasha* that was boiled in huge kettles in the meadows. After them came the young horsemen, who dashed around the village gathering eggs and then held races in which they would transfer bags filled with these delicate products. Next married mummers passed through and received refreshments which the hosts gave out generously. All three groups entertained themselves separately and prepared for competitions.

The elders (*aksakaly*) agreed on a date for the holiday and the order of celebrations for all the villages. Women and girls prepared gifts of embroidered shirts and towels for the winners and baked ritualistic small rolls (*bavursak*). The holiday itself lasted one day and ended with a race which was started by either the young boys or the old men, horse races and a national sport. Singers and musicians had waited all year for this day and had composed new songs.

Sabantui survived the Revolution, but was celebrated only in Tatar villages. In 1960 it occurred to someone in Kazan (the Tatar capital) to spread the holiday to other non-Tatar villages and to Russian cities. The period of celebration everywhere was moved from April to June 24, that is, from the period of spring sowing, when it was still linked to agrarian magic, to the period of the end of spring field work. Now it is celebrated on the day of Russian Ivan Kupala (or Ioann Krestitel). In the villages meetings were organized and leaders arrived to give awards for sowing. They also went to Russian villages to celebrate the Tatar Sabantui on the Patron Saint's Day. The holiday was not successful.

In its traditional form, the date of Sabantui was decided by respected elders of the commune. They agreed upon it together with *aksakaly* of neighboring villages, thus creating organic ties with their fellow tribesmen and demonstrating the autonomous independence of the fellow villagers. Now, control over the ritual calendar has passed into the hands of unknown people who arbitrarily change the date every year in different places.

I witnessed Sabantui in the summer of 1963 in the Ural city of Nizhni Tagil, a major metallurgical center. The Tatar population of the city was at that time close to 2 per cent.[30] On Sunday, as usual, many people gathered in the city park on the banks of the lake. On the gates to the park, a sign saying "Sabantui" had been hung. People walked around, lounged on the grass. In the evening an amateur concert was held on a stage. Two Tatar boys performed a national sport and Tatar girls sang songs. All the other performers were Russian. Judging from what Professor M. Magdeev of Kazan University writes, this was part of "integrational politics":

> Sabantui has one particular feature—its approach is impatiently awaited not only by Tatars but also by Russians, Chuvashi and Maritsy. In a word, for those who lived in the Kazan province, it gradually became a holiday of national integration. In this lies its striking distinction from religious holidays which divide people of different faiths. A Tatar would not be able to invite a Russian to a religious holiday—he would offend the participants and compromise himself. But he would invite a Russian to Sabantui. Neither the advocates of Mullah and Ishan, nor the politics of Orthodox Muslims, can disturb the friendly ties based on commonalities of agricultural life that exist between Tatars and Russians who live side by side. Sabantui is now celebrated in Sverdlovsk, Perm, Gorky, Kurgan, Cheliabin and other oblasts.[31]

The replacement of church holidays with pagan and international substitutions often produces a result that is contrary to the policy of integration and actually cultivates neighboring ethnic groups. With respect to this is the field work of A. V. Kurochkin, based on a study of calendrical holidays on the border between the Ukraine and Moldavia and published in 1987.[32]

What is distinctive here is that Moldavians and Ukrainians share one religion—Orthodoxy. Language—Romance for the Moldavians and East Slavic for the Ukrainians—separates them. Differences in their calendrical holidays have been traced back, for the most part, to the level of pagan beliefs. The sources of Moldavian magical rituals go back to ancient Thracian cattle-breeders of the Balkan peninsula, while the roots of Ukrainian paganism have been traced back to pre-Slavic agricultural cults.

These oblasts were annexed to the USSR just before World War II; thus they preserved their Christian calendrical customs right up until the 1960s. Holidays linked with the winter cycle such as Christmas, New Year and Epiphany were especially stable here.

For members of the Orthodox Church, the *sviatki* (Christmas-tide) cycle usually lasted for two weeks, from Christmas (December 24) until Epiphany (January 6). However, in these oblasts it was extended to a month, from December 13 (Saint Andrei's Day) until January 13 (the day of Saint Malan'). *Malanki*, renowned among folklorists, are held on this latter day: wearing archaic masks and bells and carrying whips, mummers go from house to house performing improvised dramas with stock characters similar to those of the *commedia dell'arte*.

Toward the end of the 1950s youth gatherings were stopped on Saint Andrei's Day. Dark clouds also gathered around Malanka. On the one hand, it began to attract unusual attention from theater critics and ethnographers: Irina Yvarova wrote about it in the journal *Theater* and Tat'iana Zlatkovskaia in *Soviet Ethnography*. On the other hand, local authorities feared ancient forms of improvisation, such as Ukrainian *shchedrovki* and Moldavian *kheiture*, in which the resurrection of Christ received much attention.

Finally in 1970 a compromise was reached. Malanka was acknowledged as a nonreligious drama which the Moldavians had borrowed from the Ukrainians.

> In the Moldavian tradition of folk performances, Malanka is famous as a heroic character—a Ukrainian girl who is killed in a fight with Tatars. The legendary Ukrainian heroes, Oleksa Dovoysh and Ustim Karmeliuk, entered into the eastern-Romance *hayduck* drama of the New Year cycle, which exists up to this day. It is characteristic that these personages exist hand in hand with their Moldavian counterparts, clearly demonstrating the sympathy and

solidarity of the workers of these two peoples in the common struggle for social and national liberation.[33]

It demands special research to determine what dictates these lines: is it a genuine interest in the origin of Malanka, or an effort by the anthropologist to save a folk drama in the same way that the Latvians struggled for Ligo and the Uzbeks for Navruz?

The celebration date of Malanka was changed (according to the wishes of activists in the region) from January 13 to December 31 thereby shortening the *sviatki* cycle by two weeks and breaking the outward tie with the church calendar. After that elements of "friendship between nationalities" began to be introduced into Malanka. G. I. Spataru observed a variation of Malanka performed by a group of amateurs with 15 youth representatives from all the republics. Instead of antique masks, they wore brightly colored headgear, decorated with state heroes of the Soviet republics and a red star, the symbol of the socialist system.[34]

Earlier, on Christmas, children and young people would go caroling, carrying a Christmas star on a pole, singing songs and wishes and receiving refreshments. The Christmas star was canceled, but texts of ceremonial songs, similar to the following, were published in regional newspapers in Ukrainian and Moldavian:

> The Party congress in spring
> Explained and announced to us
> That we are traveling by way of the furrow
> That was ploughed by Lenin
> And that this Il'ichev furrow
> Is no ordinary one.
> On this planet it became
> A landmark of happiness and labor.[35]

However, according to Kurochkin, the natural territory of Malanka narrowed to separate regions of western Ukraine (Podoli, Galitsi and Bukoviny) and northern Moldavia.

An attempt was made to introduce the popular Ukrainian holiday of Ivan Kupala into Moldavia, but other nationalities living in the republic—the (Romance) Moldavians, the (Slav) Bulgarians and the (Orthodox Turk) Gagauzy—would not accept the holiday. The favorite Moldavian spring holiday Mertsishor (March 1) was propagandized in the Ukraine, also without any success. It would appear that the Christian calendar, the *sviatki* and Easter holidays unite Ukrainians and Moldavians more strongly than the pagan holidays.

The situation is still worse among peoples of more primitive cultures who are incapable of offering opposition to reformers. The

Tuvinians professing Buddhism and Lamaism, who celebrated the spring New Year according to a lunar calendar, called it Shagaa. They observed a series of customs that they try to honor even now: they cleanse dirt from their *yurtas* (nomad's tent), prepare their best clothes, and, at sunrise on the day of the holiday, they roll in the snow until the snow becomes dirty, believing that in this way they are cleansed of their sins. To their elders they give gifts with special marks of esteem, and they put on a celebration in honor of the herdsmen. In every *yurta* they serve the herdsman the dish of honor—the leg joint, emphasizing that the herdsmen are the arms of the people and their main support. Thus they pay respect to the most important vocation among the Tuvinians.

One of the Tuva representatives at a conference in Ulan-Ude in 1962 reported:

> Our elders wonderfully recall the customs of the Shagaa. They talk about it for hours as the most treasured thing of all. This alone forces us to consider that these customs might have gone from our life too soon. They can and should be utilized in the celebration of today's New Year.[36]

Why has it become a necessity to consider the question of giving back to people their customs? The fact is, that in 1925 the New Year was introduced, in accordance with the European calendar, on January 1. New Year trees, which the people had not even heard about before, were imported, just as they had been in Central Asia, and parties were organized even at remote stations and farms. Shagaa, which once had been a real symbol of the beginning of new life in nature, was converted into the May 1 holiday or into the Stockbreeder's Holiday.

A note of anguish is sounded in the local representative's remarks as he appeals for the crippled culture of the original people to somehow be enhanced and humanized. But he makes his appeal cautiously, taking into account the desires that come from the center. He proposes the introduction of new ritual songs, the basis for which might be Tuvinian New Year greetings and Russian Christmas *koliadky* (carols). He enumerates new holidays and, to our astonishment, we again encounter the very same winter New Year celebrations, Farewell to Winter and Birch Tree Day, which we found in the provinces of Russia some ten hours' flying-time away.

But that is not all. A so-called national Naadum Holiday of Independence was also introduced in Tuva. At a conference a local representative, G. N. Kurbatskij, described it:

Socialist competitions were developed in honor of it.... Topics for reports that summed up the economic and cultural achievements of individual *khoshuns* (regions) and of the Republic as a whole were formulated. Memorial papers and documents were developed.... Naadum began with a mass meeting and parades. Members of the Party Presidium stood on a small wooden tribunal; paraders performed in front of the tribunal. Everything was red with banners and flags. *The borrowing of Soviet forms of celebration is one of the manifestations of the closeness of the TPR and the USSR.*[37] (my emphasis)

Among the Khanty in Siberia the Bear Holiday, which is connected with a bear cult, has been preserved until the present day. The bear was the totem of the Khanty, who called themselves the "clan of the old man from the holy city." Killing a bear is a crime, but people hunt it because of a possibility of expiating sin by rendering certain homages to the "Son of God." The Bear Holiday ritual exists just for this purpose.

If a male is killed, dances are supposed to continue for seven days; if a female, for five. The bear is glorified as a Son of God; insults and gibes are pronounced with the faces covered with birch-bark masks so that the bear will not recognize his "offenders." Local authorities consider it necessary to ban the Bear Holiday. At a conference in Ulan Ude, V. N. Plesovskikh said:

In the first place, the Bear Holiday possesses a vividly expressed quality of national special apartness, and in this is its principle contradiction to contemporary reality. During the years of Soviet power in the northern regions of the Ob River (in Siberia), large international collectives grew up. Representatives of nearly 20 nationalities and ethnic groups work at the enormous facilities of the fishing industry.... The Bear Holiday cannot serve in these circumstances to improve relations between nationalities, but rather to inhibit them. In the second place, the holiday remains a spontaneous celebration, the time of which there is no way to regulate. Kill a bear and they start dancing. What if they kill 10 or 15 of them in one winter? What do you do in that case? In the third place, by virtue of its conservative character, the Bear Holiday is not in keeping with the contemporary level of development of the state, the economy, and the culture of the minority nationalities of the Northern Ob.

In the present circumstances, celebrations in honor of the "master of the taiga," "wise seer," "supreme judge" must be perceived, at the very least, as mocking the real masters of our region that the Khanty and Mansi have become ...

The folk-national is not only antiquity, and among the minority nationalities of the North, it is not at all antiquity, but that which fills contemporary life and is the way of life of socialist nations and nationalities. In place of ritual holidays that have become obsolete, the creative work of the peoples of the Northern Ob has produced a new type of holiday that is socialist in content. I am speaking about the traditional olympics which take place annually in the facilities of former cultural centers in the villages of Sos'va and Kazym. The first olympics took place in 1935 and 1936 and they have been conducted ever since.[38]

S. A. Tokarev writes that a ritual self-justification of the hunters before the bear formerly formed an essential part of the Bear Holiday: "It was not I who slew you, but the Russian who made the rifle ..."[39] Might not this be a reason why the Khanty and Mansi now have to celebrate Greek olympics?

Even among the small peoples of far northeast Siberia one can observe the supplanting of traditional rituals by new Soviet rituals. Thus, in several Koryak settlements, the Nerpa Holiday merges with New Year's Day. Among the reindeer Koryaks (Tigil'skije Koryaki from the village of Sedanka), the traditional Reindeer Holiday is shifted in time and becomes a sport competition that coincides with Soviet Army Day.

As we see, only the name of the former holiday remains. And all the theoreticians of new rituals came to the conclusion that, by preserving at least some elements of traditional rituals, new holidays have a greater chance of entering the life of the people and of being preserved. Kampars and Zakovich summarize their observations in the following fashion:

> ... traditional holidays, and rituals with new contents or modern festivities based on old traditions, are accepted by the people significantly faster and more successfully than those that have been newly created. It is very important to consider traditional, progressive elements of ritual as a tactic in the struggle with outmoded and harmful customs.[40]

By 1980 we had already consumed enough heterogeneous statistics reflecting the success of an almost 20-year campaign. Unfortunately, these statistics do not indicate how many traditional holidays and ceremonies have been extinguished, syncretized with international elements, changed their names or contents, or gone underground. But they do give some idea of the extent of efforts to speed the introduction of new ceremonies.

By the end of 1977, 63 new holidays had been invented.[41] In the RSFSR lectures on new rituals had been read to four million people.[42] The Ukraine forged ahead: by 1978, 94 palaces of ceremonial events,

400 bureaus of ceremonies, 8,500 ceremonial halls and 940 workshops for ceremonial services had been opened there. Some 11,000 activists, approved by local councils, carried out these rituals as volunteers during working hours paid by the government.[43] In Uzbekistan, taking the lead in Central Asia, there were by 1979 more than 200 lecture halls and 130 people's universities of culture that propagandized the new ceremonies.[44]

The June 1983 Party plenum once again stressed the importance of new rituals and holidays in the international education of the workers. By the end of 1987, two years into Mikhail Gorbachev's rule, much had appeared in the press about the attachment that the peoples of national republics feel for their traditional customs. Sensational reports on the self-immolation of Tadzhik and Uzbek women,[45] on pilgrimages to Muslim *mazary* (graveyards),[46] and on performances of Muslim rituals in the family[47] gave rise to discussions of principles. What is the cause of these occurrences—preservation of "survivals of the past" or, on the contrary, destruction of traditional values and conflicts with modernized society?

Simultaneously there appeared interesting articles on national policy in the past, which called into question the concept of socialist nationality and the practise of artificially strengthening ethnic links in the USSR and reducing the quantity of nationalities in statistics, which gives a false picture of the consolidation of Soviet nationalities.[48]

However, the attitude toward the policy and practice of introducing new rituals has not changed at all. On the contrary, the "intensification of new ritual introduction" began to be considered as one of the main tools in the struggle with nationalistic and religious excesses. In 1986 the journal *Soviet Ethnography* carried two articles on the tasks that ethnographers face in dealing with the problems of Soviet rituals.[49] In one article the academician Bromlei wrote that ethnographers have fixed the process of "regeneration of traditional customs and rituals."

In 1987 Urazmanova wrote that in scholarly literature, "socialist ceremonies are demonstrated to have great significance but the very ceremonies which stand beneath their rituals are given relatively little value."[50] She proposed an extensive plan for the organization of massive "ceremony creation."

The politics of new rituals encountered opposition both concealed and open. The intelligentsia tried to protect the traditions of their people from the intrusions of experimenters. The activities of the intelligentsia in some cases became quite open, as when 17 Latvian Communists appealed for help from abroad. A statement of the

Ukrainian writer, Valentin Moroz, in 1968 is another example of open conflict. He wrote:

> In recent times, they have taken to creating new traditions. We are showered with new word combinations, each more nonsensical than the last: "House of Happiness," "Holiday of Laboring Springtime". . . . To try to create traditions is as senseless as to try to make a cultural revolution. "Culture" and "revolution" are incompatible, contradictory concepts. Culture signifies a centuries' old process that cannot be speeded up. Any form of revolutionary interference here is destructive. Traditions aren't created. They create themselves during the course of centuries. You can herd people together in clubs and announce some idiotic Holiday for Swineherds or Milkmaids in place of Easter, but it will not be a holiday. It will be yet another kolkhoz meeting and afterwards, yet another drinking-bout. It will lack the spiritual content, the atmosphere necessary for a holiday, and it will not last. They have crippled and made dull the atmosphere of Christmas and Easter in the Ukrainian village. They have already forgotten what Christmas is.[51]

But there are other, less hostile statements when a national intelligentsia, externally assimilating the terminology of official theories of ritual, tries to prove that this or that tradition, which is threatened with prohibition, is not linked with religion. Examples of this have been given above.

There have been examples, though not often, of articles published in the Soviet press arguing the impossibility of new rituals as a matter of principle, and the lack of scientific grounds for the theoretical premises on which they are formulated. A review of several books devoted to new rituals appeared in the article "Paper Flowers" by A. Petukhov, published in the literary journal *Novyj Mir* in 1969. The author compared descriptions taken from different books of The Initiation of Field Workers, Builder's Day, etc., demonstrating that they are extremely one-sided and poor in content. Petukhov expressed doubt that national holidays can be invented artificially. He emphasized that "despite all the inventiveness of the 'originators' and the organized efforts, 'civic rituals' have had a difficult time in finding acceptance." He wrote further:

> Undoubtedly a big turnout for a holiday is a good sign. But we cannot flatter ourselves that people come out for "Harvest Day" and "First Furrow Holiday." The fact is that these people come not as participants in a celebration, but only as spectators to an organized show; they come as people come to a concert, or to a

touring circus. And are the instances so unknown where such holidays do not succeed, and, like an unsuccessful concert, provoke a feeling of disappointment, dissatisfaction, and disillusionment?[52]

But even later the voices of sceptical researchers can be heard from time to time. For example, the well-known sociologist Yu. V. Arutjunjan wrote about the propagandists of new rituals: "While advocating new rituals, they do not understand that strictly regulated rituals, in that high degree of urbanization which has already been achieved in our country, have, in general, little promise."[53]

M. N. Mel'nikov informs us that in Siberia, where they used to celebrate a luxurious Shrovetide or Maslenitsa, the Russian population has not accepted a single one of the new holiday titles (Farewell to Winter, Winter's Meeting with Spring or Russian Winter Holiday). He writes that today's Shrovetide is "no longer like an entertainment spectacle that makes widespread use of folk traditions and symbolism.[54]

Among the broad masses of the population in general, we encounter zeal in a relatively small number of enthusiasts, cynical indifference in executive bureaucrats, and submissiveness and passive opposition in a kind of dualistic behavior toward the authorities. Dualistic behavior gives people the ability to coexist with authority. They are willing to take part in new rituals, but at the same time, sometimes secretly, they are willing to preserve traditions that are dear to them. This habit of flexibility, of avoiding taking sides, of compromise, is apparently more characteristic of that portion of the population which is deeply tied to its national roots. The research of Soviet anthropologists shows that in the large cities, and among the intelligentsia in outlying districts, new rituals are implanted with great ease as they displace traditional ones. An exception should probably be made only for a comparatively thin layer of the creative and the national intelligentsia which becomes the conscious and active defender of the cultural traditions of their people. Compromise mixtures of the forms of rituals and holidays have appeared in villages and small towns (of Russia, the Ukraine and Belorussia), in the Caucasus, the Volga lands, Central Asia, Siberia and the Far East.

Dualistic behavior is a form of adaptation used by the population of the national republics in the circumstances of a political program that seeks to equalize and integrate them. The government endeavors to overcome dualistic behavior by proposing new forms of ceremonies that will destroy the barriers between private and public life, between different religious and national groups, between city and village, etc. Common people (peasants and workers) try to preserve their traditions, but don't quarrel even with local authorities. The result is an unstable balance that shifts first one way and then the other.

Do the new rituals solve the problems which the state has set before them? In order to answer this question, we have to define the problems. They apparently coincide only in part with the struggle against "religious survivals" and for atheistic education. Many of the festivities are not intermixed with the old, religious ones, but are newly invented to give expression to Soviet values: love of country, loyalty to the Party, willingness to perform self-sacrificing labor and to defend the homeland militarily. To these are added symbolic elements which either represent folklore reminiscences that have been taken, not from the living tradition, but from literary rehashes, or are borrowed from the contemporary practice of Party-state ceremonies. Moreover, the latter has a tendency to supplant the former. Purposeful intermingling of cultural elements of various nationalities tears them away from the traditional meaning that is organic for them. A predominance of Russian folklore elements still does not, in my opinion, give reason to see Russification as the secret goal of the new rituals. National rituals are weakest of all among Russians, and the new ones, which have often been created in a void—all these Russian Birch Trees, Russian Winters, Russian Springs, Berendei (Russian fairy-tale tsars), Snowmen, Rainmen, etc.—have as much relationship to Russians today as they have to any other people. The distraction of religion, the effacement of national differences, the leveling of the traditions of town and country: all these taken together are very apparent as the goals of the politics of the new rituals. Not atheism, and not Russification, but total Sovietization is, apparently, the purpose, regardless of whether it was set consciously or spontaneously.

These holidays were devised with the aim of destroying local groups and communal solidarity and replacing them with international state solidarity, which would be accessible to the imagination of even those who were not familiar with other cultures or who knew them only through textbooks or propaganda materials distributed by regional Party instructors. The success of the campaign is twofaceted. Integration of various ethnic groups through common ceremonies has hardly been achieved. But if the aim was the destruction of old links, the atomization of religious and ethnic communities that were at one time united, and the withdrawal of ritual life from the family, then here the plan has been more successful.

The new variations offered the people abstract ties, clothed in an insufficiently accessible ideology. Objectively, this policy played an integral role in the life of local ethnic groups even if it was rejected in the everyday life of the populace.

Mikhail Gorbachev's promise of democratization and *glasnost'* promotes wishful thinking both within the country and abroad. Therefore, I will permit myself a few "ifs."

If anthropologists and the national intelligentsia are permitted to report truthfully on the real results of the introduction of new rituals, and if the peoples of all the republics are given full freedom to choose the form of ceremonial life, the situation might change. In the first place, the dead, pompous spectacle created by methodologists in the offices of atheist institutes would disappear. But then a different, even more serious problem would arise—how to relate to unforgotten religious ceremonies, which are close to the memory of the people, and which express not the importance of a multinational empire in its entirety, but rather the value of those small groups which the people understand and experience as their own.

Notes

1. L. N. Saburova, "Literatura o novykh obriadakh i prazdnikakh za 1963-1966," *Sovetskaya etnografhia*, no. 5 (1967).

2. Nikita Struve, "Pseudo-Religious Rites Introduced by the Party Authorities" in William C. Fletcher and Anthony I. Strover (eds.), *Religion and the Search for New Ideas in the USSR* (New York: Frederic A. Praeger, 1967), pp. 44–48; David E. Powell, "Rearing the New Soviet Man" in Bodhan R. Bociurkiv and John W. Strong (eds.) *Religion and Atheism in the USSR and Eastern Europe* (London: Macmillan Press, 1975), pp. 151-67; Christel Lane, *The Rites of Rulers* (Cambridge University Press, 1981); Christopher A. P. Binns, "The Changing Face of Power: Revolution and Accommodation in the Development of the Soviet Ceremonial System," *Man*, no. 15 (1979), pp. 585-606, and no. 15 (1980), pp. 170-87.

3. Except L. N. Saburova, "Novoe i traditsionnoe v prazdnikakh i obriadakh narodov SSSR," *Sovremennye Etnicheskie protsessy v SSSR* (Moscow: Nauka, 1975), pp. 383-404.

4. K. V. Chistov uses the term "secondary folklore" to denote folk creations which are converted by progressive culture and which were sometimes returned to the agricultural population through rituals implanted from above. See *Sovremennye etnicheskie protsessy* (Moscow: Nauka, 1975), p. 351.

5. L. Trotsky, *Problems of Everyday Life* (New York, 1973).

6. V. Veresaev, "Ob obriadakh starykh i novykh," *Polnoe sobranie sochinenii*, vol. 8 (Moscow, 1930).

7. N. A. Belyk, "Vnedrenie novykh grazhdanskikh obriadov—delo vsekh gosudarstvennykh organizatsii" in *Voprosy preodoleniia perezhitkov proshlogo v bytu i soznanii liudei i stanovleniia novykh obychaiev i traditsii*. Conference proceedings (Ulan-Ude, 1968).

8. L. I. Brezhnev, *Otchetnyi doklad Tsentralnogo Komiteta KPSS XXIV s'iezdu Kommunisticheskoi Partii Sovetskogo Soiuza* (Moscow: Gospolitisdat, 1971) p. 135.

9. N. P. Lobacheva, *Formirovanie novoi obriadnosti Uzbekov* (Moscow: Nauka, 1975), p. 3.

10. *Nauka i religiia*, no. 2 (1979), p. 3

11. I. V Remizov, "Sotsialisticheskie tradizii i besreligiosnye prazdniky kak sredstvo ateisticheskogo vospitania," *Voprosy kommunisticheskogo vospitania*, no. 1 (1965), Izvestia Voronezhskogo gosudarstvennogo pedinstituta, vol. 50, p. 163.

12. V. A. Rudnev, *Sovestskiie obychai i obriady* (Leningrad: Lenizdat, 1974) p. 131.

13. Ibid., p. 134.

14. N. Markevich, *Obychai, poveria Malorossii* (Kiev, 1960), p. 21.

15. V. I. Brudnyi, *Obriady vchera i segodnia* (Moscow: Nauka, 1968), pp. 94–6.

16. A. V. Kurochkin, "Kalendarnye prazdniki na ukrainsko-moldavskom pogranich'e i ikh sovremennye sud'by," *Sovetskaya etnografia*, no. 1 (1987), pp. 24–35.

17. Lev Kopelev and Dzidra Kalnyn, "Ligo znachit Radost!" in *Druzhba narodov*, no. 7 (1966), pp. 252–3.

18. "Obrashenie latviiskykh kommunistov k Rukovoditeliam riada inostrannykh kompartii" in *Natsionalnyi vopros v SSSR* (New York: Souchasnist, 1975), p. 200.

19. *Sovetskaya Latvia*, June 23, 1959; quotation from P. P. Kampars and N. M. Zakovich, *Sovetskaya grazhdanskaya obriadnost* (Moscow: Mysl', 1967).

20. Lobacheva, *Formirovanie*, p. 117.

21. Sh. U. Ustaev, "Novyi god (Navruz) v mifologicheskikh vozzreniakh tadzhikov i uzbekov," *Sovetskaya etnografia*, no. 6 (1985), p. 98.

22. A. M. Rakhimov, "Ob ispolsovanii narodnykh traditsyi v novykh prazdnikakh i ritualakh" in *Voprosy nauchnogo ateisma*, "Danish," Dushanbe, pp. 80–8.

23. O. A. Sukhareva, *Islam v Uzbekistane* (Tashkent, 1960), p. 27.

24. G. P. Snesarev, *Relikty domusylmanskikh verovanii i obriadov uzbekov Khoresma* (Moscow, 1969).

25. L. Drobizheva, "My zhivem v mnogonatsional'noi strane," *Moskovskie Novosti*, no. 22, May 31, 1987.

26. N. S. Sarsenbaev, "Novye obriady i idealy kommunizma" in *Voprosy preodoleniia perezhitkov proshlogo v bytu i soznanii liudei*, Conference proceedings (Ulan-Ude), p. 51.

27. N. P. Lobacheva, op. cit., p. 129.

28. M. Mirrakhimov, "Navruz: segodniashnii den' drevnego prazdnika," *Nauka i Religiia*, no. 5 (1983), pp. 17-20.

29. R. K. Urazmanova, "Traditsionnie trudovie prazdniki i obriadi tatar i ikh rol' v vospitanii molodeji" in *Sovremennie etnosotsialnie protsessi na sele* (Moscow: Nauka, 1986), pp. 222-5.

30. V. U. Krupianskaya, O. P. Budina, N. S. Polishuk and N. B. Uhneva, *Kultura i byt gorniakov i metallurgov Nizhnego Tagila, 1917-1970* (Moscow: Nauka, 1974), p. 20.

31. M. Magdeev, "Prazdniki, obriady, traditsii," *Molodaya gvardiia* (Moscow, 1976), p. 96.

32. A. V. Kurochkin, "Kalendarnye prazdniki na ukrainsko-moldavskom pogranich'e i ikh sovremennye sud'by," *Sovetskaya etnografia*, no. 1 (1987), pp. 24-35.

33. Ibid., p. 32.

34. G. I. Spataru, *Istoricheskaya moldavskaya narodnaya drama* (Kishinev, 1980), p. 76.

35. Moldavane, "Shtiintsa" (Kishinev, 1977), p. 307.

36. G. N. Kurbatskii, "Novaya obriadnost v Tuve" in *Voprosy preodoleniia perezhitkov proshlogo v bytu i soznanii ludei i stanovleniia novykh obychaiev i traditsii* (Ulan-Ude, 1968), pp. 196-9.

37. Ibid.

38. V. I. Plesovskikh, "O nekotorykh religioznikh perezhitkakh i ustarevshikh bytovikh traditsiakh narodnostei khanty i mansy" in *Voprosy preodoleniia perezhitkov proshlogo v bytu i soznanii liudei*, Conference proceedings (Ulan-Ude), 1968, p. 100.

39. S. A. Tokarev, *Etnografia narodov SSSR* (Moscow: Moskovskii Universitet, 1958), p. 480

40. P. P. Kampars and N. M. Zakovich, *Sovetskaya grazhdanskaya obriadnost* (Moskva: Mysl', 1967), p. 94.

41. "Estafeta" (Vtoroe Vsesoyuznoe soveschanie-seminar no sotsialisticheskoi obriadnosti), *Nauka i religiia*, no. 2 (1979), p. 9.

42. Ibid., p. 7.

43. Ibid., p. 9.

44. U. Fyshevsky, "Ispolzuia vse luchshee," *Nauka i religiia*, no. 7 (1979).

45. L. Makhkamov, "Ten' parandzhi," *Izvestia*, June 7, 1987; Adyl

Yakybov, "Tragediia v kishlake," *Literaturnaya gazeta*, August 19, 1987.

46. "Sheikhi na Suleiman—gore," *Sovetskaya Kirgiziia*, May 26 1987. In response to criticism, S. Bakhapova, Secretary of the Oshskii obkom of the Kirgiziia Communist Party, said: "In the bureau of the Party *obkom* a 'complex plan for the strengthening of atheistic education and the introduction of new nonreligious ceremonies, rituals and traditions into everyday life for the years 1987-1990' was approved."

47. I. Irisbaev, "Pochemu zhivy predrassudki," *Pravda Vostoka* (Uzbekistan), August 25, 1987.

48. Mikhail Kriukov (zaveduiuschii sektorom instituta Etnografii ANSSSR), "Sto natsii i narodnostei, "*Moskovskie Novosti*, August 9, 1987.

49. Yu. V. Bromlei and A. E. Ter-Sarkisiants, "Sovetskaya etnograficheskaya nauka na rubezhe dvukh piatiletok," *Sovetskaya etnografia*, no 2 (1986), pp. 3-24; N. P. Lobacheva and M. Ya. Ustinova, "Zadachi etnograficheskoi nauki v razrabotke, vnedrenii i sovershenstvovanii sotsialisticheskoi obriadnosti (semeinyi tsikl)," *Sovetskaya etnografia*, no. 2 (1986), pp. 24-35.

50. R. K. Urazmanova, "Eshche raz o zadachakh etnograficheskoi nauki v razrabotke, vnedrenii i sovershenstvovanii sotsialisticheskoi obriadnosti," *Sovetskaya etnografia*, no. 3 (1987), p. 74.

51. Valentin Moroz, "Selo Kosmach" in *Nationalnyi vopros v SSSR* (New York: Souchastnist, 1975), p. 72.

52. *Novy Mir* no. 6 (1969), p. 274.

53. Yu. V. Arutjunjan, "O nekotorikh tendentsiakh v ismenenii kulturnogo oblika natsii," *Sovetskaya etnografia* no. 6 (1973).

54. M. N. Mel'nikov, "Poesia narodnikh obychaev," *Sibirskie ogni*, no. 4 (1966).

Chapter 8

Regional Population Redistribution and National Homelands in the USSR

Lee Schwartz

Introduction

The jurisdictional formation of the ethnic mosaic comprising the modern Soviet state was characterized by two distinct processes of administrative decision-making. First, there was the granting of nominal autonomy for the large, historically self-conscious or politically distinct nations located on the outskirts of the old Russian Empire. Second, there was the union-wide imposition of an administrative substructure also based on national-territorial jurisdictions. In the first case, many of the peripheral groups had attempted to secede from the newly formed Soviet state by exercising the right of self-determination, and a federal compromise was necessary in order to achieve a viable union. The decision to apply a nationality basis to tertiary administrative units as well, however, was based on a different set of conditions altogether. Groups which previously had little or no sense of national self-consciousness were granted explicit political units toward which they could identify. There now existed defined and legitimized territories serving as national homelands for their indigenous peoples. This paper is concerned with investigating the latter of these two decisions, in terms of its intent and the resulting consequences on the population redistribution of the various minority nationalities in the Soviet Union. The specific focus will be that of the national homelands below the union republic (SSR) level—the autonomous republics (ASSRs) and autonomous oblasts (AOs).[1]

National homelands, particularly when legitimized by institutional features supporting cultural and political autonomy, have the potential to generate territorial attachments which may be reflected by patterns of migration and settlement. The sense of territoriality associated with a particular national group is especially salient in the Soviet Union, where over 100 different peoples live within a jurisdictional structure based on national autonomy. Under such conditions, the distinctions between nation and national homeland may become obfuscated.

While the Russian nation, as well as most of the larger nations on the periphery of the Russian Empire, were already politically or ethnically self-conscious by the time of the formation of the USSR,[2] many of the smaller nationalities had their territorial self-awareness substantially bolstered by the granting of autonomous units. These latter regions (AOs, ASSRs) comprised peoples of generally lower levels of national self-awareness than those of the constituent republics (SSRs). It can be argued that many of these smaller groups were still in their pre-national stages at the time of the formation of the Soviet Union, and that the jurisdictional character of the union increased the importance of their identification with specific territories of political legitimacy. Whether such territories were based on historical legacy or actual population distribution, the newly created national homelands had the potential to serve as units of territorial attachment.

This paper is distinguished by the fact that it concentrates on the patterns exhibited by the populations of the smaller national minorities inhabiting the ASSRs and AOs of the Soviet Union. Most work along similar lines has focused on the larger economic regions or the SSR level. In general, the constituent republics have relatively high degrees of cultural development, historical feelings of territoriality if not national self-awareness, and low levels of Russian in-migration, especially in the less-developed areas. Given such conditions, policies would tend to have little influence on firmly established patterns of nationality-based population behavior. The long-term effects of Soviet nationality policies should, however, be more pronounced for the less-developed populations of the national subunits than for those of the union republics. That is why this study limits its scope primarily to the indigenous populations at the ASSR and AO level of autonomy.

The purpose of this study is twofold. First, to determine to what degree the original political borders of these Soviet national autonomies demarcated legitimate homelands based on the population distribution existing at the time they were formed. To do this, the homelands will be viewed in terms of the rationale behind their creation; that is, the national autonomies will be examined based on the effectiveness in which they bounded homogeneous ethnic populations. Second, the population settlement patterns of their contained nationalities will be studied over time in order to assess the effectiveness or importance of these homelands as regions of territorial attachment and as confines of institutional affiliation.

Specifically, as the Soviet Union has become increasingly developed economically, with greater contact among national groups, what effect did the decision to base tertiary administrative units on nationality have on the regional population trends of their titular nationalities? Furthermore, how much of this redistribution is related to Soviet policies, either past or present, and was this redistribution the result of nationality policies, or policies based on other related socioeconomic factors, or perhaps not the result of identifiable policies at all?

Nations and Homelands

Before proceeding further, it might be helpful to provide a brief insight into the relationship between the terms "nation," and "homeland" from the Marxist-Leninist perspective, which describes the peculiarities of the Soviet context of the national homeland. The Marxist-Leninist conception of the evolution of national groups proceeded from the establishment of a linguistic community and the development of a consciousness of "peoplehood" (*narodnost'*), through the operation of the forces of capitalism leading to the formation of a bourgeois nationality (*natsional'nost'*), to a true socialist nation (*natsiya*) free of all vestiges of class or property.[3]

Marxism views the nation as an exclusively historical phenomenon which is a function of economic development. The Marxist position holds that nation and class are functionally equivalent; ethnic groups, or nonprogressive nations (i.e. *narodnosti*) will be assimilated to the roles and positions of social classes. As long as classes existed, the consciousness of the individual would be conditioned primarily by the class to which he belonged. As a doctrine Marxism disdains the temporary, transitional stage of small national groupings, showing preference for large economic units which are historically more progressive. According to Lenin as well, the real social unit was not the national state, but the class, which knows no national frontiers. The Marxist-Leninists viewed nationalism as a social force utilized by capitalists to maintain their hold on society. Nevertheless, Lenin recognized that nationalism was a vital and powerful ally to consider in the Bolshevik struggle for socialist revolution.

The following remarks by anthropologist Fredrik Barth help to further an understanding of the relationship between the concepts of nationhood and territory particularly relevant to this study:

> The critical focus becomes the ethnic [nationality] "boundary" that defines the group, not the cultural stuff it encloses.... The features that are taken into account are not the sum of the "objective" differences, but only those which the actors themselves regard as significant....
>
> The cultural features that signal the boundary may change, and the cultural characteristics of the members may likewise be transformed, indeed even the organizational form of the group may change—yet the fact of continuing dichotomization between members and outsiders allows us to specify the nature of continuity and investigate the changing cultural form and content.[4]

Of pertinent meaning to this study is the concept that once a group is territorially bound, the political unit becomes the means by which the cultural content of the nationality is maintained.

The territorial aspect of nationality is represented by the national homeland. It stands to reason that once an ethnic group recognizes its uniqueness it will seek to identify with an area of habitation that will allow it to maintain, legitimize and consolidate its nationality. Or, as Karl Deutsch might have put it, an ethnic group (*narodnost'*) would be considered a nationality (*natsional'nost'*) once it gained "the ability to propel its cohesiveness toward political, economic or cultural autonomy."[5] A national homeland thus becomes regarded as a space to which identity is attached by a distinctive group of people who hold or covet that territory and who desire to have full control of it for the group's benefit.[6]

Within the Soviet Union there exists a wide variety of economic, cultural and historical conditions which contribute to different behavior among the inhabitants of administrative units organized on the same principle of national autonomy. Soviet scholarship recognizes the importance of understanding the regional diversity of such units:

> ... the republic is not a "universal model" for the entire Union. Many of its peculiarities are the product of the specific character of its cultural development, the length of the international contact of the ethnic groups, and the level of development of nations.[7]

In addition, symbols such as a flag, national anthem, state seal (emblem) and official history all comprise part of a set of objects—or iconography—which serve to strengthen the bonds already existing among similar people living within the boundaries of a given unit. These symbols, plus such constitutional rights as an education in native-language schools and political representation in the Council of Nationalities of the Supreme Soviet, point to the value of the institutional confines of nationality provided by the trappings of autonomy granted to the various national groups in the USSR.

Soviet ideology has postulated that as the state progresses towards pure Communism, nationality distinctiveness will decrease, ethnic conflict will diminish, and, eventually, a new "Soviet man" will be created. While in recent years the unidirectional nature of this position has wavered, the belief remains that as the state develops economically, national self-consciousness and differentiation will tend to decrease. This hypothesis is often supported by pointing to such factors (i.e. socioeconomic indicators of modernization) as equalizing levels of education, an increase in intermarriage, and the use of the Russian language by a growing number of people. In addition, popular objective expressions of nationality, such as religion, literature and folklore, have often diminished measurably with increasing modernization.

Operating at the same time, however, are some of the more psychological realities of national self-consciousness which oppose the tendencies towards assimilation and acculturation. A most important characteristic of modernization (economic development) which heightens self-awareness is the process of increasing migration and the resultant contact between different nationality groups. When two groups enter into competition in the same geographic area, it seems logical that the native, or indigenous, groups may exhibit a renewed identification with the territory it occupies as a "national homeland," despite the fact that many of the group's cultural traditions are fading. A study of settlement patterns brought about by interregional migration is one means of measuring a concept as intangible as one's national identification.

Hypotheses such as these can be tested in the context of the Soviet Union, where the numerically dominant Russian population has been moving into the peripheral and internal non-Russian territories over the course of several centuries. It has only been for the past 60 years, however, that the state has been administratively organized on the basis of the national distribution of the population. The system of national homelands in the USSR, therefore, conveniently coincides with the Soviet period of intense modernization and economic development.

Formation of the Soviet Union

The Soviet Union, as it emerged in 1923, can be viewed as a compromise between doctrine and reality. The force of nationalism among the non-Russian minorities proved itself to be more powerful than Lenin had foreseen, leading to the eventual implementation of the federal compromise. The federal solution sought to reconcile the Bolshevik striving for centralization with the recognition that nationalism was a force that survived the Revolution and would have to be given strong consideration by the new regime. Lenin made it clear that federalism was only to be a temporary solution, with the Russian national leading the way towards the eventual equalization of all nationalities. Still, the promise of self-determination had proved to be a successful strategy by which the Bolsheviks gained support, especially with the outbreak of revolution and the onset of civil war. The nature of the future direction of Soviet nationality policy was to be "national in form but socialist in nature," meaning that the development of outward forms of national culture was encouraged only when geared towards the overall needs of the Communist Party and Soviet state.

The diversity in ethnic and cultural backgrounds of the Soviet population was reflected in the administrative and territorial organization imposed by the Bolshevik regime. On December 30, 1922, the First Congress of Soviets unanimously approved the Declaration and Treaty establishing the Union of Soviet Socialist Republics. The first USSR Constitution, ratified on January 31, 1924, allowed the six original constituent republics to maintain and develop their own national customs, languages and institutions, preserving the national character of their homelands.[6] At the same time, areas within these union republics which contained relatively concentrated populations of other distinct minority nationalities were granted "autonomous" republics, oblasts (regions), and other nationality-based administrative subunits. The status of the autonomous units was to be determined by a combination of factors, such as numerical size and concentration of the indigenous nationality, level of socioeconomic development and geographic location.

The degree of autonomy allocated these units was described in the 1924 constitution, which also established an All-Union Soviet (Council) of Nationalities. This half of the government's legislative branch at first comprised five representatives from each union and autonomous republic and one representative from each autonomous oblast.[9] The boundaries finally recognized by the third All-Union Congress of the Soviet Union (May 20, 1925) contained a great number and variety of distinct and separate national groupings, both large and small. Depending on the various sources consulted, the population of the USSR at this time included between 146 and 188 different nationalities and ethnic groups, speaking anywhere from 104 to 200 distinguishable languages.

The 24 census units of 1926 were further delineated into 15 autonomous republics and 16 autonomous oblasts, delimited according to the national composition of the population. The first Soviet (1926) census listed 188 different nationalities with wide racial, cultural, geographic and linguistic differences. Fourteen nations were over one million strong; the top five groups totaled 84 per cent of the Soviet population with no other single group reaching as much as 2 per cent of the total. Thirty of the 188 nationalities formed nearly 98 per cent of the population.[10] The administrative substructure of autonomous republics and autonomous oblasts was based on the larger and more regionally concentrated of these nationality groups that were settled within the vast and diverse land mass of the Soviet Union.

The Autonomous Subunits

Prior to Soviet authority, the administrative substructure had been formed without regard to the ethnic composition of the population. The first formal provision for national autonomy below union republic level appeared in the post-Revolutionary RSFSR Constitution of July 10, 1918, which states:

> The soviets of regions which are distinguished by special customs and national compositions, may unite in autonomous oblast unions, at the head of which, as at the head of any oblast association which may be formed in general, will stand oblast congresses of soviets and their executive organs.
>
> These autonomous oblast unions enter into the RSFSR on a federal basis.[11]

By applying the concept of self-determination within a federation system, the Soviet authorities created a state substructure comprised of numerous autonomous territories derived on the basis of nationality. With the creation of lower-level autonomous units, the old divisions of the Russian Empire gave way to new ones which had the potential to revitalize the history and spirit of a number of peoples.

The autonomous republics and oblasts remained distinct from one another and entered the union indirectly, through the federation of which they were a part.[12] After the adoption of the 1925 RSFSR constitutional amendments, the autonomous republics occupied a special position within the Soviet administrative framework and were regarded as possessing a certain degree of political competency and self-sufficiency. The organs of state authority of these ASSRs, as stipulated in the Soviet Constitution, consisted of local and central congresses of soviets and their respective executive committees.[13]

Although the general qualifications for union republic status had been set forth by Stalin,[14] the distinction between autonomous republics and oblasts was less clear. The autonomous oblasts had, however, considerably less autonomy than the autonomous republics, with no particular distinguishing features provided for them in the Soviet Constitution.[15] Most of the so-called autonomy of these regions was only operative with respect to local matters of language and culture.

Post-revolutionary political expediency made it necessary to recognize the autonomy of various nations in the USSR, and to concede the independence of Latvia, Lithuania, Estonia, Finland and Poland. The large nations which were initially granted SSR status had for the most part already firmly established their homeland regions at the time of the formation of the Soviet Union. The existence of these areas was largely indisputable; the problems they posed for unification were historical ones inherited from Tsarist times.

The imposition of lower levels of national autonomy, however, based on political, strategic, numerical or geographical considerations, tended to be associated with peoples of less-developed national self-consciousness. The decision to create further, subsidiary, ethnic jurisdictions, and the consequences of such a move, make the concept of national homeland one which merits especially careful consideration at the level of autonomous republic and autonomous oblast.

It should be mentioned that the policy of granting administrative autonomy to nationality groups identified as being regionally distinct ran contrary to several concurrent movements for national agglomeration. In contrast with the nations of the European periphery and Transcaucasia, most of the groups involved with movements for amalgamation—primarily Turkic and other Muslim peoples of Central Asia, the Volga-Urals, and the northern Caucasus— were of less-developed self-awareness, had little proletarian, industrial or urban strength, and did not border a foreign power. In these instances, the eventual national-administrative substructures were generally imposed from above, the result of conscious policy decisions by Soviet leaders. The choice to create these units often served to reverse trends towards assimilation, giving groups a renewed (or newly created) focus towards a territory, language and cultural institutions, which were now formally recognized. Despite arguments as to the justifications of these imposed jurisdictions,[16] such autonomous units (e.g. Bashkir ASSR; Ingush AO) were now legitimized as national homelands in areas where they previously had no territorial-administrative recognition.

Whether the federal state structure was established for pragmatic or ideological reasons, and regardless of whether the units themselves were viewed as theoretically transitory or permanent, there was now the potential that several of the nationalities in the Soviet Union would begin to see the arrangement as a long-term if not permanent one, assign importance to it, and resist attempts to change it. In this manner the legal, political recognition within a federal state of a territory based on the national composition of the population would tend to reinforce further a group's perception of a legitimate claim to privilege in its own homeland.

Assessing the Original Boundary Demarcations of the ASSRs and AOs

Regardless of how significant the formation of national homelands has been in affecting the subsequent population redistribution in the USSR, it is important to ascertain the facts of how and where their borders were originally demarcated, and whom they contained. This is partly because various writers have suggested that the national units in the Soviet Union were delimited as part of a general process of Russification, or gerrymandering, whereby the Soviet authorities intentionally sought to diminish the numerical strength of the national minorities within their titular domains by drawing the boundaries in a manner more favorable to the Russian or a third nationality.[17] Such charges should be answered before subsequent patterns are investigated. If one is to determine the value a national autonomy has as a homeland capable of generating emotional and demographic attachments, a judgment must first be made as to how legitimate such units were at the time of their jurisdictional inception. Fortunately, the first postrevolutionary (1926) Soviet census provides information on population, nationality and territory sufficiently detailed to conduct an investigation based on the population composition of the small, predominantly rural districts (volosts) which were contiguous to the actual boundaries. It should be remembered that this study is primarily concerned with the secondary (ASSR and AO) level of national autonomy,[18] in order to study those units which, based on the nature of their contained populations, would appear more susceptible to the influence of policy decisions.

Distribution of the Soviet Nationalities in 1926

By the end of the nineteenth century, the external borders of the Russian Empire's peripheral acquisitions had become more-or-less fixed. By the time of the 1926 census, the internal borders of the national subunits had also been delimited, superimposed by authorities from above, often years after historical settlement patterns had been established. Most of these ethnically based jurisdictions had previously never existed as distinct (no less autonomous) administrative units. This was in stark contrast with the boundaries of the constituent republics, which tended to conform to either the physical landscape, military defense lines or diplomatic treaties.

Table 8.1 lists all of the national autonomies in the Soviet Union and their populations at the time of the first all-union census (1926). Additionally, the table indicates the percentage of the total population of the autonomous unit comprised by the titular group, as well as the degree to which the homeland incorporates the total union-wide numbers of the particular nationality. The 29 numbered subunits constitute the entire range of the 1926 autonomous Soviet jurisdictions below SSR (union republic) level which were organized on the basis of nationality. Several of these tertiary administrative units, although formed on the basis of the national composition of the population, nevertheless had Russian numerical pluralities. While not all of these units bore the name of the nationality group upon which they were based, they were unique in that each was created due to the particular composition of the population; that is, with few exceptions, these "homelands" were populated predominantly by a single non-Russian nationality. Only four of the 29 subunits did not bear the name of the nationality upon which they were based.

Table 8.1 includes the titular groups *concentration* percentages of the autonomous republics and oblasts, as well as the nationality *containment* levels of these units (figures for the union republics are also provided here). Eighteen of these national autonomies had a majority population of their native group, with 12 of these having titular group composition levels of 75 per cent or higher. Only three of these administrative subunits, all in the RSFSR, had a Russian majority; 13, however, had a Russian minority population of greater than 10 per cent.

In terms of the proportion of the various nationalities' union-wide populations incorporated within these homelands, 20 of the jurisdictions contained a majority of the group's total Soviet population; 18 of these majorities exceeded 75 per cent. Significantly, only one of the nine units which did not comprise the bulk of that nation's union-wide population had a Russian majority (the Karelian ASSR). Most of the reasons for the lack of a majority in the other cases were due either to discrepancies in nomenclature or definition, or the fact that the nationality already had another autonomous unit that contained the majority of its population.[19]

The percentages in Table 8.1 reveal the levels of concentration and containment of the indigenous nationalities within the system of national autonomies in the USSR in 1926. In several cases, when either of these two figures are considered alone, they do not neces-

Table 8.1 National-Territorial Jurisdictions with Populations and Levels of Concentration and Containment of Titular Groups: USSR, 1926

	Unit	Population (000)	% of Unit	Titular Group In Unit as % of Total	Russians As % of Unit
I.	Russian Soviet Federated Socialist Republic	100,891.2	73.4	95.2	73.4
	RSFSR excluding Kazakh and Kirgiz ASSRs, listed separately below	93,395.2	77.8	93.4	77.8
	Including:				
	1. Karelian ASSR	269.7	37.4	40.6	57.1
	2. Komi AO [ASSR][a] (Zyryan)[b]	207.3	92.3	84.5	6.6
	3. Tatar ASSR	2,594.0	44.9	39.9	43.1
	4. Chuvash ASSR	894.5	74.7	59.8	20.0
	5. Volga-German ASSR [eliminated in 1944]	571.8	66.4	30.7	20.4
	6. Kalmyk AO [ASSR]	141.6	75.6	82.8	10.7
	7. Votyak AO (Udmurt ASSR)	756.3	52.3	78.5	43.3
	8. Mari AO [ASSR]	482.1	51.4	57.9	43.6
	9. Permyak Okrug [Komi-Permyak Autonomous Okrug]	152.5	77.0	78.6	22.8
	10. Bashkir ASSR	2,694.9	23.7	89.3	39.8
	11. Crimean ASSR (Tatar) [eliminated in 1944]	713.8	25.1	6.1	42.2
	12. Adygey-Circassian AO (Cherkesy) [Adygey AO]	114.2	44.5	77.9	26.0
	13. Ingush AO [Chechen-Ingush ASSR]	75.1	93.1	94.4	1.2
	14. Chechen AO [Chechen-Ingush ASSR]	309.9	94.0	91.1	2.9
	15. Kabardino-Balkar AO [ASSR]	204.0	76.3	89.9	8.4
	16. North Ossetian AO [ASSR]	152.4	84.2	47.1[c]	6.6

Table 8.1 *Continued*

Unit	Population (000)	Titular Group % of Unit	Titular Group In Unit as % of Total	Russians As % of Unit
17. Karachay AO [Karachay-Cherkess AO]	64.6	81.3	95.3	1.7
18. Circassian AO (Cherkesy) [Karachay-Cherkess AO]	37.0	7.2	4.1	4.0
19. Dagestan ASSR (31 ethnic groups)	788.1	64.5	88.5	12.5
20. Oyrot AO (Altay) [Gorno-Altay AO]	99.7	35.7	91.3	52.0
21. Khakass Okrug [AO]	88.9	49.7	96.3	46.6
22. Buryat-Mongolian ASSR [Buryat ASSR] [Aga-Buryat Autonomous Okrug] [Ust-Orda Buryat Autonomous Okrug]	491.2	43.8	90.5	52.7
23. Yakut ASSR	289.1	81.6	98.0	10.4
II. Kazakh ASSR [SSR]	6,503.0	57.1	93.6	19.7
Including:				
24. Karakalpak AO [became an ASSR in the Uzbek SSR]	304.5	38.1	79.4	1.6
III. Kirgiz ASSR [SSR]	993.0	66.0	86.7	11.7
IV. Belorussian SSR	4,983.2	80.6	84.8	7.7
V. Ukrainian SSR	29,018.2	80.0	74.4	9.2
Including:				
VI. Moldavian ASSR	572.3	30.1	61.8	48.5
Transcaucasian SFSR:	5,861.5	81.6	87.0	5.7

Table 8.1 *Continued*

	Unit	Population (000)	Titular Group % of Unit	In Unit as % of Total	Russians As % of Unit
VII.	Azerbaydzhan SSR	2,314.6	62.1	84.3	9.5
	Including:				
	25. Nakhichevan ASSR (Azeri)	104.9	84.3	5.2	1.8
	26. Nagorno-Karabakh AO (Armenian)	125.3	89.1	7.1	0.5
VIII.	Armenian SSR	880.5	84.5	47.4	2.2
IX.	Georgian SSR	2,666.5	67.0	94.2	3.6
	Including:				
	27. Abkhaziya DSSR [ASSR]	201.0	27.8	98.2	6.2
	28. Adzhariya ASSR	132.0	53.7	99.2	7.7
	29. South Ossetian AO	87.4	69.1	22.2[c]	0.25
X.	Uzbek SSR (not including Tadzhik ASSR)	5,272.8 / 4,445.6	65.9 / 74.2	89.0 / 84.5	4.7 / 5.4
XI.	Tadzhik ASSR [SSR]	827.2	74.6	63.0	0.7
XII.	Turkmen SSR	900.0	70.2	94.2	8.2

Source: USSR, *Vsesoyuznaya Perepis' Naseleniya 1926 Goda* (Moscow: Tsentral'noye Statisticheskoye Upravleniye SSSR, 1928), vols. 1–17, Table X.

[a] Brackets indicate that, since 1926, there has been a change in the status, framework, or name of the autonomous subunit.

[b] The name which appears in parentheses is that of the nationality upon which the jurisdiction is based, when not evident from the title of the unit.

[c] If the figures for both Ossetian-based jurisdictions had been combined, 69.3 per cent of the total Soviet Ossetian population would have been contained within these two national autonomies.

sarily justify the union-wide establishment of national-territorial jurisdictions at the tertiary level of administration. Considered together, however, and given the nature of the geographically diverse Soviet population, the dual criteria of concentration and containment seem sufficient in most cases to legitimate these lower-level national autonomies as homelands of regionally concentrated indigenous populations.

Any analysis of these categories must be considered in the context of certain supposed policy goals of Soviet planners and administrators. Specifically, it will be assumed here that the nationality jurisdictions were planned to include, within the borders of a single uninterrupted land mass, as much of an ethnic group's homogeneous union-wide population as was feasible. This would be consistent with the stated goal of forming regional autonomies so as to encourage the separate cultural development, rather than consolidation, of certain "backward" ethnic groups within the Soviet Union.[20] The effective enactment of such a plan would result in the creation of legitimized national homelands for the widely distributed ethnic minorities of the USSR.

Judging the Delimitation of the Original Homeland Boundaries

The percentages presented in Table 8.1 make it apparent that most of the ASSRs and AOs as originally constituted conformed to general criteria relating to nationality concentration and containment. The detailed ethnic and regional population information presented in the 1926 census makes it possible to undertake an even more precise inquiry into the nature of these national homelands. Specifically, the data are available to conduct an empirical analysis of the populations living immediately contiguous to the boundaries of the national-territorial units. What follows is a study of the effectiveness of the actual political borders of the autonomous republics and oblasts, as originally demarcated, and a comparison of these with the boundaries of the more historically secure and clearly legitimized union republics. The implications of such an analysis are important because a choice was involved in determining autonomous jurisdictions for the populations of less-developed national self-awareness; the decision by Soviet policy-makers to bound and legitimize pockets of ethnic group concentrations would have obvious consequences for future Soviet nationality relations.

In order to make a judgment about the effectiveness of Soviet national-territorial boundary demarcation, it was decided to "redraw" the borders of the ASSRs and AOs according to a set of criteria which more rigidly adhered to the distribution of the national minorities. This reconstitution of the national boundaries was not actually done physically for each of the units, but was a hypothetical reconstruction based on statistical information provided by the 1926 Soviet census.

Regional Population Redistribution and National Homelands   135

The most precise method for a restructuring of the national boundaries would have to be conducted at the smallest of all possible census units for which ethnic data are available. For the 1926 census this would be the level of volost.[21] There were literally thousands of these predominantly rural regions in the USSR, with the population of any urban centers that fell within their confines listed separately in the census. The numbers of people they contained ranged from several hundred to tens of thousands, and their area varied from ten to several thousand square kilometers, depending where they were located.

By using comprehensive data collected at the volost level, each nationality boundary of the Soviet Union could be surveyed and rearranged to achieve the most homogeneous unit possible, based purely on the ethnic composition of the immediately surrounding population. Such a process intentionally ignores all boundaries based solely on physical features. By drawing hypothetical boundary lines to include zones populated primarily by the titular nationality, while carving out the border volosts where other groups persisted, "optimum" national-territorial jurisdictions are created. Such units are designed to maximize the levels of titular group nationality concentration and containment within areas of feasible territorial contiguity.

A detailed accounting of the 1926 census revealed that of more than one thousand distinct border districts examined, only 11.4 per cent (132 of 1,162) would have had to be transferred to neighboring units based on the optimum criterion used to describe the units listed in Table 8.2.[22] The main criterion used for transferring border units was simple. All that was required was for a border volost, or other similar local jurisdiction, to have a plurality concentration of the particular nationality whose titular unit was located directly across its external border. This condition excluded the transfer of a unit which had a plurality concentration of a nationality other than the titular one, but different from that of any bordering group as well. Also excluded from this re-districting were numerous enclaves of national populations located nearby, but not directly contiguous with the border of their titular jurisdictions. The several cases where noncontiguous ethnic borders already existed (e.g. Buryat-Mongolian ASSR, Bashkir ASSR, Nakhichevan ASSR) showed a remarkable conformity to the national population composition.

It is perhaps surprising that so few border districts would change jurisdictions based on the national composition of their populations. Closer scrutiny reveals that of the 132 border volosts which did qualify for transfer, 68 per cent (90) lay within only 6 of the 29 subunits. This would seem to indicate that Soviet authorities did a

Table 8.2 Per Cent Change in Nationality Concentration and Containment Levels of "Optimum" National-Territorial Subunits, 1926

"Optimum" Unit*	Net Change in Number of Border Units	Net Change in Total Population	Net Change in Titular Group Population	Nationality Concentration Level of "Optimum" Unit (in %)	Per cent Change in Concentration	Nationality Containment Level of "Optimum" Unit (in %)	Per cent Change in Containment
1. Karelian ASSR	−10 (+0/−10)	−52,050	−943	45.9	+22.7	40.2	−0.1
2. Komi AO	−3 (+0/−3)	−4,617	−282	94.2	+2.1	84.4	−0.1
3. Tatar ASSR	−15 (+2/−17)	−321,494	−66,198	48.3	+7.6	37.7	−5.5
4. Chuvash ASSR	−2 (+1/−3)	−103,959	+14,694	86.3	+15.5	61.1	+2.2
5. Volga-German ASSR	−1 (+0/−1)	−55,831	−6,074	72.4	+4.0	30.2	−1.6
6. Kalmyk AO	0 (+0/−0)	0	0	75.6	0.0	82.8	0.0
7. Votyak AO	−3 (+0/−3)	−59,841	−17,089	54.4	+4.0	85.2	−3.8
8. Mari AO	−5 (+0/−5)	−270,604	−104,803	67.7	+31.7	33.4	−42.3
9. Permyak Okrug	−1 (+0/−1)	−24,741	−619	91.4	+18.7	78.1	−0.6
10. Bashkir ASSR	−22 (+0/−22)	−470,050	−73,163	25.4	+7.2	79.1	−11.4
11. Crimean ASSR	0 (+0/−0)	0	0	25.1	0.0	6.1	0.0
12. Adygey-Circassian AO	−2 (+0/−2)	−46,855	−8,817	62.4	+40.2	64.4	−17.3
13. Ingush AO	0 (+0/−0)	0	0	93.1	0.0	94.4	0.0
14. Chechen AO	0 (+0/−0)	0	0	94.0	0.0	91.5	0.0

15. Kabardino-Balkar AO	−1 (+0/−1)	−9,355	−44	79.9	+4.7	89.8	−0.02
16. North Ossetian AO	−1 (+0/−1)	−19,238	−2,911	94.2	+11.9	46.1	−0.2
17. Karachay AO	0 (−0/+0)	0	0	81.3	0.0	95.3	0.0
18. Circassian AO	−2 (+0/−2)	−36,996	−2,655	0	−7.2	0	−4.1
19. Dagestan ASSR	0 (+2/−2)	−58,674	+739	69.8	+8.2	88.6	+0.1
20. Oyrot AO	−1 (+0/−1)	−11,388	−3,388	38.2	+7.0	83.0	−9.1
21. Khakass Okrug	−2 (+0/−2)	−26,616	−6,846	60.0	+20.7	81.8	−15.6
22. Buryat-Mongolian ASSR	−13 (+0/−13)	−93,269	−4,783	52.8	+20.5	88.5	+2.2
23. Yakut ASSR	−1 (+0/−1)	−19,896	−848	87.3	+7.0	97.7	−0.3
24. Karakalpak AO	−16 (+0/−16)	−178,297	−14,997	80.1	+110.2	69.1	−13.0
25. Nakhichevan ASSR	0 (+1/−1)	+12,362	+5,908	80.5	−4.5	5.5	+5.8
26. Nagorno-Karabakh AO	0 (+1/−1)	+323	+8,874	96.0	+7.7	7.7	+8.5
27. Abkhaziya ASSR	−10 (+0/−10)	−18,116	−637	30.2	+8.6	97.1	−1.1
28. Adzhariya ASSR	0 (+0/−0)	0	0	53.7	0.0	99.2	0.0
29. South Ossetian AO	+1 (+4/−3)	+33,986	+48,219	89.5	+29.5	39.9	+79.7

Source: USSR, *Vsesoyuznaya Perepis' Naseleniya 1926 Goda* (Moscow: Tsentral'noye Statisticheskoye Upravleniye SSSR, 1928) vols. 1–17. Table X.
*For a description on how the "optimum" national-territorial jurisdictions were formed, see text.

reasonably accurate job in demarcating most of the national homeland territories according to the 1926 ethnic distribution.

Table 8.2 details results of the rather painstaking process involved in such a re-districting of the ASSRs and AOs based solely on population criteria. The two primary determining factors considered were, once again, those of nationality containment and concentration levels. After the boundaries were hypothetically redrawn according to the number of border units transferred, the net changes in both total and titular group populations of the new, optimum units were calculated. These were used to determine per cent differences in both concentration levels and union-wide containment levels for each of the nationality jurisdictions. An evaluation of these findings helps to determine more precisely the degree to which the originally drawn national boundaries fit the existing population distribution of the newly organized Soviet state.

How Well Were the Borders Drawn?

What is immediately evident from Table 8.2 is that the reconstructing of the national boundaries for the most part *excluded* more regions than were added to the newly created optimum units. What resulted, in general, was a gain in concentration levels at the expense of containment. This seems logical owing to the fact that because more regions were subtracted than were added, the national populations of the new units would tend to be smaller, but more concentrated. Because the regions taken away were composed of pluralities of *other* nationalities, it can also be seen how gains in concentration would usually be more significant than would comparative losses in containment.

Indeed, a survey of the changes in containment levels shows that an application of more rigid national criteria for boundary demarcation nearly always resulted in lowered levels of containment for the optimum national-territorial units. The only case where the nationality containment was appreciably raised was in the South Ossetian AO, and this deviation is easily accounted for by the fact of its unique location across the border of a jurisdiction (the North Ossetian AO) containing the same titular nation.

In terms of nationality concentration, several of the units showing a relatively significant increase (e.g. Khakass Okrug, Mari AO) became less than ideal creations, when one considered the fact that in these cases the optimum units showed even larger proportionate decreases in containment levels. It was necessary, therefore, in attempting to judge the effectiveness of a unit's ethnic "fit," to once again consider the combined influence of changes in nationality containment and concentration levels.

Regional Population Redistribution and National Homelands 139

By applying these factors together, it was possible to determine which optimum units had a large proportionate increase in nationality concentration with a correspondingly small decrease in containment. Such a situation would indicate that, at least based solely on ethnic criteria, the homeland boundaries could have been drawn more accurately than they originally were. According to Table 8.2, those jurisdictions which conformed to this pattern were the Karelian ASSR (1), the Permyak Okrug (9), the North Ossetian AO (16), the Buryat-Mongolian ASSR (22), and the Karakalpak AO (24).[23] In addition, the Chuvash ASSR (4) showed a significant increase in concentration with a rise in containment as well, while the Circassian AO (18) showed a decrease in both levels. Each of these latter situations would also have called for a reconstruction of the existing borders if only ethnic criteria were applied.

Based on the parameters established, therefore, a reconstruction of the subunit boundaries to conform to optimum criteria would have resulted in a better "fit" for only 7 of the 29 (24 per cent) national-territorial jurisdictions. Of the remaining 22, 12 had a less than 10 per cent increase in concentration, without a significant decrease in containment; 3 had a large increase in concentration, but at the expense of the containment levels; and 6 showed no change in the borders at all, based on the concentration and containment levels of the surrounding regions. (The South Ossetian AO is not considered in this classification because the reconstruction of its borders included territory from the North Ossetian AO; both subunits were based on a large majority of the Ossetian nationality). Overall, 18 of the 29 subunits had changes in both concentration and containment levels of less than 10 per cent.

According to Boggs, "one of the principal reasons for making any study of boundaries is the desire to determine what kind of boundaries have proven to be 'good' and which have been found out to be 'bad'."[24] Applying these rather basic terms to the Soviet case, most of the originally drawn boundaries of the ethnic subunits appeared to be quite "good" based on the criteria used in this study. Without a framework for comparison, however, such an evaluation of these subunits would be inconclusive.

The most pertinent and readily available comparison would be with the internal boundaries of the union republics.[25] These borders included the frontiers between the SSRs as well as those within the individual constituent republics that bordered their contained tertiary-level national autonomies. Altogether 1,386 border volosts were examined, and, of these, 236 (17.0 per cent) qualified for transfer based on the same criterion established for Table 8.2. Because the RSFSR is so large, it was broken down into its 12

Russian-based census regions. Similarly, the Ukraine was analyzed based on its six Ukrainian subregions. Table 8.3 presents a summary of the number and location of border units which would have required a change in jurisdiction in order to meet the requirements of concentration and containment necessary to satisfy the establishment of optimum boundaries.

Altogether, the number of units considered in Table 8.3 totalled 27, only two fewer than those in the subunit classification. (The Table 8.3 units included those ASSRs which would eventually become full union republics.) A survey of the border changes involved in creating optimum union republics allows for some comparison between the delimitation of these territories and those of the autonomous republics and oblasts listed in Table 8.2. The *numbers* of border units exchanged in each of the data-sets were actually quite similar, and a comparison of these proved interesting. Closer examination indicated that there were in fact fewer proportionate changes necessary (11.4 to 17.0 per cent) in reconstructing the boundaries of the tertiary subunits than for those of the constituent republics. Many of the SSR boundaries were historical vestiges, their territories having been previously delimited as national homelands in one form or another, some for many years. Based, therefore, on the experience of bounding the major Soviet nationalities within their own autonomous jurisdictions (SSRs), the limits of the lower-level autonomies (ASSRs and AOs) compared quite favorably.

Because the populations of the SSRs were much greater than those of the autonomous republics and oblasts, a similar number of border units exchanged did not have as much of an impact upon the population composition and containment levels of the larger jurisdictions. In fact, out of the 27 units, there was only one case (Moldavian ASSR) where the optimum boundaries would have made a difference of greater than 5 per cent in *either* containment or concentration levels.

Therefore, a simple t-test was performed to determine the significance of the difference between the two means of the total number of border districts that all units at each level of national autonomy (i.e. union republic v. ASSR and AO) were required to exchange. The calculated t value of 1.79 indicated no significant difference at either the 1 or 5 per cent level. This leads to a rejection of the notion that the boundaries of the union republics were significantly more effective in their demarcation of homeland territories than were those of the autonomous republics and oblasts in 1926. Although this nonparametric test is far from conclusive, it lends support to the argument that the policy of demarcating the original national homeland

Table 8.3 Change in the Number of Border Districts to Conform with the Criteria for "Optimum" Units: SSRs, 1926

Unit	Total Number of Border Districts	Number of Border Districts Added	Number of Border Districts Subtracted	Net Change in Number of Border Districts
RSFSR:	346	95	26	+69
Northeastern	4	3	0	+3
Leningrad-Karelia	8	7	0	+7
Western	27	4	1	+3
Central Ind.	12	0	0	0
North Caucasus	42	9	5	+4
Siberia	42	26	0	+26
Central Chernozem	22	2	13	−11
Central Volga	48	10	3	+7
Lower Volga	32	8	2	+6
Vyatka Rayon	27	10	1	+9
Ural Oblast	57	16	1	+15
Far East	25	0	0	0
Ukrainian SSR:	72	26	3	+23
Steppe	17	18	0	+18
Forest	19	1	1	0
Right Bank Dnepr	11	4	0	+4
Left Bank Dnepr	18	1	1	0
Dnepr Industrial	0	0	0	0
Mining Industrial	7	2	1	+1
Belorussian SSR	32	0	4	−4
Armenian SSR	16	3	1	+2
Georgian SSR	58	9	8	+1
Azerbaydzhan SSR	29	3	7	−4
Uzbek SSR	49	4	3	+1
Turkmen SSR	9	1	3	−2
Moldavian ASSR	8	0	5	−5
Kirgiz ASSR	34	1	1	0
Tadzhik ASSR	15	2	1	+1
Kazakh ASSR	90	6	24	−18

Source: See *Source*, Table 8.2.

territories of the USSR, given the existing ethnic population, was rather effectively carried out at all levels.

Tracing the National Homeland Populations over Time

Now that the jurisdictional validity of the Soviet national homelands has been assessed, it remains to be seen what effect the decision to create a secondary level of national autonomy had on the population redistribution of the national minorities over the years. Did the established autonomous republics and oblasts maintain a focus as homelands of national attachment as measured by the ensuing settlement patterns of the indigenous groups?

In general, Soviet authorities made an effort over the years to alter the name, status, or organization (but usually not the political borders) of the lower-level autonomies in response to changing conditions or new information. As a group inhabiting an autonomous oblast became sufficiently advanced, culturally and economically, the status of the unit was to be promoted to the next level of autonomy, that of ASSR.[26] In fact, the 1936 Soviet Constitution promoted several of the more populous autonomous oblasts to autonomous republics. It is interesting to note that, although there have been many changes over the years in the *rank* of these nationality-based units, changes in their boundaries have been relatively slight. On the other hand, the *non*-national territorial-administrative structure has been characterized by extensive changes in the internal boundaries of its component units, with the ruling consideration generally being administrative efficiency.[27]

In sharp contrast, therefore, with the dynamic character of the ever-changing boundaries of the non-national administrative substructure (i.e. oblasts), the geographic configuration of the national-territorial jurisdictions in the Soviet Union has remained quite static. Any major changes would have challenged the fundamental concept of containing significant concentrations of the various Soviet national minorities in areas as compact as possible.

The points of reference for tracing the changing population composition and containment levels of the ASSRs and AOs will be the union-wide censuses of 1926, 1959, 1970 and 1979.[28] Even a study based on these years, where statistics are relatively readily available, presents problems of maintaining a continuous and comparable dataset for evaluating the changing Soviet population. Among the difficulties confronted in attempting to trace the trends in redistribution over time is the 33-year gap between the 1926 and 1959 censuses, during which time severe disruptions in Soviet population trends were caused by forced collectivization, purges and the population losses associated with World War II, including direct war deaths, emigration, deportations, transfers and the population deficit resulting from births prevented.

Further compounding the difficulties in measuring these populations were the changes in the actual boundaries of some of the subunits, the redefinition of certain groups listed in the 1926 census, the creation of a new level of national autonomy (the nationality okrug), and the elimination altogether of several of the original autonomous oblasts and republics. Many of these problems resulted from the deportation of nationalities that occurred during World War II. Specific groups accused of collaborating with Nazi Germany included the Crimean Tatars, the Volga Germans, the Kalymks, Chechen, Ingush, Karachay and Balkar nationalities. All of these peoples were deported to the east either during or after the war, primarily to regions in Central Asia and Kazakhstan.[29] By the late 1950s these groups, with the exception of the Germans and the Crimean Tatars, were allowed to move back to their homelands. Compounding the difficulties of territorial and definitional comparability are the increasing paucity in the data published for succeeding census years and problems caused by assimilation and reidentification which are present in any census count.

By far the most salient feature of the nationality redistribution pattern—a feature which has characterized the post-Revolutionary population of the Soviet Union—has been the dispersal of Russians into non-Russian areas. The bulk of this flow migrated into urban areas, which is not surprising in light of the fact that the rate of Russian urbanization during this time was exceptionally rapid. In terms of the regional redistribution of the population, the greatest shifts were caused by the Russian population moving to other Russian areas within the RSFSR, particularly the North Caucasus, West Siberia and the Far East. In addition, there was a substantial increase of Russians moving into the non-Russian nationality units within the RSFSR, which by 1979 contained 10.6 million Russians, approximately one-half of their aggregate population. While the total numbers of Russians that had over the years relocated to the other union republics was greater than those living in the less populous ASSRs and AOs, the former figure (23.9 million) represented a far smaller *share* (19.1 per cent) of the total populations of the SSRs than that of the nationality subunits.[30]

Because of the territorial changes that occurred in the boundaries of the nationality subunits between 1926 and 1959, the 29 ASSRs and AOs listed in Table 8.2 are not entirely appropriate for investigating subsequent patterns in the ethnic population distribution. Instead, the 1959 census units, which remain virtually unchanged to the present day, will be the parameters used for tracing the population redistribution of the Soviet national autonomies between 1926 and 1979. Of the 26 autonomous jurisdictions remaining from the original data-set, nine had been upgraded from their status as autonomous oblasts in 1926 and comprised eight reconfigured autonomous republics by 1959.[31] Two units (the Komi-Permyak and Khakass Okrugs) had been granted autonomous status, while two others (the Votyak and Oyrot Autonomous Oblasts) were renamed.[32] In addition, the five North Caucasian national autonomies, which had been dissolved during World War II, were reconstituted into three jurisdictions with altogether different borders than previously.

In the meantime, the Mordvinian nation had been organized as an autonomous oblast which in 1934 was elevated to the status of autonomous republic. Finally, it should be noted that there are three more recent formations which, along with the autonomous (formerly nationality) okrugs, are for various reasons not included in this study. They are the Yevrey and Gorno-Badakhshan AOs, and the Tuvin ASSR.[33]

As mentioned previously, the most complex problems of territorial comparability arise when attempting to compare the subunit populations between the census years of 1926 and 1959. Fortunately, a study conducted by Ralph Clem has already addressed this difficulty, and has corrected the territorial allocations of the Soviet political administrative structure so that the 1926 ethnic population distribution was presented within the boundaries of the 1959 units.[34] These are the populations and jurisdictions which will be used as the basis for the following analysis.[35]

The actual number of autonomous subunits considered in the remainder of this paper totals 25, including 18 autonomous republics, 6 autonomous oblasts, and 1 autonomous okrug (Komi-Permyak).[36] This contrasts with the 29 units which comprised the original 1926 data-set. Apart from the reorganization which took place in the North Caucasus region, most changes that have occurred since these regions were originally constituted were in title and status only.

For the purposes of this analysis, the national autonomies at the tertiary administrative level (ASSRs and AOs) will be divided into four groups, according to their geographic proximity. The population concentration and containment levels of these units will then be examined based on the four successive Soviet censuses for which data are available: 1926, 1959, 1970 and 1979. Tables 8.4 and 8.5 trace the population concentration and containment levels from 1926 to 1979

Table 8.4 Change in Population Composition, Autonomous Subunits, 1926–1979

Political Unit	Population Composition Percentage							
	Titular Group				Largest Minority Group			
	1926	1959	1970	1979	1926	1959	1970	1979
I. Northern Europe and Siberia						Russians		
Karelian ASSR	22.6	13.1	11.8	11.1	35.6	63.4	68.0	71.3
Komi ASSR	74.2	30.4	28.6	25.3	24.3	48.4	53.0	56.7
Yakut ASSR	85.0	46.4	43.0	36.9	9.0	44.2	47.0	50.4
Buryat ASSR[a]	37.1	23.8	25.4	26.2	60.0	70.3	69.5	68.5
Khakass AO	49.7	11.8	12.4	11.5	46.6	76.5	78.4	79.4
Gorno-Altay AO	37.2	24.2	27.8	29.2	52.0	69.8	65.6	63.2
Komi-Permyak Autonomous Okrug	77.0	58.0	58.0	61.4	22.8	32.9	36.0	34.7
II. Volga-Urals								
Bashkir ASSR	22.7	22.1	23.0	24.3	40.4	42.4	40.5	40.3
Mari ASSR	49.5	43.1	43.6	43.5	45.6	47.8	46.9	47.5
Mordvinian ASSR	31.0	35.8	35.5	34.2	62.4	59.0	59.0	59.7
Tatar ASSR	48.5	47.2	49.0	47.6	43.3	43.9	42.4	44.0
Udmurt ASSR	41.1	35.6	34.0	32.1	55.0	56.8	57.0	58.3
Chuvash ASSR	74.6	70.2	70.0	68.4	20.0	24.0	24.4	26.0
III. North Caucasus								
Dagestan ASSR	56.7	69.3	74.2	77.8	10.0	20.1	14.7	11.6
Kabardino-Balkar ASSR	67.6	53.4	53.6	54.5	13.1	38.7	37.2	35.1
Kalmyk ASSR	69.7	35.1	41.0	41.5	14.9	55.9	45.8	42.6
North Ossetian ASSR	55.2	47.8	48.7	50.5	22.0	39.6	36.6	33.9
Chechen-Ingush ASSR	61.9	41.1	58.5	64.6	26.2	49.0	34.5	29.1
Adygey AO	44.5	23.2	21.0	21.4	26.0	70.4	72.0	70.6
Karachay-Cherkess AO	77.2	33.1	37.2	39.1	2.6	51.0	47.0	45.1
IV. Transcaucasia and non-Slavic South						Nationality of the Presiding Republic		
Karakalpak ASSR	31.7	30.6	31.1	31.1	36.1	28.8	30.3	31.5
Nakhichevan ASSR	84.3	90.2	94.0	95.6	10.8	6.7	2.9	1.4
Nagorno-Karabakh AO	89.1	84.4	80.7	75.9	10.2	13.8	18.1	23.0
Abkhaz ASSR	27.8	15.1	15.8	17.1	33.6	39.1	41.0	43.9
South Ossetian AO	69.1	65.8	66.5	66.4	26.9	27.5	28.3	28.8

Sources: See *Sources*, Table 8.6 (p. 150).
[a]Figures for this unit include the populations of the Aga-Buryat and Ust-Orda Buryat Autonomous Okrugs, which were separated from the Mongol-Buryat ASSR in 1927.

Table 8.5 Change in Population Containment, Autonomous Subunits, 1926–1979

Political Unit	% of Total USSR Ethnic Group Population Contained			
	1926	*1959*	*1970*	*1979*
I. Northern Europe and Siberia				
Karelian ASSR	37.8	51.1	57.6	58.7
Komi ASSR	82.2	85.4	85.8	85.9
Yakut ASSR	93.0	95.5	96.5	95.7
Buryat ASSR[a]	90.5	80.6	82.7	81.7
Khakass AO	96.3	85.7	82.1	80.9
Gorno-Altay AO	91.3	84.0	83.8	83.7
Komi-Permyak Autonomous Okrug	78.6	87.5	80.6	70.0
II. Volga-Urals				
Bashkir ASSR	79.3	74.6	72.0	68.2
Mari ASSR	56.9	55.4	50.0	49.3
Mordvinian ASSR	25.8	27.9	28.9	28.4
Tatar ASSR	43.3	27.1	25.9	26.0
Udmurt ASSR	83.3	76.2	68.7	67.2
Chuvash ASSR	58.4	52.4	50.5	50.7
III. North Caucasus				
Dagestan ASSR	74.1	78.0	77.7	76.5
Kabardino-Balkar ASSR	87.1	78.6	93.1	93.6
Kalmyk ASSR	78.5	61.2	80.4	83.3
North Ossetian ASSR	53.4	52.2	55.2	55.2
Chechen-Ingush ASSR	90.4	55.7	80.8	79.2
Adygey AO	77.9	82.7	81.6	79.5
Karachay-Cherkess AO	85.8	82.2	84.1	80.9
IV. Transcaucasia and non-Slavic South				
Karakalpak ASSR	78.5	90.4	92.2	92.9
Nakhichevan ASSR	5.2	4.3	4.3	4.2
Nagorno-Karabakh AO	7.1	3.9	3.4	3.0
Abkhaz ASSR	98.2	93.5	92.8	91.4
South Ossetian AO	22.2	15.4	13.5	12.0

Sources: See *Sources*, Table 8.6.
[a] Figures after 1926 include totals from Aga-Buryat and Ust-Orda Buryat Autonomous Okrugs.

Regional Population Redistribution and National Homelands 147

for these autonomous jurisdictions as units appropriate for emotional attachments based on national self-consciousness.

Regionally, there are certain trends in the patterns of concentration and containment distinguishable between 1926 and 1979. These patterns seem most pronounced and consistent in Northern Europe and Siberia. All of the autonomous republics and autonomous oblasts in this category contain numerically small populations so that even a relatively modest influx of Russians will, by sheer force of numbers, cause the population concentration of the indigenous group to diminish comparatively. Since the years of their formation, in fact, each of these national autonomies experienced a significant decrease in the population composition of its titular group, with a corresponding increase in the number and percentage of Russians. The population *containment* levels of these Northern European and Siberian subunits, however, have not undergone significant change over the years; no pattern or direction is discernible. This is because Russian in-migration has had little effect on the share each jurisdiction contains of the union-wide population of its titular nationality. One apparent exception is the Karelian ASSR, but the increase between 1926 and 1959 in the containment level of Karelians living within the borders of the Karelian ASSR can be largely attributed to the fact that a large portion of the original Soviet Karelian population was transferred to Finland in the aftermath of World War II.[37] Between 1926 and 1959 the total Karelian population in the USSR actually decreased by 32.6 per cent, from 248,120 to 167,278.[38] The fact that the number living in the Karelian ASSR diminished by only 8.9 per cent during this same period would account for a large portion of the nearly 40 per cent increase in the population containment level of Soviet Karelians living within their national homeland.

Of the four geographic categories, the Volga-Urals appears to be the most stable in terms of the population composition of the individual autonomous republics. While the percentage composition of the various republics varies widely, the changes between 1926 and 1979 are minimal. The trend is generally in the direction of a slightly decreasing concentration of the indigenous group, although a quick observation reveals that this is not necessarily due to an influx of Russians, as is the case with the units in Northern Europe and Siberia. The containment levels, on the other hand, show evidence of a downward trend, indicative of the increasing out-migration which is associated with the socioeconomic modernization occurring among these particular nationality groups. This modernization is also indicated by comparatively higher regional rates of intermarriage, investment, education and linguistic Russification.

The only one of the Volga-Urals subunits which did not show a downward trend in the level of containment was the Mordvinian ASSR. The total Mordvinian population of the Soviet Union is one of the largest and most widely dispersed of all the Soviet ethnic minorities. The fact that the Mordvinian population was so great (1.3 million in 1926, ranking 11th of all groups) led the Soviet authorities to create a Mordvinian autonomous jurisdiction in 1934. Because this unit did not come into existence until more than a decade after the 1926 census count, it is difficult to attach any meaningful significance to the figures for its 1926 population. And because the Mordvinian population has been historically dispersed over a wide territorial expanse, the percentage contained within the Mordvinian ASSR has remained consistently rather low throughout the years.

There are two distinct time periods observable in terms of the trends in the population composition and containment levels of the subunits within the third major geographic category, the North Caucasus. First, between 1926 and 1959, both levels tended to go down as a result of administrative reorganization, expulsions of indigenous group and a significant influx of agricultural settlers. Since 1959 this trend has generally been reversed. In terms of explaining the increase in population containment levels, a variety of reasons are postulated as to why the relatively underdeveloped native peoples of the North Caucasus have been reluctant to leave their homelands. Their levels of education, intermarriage and linguistic assimilation have remained relatively low over the years; many of these groups have also maintained their Muslim traditions and sedentary agricultural lifestyles. This slowness to modernize has combined with a geographic isolation provided by the peaks and valleys of the Greater Caucasus Mountains effectively to tie these people to their homeland territories over the years.

In addition, much of the recent rise in both concentration percentages and containment levels has been caused by the differential natural increase between the indigenous groups and other, predominantly Russian and Ukrainian, peoples. The nationality groups of the North Caucasus have rates of natural increase which are among the highest in the entire Soviet Union.

The fourth geographic category, labeled Transcaucasia and the non-Slavic South, includes all those nationality subunits not contained within the Russian Republic. This category lacks any unifying criteria other than a location beyond the borders of the RSFSR and is, in this sense, not a homogeneous classification. The five subunits which comprise this residual category are found within three separate republics, each characterized by pronounced and distinct geographic

Regional Population Redistribution and National Homelands 149

and demographic qualities. Of the five autonomous regions, three are based on nationalities which have a majority of their population contained within the confines of another titular jurisdiction. A fourth (the Abkhaz ASSR) has, since its formation, maintained an extremely low titular group population concentration, currently below 20 per cent. Of all the subunits in this last category, the Karakalpak ASSR is the only one which seems to possess the necessary requirements of concentration and containment that qualify it to fulfill the function of national homeland. Because of the dissimilarities in the ethnic population characteristics and distribution among the subunits of Transcaucasia and the non-Slavic South, it would appear impossible to find representative patterns for this category based on geographic or demographic similarities. Eliminating the regions in this latter category from future consideration leaves 20 autonomous regions, all of which lie within the RSFSR. In each instance it is the Russian nation which comprises the largest "other" group living within the territorial confines of the national subunit.

Population Redistribution: Index of Diversity

The last task remaining in this study is to evaluate the population redistributions of nationalities within the Soviet autonomous homelands of the RSFSR through the use of a diversity index. As an alternative measure for evaluating population trends, the specific measure used reduces the impact of large numbers and presents a measure of concentration/diversity on a scale of zero to one.[39] By using a logarithmic scale to lessen the influence of large numbers of Russians, the index can reveal patterns which isolate the behavior of an entire matrix of local groups despite a numerical Russian dominance.

Table 8.6 presents the result of such an effort, listing the changing levels of diversity for 20 autonomous regions within the RSFSR between the census years of 1926 and 1979. As opposed to the measures of concentration (percentages), these indices indicate that, despite Russian in-migration, the population distributions of the national homelands are nevertheless moving towards a situation of increasing measured diversity (evenness). Furthermore, the units of the Volga-Urals have become more heterogeneous than those of either the North Caucasus, Northern Europe or Siberia; this is what would be expected due to the associated patterns of socioeconomic development that tend to influence population behavior. By its nature, the diversity measure also incorporates pertinent factors

Table 8.6 Change in Index of Diversity: Autonomous Subunits, 1926–1979

Political Unit	Index of Diversity			
	1926	1959	1970	1979
I. Northern Europe and Siberia				
Karelian ASSR	0.46	0.56	0.41	0.53
Komi ASSR	0.33	0.47	0.50	0.61
Yakut ASSR	0.34	0.46	0.50	0.58
Buryat ASSR[a]	0.35	0.42	0.45	0.46
Khakass AO	0.45	0.42	0.37	0.46
Gorno-Altay AO	0.52	0.51	0.54	0.64
Komi-Permyak Autonomous Okrug	0.51	0.57	0.58	0.62
II. Volga-Urals				
Bashkir ASSR	0.58	0.66	0.71	0.74
Mari ASSR	0.49	0.55	0.58	0.63
Mordvinian ASSR	0.28	0.54	0.55	0.72
Tatar ASSR	0.40	0.48	0.54	0.60
Udmurt ASSR	0.46	0.53	0.55	0.65
Chuvash ASSR	0.36	0.46	0.50	0.62
III. North Caucasus				
Dagestan ASSR	0.29	0.40	0.38	0.43
Kabardino-Balkar ASSR	0.46	0.52	0.50	0.52
Kalmyk ASSR	0.45	0.52	0.54	0.54
North Ossetian ASSR	0.62	0.53	0.55	0.56
Chechen-Ingush ASSR	0.40	0.51	0.53	0.50
Adygey AO	0.58	0.47	0.46	0.49
Karachay-Cherkess AO	0.66	0.59	0.55	0.53

Sources: USSR, *Vsesoyuznaya Perepis' Naseleniya 1926 Goda* (Moscow: Tsentral'noye Statisticheskoye Upravleniye SSSR, 1928), vols. 1–17, Table X; Ralph S. Clem, "The Changing Geography of Soviet Nationalities and Its Socioeconomic Correlates" (Ph.D. dissertation, Columbia University, 1976), pp. 322–51; USSR, Tsentral'noye Statisticheskoye Upravleniye SSSR, *Itogi Vsesoyuznoy Perepisi Naseleniya 1959 Goda* (Moscow: Gosstatizdat, 1962), vols. 1–16, Table 54; USSR, Tsentral'noye Statisticheskoye Upravleniye SSSR, *Itogi Vsesoyuznoy Perepisi Naseleniya 1970 Goda* (Moscow: "Statistika", 1973), vol. IV, pp. 20–320, Tables 4–29; USSR, Tsentral'noye Statisticheskoye Upravleniye SSSR, *Chislennost' i Sostav Naseleniya SSSR* (Moscow: Finansy i Statistika), pp. 76–136.
[a] Figures after 1926 include totals from Aga-Buryat and Ust-Orda Buryat Autonomous Okrugs.

which tend to influence redistribution, such as ethnic reidentification and differential natural increase.

The main utility of the diversity measure lies in its value as an indicator of broad patterns and general trends. The absolute figures derived for each of the different regions are not necessarily comparable, owing to differences in the size and composition of the individual units. Still, the numbers do reveal certain overall aspects of regional population redistribution in the national homelands that are not observable by a study of concentration and containment levels alone.

The data clearly reveal the fact that between 1926 and 1979 the populations within the confines of the national autonomies at the level of ASSR and AO have become more evenly distributed. This has occurred even in areas with small populations where Russian in-migration has been traditionally strong, meaning that there has either been an influx of other nationalities as well, or that the absolute numbers of the indigenous groups have also significantly increased.[40] In such situations the diversity index proves more revealing than measures of the changing relative percentages of the titular and Russian groups. Regionally, the Volga-Urals show the greatest average increases in the diversity measures, while the North Caucasus grouping has had the least average change, and in some cases even reveals an overall decrease in the index.

While the general trend towards increasing diversity appears quite evident from the time of the earliest until the most recent Soviet census, changes occurring within each of the various intercensal time periods are much less apparent. Between 1926 and 1959 the differences in the index were greatest, whether in the direction of increasing concentration or growing diversity. Although this change was in several cases dramatic, a large part of the differential is attributable, not to natural population movements associated with the impact of gradual modernization, but to the forces of resettlement associated with collectivization, the war effort, economic reorganization and a policy which forced heavy industrialization upon the Soviet economy.

The most notable feature of the 1959–1970 time period is that the magnitude of change in the index was less, perhaps indicative of a stabilization that was occurring in Soviet population redistribution. The overall trend in Russian migration patterns during these years was characterized by a gradual shift westward, after several decades of Russian out-migration to the east and south. This was taking place during a time of fairly rapid economic growth occurring now in an atmosphere of relative political stability.[41]

Conclusion

By giving constitutional recognition to the languages and territories of individual nationalities, the federated political administrative system of the USSR provided national homelands with the potential to play influential roles in governing future relations, including population processes, among the numerous peoples of the multiethnic Soviet state. A federal structure inevitably brings to the forefront the issue of territoriality, which is directly related to the desire to legitimize traditional national homelands. Along with the concepts of regionalization and equalization, this "territorial imperative" contributes to making the notion of an ethnic homeland a powerful political force in most countries today. And when ethnic groups and their homelands are linked within a federal system to the very structure of the state, issues that might otherwise have been "regional" become "ethnic" instead.[42]

A number of sociological surveys conducted within the Soviet Union established that residence either within or outside one's homeland tends to influence attitudes and behavior.[43] Homeland residency influences the willingness to learn a second language, the propensity to enter into interethnic marriages, the choice of national identity by children who are products of mixed marriages, and attitudes towards other national groups.[44]

The formal implementation of the system of national homelands was especially important in that it provided for education and a local press in the native language, as well as the teaching of national history. Yuriy Bromley, a prominent Soviet demographer, recognized the value of autonomous homeland units by asserting: "National-state construction, and above all the formation of Union and Autonomous Republics, created particularly favorable conditions for the sociocultural development primarily of the previously backward peoples."[45]

On the one hand, therefore, there is the view that the Soviet federal system will lead to an erosion of ethnic identity among the non-Russian nationalities and their eventual amalgamation as part of a Russian or "Soviet" nation. This type of assimilation is to be brought about by raising the cultural levels and international awareness of the minority groups (or, as posited by those critical of the Soviet federal system, by the continued repression of backward peoples).

On the other hand, there is the retrospective viewpoint that the Soviet national federation, although devised to mollify nationalism and secure the cooperation of ethnic minorities, has instead intensified nationalism by providing it with formal institutional outlets.[46] Such an argument can lead to the conclusion that the federal structure of the USSR will eventually cause the country to be torn apart by interethnic strife and conflict.[47] From this latter viewpoint, regional inequalities are regarded as a major factor in the ethnic discontent of multinational countries. Cynthia Enloe has written: "In a federally divided multiethnic society achieving national development is easier than distributing it equally. Eventually development gaps between states or republics exacerbate ethnic animosities to the point that the nation's aggregate development may be jeopardized."[48]

Regardless of the point of view, the structure of the Soviet state did provide various ethnic groups, both large and small, with well-defined, distinct territories which had the potential for emotional attachment and national identification. Once a land area had been demarcated according to nationality distinctions, it became a tangible focus towards which a group could channel its nationalism. Because a national administrative unit formally represented the language, tradition and culture of its titular group, it was able to function as a homeland in both the emotional and geographical sense of the word. The national homelands in the Soviet Union tended to contain fairly homogeneous ethnic populations, whether they comprised historically self-aware, or nonhistoric and unaware, members.

It is difficult to make a clear distinction between settlement patterns and emotional attachments to one's national homeland. The importance of the territorial aspect of nationality has, however, been increasingly recognized by the Soviet leadership and local press.[49] While it is difficult to measure the actual impact of national homelands on population redistribution in the face of a modernizing economy, the permanent nature of their (the homelands') existence seems firmly entrenched and widely accepted. This mutual compatibility is underscored by the following comments:

> It seems to me that the idea of the fusion ['*sliyaniye*'] of nations has suffered in large part from a vulgar-Utopian interpretation which assumed that fusion meant the total eradication of all linguistic and ethnic differences among national groups . . . . As the 26th CPSU Congress pointed out, social classes will largely disappear while we are still in the process of developing socialism. The same cannot be said of socialist nations, which are more stable social and ethnic entities. As for the racial, national and ethnic differences among major population groups and individuals, these will undergo substantial changes, of course, as a result of *migration* and the constant *intermixing* of the population, but in principle they are indestructible. Only given this condition can we realistically conceive of the future fusion of nations.[50]

Regardless of their territorial value as national homelands, the autonomous subunits of the Soviet Union remain important as *institutional* confines of ethnicity in terms of local political, cultural and social expressions and aspirations. Concerning their relationship to the regional population redistribution of the titular groups, the most salient observation that can be made from this study is that the populations they bound have continued to behave by and large along the lines of historically and traditionally established patterns, despite significant changes in their levels of socioeconomic development. The time period being studied, even counted from the beginning of the Soviet era, is relatively brief in terms of revealing changes in population behavior. Forces once firmly established tend to continue with a good deal of internal inertia. Even in the case of the Soviet Union, where the administrative jurisdictions are based on the nationality composition of the population and the economy is centrally planned, population behavior has tended to be resistant to official policies. The decision to grant national autonomy to Soviet tertiary-level units, therefore, while apparently having had some measured significance on the process of population redistribution of the indigenous peoples, is perhaps most important for the fact that it has served to legitimize the cultural, political, social and geographic expression of minority nationalities.

Notes

1. Altogether, there are 53 national autonomies in the USSR today, of which 15 are union republics, 20 are autonomous republics, and 8 are autonomous oblasts. This paper does not include figures for the smallest of the national autonomous formations in the Soviet Union, the autonomous okrug (called nationality okrug prior to the 1977 Constitution). This omission is due to the fact that the minority populations contained within these ten units are relatively small numerically and diluted in terms of their concentration.

2. Regions such as the Baltics and Transcaucasia were inhabited by peoples with a history of political autonomy on the land as well as a sense of national distinctiveness. The Ukraine, while a region of historic territorial and ethnic ambiguities, actively moved towards political secession and independence during the years of civil war immediately following the Revolution. Most of the territory of Central Asia was politically administered by the three khanates of Bukhara, Kokand and Khiva, all of which were protectorates of the Russian Empire in the late nineteenth century.

3. Konstantin Symmons-Symonolewicz, *Modern Nationalism* (New York: The Polish Institute of Arts and Sciences, 1972), p. v.

4. Fredrik Barth, *Ethnic Groups and Boundaries* (Boston: Little, Brown, and Company, 1969), pp. 14–5.

5. Karl W. Deutsch, *Nationalism and Social Communication* (New York: John Wiley and Sons, Inc., 1953), p. 3

6. David B. Knight, "Identity and Territory: Geographical Perspectives on Nationalism and Regionalism," *Annals of the Association of American Geographers*, vol. 72 (December 1982), p. 526.

7. Yu. V. Arutyunyan, "Konkretno-Sotsiologicheskoye Issledovaniye Natsional'nykh Otnoshenii," *Voprosy Filosofii* no. 12 (1969), p. 138.

8. The six original constituent republics included the three predominantly Slavic republics of Russia, Belorussia and the Ukraine; the Transcaucasian Federation of Georgia, Armenia and Azerbaydzhan; and the Uzbek and Turkmen republics comprising much of the territory of today's four Soviet Central Asian republics.

9. A. Alimova (ed.), *Istoriya Sovyetskoy Konstitutsii* (Moscow: Akademiya Nauk SSSR, 1936), p. 259.

10. USSR, *Vsesoyuznaya Perepis' Naseleniya 1926 Goda*, vol. 17, Table X (Moscow: Tsentral'noye Statisticheskoye Upravleniye SSSR, 1928), pp. 42–5.

11. Alimova, *Istoriya Sovyetskoy Konstitutsii*, section II, ch. 5, par. 11, p. 69.

12. For a description of various degrees of Soviet autonomoy, see Konstantin Arkhipov, "Types of Soviet Autonomy," *Vlast' Sovyetov*, no. 10 (1923), p. 36.

13. Alimova, *Istoriya Sovyetskoy Konstitutsii*, pp. 265–6.

14. The three criteria Stalin considered to be necessary preconditions for SSR status were: (1) a periphery location; (2) a population of one million or more; and (3) a majority population of a single nationality. Since the formation of the Soviet Union all of these conditions but the first have been broken on occasion.

15. See Walter R. Batsell, *Soviet Rule in Russia* (New York: The Macmillan Company, 1929), pp. 622–3; 649–51.

16. See, for example, Alexandre Bennigsen and Chantal Lemercier-Quelquejay, *Islam in the Soviet Union* (New York: Frederick A. Praeger Publishers, 1967); Richard Pipes, *The Formation of the Soviet Union: Communism and Nationalism, 1917–1923* (Cambridge, Mass.: Harvard University Press, 1954).

17. See, for example, Walker Connor, *The National Question in Marxist-Leninist Theory and Strategy* (Princeton, New Jersey: Princeton University Press, 1984), pp. 302–3; and Walter Kolarz, *Russia and Her Colonies*, 4th ed. (New York: Archon Books), 1967).

18. The autonomous republics and autonomous oblasts, while being *tertiary*-level administrative units below both the primary (union-wide) and secondary (SSR) levels, occupy a *secondary* position (to the union republics) in the context of the autonomous nationality regions.

19. For examples, the Nakhichevan and Crimean ASSRs and the Nagorno-Karabakh AO were all based on ethnic populations which

happened to comprise the dominant group of one of the far more populous republics. The two Ossetian autonomous oblasts were geographically separated by the high crest of the Greater Caucasus Mountains, making logical their separate jurisdictions. If taken together, their populations would have contained nearly 70 per cent of the total Soviet Ossetian nationality. And in the case of the Circassian AO, the Circassian (Cherkess) people was split primarily between two nationality subunits, each of which bore its name.

20. This policy is stated in the resolutions adopted by the Communist Party at its 12th Congress in 1923 and is also listed in J. Stalin, *Natsional'nye Momenty v Partiinom i gosudarstvennom stroitel'stve* (Moscow, 1939), pp. 31–43. (See also Batsell, *Soviet Rule in Russia*, p. 644).

21. *Volost'* was the most common name used to describe the smallest of census units. Local variations delineating areas of similar size and status included *rayon*, *sel'sovyet*, *temy*, and *canton*. In the hierarchy of Soviet administration, the next highest levels of territorial organization were the *uyezd* and *guberniya*, under whose authority the volosts fell.

22. USSR, *Vsesoyuznaya Perepis' Naseleniya 1926 Goda*, vols. 1–17.

23. For the purposes of this evaluation, the 10 per cent level was arbitrarily chosen as a cut-off point to determine a significant proportionate change in the concentration level.

24. S. W. Boggs, *International Boundaries: a Study of Boundary Functions and Problems* (New York: Columbia University Press, 1940), p. 21.

25. Including the peripheral borders of the Soviet Union would not be relevant here, since these were not the result of a conscious policy decision.

26. A new level of national-territorial jurisdiction, the nationality okrug, was created in 1925 to include many of the small, less-developed peoples living mostly on the Asiatic fringe of Russia. These NOs, based on distinct ethnic groups but with little national autonomy, were introduced too late to appear in the 1926 census. The designation of nationality okrug was changed to that of autonomous okrug in ch. 11, art. 88, of the 1977 Soviet Constitution. See "The New USSR Constitution," *Current Digest of the Soviet Press*, no. 29 (November 9, 1977), p. 8.

27. See J. A. Morrison, "The Evolution of the Territorial-Administrative System of the USSR," *The American Quarterly on the Soviet Union*, vol. 1 (November 1938), pp. 25–7; also Theodore Shabad, "The Administrative-Territorial Patterns of the Soviet Union" in W. Gordon East and A. E. Moodie (eds.), *The Changing World* (Yonkers-on-the-Hudson, New York: World Book Company, 1956), pp. 365–84.

28. For the Soviet census conducted on January 17, 1939, only preliminary results were issued. A tabulation for the entire population was never published; partial data were released, comprising less than ten pages of tables. Because of its lack of detail, therefore, the 1939 Soviet census is of little use for population analysis.

29. See Robert Conquest, *The Nation Killers* (New York: The Macmillan Company, 1970).

30. USSR, *Chislennost' i Sostav Naseleniya SSSR* (Moscow: Finansy i Statistika, 1984), pp. 71–141. Of the 23.9 million figure, a net of 18.7 million Russians relocated in the years between 1926 and 1979 [Viktor Kozlov, *Natsional'nosti SSSR* (Moscow: Finansy i Statistika, 1982), p. 84].

31. These eight are the Komi, Kalmyk, Udmurt, Mari, Chechen-Ingush, Kabardino-Balkar, North Ossetian and Karakalpak AOs.

32. The Votyak AO became the Udmurt AO in 1932 and was elevated to the status of ASSR in 1934. The Oyrot AO was renamed the Gorno-Altay AO in 1948. See USSR, *Administrativno-Territorial'noye Deleniye Soyuznykh Respublik* (Moscow: Izdatel'stvo Sovyetov Deputatov Trudyashchikhsya, 1974), pp. 23, 241.

33. Although constituted as an autonomous oblast, the Gorno-Badakhshan region has actually maintained a Tadzhik majority of greater than 90 per cent. Because it falls administratively under the jurisdiction of the Tadzhik ASSR, there seems no logical reason to consider it separately in a study of national homeland jurisdictions. The Yevrey AO, formed in 1934 ostensibly as a Jewish national homeland, has never achieved even as much as a 10 per cent population concentration of Jews, and contains an insignificant fraction (less than 1 per cent) of the total Soviet Jewish population. The territory of the Tanu-Tuva ASSR was not fully incorporated into the USSR until after World War II, prior to which time no data are readily available.

34. Ralph S. Clem, "The Changing Geography of Soviet Nationalities and Its Socioeconomic Correlates," Ph.D. dissertation (Columbia University, 1976).

35. Unfortunately, an in-depth boundary analysis is not possible for the 1959 subunits owing to the lack of a detailed regional ethnic breakdown in the census.

36. The Permyak Okrug had by February 1925, already been reconstituted as the Komi-Permyak Nationality Okrug. Of the ten autonomous okrugs existing today, this is the only one which has a population exceeding 50,000; this homeland is therefore included along with the autonomous republics and autonomous oblasts throughout the remainder of this paper.

37. Joseph B. Schechtman, *European Population Transfers, 1939–1945* (New York: Oxford University Press, 1946), p. 388.

38. USSR, *Vsesoyuznaya Perepis' Naseleniya 1926 Goda*, vol. 17, table X; also USSR, *Itogi Vsesoyuznoy Perepisi Naseleniya 1959 Goda, Svodnii Tom* (Moscow: Gosudarstvennoye Statisticheskoi Izdatel'stvo, 1962), p. 186.

39. For the specific measure used, see Shannon's index in C. Shannon and W. Weaver, *The Mathematical Theory of Communication* (Urbana: University of Illinois Press, 1949).

40. When these same measures were calculated without using the figures for the Russian population, the trends remained unchanged, although the

indices were, as expected, lower (indicating a greater concentration of the local group).

41. The fact that the 1979 results seem in several cases to indicate a resumption in the direction of the earlier trend (towards diversity) is partly the result of the paucity of ethnic data available from the 1979 census. This unfortunate deficiency makes difficult any detailed comparison based on comparably defined regions of ethnic population settlement for the most recent period of Soviet history.

42. Ralph S. Clem, "The Ethnic Dimension of the Soviet Union" in Jerry G. Pankhurst and Michael Paul Sacks (eds.), *Contemporary Soviet Society: Sociological Perspectives* (New York: Praeger, 1980), p. 56.

43. Arutyunyan, "Konkretno-Sotsiologicheskoye Issledovaniye Natsional'nykh Otnoshenii"; L. N. Tarent'yeva, "Nekotoriye Storony Etnicheskikh Protsessov v Povolzh'ye, Priural'ye i na Yevropeyskam Severe SSSR,' *Sovyetskaya Etnografiya*, no. 6, (1972), pp. 38–51.

44. Connor, *The National Question in Marxist-Leninist Theory and Strategy*, p. 40.

45. Yu. V. Bromley, *Ethnic Processes* (Moscow: Academy of Sciences, 1983), p. 27.

46. Frank Lorimer, *The Population of the Soviet Union: History and Prospects* (Geneva: League of Nations, 1946), p. 54.

47. A third viewpoint, suggested by Ralph Clem, is that "the ethnoterritorial nature of the Soviet federation may allow for an expansion of ethnic interests to more closely approximate the constitutional prerogatives of the nationalities. In other words, the minorities may be able to use the system to their own advantage" (Clem, "The Ethnic Dimension of the Soviet Union," p. 56).

48. Cynthia Enloe, *Ethnic Conflict and Political Development* (Boston: Little, Brown, and Company, 1973), p. 116.

49. See, for example, Martha Brill Olcott, "Yuri Andropov and the 'National Question'," *Soviet Studies*, vol. 37 (January 1985), pp. 103–17.

50. R. I. Kosolapov (ed.), *Sotsial'naya Politika i Natsional'nye Otnosheniya* (Moscow: Mysl', 1982), pp. 10, 15.

Appendix 8.1   Hypothetical Formation of a Mordvinian ASSR

The Mordvinian nation, the largest minority in the Middle Volga without its own autonomous region, was granted an autonomous oblast at the beginning of 1930. This became the Mordvinian ASSR on December 20, 1934. Although the sizeable Mordvinian population ranked 11th in number among all Soviet peoples, it was dispersed widely enough to prevent recognition of significant regional concentrations. Nevertheless, 64.4 per cent of the total Mordvinian population was located throughout the Middle Volga region.

Regional Population Redistribution and National Homelands 159

HYPOTHETICAL FORMATION OF A MORDVINIAN ASSR

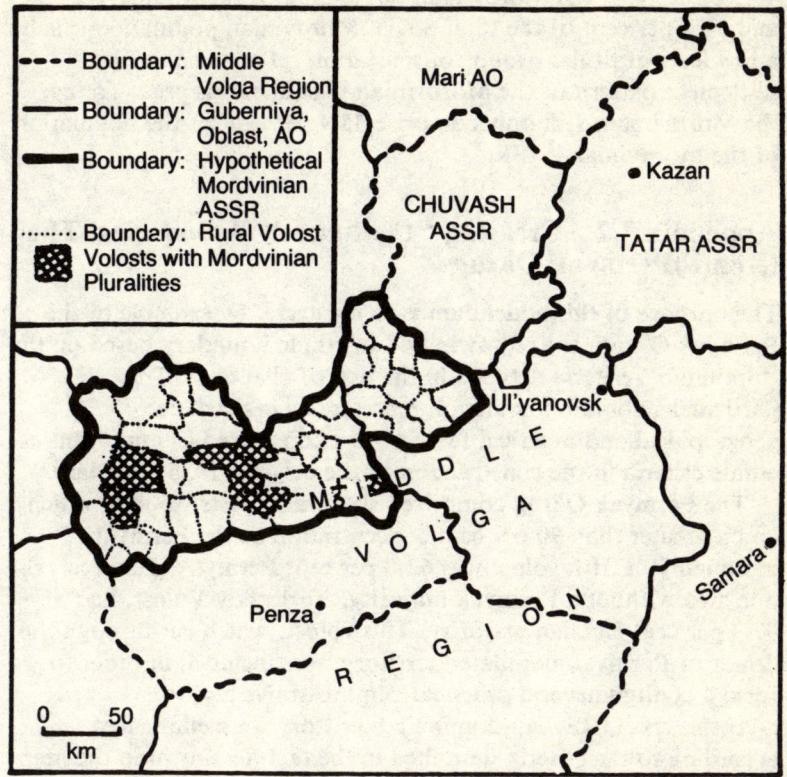

It was only once the results of the 1926 census became available that Soviet planners were able to identify precisely the distribution of the Mordvinian population for the purpose of demarcating a region of national autonomy for this numerically significant nationality. The map above is a hypothetical re-districting of boundaries drawn to form a jurisdiction that encompasses a substantial portion of the Middle Volga's Mordvinian population. Although this was not the exact scheme which was adopted, the borders of this hypothetical region closely approximate the actual boundaries of the Mordvinian ASSR today.

Four of the five uyezds which comprise the newly formed region are located in Penza guberniya, or province; the remaining one was taken from Ul'yanovsk guberniya (the Middle Volga contains four guberniya and two ASSRs). Only 6 of the 49 local volosts which

160 *Lee Schwartz*

make up this region have Mordvinian majorities and its total area contains a 27.4 per cent Mordvinian population. This represents 46.9 per cent of the Mordvinian population of the Middle Volga and 31.1 per cent of the total Soviet Mordvinian population. Such a low level of titular group concentration reflects the diffuse settlement pattern of the Mordvinian people in this area. Today, the Mordvinians still only comprise 35.4 per cent of the population of the Mordvinian ASSR.

Appendix 8.2 Creating "Optimum" Boundaries: The (Komi-)Permyak Okrug[a]

The purpose of this addendum is to illustrate, by example of the Permyak Okrug, the redrawing of an ethnic boundary based on the "optimum" criteria detailed in the text of chapter 8. This particular national jurisdiction represents a case where geographical and practical factors were considered as important as ethnic criteria in the construction of the original 1926 boundary.

The Permyak Okrug comprised six rural volosts, four of which had a greater than 90 per cent concentration of the Permyak nationality; a fifth volost was 62.0 per cent Permyak. However, the one area without a Permyak majority, Yurlinskiy Volost, had a 97.3 per cent Russian majority. This volost, which cut through the center of Permyak-populated territory, was included in order to form a contiguous and practical administrative region.

If this sixth, Russian-dominated territory were eliminated according to the criteria described in the text (as shown in the map opposite), the Permyak majority in its titular sub-unit would jump from 77.0 to 91.4 per cent. Considered in light of the odd shape which would have resulted, however, and the lack of information available at the time, the resulting compact boundary of the original Permyak Okrug appears to be a logical compromise between geography and ethnic composition.

[a] The parentheses are used to show that, although this region appears simply as the Permyak Okrug in the census of 1926, when it became a national okrug, the term Komi was added as a prefix. Today, this same territory is called the Komi-Permyak Autonomous Okrug.

CREATING "OPTIMUM" BOUNDARIES: THE (KOMI-) PERMYAK OKRUG

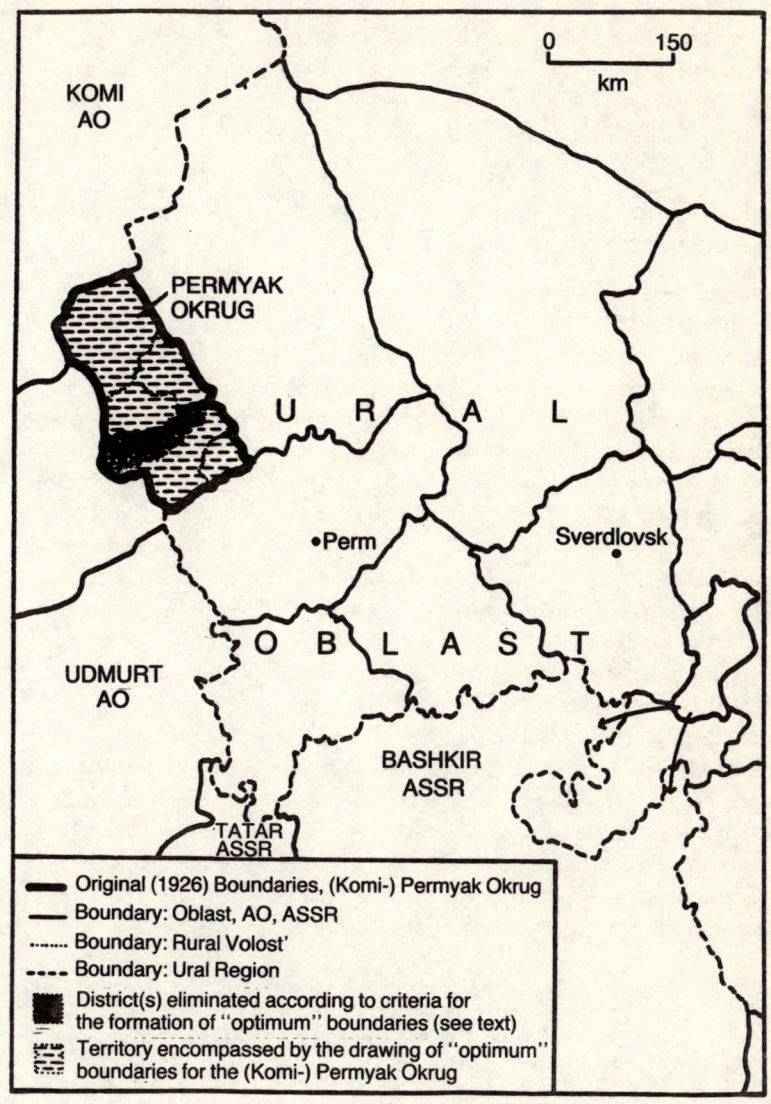

PART III

Observing Soviet Nationality Policies in Action

Chapter 9

Territorial Units as Nationality Policy

Allan Kagedan

> The Union of Soviet Socialist Republics is an integral, federal, multinational state formed on the principle of socialist federalism.... The USSR ... draws all its nations together for the purpose of jointly building Communism. (Soviet Constitution, 1977, Article 70)

The unrest that gripped the Armenian and Azerbaijanian Soviet Socialist Republics (SSRs) in 1988 revealed that tension is besetting Soviet federalism. The SSRs were in dispute over the status of Nagorno-Karabakh, an autonomous oblast which both SSRs claimed as their own. Their argument, which attracted Mikhail Gorbachev's personal attention, was driven by ethnic assertiveness on the part of Armenians and Azeris. But, not surprisingly, it was an issue in the administrative-territorial system that provided the spark to ignite the bitter, even violent, exchange.

Soviet territorial units were conceived originally as a means of satisfying undesirable ethnic sentiments. For Bolsheviks, who believed the *Communist Manifesto* dictum that working men had no country, federalism was an unhappy compromise.[1] The new Soviet leaders decided to accommodate the nationalities that had declared their territories independent during the 1918–1921 Civil War, a group that included Azeris, Bashkirs, Daghestanis, Georgians, Ukrainians and peoples of Transcaucasia. Moscow decided to offer the non-Russian nationalities the carrot of a territorial unit named for them to induce their acceptance of Soviet rule. Unable to eliminate national consciousness and unwilling to ignore it, the ever-realistic Bolsheviks opted to control this phenomenon.

Their instrument was Soviet federalism, a complicated arrangement of administrative-territorial units, each one serving as a license for ethnic expression within its boundaries. In designing the system, the Bolsheviks, led by Vladimir Lenin, relied on Marx's teaching that gradually class identity would replace ethnic sentiment. But the Bolsheviks believed that in the interim, national attachments should be permitted to wither away. "National differences," Lenin wrote, "and antagonisms between peoples are daily more and more vanishing owing to economic and technological advances. Socialism will cause these differences to vanish."[2] Soviet leaders predicted failure for any effort to stamp out ethnic identity. Worse, a campaign against national consciousness would trigger a bitter counter-reaction: separatism. As long as ethnic sentiment remained potent, the Soviet state should recognize it and control it: in other words, license it.

To control behavior, modern societies, among other things, issue licenses. Usually, licenses serve to restrict behavior which may—if pursued improperly—be dangerous. Thus, states issue drivers' licenses, liquor licenses, but, more to the point here, hunting licenses. Western societies are ambivalent toward hunting. It may serve a useful ecological purpose in limiting the size of herds and is popular among sportsmen. But since its instrument is a gun, and its aim is to kill, Western societies restrict the time and place where sportsmen can hunt. Should a hunter exceed the provisions of his license, the authorities can withdraw it. Licensing is a means of state control.

The Soviet administrative-territorial system is a licensing regime for ethnic sentiment. It permits Soviet leaders to instruct nationalities where they might exercise cultural and other rights (in the territory named for them), and prescribes that if the nationality member leaves that territory, his rights are diminished. Moscow uses federalism to reward or punish leaders of administrative-territorial units named for nationalities by controlling appointments within that unit's administrative structure. Local leaders' dependence on, and loyalty to, Moscow is thus assured. Equally, the Kremlin can dismantle a unit to punish an ethnic group; or create or upgrade a unit to garner support for a foreign or domestic policy goal.

A policy targeted at influencing the whole national question in the USSR through government action, the formation of administrative-territorial units fits Edward Allworth's definition of a nationality policy. In Allworth's scheme, this is a positive policy since it gives recognition to ethnic differences.[3]

The Soviet administrative-territorial system is complex.[4] At its peak is the federal government, the USSR. It possesses authority over the formation of new subordinate units, internal boundaries, local administration, laws, social and economic policy, education, the union-wide budget, war and peace, state security, international relations, foreign trade and other union-wide matters.

Subject to the overriding rights of the USSR, an SSR has its own constitution, participates in the deliberation of union-wide bodies, governs lower-level administrative units within its borders, and coordinates the activity of economic enterprises located within it. Each of the 15 SSRs possesses its own flag or official seal and constitution, subordinate to the USSR Constitution. Some SSRs boast their own foreign ministries, and two, the Ukrainian and Belorussian, hold seats in the United Nations. These UN delegates, like their colleagues in the foreign ministries and foreign offices of all the other republics, do not pursue policies independent of the USSR.

Republics possess legal codes, but these are subordinate to federal codes. Light industry is administered by joint union-wide and republic bodies. SSR officials implement central decisions locally. They also contribute to union-wide decisions by reporting on local conditions and assessing local reactions to a decision. Moscow might consult SSR officials about where in an SSR to locate a factory. Similarly, a decision to eliminate or introduce university-level teaching of a local language might demand consultation with republic leaders.

The republics' importance rests less in their capacity to wield political power than in their ability to serve as areas licensed for ethnic cultural life and ethnic educational and occupational advantage. Always sounding-boards for Soviet leaders in nationality policy, republics may trigger a rebuke from Moscow if they stray from the rules and become advocates for their nationality.

Below the SSRs are a range of smaller units. First come the 16 autonomous soviet socialist republics (ASSRs), which possess a constitution (subordinate to the constitution of the SSR in which it is located) and a supreme court. The ASSR is represented in union-wide bodies and it must consent to any change in its territory. ASSRs are located in the RSFSR; the sole exception, Nakhichevan, is in the Azerbaijanian SSR. The autonomous oblast (AO) or region is next down the ladder, and it, too, is subordinate to its parent SSR. The eight autonomous oblasts pass some of their own laws, and their governmental structures are supposed to function in the language of the ethnic group for which the unit is named. AOs are found in the RSFSR (5), the Georgian SSR (1), the Azerbaijan SSR

(1) and the Tadjik SSR (1). The lowest ranking autonomous unit is the autonomous okrug, or area, which exists for the small peoples of the North; okrug decisions on local matters are subject to the approval of higher bodies.

Another echelon of territorial units are purely administrative. These are the krais, the raions and the local soviets, which may be as small as a farming colony. Though originally conceived as economic units, these administrative units were given in many cases an ethnic character. Thus, in the 1920s and 1930s, for instance, the Russian Republic encompassed a multitude of administrative-territorial units, including a Crimean Tatar ASSR, a Jewish AO, a German raion and a Polish soviet.

Contradictions abound in the Soviet administrative-territorial system.[5] Territorial and ethnic boundaries in many cases do not coincide. The Kazakh SSR is more Russian in population than Kazakh. The Turkic and Persian populations of the Central Asian Republics do not fit into four neat divisions. To a degree, the administrative-territorial sub-units are intended to compensate for discrepancies between territorial boundaries and ethnic populations. Yet millions of Soviet citizens, beneficiaries of economic opportunity or victims of upheavals in Soviet history, live outside their namesake territories.

Real power, moreover, resides less in territorial structures than in the Communist Party of the Soviet Union (CPSU):[6] "The leading and guiding force of Soviet society and the nucleus of its political system, of all state organs and public organs . . . ." The Party's task is to determine the "general perspectives of the development of society and the course of the home and foreign policy of the USSR . . . ." In the ideological sphere, the Party is charged with implanting "a planned systematic and theoretically substantiated character to the struggle for the victory of Communism." The CPSU tries to achieve these aims by creating branches at a range of administrative-territorial units, from SSRs to village soviets.

Federalism worldwide involves a limited devolution of power from the central government to regional governments. The division of powers varies widely even between neighboring federal states: Canadian provinces possess much broader powers than American states. In the Soviet system, the supreme power of Communist Party unity mutes debates over divisions of authority between the natural adversaries—governmental structures such as the USSR and the SSRs. But the Communist Party's unifying influence is compromised by the fact that the administrative-territorial system has the task of influencing the nationality question, and the territorial units have become vessels of ethnic consciousness. Soviet-style federalism would enjoy easier sailing in a monoethnic society than in the ethnically divided society with which it must contend. Since 1917, the Soviet federal system, broadly speaking, has been challenged from three directions: Marxist-Leninist ideology; national security; and ethnic self-assertiveness. Historically, the Marxist-Leninist challenge has surfaced and resurfaced throughout Soviet history, national security concerns have been most salient during World War II, and ethnic group demands have sharpened since Mikhail Gorbachev assumed power in 1985.

Marxism, which emphasizes class consciousness and economic determinism, and Leninism, which applies Marxism to Soviet conditions, have been unhappily married to the administrative-territorial system. For Marxists, ethnic attachments count for less than class affiliation. Since the worker knows no fatherland, a socialist government progressing toward Communism is bound to diminish, and ultimately eliminate, ethnically based territorial units. To be sure, Soviet ideologists have accepted the continued existence of these units, much as they have coped with other unwanted phenomena. Inasmuch as (nonantagonistic) classes still exist, they reason, so may territorial units, constituents of the class superstructure. But even this rationalization of the territorial system does not go so far as to value the multitude of ethnic territories comprising the USSR.

Marxist-Leninist-driven efforts to compromise the federal system span Soviet history. In 1923 Iosif Stalin, who served in the 1920s as head of the Commissariat of Nationalities, put forward a plan to incorporate all the other republics into the Russian SSR. If accepted, Stalin's plan would have drained the federal system of even the limited meaning with which Lenin had invested it. Republic leaders protested against Stalin's proposal; many of them would pay for their openness later. More important, the ailing Lenin condemned the Stalin plan, declaring it to be motivated by Russian chauvinism. And one chauvinism, Lenin and his followers believed, begat others, which together would consume the Soviet experiment.[7]

The 1920s also saw an economically based challenge to the elaboration of the administrative-territorial system. Gosplan, the Soviet planning agency, proposed to subdivide the SSRs into economic zones called oblasts, and smaller economic districts called raions. The republic leaders objected and the oblast subdivision was abandoned; the raions were created but many assumed an ethnic coloration.[8]

The promulgation of the 1936 Constitution offered Stalin another opportunity to mold the territorial system to his liking. This time he possessed the power to achieve his goal. The new Constitution strengthened union-wide control of the SSRs by authorizing the federal legislature to establish the fundamentals of law to which the SSRs were required to conform. After Stalin's death, Soviet leaders restored the SSRs' law-making power but Brezhnev reversed this in the 1970s.[9]

Perhaps the boldest Marxist-Leninist challenge to the administrative-territorial system came in the CPSU's statement in its 1961 Program:

> The borders between the USSR's union republics are increasingly losing their former significance. Since all the nations are equal, their life is organized on a single socialist foundation . . . and they are all united into one family by . . . a single goal—Communism.[10]

This statement ignited a debate within the Soviet academic community that lasted into the middle of the 1970s and concluded with the 1977 Constitution's reaffirmation of federalism. The anti-federalists were more traditional Marxist-Leninists, who believed that federal arrangements were temporary, and felt that it was time to reform the current system. The federal system was no longer needed, one of their number, P. G. Semenov, wrote, because "the mutual assimilation of nations in essence denationalizes national-territorial autonomous units and even union republics. This brings Soviet society nearer to the point at which the full state-legal merging of nations will become a matter for the foreseeable future."[11]

The counterattacking commentators, whose view ultimately prevailed, argued that although the nationality question had largely been solved, problems of national relations remained. These stemmed from the ideological immaturity of the nations and imperialist propaganda. In addition, federalism proved that an internationalist spirit animates the policies of the Soviet leadership. Thus, the notion of eliminating the federal structure was premature and perilous. As one Soviet scholar put it:

> . . . during the discussion of the draft Soviet Constitution of 1977, various proposals were put forward that were based on the wrong assessment of the stage reached by Soviet society in its development. . . . The greater unity of the multinational Soviet people in no way means the abolition of nations and nationalities residing in the USSR.[12]

As in the 1920s, Soviet leaders wished to retain the federal system to license the powerful ethnic sentiments confronting them.

National security emerged as a challenge in the Soviet federal system in the 1940s. Stymied in his 1920s bid to form the Soviet federal system, Stalin did not shrink from altering it in the 1930s, as mentioned, and in the 1940s. In the initial phases of World War II, the Red Army suffered a series of crushing defeats which left large segments of Soviet territory in Nazi hands. The Nazis held portions of Belorussia, the Ukraine, the Crimean ASSR, and the Caucasus. Though their research on this period is scant, historians have presented a mixed picture of relations between the invaders and the Soviet peoples they encountered. Some Belorussians, Ukrainians, peoples of the Caucasus and others joined forces with the German invaders against the Red Army in order to win their independence, while others fought the occupiers. But Nazi indifference, even hostility, to the nationalities' cause, and the ultimate defeat of the Nazis by the Allies, turned this display of national assertiveness into a hollow gesture.[13] Pointing to the collaborators, Moscow decided to punish whole peoples for the misdeeds of some of their members.

The first casualty of wartime administrative-territorial change[14] was the Volga German ASSR, which was dissolved in August 1941, on the heels of the Nazi invasion of the Soviet Union. This established a pattern, soon to become familiar a few years later, in which whole communities—men, women and children—were herded into boxcars on one night's notice, if that, transported hundreds or thousands of miles from their homes, and deposited in isolated sites resembling prison camps. After the Red Army had recaptured the Caucasus, Moscow abolished the Caucasian Karachai AO (November 1943), the Kalmyk ASSR (December 1943), the Checheno-Ingush AO (February 1944), the Kabardino-Balkar ASSR (March 1944), and the Crimean Tatar ASSR (May 1944). The war also claimed smaller administrative-territorial units, such as the five Jewish districts of the Ukrainian SSR and Crimean Tatar ASSR, whose populations were either killed or evacuated to the Soviet interior. The authorities explained that the abolitions and deportations occurred because the populations had collaborated with the enemy. Moscow planned to replace the ousted residents with presumably more loyal Russians and other Slavs.

Following Stalin's death and the revelation of some of his crimes in Nikita Khrushchev's 1956 "secret speech," the Kremlin partially moved to redress wartime wrongs. The Checheno-Ingush ASSR was re-established in November 1956, followed by the Kalmyk AO, the Karachai-Cherkess AO, and the Kabardino-Balkar AO in 1957. However, the Crimean Tatar and Volga German ASSRs were neither reconstituted nor replaced. And a proposal to re-establish the abandoned Jewish districts was quashed. Loyal to the established administrative-territorial system, the reformist Soviet government was unwilling to forego all the "gains" that the war had bestowed. By removing territorial units from the Soviet map, the national-security-related tension present in the Soviet system did Marxism-Leninism's bidding. The fewer units, traditional Marxists believed, the better.

Indeed Soviet federalism may have realized its creators' dream and gradually passed into history were it not for a third, countervailing, tension: ethnic assertiveness. During the Civil War period, a number of nationalities, including Ukrainians, Georgians, Armenians, Azeris and others, declared themselves independent and resisted incorporation into the Soviet Union. Once defeated, the non-Russians lobbied successfully against Stalin's autonomization plan. Aided by the administrative-territorial system, the nationality elites began to establish themselves as the leaders of their peoples.

The purges of the late 1920s and 1930s left the republics with fewer personnel with a pre-Soviet nationally conscious past and a diminished appetite to challenge Moscow's authority. Except for the wartime collaboration of some members of nationality groups with the Germans, it was not until the Khrushchev era that the nationalities renewed their quest for broader autonomy.[15] The Crimean Tatars pressed for the reconstitution of their unit by circulating petitions among their ethnic fellows, presenting these to Soviet and international bodies, and meeting with and protesting against the authorities. Dissenters in the Baltic SSRs of Latvia, Lithuania and Estonia, which were incorporated into the Soviet Union during the 1940s, demanded greater autonomy—even freedom from Soviet rule. They called for the guaranteeing of their rights to use their native language, to display national symbols, like the national flags, and to reduce Slavic migration into the SSRs. The stirrings of the non-Russian nationalities in the 1960s and early 1970s were powerful enough to lead nationally conscious Russian writers like Alexander Solzhenitsyn to call on each nationality to choose whether it wished to remain a part of the Soviet Union.[16]

Despite a police crackdown on demonstrations, ethnic assertiveness continued in the late 1970s as well. In 1978 Soviet officials undertook a review of the SSR constitutions to ensure their conformity with the newly concluded basic law. A proposal to alter Article 75 of the Georgian SSR's constitution, which named Georgian as the unit's official language, and to invest Russian and other languages spoken in the SSR with the same status as Georgian, provoked mass demonstrations among the Georgian population. Moscow backed down. Another instance of ethnic assertiveness in defense of SSR prerogatives came in 1979. A rumor spread in the Kazakh SSR that the central authorities were contemplating the formation of a Volga German ASSR in the Kazakh republic. Mass protests followed, and the government, in the unlikely event that it was weighing this notion, shelved the idea.[17]

The determination of ethnic groups to harness the administrative-territorial system for their own needs has intensified since Mikhail Gorbachev assumed power in 1985.[18] Indeed by 1988 ethnic group assertiveness had become the primary challenge to Soviet federalism. One reason for this is Gorbachev's reformist policies of *glasnost'* and *perestroika*, which have emboldened ethnic groups to test Moscow's tolerance level.

The first large-scale expression of ethnic assertiveness under Gorbachev was touched off by a personnel change he engineered. On December 16, 1986, the Kremlin-appointed Gennady Kolbin, an ethnic Russian, replaced Dinmukhed Kunaev, an ethnic Kazakh, as First Secretary of the Communist Party of the Kazakh SSR. Soon after news of the change broke, Kazakhs filled the streets of Alma-Ata, the SSR capital, and began a demonstration that claimed one life and resulted in some 200 injured. Though the Kremlin did not retract the Kolbin appointment, it would be reasonable to assume that the event warned Moscow to avoid tampering with SSR prerogatives, even if this meant tolerating inefficiency and mismanagement.

Under Mikhail Gorbachev, the Crimean Tatars have renewed their attempt to reconstitute the Crimean Tatar ASSR. IN 1987 and 1988 the group demonstrated frequently in Moscow and in its Central Asian places of residence. The Soviet government responded by appointing a Commission, headed by Andrei Gromyko, to consider their case. In its June 1988 final report,[19] the Commission recommended that, while Crimean Tatars should be permitted, as individuals, to resettle in the Crimea, no special government assistance should be extended to the group as a whole to permit it to do so. Nor should the Crimean Tatar demand for autonomy be satisfied, the Gromyko Commission advised; indeed, "extremists" made this request. What was of primary importance, according to the Commission, was that "the country's existing administrative and territorial division, which was established many decades ago and is codified in the USSR Constitution, enables us to successfully accomplish the tasks of economic and social development of all the country's nations and nationalities."

An analogous issue arose regarding the Nagorno-Karabakh AO, located in the Azerbaijanian SSR. In 1921 Nagorno-Karabakh, whose population is predominantly Armenian, was included in the Azerbaijanian SSR. This incorporation has long been the object of Armenian protest. It is alleged that Armenians living in Nagorno-Karabakh have suffered economic and cultural discrimination at the hands of the Azerbaijanian authorities. These long-held grievances prompted numerous demonstrations of tens of thousands of Armenians and counterprotests by Azeris. In February 1988, 32 residents of Sumgait, a town in Nagorno-Karabakh, were killed during Armenian–Azeri fighting. In July 1988 striking Armenians shut down Yerevan's Zvarnots Airport.

The protests occurred against a background of conflicting resolutions favoring the annexation of Nagorno-Karabakh with the Armenian SSR, brought forward by legislative bodies in those two units, and rejection of this by the Azerbaijanian SSR. The matter was then taken up by a special session of the Supreme Soviet in July 1988. The session considered a draft resolution, ultimately approved, that rejected the annexation proposal. The viewpoints expressed at the meeting merit attention because they illustrate the nature of the debate between an SSR and central government.[20]

The Armenian SSR's position was that the 1920s decision to include Nagorno-Karabakh in the Azerbaijanian SSR was unjustified, and had led to decades of denial of economic and national rights to Armenians living there. It was necessary to redress this wrong. Article 11 of the Soviet Constitution provides that "State property, i.e. the common property of the Soviet people, is the principal form of socialist property. . . . The land, its minerals, waters, and forests are the exclusive property of the state. . . ." If all territory is state owned, then the state had the right to determine how to divide territory among the republics. The Armenians of Nagorno-Karabakh will not be satisfied with material benefits to the detriment of their "national, cultural and spiritual development," the Armenian representatives claimed. While the preferred option, they said, was to permit Nagorno-Karabakh to join the Armenian SSR, other possibilities, which would reduce Azerbaijanian influence on Nagorno-Karabakh, were: to place Nagorno-Karabakh under the supervision of the RSFSR; to upgrade its status to an ASSR level; or to place it under the supervision of central government representatives. Armenian representatives expressed concern that, should none of these options be chosen, louder protests and bloodier violence would ensue.

The Azerbaijanian representatives, in addition to denying that their SSR had discriminated against Armenians in Nagorno-Karabakh, rejected the Armenian call for annexation on the basis of Article 78 of the Soviet Constitution, which reads: "The territory of a union republic may not be altered without its consent. The boundaries between union republics may be altered by mutual agreement of the republics concerned, subject to ratification by the USSR."

The reference to Article 78 is misleading, if technically valid. The central Soviet authorities, if they wished, could force the Azerbaijanian SSR to agree to relinquish Nagorno-Karabakh. But the Kremlin chose not to. Why? As Mikhail Gorbachev said (at a July 1988 session of the Supreme Soviet): "We must find an answer to this question that will become a precedent for many other questions arising in the sphere of relations between nationalities." In other words, by bowing to Armenian demands, Moscow would be setting a dangerous precedent. Soon, other demands for territorial realignment would spring up, fueling new crises. Who would guess how many nationalities were dissatisfied with the status of their namesake territories? Each demand for change would trigger a counterdemand, heightening tension between nationalities and further embittering non-Russians toward Moscow. In the Soviet administrative-territorial system, there is little room for flexibility; change produces winners and losers.

In his remarks to the plenum, Gorbachev found fault with both sides, though the burden of criticism fell more heavily on the advocates of territorial change, the Armenians, whom he accused of using "antidemocratic" methods. Lev N. Zaikov, Moscow Party Committee First Secretary, added a traditional Marxist-Leninist position, stating that the "recarving" of boundaries could "break mutual economic ties and slow development of the united national-economic complex. Why should we replace one braking mechanism with another?" Since all republic boundaries were unhelpful obstructions to the progress of socialism, why further complicate the situation?

In the cases of the Crimean Tatars and the Armenians, Moscow rejected ethnic group demands for change. The Soviet leaders have a strong impulse to conserve the system; recent events in the Baltic republics, however, seem to indicate that Moscow may be open to reinvigorating it.

When Moscow absorbed the Baltic republics of Latvia, Lithuania and Estonia in the 1940s, it was natural to grant them SSR status. This enabled the Kremlin to depict its takeover of the regions as a free association of these republics with the USSR. The newly appointed republic leaders, Moscow hoped, would help to subordinate the population to Soviet rule. While some Baltic residents have welcomed the carrot of republic status, Moscow also used the stick—thousands of persons judged to be politically unreliable were arrested and deported—opening a wound among the Baltic peoples that has never healed.

The Sovietization of these newest republics continued for the following three decades. Moscow purged the republic communist parties of suspected "nationalists." Encouraged by the central government, the leadership of the Baltic republics promoted Russian-language schooling and use. In what many felt was a deliberate policy to dilute the national identities of the republics, Moscow sited factories in Estonia, Latvia and Lithuania and encouraged Russian and other Slavic laborers to settle there. By the 1980s the Slavic population of the Baltic republics was 50 per cent in Latvia, 20 per cent in Lithuania and 35 per cent in Estonia.

Since the 1950s underground national movements in the Baltic republics have aimed to preserve the local language and culture, to secure the dominant position of the local population, and to give content to the constitutionally provided paper autonomy of the SSRs. Some Baltic dissidents even advocated independence from the USSR. The Gorbachev era has seen Baltic activism soar to new heights. Tens of thousands of Balts demonstrated in 1987 and 1988 to press their cause. In 1988 Balts formed citizens' groups, reportedly with thousands of members, to demand economic self-rule, official recognition of the predominance of the local languages, restriction of immigration, enhancement of republic administrative authority, and the establishment of ethnically based army units.[21]

At the time of writing, Moscow is not acting against proponents of these proposals and has hinted that it is willing to consider them. The citizens' groups count among their members significant numbers of Communists who participated, it seems, with the CPSU's blessing. Neither the Baltic press nor the republic communist parties have shown hostility toward the movements.

A resolution on the nationality question adopted by the CPSU plenum on July 9, 1988, also showed an openness to change. The resolution, in the first place, conceded, that "natural growth of national self-awareness is underway" in the USSR. It called for: an extension of the rights of SSRs and autonomous entities by clarifying their jurisdication as compared with the jurisdiction of the USSR; greater budgetary authority for the SSRs; the establishment of commissions on ethnic relations at union-wide and local levels; clarification of the laws on AOs and okrugs; an improved program to foster Russian–local-language bilingualism; and the expansion of legal guarantees for ethnic group members living outside their namesake territories.[22]

At the same time, the resolution restates the standard Soviet formulation that "a new historical community—the Soviet people—has come into being." It asserts that "any gravitation towards national isolation" in economic matters "can only cause economic and cultural impoverishment." Russian remains the only language used across the USSR. Furthermore, the CPSU has opposed redrawing republic boundaries or granting an autonomous unit to a displaced people, like the Crimean Tatars. In an October 1988 interview Alexandr Yakovlev, head of the Central Committee on International Relations and said to be close to Gorbachev, rejected out of hand Baltic demands for a separate currency, and for independence from the USSR.[23]

The Soviet Communist Party, led by Mikhail Gorbachev, seems to be willing to inflate the administrative prerogatives of administrative-territorial units in recognition of the assertiveness of nationalism. It is prepared to deepen the symbolic stature of units for the ethnic groups that occupy them. By so doing, presumably, the CPSU hopes to squelch the emergence of secessionist sentiment, and imbue the Soviet people with patriotic feelings that will inspire economic productivity.

If so, the 1990s may see a swing of the pendulum away from a Marxist-Leninist policy line of weakening the administrative-territorial system and toward its strengthening, geared to satisfying ethnic demands. Far from withering away, as Lenin had hoped, the administrative-territorial system may assume a pivotal role in the Soviet future.

Notes

1. Cited in John Hazard, "Socialism and Federation," *Michigan Law Review*, April–May 1984, p. 1,185.

2. Vladimir Lenin, "Kriticheskie zametku po natsional'nomu voprosy," *Sochineniia*, 3rd ed., vol. 17 (Moscow: Partizdat, 1935), p. 145.

3. See "A Theory of Soviet Nationality Policies," ch. 3 of this volume, by Edward Allworth.

4. Boris Topornin, *The New Constitution of the USSR* (Moscow: Progress Publishers, 1980), pp. 258–64.

5. Gregory Gleason, "The Development and Role of Soviet Federalism," (University of Miami, April 1987), pp. 5–7.

6. Topornin, *The New Constitution of the USSR*, pp. 234–6.

7. "Dvenadtsatyi s"ezd RKP(b), 17–25 April 1923," *Steograficheskii Otchet* (Moscow: Izdatel'stvo Politicheskoi Literatury, 1968), pp. 447–9.

8. G. S. Gurovitch, F. I. Ivanov, V. N. Makimovskov (eds.), *Sotsialisticheskoie Gosudarstvennoe Stroitel'stvo* (Moscow: Izdatel'stvo Vlast' Sovetov, 1930), p. 8.

9. Hazard, "Socialism and Federation," pp. 1,191–3.

10. "Programma Kommunisticheskoi Partii Sovetskogo Soiuza," *Kommunist*, vol. 12 (1961) p. 84.

11. P. G. Semenov, "Programma KPSS o razvitii sovetskikh natsionalno-gosudarstvennykh otnoshenii," *Sovetskoe gosudarstvo i pravo*, vol. 12 (1961), p. 25.

12. Topornin, *The New Constitution of the USSR*, p. 150.

13. Alexander Alexiev and S. Enders Wimbush, *Ethnic Minorities in the Red Army* (Boulder: Westview Press, 1988), pp. 108-16.

14. The history of the wartime deportations may be found in Alexander Nekrich, *The Punished Peoples* trans. George Saunders (New York: W. W. Norton, 1978).

15. The development of Soviet dissidence is chronicled in Ludmilla Alexeeva, *Soviet Dissent* (Middletown: Wesleyan University Press, 1985), pp. 137-60, 60-102.

16. Alexeeva, *Soviet Dissent*, p. 443.

17. Ludmilla Alexeeva and Valery Chalidze, *Mass Rioting in the USSR* (Silver Spring, Maryland: Foundation for Soviet Studies, 1985), pp. 132-3.

18. Alexeeva, *Soviet Dissent*, pp. 106-16; Allan Kagedan, "Gorbachev and the Nationalities: Soviet Ethnic Protest, December 1986-December 1987," ORAE Extra-Mural Paper, no. 47 (Dept. of National Defence, Canada, April 1988).

19. *Pravda*, June 9, 1988, p. 6.

20. *Pravda*, July 20, 1988, pp. 1-4

21. Radio Free Europe, *Research Reports: Baltic Area*, SR 9, 10 (August, September 1988).

22. 19th All-Union Conference of the CPSU, *Documents and Materials* (Moscow: Novosti Publishing House, 1988) pp. 146-51.

23. *New York Times*, October 28, 1988, p. A8.

Chapter 10

The Famine of 1932–1933: A Watershed in the History of Soviet Nationality Policy

James E. Mace

It is obvious that Soviet nationality policy underwent a complete reversal in the 1930s. In the late 1920s the policy of indigenization (*korenizatsiia*), a policy of bending over backward to placate the Soviet Union's non-Russians, was at its quantitative height. It was a three-pronged policy: foster the development of the local language and culture; recruit members of the indigenous national group into the Party and state apparatus; and employ the local language in all Party and state business. This, in turn, led to an attempt to "de-Russify" the cities of the non-Russian republics by encouraging Russified urban dwellers to learn the local language and by attempting to prevent urbanization from leading to Russification. Schoolchildren learned their Russian history from the textbooks of M. N. Pokrovskii, who taught that the Russian Empire had been a prison of nations built on looting the less powerful.[1] And at the same time, those belonging to the larger non-Russian groups were also taught the history of their own particular nation. At least some of the non-Russian literatures and cultures in the 1920s went through a period of unprecedented creativity, thanks in no small measure to official encouragement and financial support. The Party officially considered Russian great-power chauvinism a greater ideological danger than local nationalism. Politically, a strong Soviet Ukraine did everything it could to try to ensure that the prerogatives of the union republics were taken seriously by central authorities.

All this changed in the 1930s. Indigenization became a dead letter. The local language was no longer favored in the cities. National histories were replaced by a rewritten "history of the USSR," bearing a distinctly Russian cast, while non-Russian histories virtually disappeared. The non-Russian writers most read in the 1920s were either silenced or the content of their works was made virtually indistinguishable from Russian socialist realism. Local nationalism displaced Russian chauvinism as the greater danger, and much hitherto official policy in the union republics was now condemned as "bourgeois nationalist deviation." Soviet Ukraine, earlier the bulwark of centrifugal union republic aspirations, was transformed into a "model Soviet republic," its elites closely guarded against any manifestation of "national deviationism."

In the 1920s the Ukrainian SSR enjoyed greater relative autonomy than any other Soviet republic. Some Ukrainian Communists openly called for Ukraine to distance itself from Moscow in politics, culture and economics.[2] Official spokesmen, like Mykola Skrypnyk and Hryhorii Petrovs'kyi, tended to take the lead in protesting any encroachment by central authorities on union republic prerogatives, making the Ukrainian SSR a leader of non-Russian and republic political interests in the union as a whole. And not all influential Ukrainians were in Kharkiv, capital of the republic: from 1926 to the Great Purge, Hryhorii Hryn'ko (Grigorii Grin'ko) held some of the most powerful economic posts in the Soviet Union. Hryn'ko had come to Communism as a Borot'bist, member of the Ukrainian revolutionary group which was merged with the Ukraine's Bolsheviks in 1920. In fact, it was he who negotiated the merger.

Ukraine's clout as a union republic merely reflected its size and importance. Of 69 million non-Russians in the Soviet Union in 1926, 31 million were Ukrainians, who outnumbered the next largest nationality by almost seven to one.[3] In 1931 the Ukrainian SSR had 31.4 million inhabitants, while the other five non-Russian union republics together had only 18.7 million inhabitants.[4] In industry and agriculture Ukraine was also the most productive part of the Soviet Union. Keeping such a large and powerful entity in line was no easy task for the Kremlin. It is hardly surprising, then, that Ukrainization—the Ukrainian version of indigenization—developed farther and more fully than any other version of the policy.

Toleration of Ukrainian self-assertion was, of course, a function and major component of nationality policy, which in turn reflected policy toward the countryside. After all, it was the countryside, not the Russified cities, which made the so-called borderlands non-Russian, and the "national question" was seen, as Stalin himself put it, as "essentially a problem of the peasantry."[5]

Crushing the peasantry, in turn, allowed Stalin to curtail the self-assertion of the overwhelmingly rural non-Russians. Since the Ukrainian problem was by far the largest single component of the nationality problem, crushing the Ukrainian peasantry was crucial to Stalin's new Russocentric nationality policy. Seen in this light, the famine of 1932–1933 was a crucial event in the contemporaneous reversal of Soviet nationality policy, and the policies that produced and exacerbated the famine were closely connected with considerations of nationality policy. Neither the new nationality policy nor the famine itself can be understood without reference to the other. They were two sides of the same coin.

Stalin's 1925 statement linking the nationality problem and the peasant problem was not merely descriptive; it is a key to Bolshevik thinking about both issues. Nor was it original: as early as 1919, the Eighth Party Congress discussed the nationality question as a facet of the peasant problem.[6] The Tenth Congress, which proclaimed the New Economic Policy (NEP), also ordered Bolsheviks to overcome their latent Russian chauvinism and actively support the development of non-Russian cultures.[7] In the discussion preceding the latter resolution's adoption, Stalin went so far as to speak of the "inevitability" of Ukraine's cities ultimately becoming Ukrainized.[8] Indigenization was adopted two years later precisely in order to avoid antagonizing the non-Russian peasantry along national lines.[9] And 1925, the high point of NEP, was when Moscow forced the still predominantly Russian Communist Party (bolshevik) of Ukraine (CP[b]U) to take Ukrainization seriously by appointing a new First Secretary, Lazar Kaganovich, who immediately set about Ukrainizing the Party, state and trade union apparatuses, as well as making Ukrainian the language of command in local Red Army units.[10] The fact that some Ukrainian Communists wanted to go even faster and farther does not alter the fact that Moscow was forcing the CP(b)U as a whole to go farther than most of its members would have wished.

The forced collectivization of agriculture altered the political constellation upon which earlier nationality policy had been based in two ways, by necessitating the centralization of authority in Moscow and by negating the political expediency of indigenization. Indigenization implied concessions to centrifugal aspirations in the Soviet political structure. It weakened the main centripetal force of Russian culture in the cities and political *apparats* of the periphery, which were to "take root" in non-Russian soil and thereby gradually cease to be Russian. It legitimized attachment to non-Russian nations and their cultures as something other than "bourgeois nationalism." Collectivization, however, was decreed and carried out at the insistence of the center, often in the face of much local opposition, and this required the center to take more and more power at the expense of the union republics and other intervening levels of authority. It meant completely reorganizing life in every village throughout the Soviet Union, which implied a hitherto unknown level of social penetration by the leadership in Moscow, a truism embodied in the Soviet saying of the late 1930s that no more than three people ever stood between

Stalin and the lowliest collective farmer. As to the second reason, indigenization had been based on the same political necessities as had NEP—the need to placate peasants, with indigenization aimed at non-Russian peasants and the national intelligentsia which had commanded substantial peasant allegiance during the Civil War. Collectivization meant abandoning any attempt to placate peasants; it was a war against the peasantry, abrogating the agrarian peace of which NEP and indigenization had been the cornerstones.

In the ideological sphere in Ukraine, the five-year plan meant attacking people and ideas that had hitherto enjoyed official sanction. Until mid-1928 those who had been attacked as "national deviationists" in the CP(b)U—most notably the politician Oleksander Shums'kyi, the writer Mykola Khvyl'ovyi and the educator *cum* economist Mykhailo Volobuiev—had all in some way criticized official policy. But a few months after the Shakhty Trial ushered in the Cultural Revolution, the ideological *Piatiletka*, the leading Ukrainian official historian, Matvii Iavors'kyi, came under attack for "portraying the history of Ukraine as a distinct process," that is, as something significantly different from Russian history. A good many Ukrainian Communists had hitherto taken it for granted that theirs was a separate country, a member of a Soviet Union composed of those nations in which Soviet rule had been established, a Soviet Union which only coincidentally more or less corresponded with the geography of the old Russian Empire. In this view, Ukraine did things differently precisely because it was a different country. The Moscow-orchestrated campaign aimed at denying Ukraine a separate history boded ill for those with this view, for how can a country be distinct without its own history?[11]

The first wave of collectivization was followed in Ukraine in the spring of 1930 by the Union for the Liberation of Ukraine show-trial of 45 prominent Ukrainian so-called bourgeois nationalist intellectuals. Before the trial thousands more intellectuals were arrested, and the Ukrainian Autocephalous Orthodox Church was forcibly "self-liquidated."[12] This attack on the national intelligentsia, which had provided leadership to the Ukrainian movement during the Revolution, had two implications. First, hitherto permissible national self-assertion in the cultural sphere was cast beyond the pale as "wrecking." Second, concessions which had been conceded to the intelligentsia were withdrawn in tandem with the dismantling of NEP. The suppression of the nationally minded church, which had successfully penetrated about a third of Soviet Ukraine's villages, went hand in hand with the first wave of dekulakization, which also tended to disenfranchise the most nationally conscious stratum of the

Ukrainian village. That they occurred as part of the All-Union antireligious campaign, which did not liquidate the Russian Orthodox Church, and as part of the Stalinization of the intelligentsia, which made Moscow-based "radical" ideas dominant, does not alter the fact that in Ukraine they had different national implications, different ends, and were carried out differently than in Russia.

Stalin's March 1930 "Dizziness from Success" speech, which signaled a temporary retreat from forced collectivization by denouncing violations of the principle that collectivization should be voluntary, had its nationality policy counterpart in his July report to the 16th Party Conference, where he denounced those who expected an early convergence and merger (*sblizhenie i sliianie*) of nations in the Soviet Union. Stalin now found that Lenin had "always stood for *helping* the peoples of the USSR to develop their own national culture." Great Russian culture could claim no privileges whatever, for "Great Russian chauvinism" was "the greatest danger to the Party in the sphere of the national question."[13]

The dialectical juxtaposition of Great Russian chauvinism and local nationalism was analogous to that of Right deviationism and Left distortionism in agrarian policy. The Party was always supposed to fight "on two fronts" against both "deviations," but, since any conceivable policy could always be denounced as a deviation in one direction or the other, giving one priority over the other as the main danger of the moment was Stalin's way of signaling policy shifts. Never one to give direct public orders if he could avoid it, Stalin forced his subordinates to evolve a "sixth sense" about what he wanted from such shifts in emphasis while maintaining the myth of continuity in the Party line. And, just as his criticism of "Leftist practice" in forced collectivization meant that peasants would be allowed to leave the collective farms temporarily, emphasizing Great Russian chauvinism as a greater danger than non-Russian nationalism meant a temporary return to some toleration of non-Russian national self-assertion.

In 1932 a chain of events took place which would shift the balance the other way. In February of that year Molotov officially acknowledged that the 1931 drought in the Volga Basin, Western Siberia and Kazakhstan had damaged the grain crop.[14] Limited aid was even sent. But no such difficulties were acknowledged in Ukraine or the North Caucasus, where they certainly also existed. In March, after the complete fulfillment of the procurements quota for the 1931 crop in the North Caucasus *krai*, "shock-work methods" had been employed to take an additional 40,000 metric tons of seed grain, which had been shipped as drought relief beyond the Volga.[15] Surely, had Ukraine been able to meet its quota, a similar supplement to the plan would also have been imposed on it. After all, when famine had struck the Volga Basin and the Ukrainian steppe a decade earlier, Moscow requested aid only for the Volga, and the Ukrainian SSR had to send half its grain reserve to the Volga, with even starving regions like Mykolaïv (Nikolaev) having to participate.[16]

Except for Kazakhstan, the areas where hardship was admitted and perhaps even ameliorated differed from those where it was not, most likely because the latter were considered politically suspect on national grounds. Kazakhstan, where mass starvation had begun in 1930 in connection with the forced "sedentarization" of nomadic herdsmen, in 1932 received two million *poods* of grain, released by the central government as food and seed to its nomads and semi-nomads.[17] True, Kazakhstan created some problems with revived anti-Soviet resistance. But then, with perhaps a third fewer Kazakhs left than had earlier inhabited the USSR, any problem there was largely solved.[18]

The other response to the difficulties of the 1931–1932 crop year was a series of all-union concessions known collectively as the May reforms. These included a decrease in the grain quotas to roughly what had actually been procured from the 1931 crop and the legalization of private grain trade after procurement quotas had been met (i.e. not before January 15, 1933) as an incentive to peasants. Combating Left distortions overshadowed Right deviations with the introduction of a campaign "for socialist legality" in dealing with peasants.[19]

The turning point in peasant policy came in the summer of 1932. In July, at the Third All-Ukrainian Party Conference, virtually every one of Ukraine's top Communists cited "food supply difficulties" in various parts of Ukraine.[20] But Viacheslav Molotov, sent to Kharkiv as Stalin's personal emissary, specifically cited Trans-Volga difficulties as a major reason why Ukraine had to meet its obligations to procure grain for the central authorities. He also denounced any notion that the quotas in Ukraine might be too high as an "anti-Bolshevik idea" that had to be repulsed.[21] Meanwhile, Stalin's other emissary, Kaganovich, made it clear that, "Above all, all efforts must be directed at successfully bringing in the harvest and totally fulfilling the grain procurements plan."[22] The Conference accepted the grain procurements quota Moscow insisted on—356 million *poods*.[23]

Subsequent months witnessed a series of repressive measures which reversed the May concessions. Best known is the law of August 7, 1932, "On Safeguarding Socialist Property," which authorized the use of the death penalty or a ten-year prison term in cases where a peasant "stole" an ear of wheat or a sugar-beet root from the crop he had helped produce.[24] Though the law was in force for less than half the year, fully 20 per cent of all persons convicted in Soviet law courts in 1932 were sentenced under it, and Stalin hailed it as the basis of "socialist legality at the present moment."[25]

From the very beginning of the 1932 procurements campaign, the impossibility of Ukraine meeting its quota was obvious. As early as August 3 it was announced that the initial results of the July procurements had been "highly unsatisfactory," only 15.6 per cent of the plan and 5.3 times less than had been procured in the same period of the previous year.[26] The Party was told, "The class struggle surrounding the grain procurements has sharpened with particular force. The *kulak*, defeated but not yet completely eliminated, does and will continue to insanely resist the grain procurements." He could be overcome only through "unrelenting struggle against the *kulak* and against his agents." The main thing was to "guarantee victory in the struggle for bread." "Right opportunism" was elevated to the main danger.[27] The new policy quickly wreaked havoc in the already impoverished countryside. On September 5 an official report noted that many peasants were fleeing the collective farms, the migration in some places assuming a "mass character," largely because of "distortions of the Party line" committed during the grain procurements.[28]

Officials who lagged in seizing grain were punished, at first by censure or removal, later by arrest. On September 16 the Odessa *oblast'* Party bureau censured four *raion* Party organizations for non-fulfillment of the grain procurements quota. On October 5 the Kiev *obkom* secretariat was censured for non-fulfillment, and at the *raion* level eight Party committees were censured and another 12 were singled out with a warning to their secretaries. From June 1 to October 1 a total of 121 of Ukraine's 494 *raion* government heads were replaced. From July 1 to November 1, 47 *raikom* secretaries were replaced. And the *raion* did likewise with recalcitrant village authorities, replacing them with those more willing to seize grain.[29]

As the republic pressured its local and regional officials, so Moscow pressured the republic. In October 1932 Ukraine's Party apparatus was "strengthened" by the transfer of Mendel' Khataievych from the Middle Volga *obkom* to the post of Second Secretary of the CP(b)U. Simultaneously, the first deputy head of the All-Union OGPU, Ivan Akulov, became head of the Donbas *obkom*:[30]

The appointments were clearly intended to speed up the procurements. As Stalin's man in Ukraine, Khataevich emphasized that:

> ... the issue of the grain procurements ... is an issue of primary importance. We must guarantee the complete delivery of bread to the working class and the Red Army. *So long as the annual grain procurements plan is not wholly fulfilled, this task will be primary and decisive.*[31]

On November 20 the Ukrainian Soviet government ordered the verification of all bread resources on the collective farms, made further distribution of food to collective farmers before the complete fulfillment of the grain procurements a crime, ordered the immediate seizure of "stolen" bread, and made collective farm board members responsible for the misappropriation of foodstuffs subject to the law of August 7.[32] A second decree authorized village Soviets to levy on individual farmers who "perniciously" failed to meet their grain quota an additional meat delivery quota equal to their regular meat quota for a 15-month period.[33]

On December 6, following an expedient already tried in the Kuban, an initial six villages were placed on the "blacklist" (*chorna doshka*) and subjected to an economic blockade consisting of: (1) closing all stores and removing their goods from the village; (2) imposing a complete ban on all trade, including that in food; (3) calling in all loans and advances, including food; and (4) thoroughly purging local officials and the collective farm (exclusion from the collective farm at that time meant a *de facto* sentence of death by starvation).[34] On December 13, 82 *raions* were blacklisted, and the Ukrainian Central Committee ordered the Dnipropetrovsk and Kharkiv *obkoms* to expropriate immediately 1,500 individual peasants who had not met their quotas.[35]

On December 10 the Ukrainian SSR authorities officially blamed the shortcomings on the failure of *oblast'*, *raion* and village organs of power to mobilize Soviet society "against the sabotage of the grain procurements by the *kulaks* and their agents, the remnants of the Petliurists and Makhnovists." *Raion* and village authorities were ordered to seize "illegally distributed" grain from all collective farms which had not fulfilled the quota, to force the tight-fisted (*tverdozdavtsi*) to immediately give up their imagined hoards of grain, and to enforce on uncollectivized peasants who "maliciously undermined" the grain procurements the punitive meat quotas authorized in the November 20 decree. Threshing was to be speeded up under state supervision, collective farms and their officials purged of so-called *kulak* counter-revolutionary elements, and more people sent to the countryside to seize grain.[36]

Lax local officials were now arrested. On December 14 *Visti* described two such cases awaiting trial by a people's court. One culprit from Odessa *oblast'*,

> instead of struggling for bread in a Bolshevik manner, went with the hostile class element, obstructed investigation of matters for which the *kulaks* and tight-fisted were responsible, and let them off with a slap on the wrist. This was actually giving aid to the *kulak* in his struggle against the grain procurements.

The second was a former *raikom* secretary from Kiev *oblast'*, who had allegedly impeded the grain procurements by playing up to the *kulaks* and the tight-fisted, letting them evade punishment and ameliorating their lot. *Oblast'* prosecutors were ordered to be "vigilant" in the search for such "criminals."[37]

More cases followed. On December 21 the CP(b)U Central Committee removed ten leading *raion* officials from their posts "for total inaction" and "failure to carry out measures to break the *kulak* sabotage of the grain procurements." A joint Party–state decree ordered the expulsion from the Party and arrest of five directors of state farms "for criminally frustrating the task of the Party and state in the grain deliveries."[38] A week later the entire leadership of Kobeliats'kyi *raion*, Kharkiv *oblast'*, received sentences of two to ten years' imprisonment for supposedly organizing "*kulak* sabotage of the grain procurements."[39]

In spite of such "encouragement," at the beginning of 1933 Ukraine had procured only 74.5 per cent of its grain quota, which had by then been reduced to 300 million *poods*, and none of Ukraine's *oblasts* had fulfilled their quotas.[40] It is doubtful if there was very much left to seize by this point, given the level of repressions meted out to those charged with its seizure, and, given this, any lowering of the quota short of completely suspending the enforcement of the procurements was of no significance. Yet the seizures continued along with the dismissals and arrests of local officials who had been denounced for "inactivity" or acting as the "agents" of the *kulaks*, the "tight-fisted" and the "saboteurs" of grain procurements.

Stalin addressed the procurements breakdown at a January 1933 joint plenum in Moscow. While there had been harvest losses in Ukraine and the North Caucasus, he declared, they were far less than in the preceding year, and therefore, they could not be the cause of the procurements shortfall. Rather, many Communists had not realized that the collective farmer was still petty bourgeois and the collective farms were full of hidden class enemies and counter-revolutionaries.[41] According to Stalin, members of various counter-revolutionary organizations had been able to worm their way into the collective farms, turning them into veritable nests of counter-revolution, such that in many of them well-masked anti-Soviet elements were organizing wrecking and sabotage. These hidden wreckers

> ... do not say "down with the grain procurements." They are "for" the procurements. They "only" allow themselves the demagogy of demanding that the collective farm keep a forage reserve three times greater than really necessary, that the collective farm keep an emergency reserve three times greater than really necessary, that the collective farm distribute for food six to ten pounds of bread a day to each worker, and so forth.[42]

Such denial of reality was typical of Stalin: the bread was merely being hoarded by the hidden class enemy, and the Communists had to take it. This was pure fantasy on two counts: not only was there no bread to take, the persistence of the "class enemy" was also a myth. The Party itself had implicitly recognized the latter by ordering a halt to the mass deportation of *kulaks* in May 1932: afterwards only individuals, not families, could be deported.[43] But a month later, as the famine worsened, Stalin managed to top even this when he proclaimed the slogan: "Make every peasant a collective farmer and every collective farmer wealthy."[44]

Stalin seems to have seized the opportunity created by the famine to impose measures either directly or indirectly related to nationality policy.

First, a Party–state decision of December 14, 1932, ordered the Ukrainian Central Committee and Soviet government:

> To turn serious attention to the proper implementation of Ukrainization, to cease carrying it out mechanistically, to disperse Petliurists and other bourgeois nationalist elements from the Party and Soviet organizations, to painstakingly select and educate Ukrainian Bolshevik cadres, and to safeguard the Party's systematic leadership and control over the way Ukrainization is carried out.[45]

On the following day, by decision of the All-Union Central Committee, a telegraphed order decreed the immediate Russification of all Ukrainian institutions in the USSR outside the Ukrainian SSR.[46]

The second measure—one not usually associated with nationality policy—was taken at the January 1933 joint plenum: the creation of the political sections of the Machine-Tractor Stations and State Farms. This greatly undermined the power of territorial Party and state authorities by placing the rural population largely under the control of an apparatus independent of territorial authorities.[47]

The third measure was the January 24, 1933, decision of the All-

Union Central Committee to take virtually direct control of the CP(b)U. In spite of all the measures taken by the authorities in Ukraine, the Central Committee censured the CP(b)U for its failure to meet the targets set for state grain procurements, and "strengthened" the Ukrainian apparatus by appointing Pavel Postyshev as new Second Secretary over Khataevich, making him *de facto* ruler, and appointing three new *obkom* secretaries.[48] It was a real coup d'état: Stalin now controlled two of the three CP(b)U Central Committee secretaries and four of Ukraine's seven *obkoms* through the October and January appointments. And with control of the top came change at the bottom.

By October 15, 1933, massive personnel changes had been carried out. Postyshev sent his own new men to Ukraine's 494 *raions* and to the countryside: 1,340 to *raion* leadership posts, including 237 *raion* Party secretaries, 249 *raion* executive committee chairmen, and 158 *raion* control commission chairmen. At the same time, 643 machine tractor station political sections and 203 state-farm political sections were organized, staffed by 3,000 "leading workers." Another 10,000 were sent directly to the collective farms, 3,000 of whom took over as either *kolkhoz* chairmen or secretaries of *kolkhoz* Party organizations.[49] Hryhory Kostiuk aptly described the total picture as "that of a wholesale occupation of key posts in the country by the staff of Stalin's satrap."[50]

Postyshev met initial opposition from within the CP(b)U but quickly overcame it. A plenum called immediately after his arrival lasted only 20 minutes and was conducted as a pure formality. Postyshev accused the leadership of "wanting to hide" rather than "give the Central Committee's decision its due."[51]

On February 4 Postyshev called an open joint plenum of the Kharkiv *obkom*, *gorkom*, Party secretaries of agricultural *raions* in the *oblast'*, and activists. He used it to dress down the entire CP(b)U organization for its "temporizing" in the struggle for bread. The policy was to seize as much grain as possible, ostensibly for the approaching spring sowing. He made it clear that no aid for the sowing was to be expected from Moscow. Seed for the sowing was to be seized by the same methods as it had been "procured." And since any advance distributed by *kolkhozes* which had not met their quotas, including the customary post-threshing advance, was now "illegally distributed grain," any grain in the possession of those who had not met their quotas was now officially subject to immediate seizure.[52] Postyshev added: "The task of preparing and carrying out the spring sowing requires the substantial strengthening of our repressive measures against *kulaks*, sub-*kulaks*, Petliurists, wreckers and other anti-Soviet elements."⁵³ Such enemies were also to be found within the Party, and loyal Bolsheviks were obliged to be vigilant in rooting out "wreckers" and "saboteurs" who had wormed their way into responsible posts:

> ... unverified persons have been admitted into the Party, and on the sly here and there Petliurists and White Guard elements have sneaked in. ...
> There have even been cases where Communists have led in organizing the sabotage of the grain procurements. This is the enemy within the Party executive, who organized the mass theft of grain and then advised "don't bury it in one pit, but bury the grain in dozens of pits." This is the Petliurist, the White Guard, the wrecker, who, having sneaked into the organization, has become the inspirer, organizer and leader of various malicious acts against the Soviet power and collective farm construction.⁵⁴

The February 5–7 CP(b)U Central Committee plenum gave Postyshev victory when First Secretary Stanislav Kossior gave his theoretical subordinate full public support, stating that the January 24 censure applied to "our whole Party organization in organizing and carrying out the grain procurements." The fact that a mere 225 million *poods* had been procured from the 1932 crop was inexcusable, since more had been procured from the allegedly worse 1931 harvest. Culprits were "lack of Bolshevik vigilance" and "illusion" that the plan could be met without full mobilization, which had allowed the peasants to carry out mass theft and to sell off the grain illegally before the Party even noticed it. Only in November had the CP(b)U really mobilized for the "struggle for bread."⁵⁵ And by then the class enemy had wormed his way into the regime. Echoing Stalin's January speech, Kossior declared:

> New forms of the class enemy's struggle against the grain procurements rose up in our midst. The class enemy "was sought" as before outside the collective farm, but he, having sneaked into the collective farm in such posts as storekeeper, bookkeeper, supervisor, etc., organized theft, covered up to protect the thieves, and the illegal sale of grain. ...
> When you go to a *raion* on grain procurements business, they start to pull out of every pocket figures and tables on a lower harvest, which are from start to finish put together by <u>hostile elements who have entrenched themselves in the collective farms, land sections, and the MTS</u>. But you don't find one single word about the crop that was on the root and was pulled up, stolen and hidden. Our comrades, including some plenipotentiaries, by failing to examine these false figures shoved at them, have in numerous cases become *kulak* advocates armed with these figures. In numerous

cases it has been shown that this arithmetic is *kulak* arithmetic, according to which we would not have procured even half of the grain we have procured thus far. In the hands of the class enemies, false figures and empty talk were a cover for the grain being stolen and carried off in all directions.

The Party had to expose this "*kulak* arithmetic" as a "machination of the class enemies" and not allow it "to weaken our position in the struggle for bread."[56] Many *raions* had failed to notice that collective farms had fallen "under the influence of *kulak*, Petliurist, Makhnovist and other elements," and "as a result of our complacency and lack of Bolshevik vigilance, even in the best *raions* the *kulaks* and wreckers have wormed their way into the leadership of many collective farms and organize the sabotage of the grain procurements there."[57]

Kossior blamed the *apparat* down to the *raion* level for sabotage: they had hoped for a lower plan and, when they were disappointed, sat out or sabotaged the "struggle for bread." Even those who had diverted grain from procurement to seed reserves were also "opportunists" and "agents of the class enemies." Had the *obkoms* been vigilant, the *raion* authorities would not have been able to engage in the various cases of wrecking that had now been exposed. The official policy was that "the state must be given grain first, and only later are reserves to be created."[58]

Soon after the plenum, the Central Committee's theoretical journal published a lead editorial emphasizing the same theme, calling the breakdown of the grain procurements "shameful," blaming it for its failure to enforce from the first days of the harvest the fulfillment of the peasants' "very first of their obligations—the obligation to the state in the matter of grain deliveries." It also denounced the practice of leaving seed reserves before the procurements target had been met.[59]

It soon became apparent, however, that everything had already been seized, and without aid there would be no harvest for the coming year. This led on February 25, 1933, to a seed loan from union stockpiles of 20,300,000 *poods* of grain to Ukraine and another 15,300,000 *poods* to the North Caucasus, specifically to the Kuban. The resolution stated that the loan was being extended as seed and fodder because unfavorable weather had led to harvest losses in the steppe regions. Some of the loan was indeed consumed as food, usually distributed in the collective farm fields in order to give the peasants an incentive to work on the spring sowing.[60]

Even then, the pressure on the countryside did not ease until after the harvest had been brought in. As late as June 1 the Dnipropetrovsk *obkom* announced that it was cutting the customary 15 per cent advance, distributed to the collective farmers immediately after the threshing, to 10 per cent.[61]

Unlike Khataevich, Postyshev arrived in Kharkiv with a dual mandate: not only to intensify the grain seizures (and therefore the famine) in Ukraine, but also to eliminate "national deviations," that is, the modest national self-assertion hitherto allowed Ukrainians in the USSR. This is what the December 14, 1932, All-Union Party-state decision meant. Postyshev carried it out by defeating the nationally self-assertive wing of the Communist Party of Ukraine, which had been led by Education Commissar Mykola Skrypnyk.

The weeks that followed Postyshev's arrival witnessed an extensive purge of Ukrainian cultural life.[62] On February 28 a major reshuffling of the Soviet Ukrainian government was carried out. Skrypnyk was transferred from his education post to the Ukrainian State Planning Agency, one of diminishing importance with the union's growing role in the economic sphere. He was replaced as Commissar of Education by Volodymyr Zatons'kyi, another Ukrainian Old Bolshevik, but one never known for advocating specific policies of his own.[63] On March 11 the CP(b)U Central Committee denounced the schoolbooks which Skrypnyk's Education Commissariat had approved.[64] At the end of April it sponsored a conference on the nationality question where Zatons'kyi denounced national deviations in education and Party propagandist Andrii Khvylia denounced them in linguistics.[65] Both areas had been under Skrypnyk's jurisdiction.

The final showdown between Postyshev and Skrypnyk came at the June 1933 plenum of the CP(b)U Central Committee.[66] Skrypnyk spoke first, but his speech was never published. Postyshev linked Skrypnyk to the so-called national deviations of the 1920s. He asserted that there had been a "breakdown of Bolshevik vigilance, such that wrecking counter-revolutionary elements have attained their widest field of action in Ukraine." Some had been active in agriculture, but their activities were by no means confined to that sphere: nationalist and peasant anarchist agents, known respectively as Petliurists and Makhnovists, had taken root and assumed leadership roles in various areas of "cultural construction."

> Do not think that the enemy has taken up arms only in the system of our agricultural organs. The wrecking, counter-revolutionary elements have been able to deploy their forces in other realms of socialist construction as well and not seldom in leading posts.
>
> Take the cultural front. Cultural construction in Ukraine is a most important factor in carrying out the Leninist nationality policy, has the most direct and immediate bearing on our whole daily

struggle, and for this reason numerous Petliurist [nationalist] and Makhnovist [peasant anarchist] agents had taken root and assumed leadership roles in various areas of cultural construction.

He then mentioned the Ukrainian Communists and cultural figures, whom he had arrested as spies and wreckers. Among them was the historian Matvii Iavors'kyi, whose textbooks had been obligatory in Soviet Ukrainian schools. Others were Badan, Maksymovych, Ersteniuk, Shums'kyi and Solodub. They had collectively represented the CP(b)U's contribution to the Ukrainian national cultural revival of the 1920s. According to Postyshev, they had carried out "work assigned them by various counter-intelligence services, which they served as agents" and created "a nationalist, chauvinist, bourgeois culture... hostile to the ideology and interests of the proletariat and toiling peasantry." Postyshev stated that, by means of their wrecking, "they sought to undermine and weaken the proletarian dictatorship, feverishly preparing new actions against the USSR, not excluding dreams of detaching Ukraine from the Soviet Union." These spies and wreckers had wrapped themselves in "the tattered banner" of Ukrainian nationalism, serving the interests of the German fascists, and the Polish *pans*, who hoped for the restoration of capitalism. And Skrypnyk, Commissar of Education until the end of February, was responsible:

> That realm which was up to a short time ago led by Comrade Skrypnyk (I have in mind the People's Commissariat of Education and the whole system of organs of education in Ukraine) was the most polluted with wrecking, counter-revolutionary, nationalistic elements. It was in these very organs that these wrecking elements rose, appointed by him, to the most responsible realms of the ideological front. And there was no struggle whatsoever against these elements. And even Comrade Skrypnyk was forced to recognize that here our enemies not seldom had strong and authoritative protection from some, obviously blind and deaf, "Communists."[67]

The "exposure of the national deviation headed by Skrypnyk" and the plenum was followed by a veritable competition of denunciations. Skrypnyk's erstwhile comrades vied with one another to denounce every manifestation of Ukrainian national distinctiveness that had been permitted during Skrypnyk's tenure at *Narkomosvity*. It was a competition which even Skrypnyk's suicide in July did not end.[68]

Meanwhile, Postyshev continued his speech, returning to agriculture and blaming the CP(b)U's past failure to seize the requisite quantity of bread from the starving on the lack of "Bolshevik vigilance," that is, the fact that some of Ukraine's Communists were unwilling to blame everything on the omnipresent class enemy, but instead actually complained about Moscow usurping the republic's prerogatives. He concluded by assuring the CP(b)U that with sufficient "Bolshevik vigilance" for the maneuvers of the Petliurists, Makhnovists, White Guards and other class enemies, 1933 would be the last year of difficulties.[69]

By blaming everything on "class enemies," especially those within the Party, Postyshev completed his enunciation of Stalin's policy of ignoring the human suffering and massive loss of life caused by the man-made famine, blaming the failure of the CP(b)U to seize enough agricultural produce on an impermissible lack of vigilance in discerning the maneuvers of the class enemies, and linking Skrypnyk's "national deviation" to the alleged maneuvers. It is not for us to make explicit the link between Moscow's policy toward Ukraine's countryside and its policy toward Ukrainian national self-assertion. Postyshev did so for us.

In 1933 Ukrainization was abandoned and the structures designed gradually to de-Russify the Ukraine's cities dismantled. Over the next 18 months hundreds of Ukrainian writers were shot or disappeared. Ukrainian history virtually ceased to exist for two decades. Ukrainian spelling and vocabulary, the very structure of the language itself, was radically altered to bring it closer to Russian. The November 1934 fall of the Pokrovskii school in Moscow rapidly led to an attempt to inculcate a Russian national-historical consciousness throughout the Soviet Union. Nationality policy in Ukraine as elsewhere underwent a complete reversal.

The area most similar to Ukraine in its fate is the North Caucasus *krai*, since broken up into smaller entities.[70] This region also had a nationality question, or something similar, which was no less real for the fact that the regime refused to recognize it officially as a nationality.

After the Bolsheviks seized power in central Russia, the Cossacks of the North Caucasus provided most of the troops that fought under Denikin's anti-Communist Volunteer Army. However, the Cossacks did not fight for the same thing as Denikin. A source of no little dispute with the Denikinists lay in the fact that the Cossacks evolved the rudiments of a national ideology and demanded autonomy.[71]

This was above all the case in the Kuban, where Cossack nationalism competed with Ukrainian nationalism. This area was "the heartland of the anti-Bolshevik South," and its Cossacks constituted "the backbone of the Volunteer Army."[72] Even the Russian "line

Cossacks" (*lineitsy*) hoped for some sort of regional autonomy, while the majority, the former Black Sea Cossacks, were conscious of their Ukrainian heritage and actively sympathized with the national movement led by Semen Petliura in Ukraine and many of these sought an independent Kuban.[73]

The Bolsheviks, for their part, had trouble deciding whether to try to recruit Cossacks or attempt to destroy them as a homogeneous counter-revolutionary stratum. For a time there were Cossack SSRs, one for each of the three hosts, but in early 1919, when the Bolsheviks held the Don, they adopted a policy of massive terror called "de-Cossackization."[74] This policy was abandoned, but a decree of July 18, 1923, banned the very name Cossack.[75] Lack of trust in the Cossacks is also evident in the fact that they were not conscripted into the Red Army until 1936.[76]

After 1923 Cossacks were designated as either Russians or Ukrainians, depending on their ancestry. In largely Ukrainian areas like the Kuban, the Ukrainization policy was carried out under the supervision of the Ukrainian Commissariat of Education, as it was throughout the Soviet Union.[77] To an even greater extent than in Ukraine, anti-Soviet guerrillas operated there until the mid-1920s.[78] In 1929-1930, at the same time that thousands of members of Ukraine's non-Communist intellectual, cultural and spiritual elites were arrested in connection with the so-called Union for the Liberation of Ukraine, Kuban Cossacks were also rounded up for alleged participation.[79]

Revolts against collectivization began in the Kuban in 1929 and lasted into the following year. One of the so-called "bands" in the Kuban had 4,000 "bandits" under arms, the largest such uprising we know of anywhere in the Soviet Union.[80]

As early as January 1931 the All-Union Central Committee passed a special resolution on collectivization in the North Caucasus, which was designated the first region of the USSR to have achieved total collectivization, citing "brutal class struggle" and "acute *kulak* resistance" there.[81] And no wonder. In terms of grain requisitions, the North Caucasus was ravaged as much as Ukraine. In 1930, 38 per cent of all the grain produced there was seized by the state to fulfill the compulsory procurements quota, and in 1931 the quota took up 44 per cent of the harvest. The burden was even greater on the collectivized sector: 45.6 per cent of the total harvest in 1930 and 63.4 per cent in 1931.[82]

In 1932 the grain procurements campaign fell below targets much as it did simultaneously in Ukraine. But the North Caucasus Party structure was willing to go along with Moscow's policies with less complaint than in Ukraine. At least, there is no evidence of active resistance to the quotas from high North Caucasus authorities as occurred in Ukraine in mid-1932. And, since *krai* authorities had more limited authority *vis-à-vis* Moscow than their counterparts in the Ukrainian SSR, some repressions began even earlier there. Whole Kuban *raions* were blacklisted as early as October 1932, two months earlier than in Ukraine.[83]

Soon after intervening in Ukraine in the fall of 1932, the central authorities also turned their attention to the Kuban. A top-level commission from Moscow, headed by Kaganovich, arrived in the North Caucasus on November 2 to deal with the crisis. Meeting with the North Caucasus *kraikom*, they immediately decided to reduce the quotas while stepping up efforts to meet them: the grain procurements quota was reduced from 136 million *poods*, the figure set in May,[84] to 97 million *poods*. Simultaneously, prominent officials of the *krai* were dispatched to the 31 *raions* most behind in their quotas to take charge and see to it that grain seizures were intensified.[85] The "concession" of a lower quota was by now clearly bogus: it represented only what Party officials decided it was possible to seize with the maximum effort. A former Soviet journalist later recalled that before dawn on the day after the arrival of Kaganovich's mission, the newsboys shouted the horrible headlines: "The Petliurist *kulak* saboteurs of Kuban must be finished off" and "The Petliurist–Cossack counter-revolutionary work in Kuban must be uprooted."[86]

On November 4 another decree ordered that repression be intensified in an effort to meet the quota. Three large Cossack settlements (*stanitsas*) were blacklisted, and their inhabitants were warned that "further sabotage" would compel *raion* authorities to "raise before the government the question of their exile ... to the northern regions." of the Soviet Union and the resettlement of their homes by colonists brought in from other territories. In 11 *raions* no further goods were sent to state and cooperative stores, while in ten others the goods already in the stores were ordered immediately seized and sent elsewhere. Individual farmers who refused to plant had their property seized and were threatened with deportation to the far north. "Criminal underfulfillers" and those failing to obey decrees on proper use of livestock were arrested. Cases under the law of August 7 on socialist property were speedily re-examined and prosecutions speeded up. Local Party organizations were purged of members who had "united with the *kulak* organizers of the counter-revolutionary sabotage" and become "mouthpieces for the class enemy in the Party," that is, not seizing food energetically enough.[87] Simultaneously, Moscow appointed Shkiriatov to head the commission in charge of carrying out this purge.[88]

On November 12 *kraikom* secretary Boris Sheboldaev again specifically raised the issue of exiling whole *stanitsas* from the Kuban.[89] According to later Soviet scholarship, the entire populations of the Kuban *stanitsas* of Poltavs'ka, Medvidivs'ka and others were exiled to the North.[90] From a Western account, we learn that a total of 13 *stanitsas* were exiled, and that Umans'ka and Mishativs'ka were among them.[91] This was a major operation; Poltavs'ka, which was ordered into exile on December 17, had a population of 27,000 and a Ukrainian pedagogical institute, while the population of Umans'ka was 30,000.[92] An eyewitness recalled: "Farm implements and personal belongings which people had prepared to take along with them were taken away when they were loaded into trains. Departures were usually conducted with public shootings and bloodshed."[93]

Simultaneously, "massive repressions were carried out against Party, Soviet and collective farm workers as well as against rank-and-file collective farmers." Fifteen more Kuban *stanitsas* were put on the "blacklist." In them the delivery of goods was stopped, collective farm trade was forbidden, and credit and tax payments were immediately called due. About 45 per cent of all Party members in the Kuban were purged.[94] Of the Kuban's 716 secretaries of collective farm and *stanitsa* Party organizations, 358 were removed. Whole Party organizations were disbanded.[95]

As a special threat to local officials, the Kotov affair was reopened under the November 4 decree. Kotov, who had headed a *stanitsa* Party committee in the Kuban and had secretly advanced the local Cossack farmers more food than the amount prescribed by law, was expelled from the Party and sentenced to ten years' imprisonment in October 1932. When the case was reopened, however, 15 more members of the Party committee were purged, while Kotov was executed as a counter-revolutionary.[96] Kotov became a symbol of the "enemy with a Party card in his pocket," the main target of the 1933 All-Union purge.

Stalin's January 1933 intervention in Ukraine was also paralleled in the North Caucasus. As a result of the various repressive measures taken in late 1932, the revised procurements quota for the North Caucasus was actually fulfilled, albeit at tremendous human cost.[97] On January 23, 1933, the day before Stalin's appointment of Postyshev to take the reins in Kharkiv, a special Committee on the Conduct of the Sowing in the North Caucasus was appointed. The decree establishing the Committee stated that the primary duty of authorities, from the brigade leader up, was "to combat all symptoms of *kulak* sabotage and wrecking activities." It warned that "any indulgence shown to the enemies of the people who destroy the sowings will be considered assistance to the *kulaks* and counter-revolutionary elements." The committee, headed by Sheboldaev, was given total administrative authority, and its decisions were "to be considered absolutely binding upon all organs, establishments and administrative entities of the *krai* without appeal."[98] Thus, although the *kraikom* secretary, Sheboldaev, was named chairman, this committee represented the complete by-passing of *krai* authorities by an *ad hoc* body whose decisions were to be obeyed without question or appeal to higher authorities.

The consequences of the policies carried out by Stalin's immediate subordinates in the Kuban's *stanitsas* in 1933 were identical to events in Ukraine. Accounts by eyewitnesses from the Kuban confirm those from the Ukrainian SSR. One recalled: "Krasnodar, the capital city of the Kuban, was strewn with corpses which no one bothered to pick up."[99] A Kuban Cossack named Dmytro Fesenko, from Starokorsuns'ka *stanitsa*, recalled:

> After dekulakization, mass arrests, and the exile of individuals with or without their families, the artificially created famine of 1932–1933 came to pass. After it, out of a population of 14,000, only about a thousand remained half alive. In this act of murder both collective farmers and non-collective farmers died; also village schoolteachers and even activists died. Russians from Tula, Kursk, and other regions were (then) brought into our *stanitsa*.
>
> The neighboring *stanitsas* of Voroniz'ka and Dins'ka were put on the blacklist, and their fate was the same as our *stanitsa*.[100]

A former Soviet journalist added that soon after the Kaganovich mission,

> the whole of Kuban was drenched in blood and tears as the Muscovite gangs mercilessly swept away the last kernels of grain from the Cossacks' granaries, arrested the survivors of previous arrests and packed the Krasnodar GPU dungeons, while the Kuban grain flowed into Moscow.
>
> In the late fall of 1932 Kuban was finally completely annihilated. The once-prosperous villages were now ravaged and desolate. All Ukrainian national life in Kuban was liquidated. Ukrainian schools were compelled to teach Russian only.[101]

Less information is available on the Don *oblast'* of the North Caucasus, partially because the Soviet press of the period does not indicate the existence there of special "problems" as in the Kuban. That the man-made famine did affect the Don Cossacks, Sholokov's correspondence with Stalin makes clear.[102]

Yet even in the North Caucasus, the Kaganovich delegation was sent specifically to deal with sabotage in the Kuban, even if its powers then extended over the entire *krai*. That the central authorities' most direct and invasive interventions during the famine were specifically directed against the Ukrainian SSR and the ethnically Ukrainian Kuban indicates a specifically anti-Ukrainian aspect to Soviet policies during the period.

Nationality policy (what to do about the USSR's non-Russian nations) reflected policy toward the countryside throughout the period discussed. And it was the crushing of the Ukrainian peasantry which made the crushing of Ukrainian national self-assertion possible for Stalin and his subordinates. The link between the two is evident first of all in Stalin's evolving response to the collapse of Soviet agriculture brought about by collectivization. In early 1932, when the problem was centered outside Ukraine and the North Caucasus, Stalin opted for something of a "thaw" in agrarian policy. But when the leadership in Ukraine warned Moscow of problems there, Stalin reversed his course, taking a series of actions which could only exacerbate an already bad situation and transform the hardships then existing into a tragedy costing millions of lives.

Under pressure, the CP(b)U carried out the policies that brought the famine, but it could not meet the quota. Moscow's response was to take direct control of the Ukrainian apparatus by giving Postyshev a dual mandate, to intensify the procurements, which could only have been calculated to make the famine even worse, and, at the same time, to crush any assertion of a distinct Ukrainian identity under the guise of combating national deviations. Simultaneously, Stalin dismantled the virtual cultural protectorate Ukraine's Education Commissariat had hitherto exercised over Ukrainian areas outside Ukraine and also crushed the most important such area, the Kuban.

Thus, the famine, by neutralizing the basic mass constituency of Ukrainian national self-assertion, was used to eliminate any "Ukrainian factor" in Soviet politics. As a result, the Soviet Union would never be quite the same in terms of its national-political structure. Indigenization had raised up a structural barrier to Moscow's encroachment on union republic prerogatives that was much more important than those embodied in the 1923 Constitution, by legitimizing a measure of non-Russian national self-assertion and by reinforcing its constituency. By virtue of its size and importance, the Ukrainian SSR became the natural defender of such prerogatives. With the Ukrainians broken, however, the barrier was removed, clearing the way for the structural and ideological Russocentrism characteristic of High Stalinism.

This is not the same as stating that the famine was created merely to destroy the Ukrainians. There were pressing economic motives for the extraction of as much produce as possible from the peasantry at this juncture in Soviet history. Indeed, famine had been an ongoing reality in Kazakhstan since 1930 and in the Volga Basin since 1931, and these areas too were left to their fates. But if Stalin had to conclude that some must starve in order that the state receive the grain his plans required, it made sense that as many as possible of the victims be claimed in areas that he saw as stumbling blocks to his policies of centralization and Russification. By crushing the largest and most troublesome union republic, the way was open to the Russo-centrism that became one of the essential hallmarks of the system Stalin built. And for this reason, the famine of 1932–1933 had a significance beyond the millions of lives it claimed: it also left its mark on the national structure of the USSR.

Notes

1. Marx described the period of commercial capitalism as one of primary accumulation, largely by the plundering of less-developed societies. Pokrovskii stretched out commercial capitalism in his interpretation of Russian history to three centuries, from Ivan the Terrible to the abolition of serfdom, and in some respects down to the revolutions of 1905–1917. Pokrovskii's views are lucidly and concisely expressed in Roman Szporluk, "Pokrovsky and Russian History," *Survey*, no. 53 (October 1964); Szporlukh "Introduction," M. N. Pokrovskii, *Russia in World History: Selected Essays* (Ann Arbor, 1970), pp. 1–46.

2. See, for example, Basil Dmytryshyn, *Moscow and the Ukraine, 1918–1953: A Study of Russian Bolshevik Nationality Policy* (New York, 1956), pp. 57–121; James E. Mace, *Communism and the Dilemmas of National Liberation: National Communism in Soviet Ukraine, 1918–1933* (Cambridge, MA, 1983), *passim*.

3. V. I. Kozlov, *Natsional'nosti SSSR: Etnodemograficheskii obzor* (Moscow, 1982), p. 285.

4. *Robotnicheskaia gazeta*, October 1, 1931, as quoted in John C. Wiley, Chargé d'Affaires *ad interim*, US Embassy, Warsaw, to Secretary of State, December 1, 1931; 860C.917/11; T1249; Records of the Department of State; National Archives; Washington, D.C. The other Union republics then extant were the Transcaucasian Federation, Belorussia, Uzbekistan, Turkmenistan and Tadzhikistan.

5. I. V. Stalin, *Sochineniia* (Moscow, 1946–52), vol. 7, p. 72.

6. František Silnický, *Natsional'naia politika KPSS v period s 1917 po 1922 god* (Munich, 1978), pp. 196–9.

7. "Desiatyi s"ezd RKP(b), mart 1921 goda," *Stenograficheskii Otchet* (Moscow, 1963), pp. 598-607.

8. Ibid., p. 213. Stalin also reiterated this the following month at the First All-Ukrainian Party Conference in Kharkiv. M. Ravich-Cherkasskii, *Istoriia Kommunisticheskoi Partii (b-ov) Ukraiy* (Kharkiv, 1923), p. 181.

9. See especially the arguments made to the CP(b)U on the eve of the Congress, described in Dmytryshyn, *Moscow and the Ukraine*, pp. 57-62.

10. Mace, *Communism and the Dilemmas of National Liberation*, pp. 95-7.

11. Ibid., pp. 254-63.

12. Ibid., pp. 267-75.

13. I. V. Stalin, *Stat'i i rechi ob Ukraine: Sbornik* (Kiev, 1936), pp. 212-18. Quotations pp. 214, 218.

14. *Pravda*, February 6, 1932.

15. For example, on March 18, 1932, the North Caucasus Territory reported the 100 per cent fulfillment of its plan to send 40,000 tons of seed grain to the Middle and Lower Volga, the Urals, Kazakhstan and Bashkiria, collected by "shock-work" methods. "40 tys. tonn semzerna otgruzheno," *Pravda*, March 20, 1932, p. 3.

16. H. H. Fischer, *The Famine in Soviet Russia, 1919-1923: The Operations of the American Relief Administration* (Stanford, 1927), p. 246n. M. A. Zhurbe, "Pro diial'nist' hromads'kykh orhanizatsiï Radians'koho sela po internatsional'nomu vykhovanniu trudiashchykh," *Arkhivy Ukraïny*, no. 1 (1982), p. 54.

17. A. B. Tursunbaev, "Torzhestvo kolkhoznogo stroia v Kazakhstane," *Ocherki istorii kollektivizatsii sel'skogo khoziaistva v Soiuznykh respublikakh*, ed. V. P. Danilov (Moscow, 1963), p. 294.

18. On the Kazakhstan famine, see Martha Brill Olcott, "The Collectivization Drive in Kazakhstan," *Russian Review*, vol. 40, no. 3 (April 1981), pp. 122-42.

19. *Vazhneishie resheniia po sel'skomu khoziaistvu* (Moscow, 1935), pp. 533-6.

20. For details see US Commission on the Ukraine Famine, *Report to Congress* (Washington, 1988), pp. 71-5; based on *Visti VUTsVK*, July 11-17, 1932.

21. "III Vseukraïns'ka partiina konferentsiia: Dopovid' V. M. Molotova," *Visti VUTsVK*, July 8, 1932, p. 4.

22. "III Vseukraïns'ka partiina konferentsiia: Dopovid' L. M. Kahanovycha," *Visti VUTsVK*, July 8, 1932, pp. 4-5.

23. "Rezoliutsiia III konferentsiï KP(b)U pro pidsumky vesnianoï posivnoï kampaniï, pro khlibozahotivel'nu ta zbiral'nu kampaniï i zavdannia orhanizatsiino-hospodars'koho zmitsnennia kolhospiv," *Istoriia kolektyvizatsiï sil's'koho hospodarstva Ukraïns'koï RSR, 1917-1934 rr.:*

Zbirnyk dokumentiv i materialiv u tr'okh tomakh (Kiev, 1962-1971), vol 2, pp. 603-16.

24. Text in *Vazhneishie resheniia po sel'skomu khoziaistvu*, pp. 65-6.

25. Robert Conquest (ed.), *Agricultural Workers in the USSR* (London, 1968), pp. 24-5.

26. "Lypnevyi plian khlibozahotivel' vykonano lyshe na 15.6%," *Visti VUTsVK*, August 3, 1932, p. 6.

27. "Za bil'shovyts'ku orhanizatsiiu ta udarni tempy khlibozahotivel'," *Bil'shovyk Ukraïny*, no. 15 (1932), pp. 9-11.

28. "Lyst Ukrkolhosptsentru holovam oblkolhospspilok pro usunennia prychyn vykhodu selian z kolhospiv," *Istoriia kolektyvizatsiï sil's'koho hospodarstva Ukraïns'koï RSR*, vol. 2, p. 622.

29. M. Khataievych, "Zavdannia bil'shovykiv Ukraïny v borot'bi za khlib, za orhanizatsiino-hospodars'ke zmitsnennia kolhospiv i za pidnesennia sil's'koho hospodarstva," *Bil'shovyk Ukraïny*, nos. 21-22 (1932), pp. 13-14.

30. "Plenum TsK KP(b)U," *Visti VUTsVK*, October 15, 1932, p. 1. In the summer of 1933 Akulov would be named to the newly created post of Procurator of the USSR.

31. M. Khataievych, "Zavdannia bil'shovykiv Ukraïny v borot'bi za khlib, za orhanizatsiino-hospodars'ke zmitsnennia kolhospiv i za pidnesennia sil's'koho hospodarstva," *Bil'shovyk Ukraïny*, no. 21-22 (1932), p. 33. Original emphasis.

32. "Pro zakhody do pidsylennia khlibozahotivel': Postanova Rady narodnykh komisariv USRR," *Visti VUTsVK*, November 21, 1932, p. 2.

33. "Pro orhanizatsiiu khlibozahotivel' v odnoosibnomu sektori: Postanova Rady narodnikh komisariv USRR," *Visti VUTsVK*, November 21, 1932, p. 2.

34. "Pro zanesennia na chornu doshku sil iaki zlisno sabotuiut' khlibozahotivli. Postanova Radnarkomu USRR i TsK KP(b)U," *Visti VUTsVK*, December 8, 1932, p. 3.

35. I. I. Slyn'ko, *Sotsialistychna perebudova i tekhnichna rekonstruktsiia sil's'koho hospodarstva Ukraïny (1927-1932 rr.)* (Kiev, 1961), p. 298.

36. "Pro perebih khlibozahotivel': Postanova Vseukraïns'koho tsentral'noho vykonavchoho komitetu," *Visti VUTsVK*, December 11, 1932, p. 2.

37. "Do suvoroï vidpovidal'nosti (Z postanovy Narodnoho Komisara iustytsiï ta heneral'noho prokuratora respubliky)," *Visti VUTsVK*, December 14, 1932, p. 2.

38. "Postanova TsK KP(b)U vid 21 hrudnia 1932 roku," "Postanova RNK USRR i TsK KP(b)U vid 21 hrudnia 1932 roku," *Visti VUTsVK*, December 23, 1932, p. 1.

39. M. Ohurtsov, "Neshchadnoï kary voroham z partkvytkamy v kysheni:

Prysud u spravi kolyshn'oho kerivnytstva Kobeliats'koho raionu," *Visti VUTsVK*, December 29, 1932, p. 4.

40. "Perebih khlibozahotivel' po Ukraïni za stanom na 1 sichnia 1933 roku," *Visti VUTsVK*, January 4, 1933, p. 1. Kossior in February 1933 mentioned that 225 million *poods* had actually been procured, which would indicate a final quota of 300 million *poods*.

41. Stalin, *Sochineniia*, vol. 13, pp. 216–17, 225–6.

42. Ibid., p. 230.

43. M. Bogdenko, "K istorii nachal'nogo etapu sploshnoi kollektivizatsii sel'skogo khoziaistva SSSR," *Voprosy istorii*, no. 5 (1963), p. 31.

44. Stalin, *Sochineniia*, vol. 13, pp. 236–56.

45. "Sovetskaia Ukraina—nesokrushimyi forpost velikogo SSSR (Iz rechi P. P. Postysheva na plenume TsK KP[b]U)," *Pravda*, December 6, 1933, p. 3. The text of this decree was never published except for this quotation by Postyshev.

46. Semen Pidhainy, *Ukraïns'ka intelihentsiia na Solovkakh* (n.p., Prometei, 1947), pp. 22–3.

47. Over 30 years ago Vladimir Timoshenko argued that the fact that the decision to create the political sections was taken only two weeks before Pavel Postyshev was appointed as Ukraine's ruler indicated that "it was the stubborn resistance of the forcibly collectivized Ukrainian peasants to the excessive deliveries of grain required from the collective farms that was mainly responsible for the decision . . . to create the *politotdely*." V. P. Timoshenko, "Soviet Agricultural Policy and the Nationalities Problem in the USSR," *Report on the Soviet Union in 1956: A Symposium of the Institute for the Study of the USSR (Based on the Seventh Institute Conference), April, 28–29, 1956*, ed. Jaan Pennar (Munich, 1956), p. 47.

48. The "historic" decree read: "The Central Committee considers it an established fact that the Party organizations of Ukraine have been unable to cope with the task the Party has assigned them regarding the grain procurements and the fulfillment of the plan for the grain deliveries, despite the fact that it has been lowered three times.

"The Central Committee believes that the basic regions which will determine the fate of Ukraine's agriculture and which must first of all be strengthened are Odessa, Dnipropetrovsk and Kharkiv. The Central Committee of the All-Union Communist Party resolves:

"1. To assign as Second Secretary of the Central Committee of the Communist Party (bolshevik) of Ukraine and as First Secretary of the Kharkiv *obkom* Central Committee Secretary Comrade Postyshev.

"2. To assign as First Secretary of the Dnipropetrovsk *obkom* Comrade Khataevich, also retaining him as one of the Secretaries of the CP(b)U Central Committee.

"3. To assign as First Secretary of the Odessa *obkom* Comrade Veger.

"4. To free Comrades Maiorov, Stroganov and Terekhov from the posts they have held and place them at the disposal of the Central Committee.

"5. Comrades Postyshev, Khataevich and Veger are to begin their new duties no later than January 30 of this year." "Postanova TsK VKP(b) z 24 sichnia 1933 r. ta zavdannia bil'shovykiv Ukraïny," *Bil'shovyk Ukraïny*, no. 3 (1933), p. 3.

49. "Itogi 1933 sel'skokhoziaistvennogo goda i ocherednye zadachi KP(b)U. (Rech' tov. P. P. Postysheva na plenume TsK KP(b)U 19 noiabria 1933 goda)," *Pravda*, November 24, 1933, p. 3.

50. Hryhory Kostiuk, *Stalinist Rule in the Ukraine: A Study in the Decade of Mass Terror (1929-1939)* (London, 1960), p. 28.

51. P. P. Postyshev, "Pro zavdannia sivby ta postanovu TsK VKP(b) vid 24 sichnia 1933 r.," *Bil'shovyk Ukraïny*, no. 3 (1933), pp. 70-1.

52. Ibid., p. 73.

53. Ibid., p. 75.

54. Ibid., p. 82.

55. S. Kossior, "Pidsumky khlibozahotivel' i zavdannia KP(b)U v borot'bi za pidnesennia sil's'koho hospodarstva Ukraïny," *Bil'shovyk Ukraïny*, no. 3 (1933), pp. 23, 26.

56. Ibid., pp. 26-7.

57. Ibid., p. 28.

58. Ibid., pp. 32-3, 34.

59. "Postanova TsK VKP(b) z 24 sichnia 1933 r. ta zavdannia bil'shovykiv Ukraïny," *Bil'shovyk Ukraïny*, no. 3 (1933), pp. 3-20.

60. Text in *Istoriia kolektyvizatsiï sil's'koho hospodarstva Ukraïns'koï RSR*, vol. 3, pp. 59-60.

61. "Pro postanovu Biura Dnipropetrovs'koho obkomu pro advansuvannia kolhospnykiv i ukhvalu v ts'omu pytanni TsK VKP(b) i TsK KP(b)U: Postanova IV plenumu Dnipropetrovs'komu obkomu KP(b)U," *Visti VUTsVK*, June 1, 1933, p. 2.

62. Kostiuk, *Stalinist Rule*, pp. 58-9.

63. *Visti VUTsVK*, March 1, 1983, p. 1.

64. "Pro pidruchnyky dlia pochatkovoï i seredn'oï shkoly: Postanova TsK KP(b)U z 11 bereznia 1933 r.," *Visti VUTsVK*, March 12, 1933, p. 1.

65. "Narada z pytan' natsional'noï polityky partiï," *Visti VUTsVK*, May 1, 1933, p. 2.

66. For a fuller description see US Commission on the Ukraine Famine, *Report to Congress*, pp. 92-5.

67. "Mobilizuiemo masy za svoiechasnu postavku zerna derzhavi: Promova t. P. P. Postysheva na plenumi TsK KP(b)U 10-VI 1933 p.," *Visti VUTsVK*, June 22, 1933, p. 1.

68. Mace, *Communism and the Dilemmas of National Liberation*, pp. 296-300.

69. "I have got off the track somewhat, but this whole question is directly

and intimately connected with the causes of the breakdown of the grain procurements last year in Ukraine. It is absolutely necessary to state such facts because Ukraine's Party organizations lacked Bolshevik vigilance concerning the class enemy.

"Is everything really all right with us now? Do we really not have among individual workers—including some very responsible ones—anti-Party talk to the effect that the only reason Ukraine's agriculture broke down was that the *okrug* [a Soviet level of administration between the *raion* and *oblast*] was liquidated and *oblasts* created with the special aim of "putting a paw on Ukraine and centralizing everything"? Such prattle (*balakanyna*) is hostile to us. All this is just the belching of the old hostile influence which has done great harm to socialist construction in Ukraine. A decisive struggle must be proclaimed against such anti-Party talk, and, above all, we must remember Bolshevik vigilance and not for a moment forget that it is the enemy who foists upon us this sort of explanation for the breakdown of Ukraine's agriculture.

"The lack of Bolshevik vigilance led to Ukraine's Party organizations being littered with Petliurist, Makhnovist, White Guard elements. The enemy from the Party committee, who not seldom occupied leadership posts, organized direct sabotage of last year's grain procurements in some *raions*.

"The struggle for bread is the struggle for socialism. The struggle for bread in Ukraine is the struggle for the consolidation of a socialist Soviet Ukraine. This is why it was in the struggle for bread that we especially felt the maneuvers and activities of the class enemy and his agents. It was precisely here that we felt the class enemy's greatest resistance and precisely here that all the blunders of our work presented themselves with the greatest acuteness." "Mobilizuiemo masy . . .' *Visti VUTsVK*, June 22, 1933, p. 2.

70. For more detail on the famine in the North Caucasus, see US Commission on the Ukraine Famine, *Report to Congress*, pp. 140-50.

71. The leading American historian of the anti-Soviet movement during the Civil War accused the Cossacks of evolving a "bogus nationalism," based on a "mythical past," which masked their "unwillingness to share their wealth and power with the fellow inhabitants of their rich districts." Peter Kenez, *Civil War in South Russia, 1919-1920: The Defeat of the Whites* (Berkeley, 1977), p. 112. Be that as it may, the point is that the Cossacks evolved the rudiments of a national ideology. Scholars familiar with the histories of Slavic nations should be very circumspect in labeling any nationalism as "bogus," least of all because it was based on a mythical past.

72 Ibid., p. 112.

73 Ibid., pp. 112-20, 132-9. For the viewpoint of those seeking an independent Kuban, see Vasyl' Ivanys, *Borot'ba Kubani za nezalezhnist'* (Munich, 1968).

74. Sergei Starikov and Roy Medvedev, *Philip Mironov and the Russian Civil War* (New York, 1978), pp. 101-32.

75. W. G. Glaskow, *History of the Cossacks* (New York, 1972), pp. 128-9.

76. Nobuo Shimotomai, "A Note on the Kuban Affair (1932-1933): The Crisis of Kolkhoz Agriculture in the North Caucasus," *Acta Slavica Iaponica*, vol. 1 (1983), p. 40.

77. See, for example, Mykola Skrypnyk, *Statti i promovy* (Kharkiv, 1930-1931), vol. 2, pp. 69-70, 246-7.

78. Glaskow, *History of the Cossacks*, p. 129.

79. M. Verbyts'kyi (ed.), *Naibil'shyi zlochyn Kremlia: Stvorenyi Sovets'koiu Moskvoiu shtuchnyi holod v Ukraïni 1932-33 r.* (London, 1952), p. 77.

80. Iu. S. Kukushkin, "Osushchestvlenie sel'skimi sovetami politiki likvidatsii kulachestva kak klassa," *Vestnik Moskovskogo universiteta*, no 4 (1966), p. 27.

81. "Kolektyvizatsiia na Pivnichnomu Kavkazi: Postanova TsK VKP(b) vid 10 sichnia 1931 r. na dopovid' Pivkazkraikomu." *Visti VUTsVK*, January 13, 1931, p. 2.

82. Shimotomai, "A Note on the Kuban Affair," p. 40.

83. Ibid., p. 44.

84. *Vazhneishie resheniia po sel'skomu khoziaistva*, p. 534.

85. "O vypolnenii plana khlebozagotovok po Severo-Kavkazskomu kraiu: Postanovlenie biuro Sev.-Kaz. kraevogo komiteta VKP(b), sovmestno s predstaviteliami TsK VKP(b) tt. Kaganovichem, Iagoda, Chernovym, Iurkinym i Kosyrevym ot 2-go noiabria 1932 goda," *Slomit' sabotazh seva i khlebozagotovok, organizovannyi kulachestvom v raionakh Kubani* (Rostov-on-Don, 1932), pp. 16-17.

86. Yurko Stepovy, "The Tragedy of Kuban," *The Black Deeds of the Kremlin: A White Book*, ed. Semen Pidhainy et al. (Toronto-Detroit, 1953-1955), vol. 2, p. 554.

87. "O khode khlebozagotovok i seva po raionam Kubani: Reshenie biuro Kraikoma sovmesto s predstaviteliami TsK VKP(b) ot 4 noiabra 1832 g.," *Slomit' sabotazh*, pp. 18-20.

88. "O chistke sel'skikh partorganizatsii Sev. Kavkaza: Postanovlenie TsK VKP(b) i prezidium TsKK ot 4 noiabria," *Slomit' sabotazh*, p. 21.

89. "We have stated publicly that we will exile to the Northern regions criminal saboteurs and *kulak* supporters who do not want to sow. But can it be that we have not already exiled the *kulak* counter-revolutionary elements from this same Kuban in preceding years. We did exile them and in sufficient quantity. And now, when these *kulak* remnants try to organize, sabotage and oppose the Soviet government's demands, it is more right to give the most fertile Kuban land to collective farmers who live with little land and on poor land in other regions. And they not only work it better but appreciate it more. And those who do not want to work and sully our land to the limits, we will exile them to other places. This is just. We may be told: 'How is it that you earlier exiled the *kulaks* and are

now talking about a whole settlement, in which there are collective farms and in which individual farmers of goodwill reside; how can this be?' Yes, we have to raise the question of a whole settlement, or a collective farm, or collective farmers, or individual farmers who really are of goodwill, who must in present circumstances answer for the attitudes of their neighbors. What kind of support of Soviet power is this—the collective farm, if together with another collective farm, or a whole group of individual farmers actively oppose the actions of the Soviet authorities? What kind of support is this, which does not try to smash quickly and decisively and which does not break its opposition? We demand that, if there are elements there who really are loyal to the Soviet power and the collective farm, then they must go forward with us in order to immediately smash the sabotage organized by the *kulaks* and thereby to correct the situation, then there will be no question of exile." B. Sheboldaev, "Slomit' sabotazh seva i khlebozagotovok, organizovannyi kulachestvom v raionakh Kubani," *Slomit' sabotazh*, pp. 8-9.

90. V. P. Danilov, N. A. Ivnitskii, "Leninskii kooperativnyi plan i ego osushchestvlenie v SSSR," *Ocherki istorii kollektivizatsii sel'skogo khoziaistva v Soiuznykh respublikakh*, ed. V. Danilov, p. 55.

91. Petro Ver, "Devastation of Kuban," *Black Deeds of the Kremlin*, vol. 1, p. 441.

92. Robert Conquest, *The Harvest of Sorrow: Soviet Collectivization and the Terror Famine* (New York, 1986), p. 277. The pedagogical institute is mentioned in Stepovy, "The Tragedy of Kuban," p. 555.

93. Ver, "Devastation of Kuban," *Black Deeds of the Kremlin*, vol. 1, p. 441.

94. Danilov, Ivnitskii, "Leninskii kooperativnyi plan . . . ," p. 55.

95. Shimotomai, "A Note on the Kuban Affair," p. 47.

96. Ibid., p. 48.

97. Ibid., p. 49.

98. "O meropriiatiiakh po organizatsii vesennego seva na Severnom Kavkaze: Postanovlenie Sovnarkoma Soiuza SSR i Tsentral'nogo Komiteta VKP(b)," *Pravda*, January 24, 1933, p. 1.

99. P. Petrenko, "They Ruined and Starved Kuban," *Black Deeds of the Kremlin*, vol. 2, p. 545.

100. M. Verbyts'kyi (ed.), *Naibil'shyi zlochyn Kremlia*, p. 78.

101. Stepovy, "The Tragedy of Kuban," *Black Deeds of the Kremlin*, vol. 2, p. 554.

102. N. S. Khrushchev, "Vysokaia ideinost' i khudozhestvennoe maisterstvo: Velikaia sila Sovetskoi literatury i iskusstva," *Pravda*, March 8, 1963, p. 2.

Chapter 11

Baltic Nationalism and Soviet Language Policy: From Russification to Constitutional Amendment

Romuald J. Misiunas

The language question has remained one of the principal unresolved facets of Soviet nationality policy throughout the 70 years of the existence of the system. As in many other spheres of Soviet life, the formal arrangements which were posited as a solution have merely served to mask the continued existence and indeed even exacerbation of an underlying problem which in some regions, notably the Baltic republics, has forcefully emerged in the era of *glasnost'*. While the languages of the union republics have enjoyed a formal status, the official quest for bilingualism has in effect served to water down the position of these languages.

Bilingualism is by itself apolitical. Most educated persons in some West European countries such as The Netherlands or the Scandinavian countries are in effect bilingual, a situation which does not rouse any political problems. Such a development occurred naturally without any plan or action on the part of the authorities. In the USSR, however, the official planning facet of the striving for bilingualism served to politicize the process. Any stress on the need for or use of Russian as the *lingua franca* of a giant multinational state has inevitably come to be perceived by many among the republic nationalities as advocacy of centralization. Conversely, calls for the need to develop the national languages of the republics have acquired an interpretation as "nationalism." At issue is the fate of the local cultures and the quality of local life.

This basic situation can be said to have applied to every non-Russian republic and to some of the autonomous republics as well. Several underlying historical and linguistic realities have made it a particularly acute issue in the three Baltic republics. Estonian, Latvian and Lithuanian are non-Slavic languages. The first is Finno-Ugric while the other two are the only living languages in the Indo-European Baltic group. The cultural life of the three peoples developed outside a Soviet setting during the interwar period.

Already at that time, they enjoyed a high degree of internationalization which had been achieved without a Russian medium. A distinctively pervasive feeling of cultural superiority *vis-à-vis* the Russians developed, making direct Russification unfeasible. As a result, Russification in this region has had to be much more indirect, couched in the terminology of administrative pronouncement and fiat rather than in arguments of the "cultural benefit" of knowing Russian.

The Russian presence was more pronounced in Estonia and Latvia where the *nomenklatura* elite was disproportionally heavily composed of individuals from the titular nationality who had not lived in the independent prewar republics but in the USSR, and who had immigrated after 1940. In Estonia such functionaries often spoke Estonian with a marked Russian accent, a fact which differentiated these "yestonian" cadres from the native-born apparatchiks. The Russian presence in a situation of self-perceived cultural superiority frequently led to demonstrative refusals to speak Russian in public on the part of the indigenous population. Such a development was particularly striking in Estonia, where the census of 1979 even showed a decrease in knowledge of Russian among the indigenous inhabitants of the republic.

Another reaction to the situation has been the striking effort among local linguists to minimize loan words and to keep the local languages functional in a modern setting. That included a marked tendency to nativize foreign names. The battle against loan words was an uphill one in that most technical terms did come by way of Russian. The nativization of foreign names introduced an element of inefficiency, by its very nature alien to the modernity which was being sought. The Baltic languages are written in the Latin script; the spellings of many of the nativized forms frequently precluded ready reconstruction of the originals, especially for such languages as French. Already by the early 1980s, some internal questioning seems to have arisen on how long such a linguistic holding action could be maintained and on the intrinsic value of such a basically conservative stance.

Throughout the period after their occupation and absorption into the USSR, language policy then became a political issue, an expression of local autonomy. It inevitably coincided with Kremlin interregnums or the beginning of a new Kremlin administration. In 1953 language was a significant element in the so-called Beria liberalization. In Lithuania the local leadership utilized the opportunity to purge cadres who could not speak Lithuanian. The Thaw under Khrushchev allowed the reassertion of local cultures in numerous ways. New education laws allowed parents to decide in which language their children would be taught. In the Baltic republics this made the second language, Russian, in effect voluntary. In reality, however, the pressure on the indigenous population to become bilingual was not removed, while such pressures were never exerted on the rapidly increasing immigrant populations, especially in Estonia and Latvia. In Latvia the Latvian language was made compulsory in Russian-language schools for a brief time in the late 1950s until the purges of 1959–1960 removed the majority of the local cadres and brought Latvianization to an abrupt halt. The antinationalist campaign in all three republics was most severe by far in Latvia. In 1962 nearly 5,000 students in Riga were forced to repeat the school year because of insufficient knowledge of Russian. The increase in bilingual schools even in areas without any sizable number of Russian inhabitants added to the perception of Russification among the Latvians.

Initially, the ascendancy of Brezhnev resulted in a reversal of the antinationalist campaign. The Baltic republics were even able to secure an exception to the uniform pattern of education in the Soviet Union. In 1965 the three republics became the only ones with an 11-year system of primary and secondary education in schools where the indigenous language was the language of instruction as opposed to the prevalent ten-year system. The rationale was the need for pupils to learn two languages. While many on the local level viewed this as a victory, reality may have been different in so far as the extra time was used basically to further Russian-language study.

During the later Brezhnev years, a renewed campaign for Russian-language study emerged. While these moves were most likely part of an all-union effort aimed perhaps more at Central Asia than at the Baltic republics, they were not so perceived by the Balts. The union-wide conference in Tashkent in 1978, called to consider the methods of extending the use of Russian in the public affairs and the educational systems of the non-Russian republics, roused considerable alarm. Secret instructions mandated implementation of that which officially was only under discussion. In October 1978 a leak in Estonia disclosed such "unpublished instructions" by a secret emissary from Moscow to the republic's educational officials. These instructions were supposed to be read and memorized without note-taking. The republic Central Committee was to issue the corresponding instructions on the local level. The measures called for a half-day of instruction in Russian in nursery schools. Russian was to be taught systematically from the first grade in grade school. Two subjects in secondary school were to be taught exclusively in Russian. Appropriate changes in the curricula of higher institutions were also mandated. Increased advocacy of informal use of Russian, such as in amateur theatrical groups, was recommended. Expansion of training of teachers of Russian in non-Russian-language schools was mandated. No doubt as a result of these instructions, the use of Russian in public events grew markedly. In 1980, for instance, the programs of the song festivals, which ranked among the principal mass cultural expressions of the Baltic peoples, included a highly disproportionate percentage of Russian songs.

This Russification campaign allowed certain political types to make headway. Russian-language knowledge became a particularly notable war-horse of the then Uzbek First Secretary, Sharif Rashidov, no doubt serving conveniently to camouflage his thoroughly corrupt feudal fiefdom. The most pronounced advocate of the Russian language on the Baltic scene was Latvian SSR Minister of Education Mirdza Karklins. In an article in early 1979 she expounded her views on the moral superiority of the Russian language: "Russian safeguards the effectiveness of patriotic and internationalist education, promoting the development of high moral and ideological-political qualities among pupils," she wrote, reproaching Latvians for "not adequately appreciating the value of speaking Russian among themselves."[1]

The campaign also resulted in a backlash. It was most evident in Estonia, where a drop in self-declared competence in Russian from 29 per cent (1970) to 24.2 per cent (1979) was noted in the 1979 census. One cause may have been the dying-off of an older generation which had learned Russian in Tsarist times. However, a conscious refusal to declare a knowledge of Russian may also have contributed to the drop. Riots among thousands of schoolchildren in Estonia followed the appointment of Elsa Grechkina, a Russian who did not know Estonian, as Estonian SSR Minister of Education. These were followed by an open letter to *Pravda* from 40 intellectuals and cultural figures in the republic (some quite prominent) supporting the grievances of the students. The attempt to relegate the Estonian language to a secondary status had clearly increased ethnic tension in the republic.

Reactions also broke out in Lithuania. According to *samizdat* sources, protest leaflets appeared in Vilnius University on April 18, 1979, against Order No. 1,116 of December 6, 1978, of the USSR Ministry of Higher and Specialized Education.[2] Apparently this was the same instruction that had been leaked in Estonia. It called for mandatory use of Russian in some required academic undertakings such as the writing of dissertations, which was perceived as contravening Article 36 of the Constitution of the USSR.

Native concerns over language policy continued to surface throughout the first half of the 1980s. Although it could not be expressed in the official media, sufficient intimations surfaced indicating widespread concern over the increase in the use of Russian in government offices and correspondence as well as in the media. The issue of language policy served as one of the points of crystallization for a variety of other points of discontent among the indigenous populations with the Soviet system as a whole. A resentment of the need to cater to a Slavic immigrant population, especially in Latvia and Estonia, exacerbated such dissatisfaction. The popular perception of the immigrants was low, even though many of the immigrants may have been more highly educated than the average local. The general image was set by the transient population of workers in search of the quick ruble which was flooding the Baltic republics. The interaction between the Russian immigrants and the local populations remained low. Intermarriage was relatively infrequent and the majority of offspring of such unions appeared to opt for an indigenous national self-identification.

During the final years of stagnation, and even after the ascent of Gorbachev, the increase of a Russian-language presence in national public events became especially marked. In the summer of 1985, for instance, a Red Army chorus participated in the Riga Song Festival. As late as 1987 Baltic performing groups abroad were mandated to include something Russian in their repertoires. The Lithuanian national folk ensemble Lietuva gave several concerts in France in November 1986; about a quarter of their program consisted of Russian songs and dances *à la Moiseev*. In the spring of 1987 the Estonian State Opera performed in Stockholm; the inclusion of Mussorgskii's opera *Boris Godunov* on the program was apparently *de rigueur*.

Publication policy formed a specific area of nationality discontent. The proportion of books in the local languages and in Russian provided visible evidence of disadvantages to the local languages. Certain types of publications on popular subjects were simply unavailable in the local languages. For instance, the fact that there was no automotive magazine in Lithuanian and that the Russian-language *Za rulem* was supposed to fill the gap annoyed many, especially when copies of *Russkii iazyk v shkole* were plentiful.

Discussion of publication policy became a *cause célèbre* in Estonia in early 1985. The event which underscored the extreme sensitivity of the language issue was the appearance on February 26 of an article by M. Guboglo in the Russian-language daily *Sovetskaia Estoniia*. Guboglo, a Moldavian Turk, was Academic Secretary of the USSR Academy of Sciences Council on Nationality Problems. He argued that the solution to the poor proficiency in Russian among the Estonian population was a decrease in the number of books published in Estonian. Publication in that language, he reasoned, was "artificial." "In a number of republics, publications known to be weak from artistic and scientific perspectives are included in the publication plans simply because they are written in an ethnic language." Guboglo argued, in other words, that the fact that a book was written in the native language of author and reader was insufficient as a criterion for publication in that language. In effect, it followed then that languages other than Russian, "the language of international communication," did not have the same status. Fluency in Russian would bring enlightenment to non-Russians. He went so far as to opine that the benefits of learning Russian included a general broadening of cultural habits, the development and refinement of spiritual interests and of cultural habits, and an impetus toward more active, spiritually fertile forms of cultural activity and means of self-development and self-expression by the personality. He concluded that small republican languages such as Estonian had no future except as local patois unfit for cultural, political or economic activity, which would be conducted in Russian.

The article caused a shock wave among the Estonian intelligentsia. The reaction was typical of those at the time to anything in the media: "It is not accidental." The unanswered question was why such an article, clearly at odds with officially proclaimed language policy, had been allowed to appear at all. One guess was that it had been triggered by the 1979 census results, though the time-lag was more difficult to explain. The initial response was muffled. In June 1985, in a survey of a recent meeting of the Estonian Writers Union, the Estonian cultural monthly *Looming* observed laconically that: "Probably the most discussed issue was M. Guboglo's article in *Sovetskaia Estoniia*," and proceeded to devote a full page to other, presumably less discussed, issues. At the same time, a similarly muted reference to a misunderstanding of nationality policy appeared in the party monthly *Eesti Kommunist* (February 26, 1985).

A full ten months later Savvati Smirnov, a lecturer in Russian philology at Tartu University, published a lengthy article, "Equal among equals," in the cultural monthly *Looming* (December 1985). It included a discussion of the concept of state language, the view of the Tsarist government on the question, and Lenin's ideas on the subject which had changed the compulsory policy of the old regime. Obviously, Smirnov acknowledged, a large country such as the USSR needed a language for internal communication—Russian:

> Considering the great role of the language of international communication in state life, more and more is said about the need for all the nationalities of the Soviet Union to speak Russian fluently. Often, however, [people] do not specify what is meant by the notion of fluency in a language.

That had led to a statistical anomaly—34 per cent fluency in Russian among Uzbeks and a decrease in Estonia. In the first case a very liberal interpretation of "fluency" must have prevailed; in the second, a very strict one. It is very difficult to evaluate oneself, Smirnov noted, and the more educated a person, the more likely he was to be cautious.

Smirnov also proceeded to make general observations on the role of language in a Soviet setting. It was true, he admitted, that some Soviet languages were too small for useful functions. That was not the case with Estonian. He categorized language use: (1) daily life, (2) social and political life, (3) business, (4) secondary and higher education, (5) scientific work, (6) cultural endeavors, (7) mass communication, (8) relations among the various nationalities of the USSR, and (9) international relations. All of these were accessible through Russian and all save the last through republic languages. That admittedly could change over time, but not through the fiat of language-molders such as Guboglo. Smirnov, furthermore, disagreed with Guboglo's evaluation that the desire of Estonians to have more publications in the native language was negative. It was only natural since in the USSR the Russian-language audience was served both by the central publishers as well as by local ones while no one outside Estonia provided Estonian titles. Guboglo's correlation of the increase in the number of Estonian books with a decrease in the percentage of knowledge of Russian was considered faulty: "Following this logic, we would find as much meaning in the correlation between the increase in the wheat harvest and the decrease in the number of wolves." Smirnov's article opened the way for a more extensive consideration of the language issue which has continued throughout the 1988 period of dramatic reconstruction.

Language issues have also come to the forefront in Latvia. The dissatisfaction of the indigenous population over the *de facto* secondary status of its language, which had until then only been occasionally intimated, now began to be widely discussed. Throughout 1986 this question emerged as a constant topic in the republic press and occasionally even received attention in the all-union press. At the end of the year it evoked some dramatic pronouncements.

In November 1986 Latvian CP Central Committee Secretary for Ideology Anatolijs Gorbunovs objected to some calls that had been made for the learning of Latvian to be made obligatory for all residents of the republic. He was apparently answered the following month in an interview with the leading poet of the republic, Imants Ziedonis:

> Can any citizen call himself an internationalist living in any of the national republics who knows only one language? And if this citizen is not an internationalist, can he be permitted to serve as a leader, organizer, inspirer, or example for the Komsomol and party members?[3]

In the aftermath of the disturbances in Alma-Ata, Gorbunovs apparently felt compelled to answer Ziedonis. On December 24, 1986, speaking to Latvian writers, he stated:

> I object categorically to the demand ... for the priority of the Latvian language in ... the republic and to its being opposed to the Russian language. The principle of learning the Latvian language voluntarily ... is now being [perverted and] declared obligatory for all members of the republic's non-indigenous population if their internationalist feelings, membership in the political avant-garde, and suitability for the positions that they hold are not to be cast in doubt.[4]

An even harder line was taken by E. Pelkaus in an unusually long article, "Democratization," which appeared in the Party daily *Cina* on January 14, 1987. He considered it "fundamentally wrong to make the distinction that has occasionally been made in the press [between us] the home folk and [them] the guests, who must abide by our traditions. We have a common home: the Soviet [Union], of which Soviet Latvia has been an integral part for more than four decades." Such bureaucratic pronouncements, however, failed to dampen the issue. Throughout 1987 a pattern appeared where writers and other cultural figures kept harping on the language problem while officials sought to downplay or deflect the issue.

The question was not limited to the Baltic republics alone. At the 27-28th plenum of the USSR Writers' Union, held on 1-2 March 1988, Belorussians and Ukrainians dramatically raised the problem of an imminent threat to their languages because of long-standing educational and publication policies. These were republished in the cultural press of the Baltic republics and no doubt reinforced the local pressures on this question which had been growing.

Its most unqualified expressions came from the writers. In 1987 it emerged as the principal topic of discussion at the conferences of Latvian and Estonian writers. The initial account of the Estonian Writers Union meeting in the cultural weekly *Sirp ja Vasar* (1 and 9 May) remained somewhat reticent, though the subsequent summary in the cultural monthly *Looming* (August 1986) was more informative.[5] The fact that Estonian literature was more popular in Moscow and Leningrad than among Russians in Estonia was noted. And the basically pro forma teaching of Estonian in schools with Russian-language instruction was observed. Two Russian writers, however, complained about the lack of a Russian textbook on Estonian literature and of poor reportage of Estonian cultural life in the two Russian-language dailies of the republic.

The Latvian Writers Congress in April 1987 occasioned complaints over the impoverishment of language. One participant proposed that the resolution of the conference include an appeal to the leadership of the union to acquaint itself systematically with the teaching of Latvian and its mastery in schools where Russian was the language of instruction and to inform the Ministry of Education of its findings. Another noted that "a people that loses its linguistic ability also loses its ability to think coherently. The thought–language relationship is a reflexive one." Some participants expressed concern over the insufficient number of hours devoted to the teaching of Latvian. Another general concern was for the need for books to integrate the Russian population into the richness of the local culture. Publication policy, which is intrinsically connected with language policy, also came under attack. The principal complaint was over the exaggerated size of several editions in the Russian language. While these might be profitable to the publishers, their printing in Riga depleted the republic's allotment of paper. As a result, native literary works were pushed into the background, resulting in a large backlog.

Language had become a very prominent aspect of the Latvian cultural scene. In March 1987 a language festival, the first of its kind in the USSR, was organized in Riga. Its purpose was to promote the learning and teaching of languages. The winners of regular "olympiads" (competitions among secondary school students throughout the republic in proficiency in learning Latvian, Russian, English, French and German) were brought to Riga. There they participated in special programs and attended exhibitions intended to stimulate their interest in these languages. While the scope was international, the event was apparently devoted principally to the Latvian language. This facet was most dramatically expressed by the head of the Latvian Writers' Union, Janis Peters, who in his address to the gathering noted the need to possess an excellent command of one's native language and to be intolerant of its corruption. He stressed the notion of cultural pollution:

> A contaminated language is a catastrophe of no lesser magnitude than polluted forests and rivers where life dies. Spiritual death is even more terrible than physical death. It is precisely you, engaged in cultivating language, who are encouraged to respect the life of each nation, its language, traditions and culture. Precisely you are the ones for whom hatred among nations and inequality among languages are alien. Respecting your own language, you also respect your brother among the Russians, Lithuanians, Germans and the English. . . . I urge you to be patriots of your own language and at the same time to open [yourselves] in love to other nations.[6]

In September Peters stated in a Moscow Radio broadcast that the Latvian CP Central Committee Commission on Nationality and Internationality Relations, of which he was a member, had decided that it was necessary, among other measures, to start teaching Latvian to children of the non-native population.[7]

Throughout 1987 the Lithuanians remained somewhat more muted on the language question, perhaps because the issue was not as pressing there, or perhaps because of a traditional wait-and-see attitude which has characterized the Lithuanian political and cultural elite throughout the postwar period. But during the national renaissance of 1988, it emerged with equal force in that republic as well.

The language issue has become one of the most prominent facets of the national renaissances that took place in all three republics during 1988. The numerous massive demonstrations accentuated the rise of national self-consciousness providing a dramatic backdrop for the discussion. The earlier complaints of "deformations of Leninist policy" were now replaced by demands for rectification. During the summer of 1988 in all three republics such calls merged into a push for constitutional amendments to make the indigenous languages state languages.

The resolution of the Estonian Cultural Unions of April 1–2, 1988, which served as the harbinger of Baltic self-assertiveness during the summer to come, consisted of 18 proposals for radical economic, social, ecological, demographic and political reform. None specifically touched on linguistic policies, though some were intrinsically tied to language-related activities. Point 4 called for republic units to take concrete steps to "decentralize cultural life in the Estonian SSR." In effect that would limit the roles of the Ministry of Culture and the Department of Culture of the Estonian SSR Central Committee. Point 5 called for available means to be utilized to "overcome years of falling behind in the material basis of the cultural-social sphere," which, presumably, meant cultural activity. Point 18 touched specifically on publication policy: it called for a change of policy toward Estonian literature; for an end to the printing of large editions in Russian for the all-union market, which depleted the republic's paper quota; and for republic cultural unions, societies, institutions of higher learning and other scientific and cultural establishments to receive the right to publish in the local language. Other points called for support of scholarship on national-heritage projects, and for restoration of books destroyed in the 1940s and 1950s.[8]

Two months later the Latvian Writers Union uttered a poignant cry of desperation by a national group which had been pushed to the brink of extinction by a policy of national deformation. Its resolution, to which the leaderships of the other Latvian creative unions concurred, was more radical. Included is a specific call for making Latvian the state language of the Latvian SSR.[9] The pressure on the regime on the language question in Latvia was already evident the previous month. Visiting Sweden at the head of a Soviet party delegation in May, Latvian CP First Secretary Boris Pugo admitted in an interview that all was not right. He observed that it was necessary for a cultured individual to learn from the milieu in which he lived; too many immigrants had not studied Latvian sufficiently.[10]

On July 20, 1988, the party daily *Tiesa* published a strongly worded statement by 11 members of the Lithuanian SSR Academy of Sciences which criticized the *de facto* downplaying of the Lithuanian language and called for Lithuanian to be made the state language of the Lithuanian SSR:

> The deformers of Marxism, who base themselves on the antiscientific "theory of the fusion of languages," ... have been constantly narrowing down the sphere of the usage of national languages. Up to now, the Lithuanian language was frequently displaced from the sociopolitical sphere (in the party and the government organs, especially in those of the republic) as well as in the areas of science, production and service.

One of the signatories, the linguist Vytautas Ambrazas, elaborated on the claim that there had been an active policy gradually to exclude Lithuanian from everyday public life:

> For a long time the Lithuanian language has been and is being displaced from many areas. ... It is no secret that even in top government agencies the Russian language was considered as the main one, while Lithuanian was relegated to the status of a local

language . . . . We already have a whole stratum of officials and even scientists who have deformed their language in accordance with foreign examples, but who have failed to learn a second language properly.[11]

The perception of conscious Russification was elaborated even more unequivocally by the Estonian linguist Mati Hint who claimed that the Estonian and Latvian CP leaderships had purposely encouraged immigration as a means of wiping out the national languages and cultures of these republics. There was a clear link, he observed, between chauvinism and demography; the swamping of Estonia and Latvia by Russian immigrants had not simply been a result of economically motivated undertakings by Moscow ministries. Hint proposed policies to encourage emigration by the Russian population.[12]

The question of language policy was prominent in late 1988 during the adoption, in all three republics, of constitutional amendments declaring the indigenous languages to be state languages. The Supreme Soviet of the Latvian SSR was the first to act, on October 6. The Lithuanians followed on November 17. That session of the Lithuanian SSR Supreme Soviet triggered off considerable demonstrations in the wake of a refusal to include a declaration of sovereignty analogous to the one which had been passed in Estonia the previous day. The Estonian language amendment, which had been recommended by the Presidium of the Estonian SSR Supreme Soviet on June 13, was passed on December 7, during the same session which reaffirmed an earlier declaration of sovereignty in November that had been declared unconstitutional by Moscow.

The proponents of these constitutional amendments aimed principally to explain their necessity and to mollify opposition among the nonindigenous population. The extent of the writing on the subject which appeared in late 1988 testifies to the significance of the problem. Mati Hint, for instance, addressing a meeting of Komsomol activists in Tallinn on November 10, stressed the fact that the planned Estonian law would not give any privileges to the Estonian language and would only somewhat curb the privileges which had accrued to Russian.[13] In Lithuania the linguist V. Toporov argued that unfortunately many people did not understand that making a language a state language was a recognition of the status and development of a people, not a move against another language.

> Making the Lithuanian language the state language will not make "second class citizens" of the Russians in Lithuania; however, they can make themselves into such by refusing to respect the Lithuanian

language (in the theoretical sense) and by refusing to learn it (in the practical sense). The only alternative is "secondratedness"—to feel a conqueror in a land whose language it is not necessary to learn.[14]

Another writer in Lithuania with a Slavic surname, V. Verkovich, also commented on the question as to why non-Lithuanians objected to making Lithuanian the state language. His answer was that an erroneous identification of the USSR with Soviet Russia had become widespread:

> It was very convenient and no trouble to get along only with a knowledge of the Russian language in any corner of the USSR. Knowledge of Russian by the non-Russian inhabitants of all republics was evaluated as a factor helping their integration into a unitary Soviet people.[15]

He stressed the need to publish a concrete program for the implementation of Lithuanian as a state language: this, he felt, would demonstrate to non-Lithuanians that no one was interested in taking away anyone's rights, and so remove many unfounded apprehensions.

Published opposition, for the most part, did not attack the principle of state-language status for the indigenous languages. Rather, it tended to focus on the announced details of implementation. On September 22, for instance, a spokesman for the Balto-Slavic Society of Latvia, one of several groups of Russian immigrants coalescing to counter the Latvian Popular Front, approved the idea of making Latvian the state language, but cautioned care in the practical implementation of any measures stemming from such a constitutional amendment. Such implementational opposition appears most pronounced in Estonia, where discussion of these questions long preceded the actual constitutional amendment. A. Poltev, writing from the predominantly Russian city of Narva in eastern Estonia, agreed that while a language law was necessary, the draft legislation which had been announced was inadequate in that it did not guarantee non-Estonians the right to use their own language and frequently opposed such a right in its details: "The adoption of the law, in the sense that it is proposed, will make normal activity by the Russian-language population and enterprises impossible, and it will considerably impede interrepublic contacts."[16] On December 1 N. Zhukovskaia questioned to what extent a Russian resident of Estonia would realistically be able to learn Estonian in three years if language legislation did not guarantee for any Russian speaker the opportunity to study Estonian. If that were not possible, some would simply not try, while others might emigrate. Such legislation would then meet the fate of much previous Soviet legislation—good in theory, but ignored in practice.¹⁷ Her concerns appear not to be far-fetched, given the scarcity of Estonian teachers and texts.

By February 1989 only Estonia had adopted legislation designed to implement the new status for the Estonian language. On January 18 the Estonian SSR Supreme Soviet passed a law entitling Estonians, over a period of four years, to ask a question in a government office, in some stores, and in some hospitals in Estonian and to expect to receive an answer in that language; Russians were accorded the same right in Russian. The legal spelling of names was to be in the Latin script (not by way of the Cyrillic); and patronymics were to be abolished for Estonians. Street and store signs in Estonian were to take precedence over Russian equivalents, which could not be larger in size. The only exception was for military installations.¹⁸ In effect, many Russian residents would be required to learn Estonian over the next few years at a considerable expense of time and money or leave the republic. It remains to be seen how effective the legislation will be in practice.

It is evident that the issue of language has become cardinal on the Baltic political scene because it enjoys considerable support among the population. And it is furthermore evident that the question will not be resolved readily. Implementation of the measures passed in Estonia, and of analogous measures which will probably be legislated in Latvia and Lithuania, will take a long time. The question of the status of the constituent republics of the USSR in a post-*perestroika* USSR also remains unresolved; no doubt its resolution will also affect the course of implementation of such language legislation.

Notes

1. *Sovetskaia Latviia*, January 6, 1979.

2. *Alma Mater*, III/1979.

3. *Literatura un maksla*, November 19, 1986 as quoted in *Radio Free Europe Research*, RAD/Bungs, March 3, 1987.

4. Ibid.

5. For an account of the meeting, see *Baltic Forum* (Fall 1986), pp. 65-8.

6. *Skolotaju Avize*, March 28, 1987, as quoted in Dzintra Bungs "Latvia's First Language Festival," *RFE Research*, Baltic Area, SR/3, May 8, 1987.

7. *Foreign Broadcast Information Service*, SWB, SU/8676/B/16, September 21, 1987.

8. *Sirp ja vasar*, April 8, 1988 as quoted in *Radio Free Europe Research*, RAD/Ilves, April 20, 1988.

9. *Sovetskaia Latviia*, June 11, 1986.

10. *Svenska Dagbladet*, May 21, 1988.
11. *Literatura ir menas*, July 30, 1988.
12. *RFE Research*, Baltic Area, SR/8, August 4, 1988.
13. *Molodezh Estonii*, November 11, 1988.
14. *Sovetskaia Litva*, November 10, 1988.
15. *Sovetskaia Litva*, November 16, 1988.
16. *Molodezh Estonii*, November 11, 1988.
17. *Molodezh Estonii*, December 1, 1988.
18. *The New York Times*, January 18, 1989.

Chapter 12

Islam and Nationality in Tsarist Russia and the Soviet Union

Tadeusz Swietochowski

With some 45–50 million Muslims, broadly defined, living within its borders, the Soviet Union is one of the world's major Muslim countries, ranking with Turkey, Iran or Egypt. But to what extent can Soviet Muslims be regarded as one entity? This is the major theme of this chapter.

Russian rule over the Muslims has a long history reaching back to the conquest of the Volga Tatars by Ivan the Terrible in the mid-sixteenth century. The subjugation of other Muslim peoples spanned the next three centuries, the process going on gradually with long interruptions. Under Catherine II Russia seized the khanate of the Crimea; under Alexander I, the khanates of northern Azerbaijan; under Alexander II, Turkestan, i.e. the territories of the emirates of Bukhara, and the khanates of Kokand and Khiva. The conquest of Central Asia was completed by the capture of Turkmenistan and the oasis of Merv in 1884.[1]

The conquered Muslim populations were far from forming a homogeneous mass. Spread over vast expanses, they lacked geographical contiguity, isolated from each other as they were by Christian inhabited areas. In their homelands diverse Muslim groups lived in various stages of historical development ranging from the nomadic tribes of the Kazakhs, Kirghiz, Turkmens, part of the Uzbeks and Karakalpaks, to societies that in the Tsarist era had entered the age of commercial capitalism, such as the Volga Tatars, or had even begun to industrialize, as was the case of the Azerbaijanis.

Furthermore, the Muslims of Russia lacked the benefit of linguistic unity. Although a large majority of them spoke Turkic languages, their literary idioms were Chagatai, Persian or Arabic. Even the common denominator of their identity, the religion of Islam, has shaped various groups of these Muslims to different degrees. Some, such as the Volga Tatars, Azerbaijanis or sedentary

Turkestanis, had behind them a centuries-long tradition of belonging to the Islamic civilization; others, such as the nomadic peoples of the Kazakh steppes and the Kirghiz, and some of the Caucasian mountaineers, had been converted much later, and their Islamization was still superficial. Then, there was the split between the Sunni and Shi'a branches of Islam, the latter predominant in Transcaucasia. In this multilevel diversity, it was the Russian state that provided a structure for some measure of integration among the peoples who otherwise would be unlikely to have been brought together.

The pattern of the Russian conquest varied: in some cases, notably in the Azerbaijani khanate of Ganja, the emirate of Bukhara, the khanate of Kokand and Turkmenistan, violence and bloodshed were involved. In the case of the Caucasus mountaineers there followed more than half a century of armed resistance whose symbol was Shamil. In other instances the submission to, or incorporation into, Russia was effected through negotiated treaties, as in the case of Khiva and some Azerbaijani khanates. The relationship of the subject Muslims to the Russian state was not invariably antagonistic. After a long period of brutal persecutions and forcible conversions that came in the wake of conquest by Ivan the Terrible, religious tolerance had become the norm since the reign of Catherine II. The effect was that the bulk of the Muslim population was able to cultivate its splendid isolation from almost all things Russian—a remarkable feature of coexistence under the Tsardom. The Muslims were usually exempt from military service, they were tried by their *Shari'ah* courts in noncriminal cases, retained their traditional system of education—indeed their nineteenth century literatures seem to barely acknowledge the fact of the Russian overlordship. In many Muslim-populated regions traditional loyalties—based on kinship, tribal, or alternatively local, bonds—remained undisturbed as long as they did not conflict with the interests of the Russian state.

At the same time, Russian rule brought tangible advantages to some select groups among the Muslims: the petty landowning aristocracies in Daghestan, Azerbaijan and Turkestan saw their status upgraded to the level of the Russian gentry. The economic expansion of Russia made possible the rise of the Volga Tatar commercial bourgeoisie and the Baku oil magnates, groups that would become important components of the Muslim modernizing elite.[2]

Another group which emerged from the impact of Russian rule on the Muslim societies was the intelligentsia, its first representatives making their appearance before the mid-nineteenth century. It was primarily the native intelligentsia, rather than the Tsarist administration, that acted as the transmission channel for the penetration of

European ideas into the Muslim environment. Nevertheless, the transmission was through the tainted prism of Russian civilization, and the Muslim intelligentsia accepted as its models the Russian *Zapadniks* (Westernizers), *Narodniks* (Populists), Liberals and Pan-Slavists. In fact, their conservative opponents would come to criticize them as being accomplices in the Russian assimilationist designs. To a degree out of proportion to the numbers of the intelligentsia, the history of the Russian Muslim political movements has become the history of that social force.

A special preoccupation of the intelligentsia was the question of the Muslims' group identity in face of the coming modern age. Traditionally, the ties binding Muslims together were primarily religious in nature. All Muslims were members of the *umma*, the worldwide community of believers, regardless of ethnic, linguistic, tribal or racial distinctions. The *umma* was inherently opposed to nationalism in any form, regarding it as a concept alien to the universalistic spirit of Islam, and, furthermore, a divisive force *vis-à-vis* its enemies. At the turn of the century the political program of Pan-Islamism, which called for the unity of all Muslims of the world (implicitly under the leadership of the Ottoman Empire and its sultan Abdulhamid II), tried to capitalize on the deeply rooted *umma* consciousness.[3]

Yet this consciousness did little to bring closer to one another the disparate strains of the Russian Muslims. The program of Pan-Islamism was distinguished above all by its nebulousness; and in its Abdulhamidian variety it smacked strongly of religious conservatism, which accounted for its limited appeal to the Muslim intelligentsia in Russia. As a group, they were inclined toward secularism, a proclivity stemming from the conviction that at the root of the Muslim world's backwardness was the grip of religion on all facets of communal as well as individual life. Moreover, they were increasingly influenced by theories of contemporary European nationalisms. Again, the Russian models loomed large, and in response to such movements as Pan-Slavism and Slavophilism, there emerged a defensive program for the unity of the Muslims within the Russian empire. Inasmuch as these Muslims were overwhelmingly of Turkic stock, the program amounted to the launching of an ethnocentric movement, which came to be referred to variously as Turkism or Pan-Turkism. The first term connoted concern with the ethnic and linguistic identity of the Turkic peoples; the other, the striving for their cooperation and solidarity.

The founder of the movement was the Crimean Tatar writer and journalist Ismail bey Gasprinskii, who promoted the idea of the community of all Turkish-speaking peoples, the *qavm*, but stopped short of advocating political action, the prospect of which would have been doomed in any case given the repressive climate of the Alexander III reign. The Turkic unity that Gasprinskii preached was to be of a spiritual and linguistic quality as expressed in his famous slogan: *dilde, fikirde, ishte birlik* (unity in language, thought and work). The fundamental precondition for attaining this goal was to be the creation of a literary idiom understandable to all Turks, from the Balkans to the borderlands of China. Such a common language was indeed formed in the columns of Gasprinskii's newspaper, *Tarjuman*, published in Bakhchisaray from 1883 on. It was based on the Turkish of Istanbul, i.e. Ottoman, though purified of an excess of Persian and Arabic words and written in a simplified syntax. The *Tarjuman* could be read by the well-educated in all Turkic lands, but for an average reader it was easily comprehensible only in the Oghuz subgroup, the Crimea and Azerbaijan, while most of the eastern and northern Turks would find it unintelligible without special study.[4]

In step with the communications media, the second instrument of Pan-Turkism was to be modernized education. The reform of the traditional Islamic educational system in Russia was the essence of the *jadidist* movement that had originated among the Volga Tatars and subsequently spread to other parts of the Tsarist Empire. *Jadidism*, its name derived from *usul-i jadid* (the new method), aimed at reforming the curricula of Muslim schools and their overall approach to teaching. The *jadidist* schools taught such secular subjects as geography, science and European languages, and attempted to replace the study of classical literary languages with that of the spoken idioms of Turkic peoples. With time, the original meaning of *jadidism* extended to connote the reformist frame of mind in general. The new method met with vociferous opposition from the conservatives known as the *qadimists*, who among other criticisms, accused the reformers of helping the policy of Russification.[5]

The notion of the Turkic *qavm* promoted by Pan-Turkism, and at least indirectly by *jadidism*, clearly signaled a departure from the traditional form of group identity, yet the process remained limited chiefly to the intelligentsia. Pan-Turkism depended for its spread on social communications, and it was slow in taking roots among the predominantly illiterate masses.

When the 1905 Russian Revolution improved the possibilities for the public use of the Turkic vernaculars—Azeri, Kazakh, Uzbek, Kirghiz, Tatar—Pan-Turkism found a potential rival in the current of regionalisms.[6] This current was a rapidly growing phenomenon which held a special appeal for the populist instincts of a good part of the intelligentsia. The growth of regional identities among the Turkic peoples of Russia continued after 1908, when a new upheaval in that epoch of revolutions brought the Young Turks to power in Istanbul. Unlike the regime of Abdulhamid, which it had replaced, the new ruling group soon proved itself sympathetic to Pan-Turkism and interested in the Turkic peoples across the Russian frontier. These ethnic cousins of the Ottomans were, however, increasingly concerned with their regional identities—*Qazaqchiliq, Azerichiliq, Tatarchiliq*, and Pan-Turkism was faced with the choice of whether to accommodate these particularisms or to persist in forging complete unity no matter what the odds. A leading intellectual of the second generation of Pan-Turkists, Ali bey Huseynzade, who alternated his activities between Baku and Istanbul, inveighed against the inclination toward what he perceived as parochialism implicit in the idea of regional communities: "Rise, rise above and step out of the narrow circle of nationalisms. Do not allow yourself to be turned into docile subjects of particularistic, petty nations." He called the Ottoman state the "spiritual and political head of the Islamic world" and believed that Ottoman should be used as a standard literary language for all the Turkic peoples.[7]

In his criticism of the regional particularisms, Huseynzade referred to the term *millet*, which in the period 1905-1914 came increasingly into use. The origins of the term go back to the history of the Ottoman state where it denoted a religious, non-Muslim community. Among the Russian Muslims, it was used at first in regions with diverse populations to describe a local religious group, Muslim or otherwise, which usually spoke the same language or dialect. After 1905, the term *millet* acquired the meaning of nation, in a regional and particularist sense, as distinct from the *qavm*, and even more from the *umma*, although the confusion of the terms still lingered on. One of the first attempts to define it came from the Azerbaijani political figure Mammed Emin Rasulzade, who used a clearly secular frame of reference: *millet*, in his words, was "community based on common language culture, history, as well as religion, the latter being one of its elements".[8] This definition of a nation bore resemblance to another given in the same year, 1913, by an acquaintance of Rasulzade and his erstwhile political companion, Stalin.[9]

The debate on the forms of group identity—*'umma, qavm*, or *millet*—was noticeable, though barely so, in the all-Russian Muslim congresses that were convened from 1906 on, and it became the dominant theme in the Congress that met under the conditions of unrestricted freedom in May 1917, soon after the overthrow of the Tsardom. The meeting turned into an arena for the clash between the two opposite camps on the question of unity and diversity, a controversy which sounded the echoes of the *'umma* versus *millet* debate.

Representatives of the ethnic groups which formed compact masses within particular regions, such as Transcaucasia, Turkestan, Bashkiria, Kirghizia and the Crimea, generally favored territorial autonomy. In their view, the Muslim-populated lands should become self-governing in all matters except those of vital concern for the whole of the Russian state. In the words of Rasulzade, who was their spokesman, "there is no Christian nationality, likewise there is no Islamic one".[10] He took a step even beyond Pan-Turkism by reminding the Congress that various Turkic peoples had already developed written languages, literatures, and indeed identities, distinct from one another, even though they all formed one Turkic *qavm*.

The Volga Tatars, their population dispersed over various parts of Russia, were at the forefront of the opposing camp. Unable to claim the right for a self-governing territory, they called for cultural autonomy within a centralized body that would represent all Muslims *vis-à-vis* the government. Curiously, the position of the Tatar bourgeoisie, who stood for Muslim unity and organizational centralism, found support from socialists of diverse persuasions. In their loyalty to the cause of the Russian Revolution, they came out against the fragmentation of the Muslim community, the alternative that could benefit the capitalists and landlords. The conservative Pan-Islamists, for their part, fought a rear-guard battle to stop the break-up of the *umma* into national units built on secular foundations. In the end the territorial autonomists prevailed, though far from overwhelmingly, an indication of an effective standoff on the *umma* versus *millet* issue.[11] In fact, a compromise formula went into circulation, to the effect that all the Muslims of Russia constituted one *millet*.

In the new revolutionary period, between February and October 1917, in the Muslim-populated regions there sprang up political parties and associations, such as *Alash Orda* in Kazakhstan; *Milli Firqa* in the Crimea; *Musavat, Himmat, Ittihad* in Azerbaijan; the Young Bukhariotes; and the Young Khivans. All of them in one way or another championed autonomy for their respective homelands and formed the hard core of regional governments that emerged from the disintegration of the Russian state. During the Russian Civil War, these Muslim governments, after tortuous and usually repeated switching of alignment, came to the conclusion that the Bolsheviks, in the end, represented a lesser evil than the White regimes, such as those of Kolchak and Denikin. As for the Bolsheviks, they did not face great difficulties in replacing in due course the national governments of the Crimea, Azerbaijan, Bashkiria and Kazakhstan with Soviet authorities.[12] Notable exceptions to the pattern were the North

Caucasus, the historic citadel of Muslim resistance, and Turkestan, where the Basmachi movement of armed opposition continued through most of the decade of the 1920s.[13]

Among the factors facilitating the Boshevik seizure of power was the fact that while regional nationalists controlled the local governments and political parties, conservative Pan-Islamists who stood for the *umma* enjoyed the backing of the population at large. The conservatives argued that Islam and socialism were close to each other in their universalism and the advocacy of equality and brotherhood. The defense of petty states accidentally spawned by the Revolution was not a cause worthy of fighting. Moreover, the Soviet system offered a better prospect for preserving Muslim unity. In the vocabulary of the conservatives the word "nationalist" was a term of abuse.

The issue was a cause for hesitation in the Bolshevik councils, and the Soviet policy toward the Muslims would for a long time be marked by some zigzagging, yet its general line would remain easily discernible: promotion of the *millet* over the *umma* identity, secular foundations of the communal life over the Islamic, fragmentation rather than Muslim unity.

Two major considerations tipped the scales in choosing the long-term policy. First, there was recognition of the fact that a transition from a religion-based community toward a socialist society would not be feasible. In the distinctly Eurocentric view of the Bolsheviks, nationality was an unavoidable stage in historical development, even though it was an intermediate stage and would not, it was hoped, last long. A second consideration of a less theoretical nature was the "surrogate proletariat" syndrome. The working-class in most of the Muslim lands was nonexistent, and in others such as Azerbaijan it was weak in numbers and even weaker in class consciousness. By contrast, there was in these lands a secular-minded, active and ambitious intelligentsia, the modernizing elite of the regional communities. The intelligentsia, it could be expected, would be won over to the Soviet cause far more easily than the Muslim masses, whose apathy and backwardness the Bolsheviks described without excessive inhibitions.

The chief Soviet agency in charge of implementing—and also elaborating, interpreting, and often formulating—the nationality policies was the People's Commissar for Nationalities Affairs (Narkomnats), whose head in the years 1917–1918 was Stalin. Of the top-level Bolshevik leaders, he was the only one with interest in and some knowledge of Muslim political movements, the by-product of his Transcaucasian background.[14]

Under his aegis the Narkomnats established specialized bodies dealing with Muslim affairs, various Muslim commissariats (*Muskomy*) and bureaus (*Musbiuros*). These tended to be organized on territorial bases, i.e. concerning themselves with particular regions or even provinces, and they agitated against the all-Russian Muslim movement. Whenever possible, members of the native intelligentsia, among whom there were few Communists, would be encouraged to join the work of these bodies. In such a way began the influx of the Muslim intelligentsia into the Soviet regime, a process further expanded by Stalin after the end of the Civil War. At this juncture he was displaying his political flexibility, opposing rigid application of class warfare in the national regions.

Among his appointees was Mir Said Sultangaliev, the highest ranking Muslim in the Party hierarchy and for some time the right-hand man of Stalin in the Narkomnats. While in some ways Sultangaliev acted as spokesman for Stalin's policies, in others he tried to deflect them from their disintegrating effects on the Muslim community. His ideas on changing the Party line on the nationality question among Muslims came to be known as Muslim national Communism. Reduced to its bare essentials, Sultangalievism, a term which also gained currency, was an attempt to adapt the notions of the *umma* and the Turkic *qavm* to the Soviet system. At its root was the assumption that a fundamental and unbridgeable difference existed between the worlds of Islam and of the West. From the standpoint of revolutionary strategy, the Muslim society had not developed its proletariat, therefore the dictatorship of that class is not a viable proposition for the Muslims. In their lands the proper course of action should be the formation of a Muslim national, rather than a class government, and there should be a Muslim Communist Party. In a sense all Muslims, inasmuch as they suffer oppression from colonialism, are proletariat. Even the working class of European nations derives benefits from colonial exploitation. For the expansion of Communism, the future lies not in Europe but in Asia, especially in the Islamic East. Consequently, it is imperative to arrive at a compromise between Marxism and Islam as a way of life and a set of traditions. In the Soviet state, instead of regional fragmentation, two large Muslim entities should be established on the basis of ethnic and linguistic affinities: the Bashkir-Tatar or Volga Ural, and the Turkestani republics.

As urgent matters of practical concern for the Soviet Muslims, Sultangaliev and his followers called for an end to the rural Russian colonization of the Kazakh steppe, and for the replacement of Russian officials in the local government by natives. The latter demand was accepted and explicitly endorsed by the 1923 12th Party Congress which officially launched the *korenizatsiia* (indigenization) policy. On the other hand, the same Congress was followed by the public disgracing of Sultangaliev: his ideas were condemned and he himself was arrested, albeit for a brief time.[15]

Meanwhile the process of dividing the Muslims into regional units went on and reached a crescendo after the 12th Congress. The task of creating European-type nations, by decree modern, proceeded according to the criteria which Stalin had formulated in 1913. A nation, he wrote, is a "historically evolved, stable community built on the foundations of a common language, territory, economic life and psychological make-up manifested in common culture".[16] Of these criteria, the unity of language and territory became in practice the ultimate determinants in Soviet decision-making. The task of restructuring the Muslim community of Russia was a highly complex undertaking that involved the efforts of administrators and economists, as well as scholars. The thrust of specific solutions generally favored the peoples that inhabited a territory in a compact mass, rather than those living in dispersion.

Yet in the notable case of the Volga-Ural region the effort to overcome the dispersion by the union of two closely related peoples, Bashkirs and Tatars, was disallowed. Instead, the Autonomous Bashkir Republic was created in 1919 on the basis of a vernacular with no written form. In Transcaucasia the task was rendered simple by converting independent Azerbaijan into a Soviet republic by means of military conquest. In the Caucasus the mosaic of tribes was raised to the status of officially recognized nationalities and grouped into (1) the Chechen-Ingush Autonomous Republic; (2) the Kabardo-Balkar Autonomous Republic; (3) the North Ossetian Autonomous Republic; (4) the Adyga Autonomous Region; (5) the Karachai Autonomous Region. The multilingual territory of Daghestan was formed into an Autonomous Republic in which initially Azerbaijani, and then 11 local languages, became recognized as being literary.[17]

In 1924 the National Delimitation of the Central Asian Republics was carried out with the resulting division of the region into units formed on broadly ethnic-linguistic lines, a crucial step that ended the tradition of multilingualism and created preconditions for the rise of homogeneous nations. The reform did away with the transitory People's Republics of Turkestan, Bukhara and Khorezm. The new states that came into being were the Soviet Republics of Uzbekistan and Turkmenistan, the Kazakh and Kirghiz Autonomous Republics, and the Karakalpak Autonomous District (*oblast'*).[18]

The Soviet nation-making activity was supplemented, especially after 1923, by the *korenizatsiia* policy, which amounted to more than simply promoting the natives into high positions in the Party and the government. An attempt to reconcile the nationalities with Soviet rule, *korenizatsiia* called for the equality of the non-Russian language and cultures with Russian. It sought to legitimize an urban-based Revolution in a predominantly agricultural and multiethnic state by encouraging the development of distinct national cultures.[19]

Inasmuch as *korenizatsiia* offered the promise of overcoming backwardness and economic underdevelopment in the non-Russian societies, it met the fundamental aspirations of the Muslim intelligentsia half way. Many members of this social group were appointed to positions of responsibility and influence in their republics, and under *korenizatsiia* they resumed their time-honored programs of the *jadidist*-Enlightenment character: elimination of illiteracy, growth of education and communications media, formation of literary languages based on the spoken vernaculars, equality of rights for women. All these programs were carried out to the accompaniment of a secularization policy, which during most of the 1920s remained moderate, and which focused on such issues as the integration of the *Shari'ah* into Soviet law and nationalization of the *waqfs* (pious foundations that had been the economic basis for Muslim charitable and educational activities). Only after 1928, with the consolidation of Stalin's power, did secularization turn brutal, when it was aimed at uprooting the Islamic identity and, by extension, the vestiges of *umma* consciousness.[20]

The effect of *korenizatsiia* was *rastsvet*, the flourishing of national languages and cultures, the latter with the proviso of being socialist in content. On the whole, *rastsvet* brought impressive achievements in the Muslim republics, which often had no strong traditions of national cultures (as distinct from supranational Islamic), of native literary languages, or indeed of literacy. The alphabet reforms of the late 1920s greatly facilitated the struggle against illiteracy by replacing the Arabic alphabet, ill-suited to the Turkic phonetics, with the Latin. On the other hand, these reforms deepened the differentiation among the Turkic languages as the new script highlighted phonetic distinctions which the old one was able to slur over.

The high point of *korenizatsiia*'s successes came in the period of the first five-year plan, when rapid industrialization drew large numbers of Muslims into the factories of republics and regions. Because of the massive character of the population shift, these migrants were no longer faced with assimilation to the Russian culture in their towns and cities. By 1933 *korenizatsiia* was phased out amidst the official criticisms of encouraging local chauvinism and nationalist deviations, or discriminating against the Russian language. In retrospect, these attacks on *korenizatsiia* appear as the backdrop for the purges of the Stalin era, which in the Muslim republics, among the multitude of other victims, centered on the pre-revolutionary intelligentsia with past links to Pan-Turkism, Sultangalievism, "separatism" or even Pan-Islamism. By the end of the 1930s new alphabet reforms went into effect, this time changing the Latin script into the Cyrillic. The reforms were a clear signal that a new policy was under way. Instead of promoting further the growth of distinct national identities, the emphasis now shifted to unity—indeed, uniformity. The vision for the future was the formation of a new Soviet man in whose make-up the Russian culture and language would be the weightiest component. This goal was to be achieved through a complex two-stage process. First, through *sblizhenie* (rapprochement), the term which officially came to use only after 1945. On the theory that the peoples of the Soviet Union had progressed to a higher, socialist form of consciousness, the national distinctions were losing their significance. The special role of the Russian language—no longer a tool of oppression after the October Revolution—was that of communication among the Soviet peoples, as well as the means of enriching their languages by the influx of Russian words. Along with linguistic and cultural assimilation, migrations and intermarriages would be encouraged. The transitional stage of *sblizhenie* would lead to a new dialectical quality, *sliyanie* (fusion), the vision somewhat reminiscent of Pushkin's imagery of various Slavic rivers merging into the Russian sea. The point of *sliyanie* has never been attained, and in recent years this prospect, disturbing for the non-Russian nationalities, was discreetly dropped from official use. In its stead came the new term *edinstvo* (unity), which holds the promise that diverse national cultures will survive indefinitely. Meanwhile, in the age of television, urbanization and expanding Russian-language education for the natives, the process of assimilation continues quietly at its own pace.

Within the last century of Russian rule, the general direction of the Muslim community's evolution has been from the universalism of the *umma* toward the particularism of the *millet*. Such transformation was not unique to the Russian-held segments of the Islamic world: in fact it showed remarkable similarities with the processes under way in Muslim lands outside Russia.

In the early 1920s the colonial powers of Great Britain and France resorted to comparable solutions of creating dependent Arab states on the lines of regional particularisms. At this formative period for

Soviet Muslim policy, there emerged beyond Russia's frontiers the states of Syria, Lebanon, Iraq, Transjordan and Egypt. Many, if not most, Arabs regarded these states as artificial products of the imperialist "divide-and-rule" designs, yet they proved themselves viable enough to continue their existence long after colonial rule had ended. The largest of the new Muslim-populated nation-states, Kemalist Turkey, was created without the influence of the imperialist powers, in fact struggling against them. Still, the Turkish Republic came into being through the determined effort of its Europeanized elite, which imposed its program on the population.

The similarities between the Soviet Muslim policies and those that brought about the Turkish transformations are far more striking than in the case of the Western solutions for the Arabs. In both Turkey and Soviet Russia the regimes' objectives were: the break-up of the *umma* bonds; building a sense of regional nationalism; forceful secularization; and formation of a new, vernacular-based literary language. Even the Latinization of the alphabet in Turkey closely followed the example of the Soviet republics.

The effect of the changes taking place at approximately the same period in the Soviet Union, Turkey and the Arab lands was the restructuring of the greater part of the Islamic world on the lines of nation-states, a process sometimes referred to as the nationalization of Islam. But an open question remains: to what extent did this process reflect the inner dynamics of the Islamic community, and to what extent was it imposed by a foreign power, or at best by Europeanized native elites.

Notes

1. For a general discussion of the Russian conquest of the Muslim lands, see A. Bennigsen and C. Lemercier-Quelquejay, *Islam in the Soviet Union* (New York, 1967), pp. 3–19.

2. For a recent work on the Russian Muslim policy under the Tsardom, see: A. Kappeler, "Die zaristische Politik gegenüber den Muslimen des russischen Reiches" in A. Kappeler, G. Simon and G. Brunner (eds.), *Die Muslime in der Sowjetunion and Jugoslawien. Identität-Politik-Widerstand* (Köln, 1989), pp. 117–30. On the Volga Tatar bourgeoisie, see S. A. Zenkovsky, *Pan-Turkism and Islam in Russia* (Cambridge, 1967) pp. 18–23; for a monographic work on the Azerbaijan bourgeoisie, see D. B. Seidzade, *Iz istorii azerbaidzhanskoi burzhuazii v nachale XX veka* (Baku, 1978).

3. See A. Arsharuni and Kh. Gabidullin, *Ocherki panislamizma i pantiurkizma v Rossii* (Moscow, 1931).

4. On Gasprinskii, see Zenkovsky, op.cit., pp 26-36; A. Fisher, *The Crimean Tatars* (Stanford, 1978), pp. 100-6. For a recent Soviet discussion, see L. Klimovich, "Na sluzhbe prosveshcheniia," *Zvezda Vostoka*, no. 8 (1987), pp. 173-9.

5. For a recent work on *jadidism*, see E. J. Lazzerini, "Reform und Modernismus (Djadidismus) unter den Muslimem des russischen Reiches" in Kappeler, Simon, Brunner, op. cit., pp. 35-48. See also S. Rybakov, "Novometodisty i starometodisty v russkom muzul'manstve," *Mir Islama*, no. 2 (1913), pp. 852-73.

6. For a recent work discussing this issue, see N. Devlet, *Rusya Turklerinin milli mucadele tarihi, 1905-1917* (Ankara, 1985) pp. 163-225.

7. On Huseynzade and his writings, see T. Swietochowski, *Russian Azerbaijan, 1905-1920. The Shaping of National Identity in a Muslim Community* (Cambridge, 1985), pp. 58-60.

8. Ibid., p. 75.

9. I. V. Stalin, *Sochineniia*, vol. 2 (Moscow, 1946), pp. 290-367.

10. *Der Neue Orient*, no. 10 (1917), pp. 526-7.

11. For a detailed discussion of the Congress, consult Devlet, op. cit., pp. 267-89.

12. On the Soviet conquest of the Muslim borderlands, see R. Pipes, *The Formation of the Soviet Union. Communism and Nationalism, 1917-1923* (Cambridge, Mass., 1957), pp. 155-92.

13. On the Basmachi movement, see R. Lorenz, "Die Basmatschen-Bewegung" in Kappeler, Simon, Brunner, op. cit., pp. 235-55; A. Park, *Bolshevism in Turkestan, 1917-1927* (New York, 1957), pp. 51-4.

14. For a recent monographic work on the Narkomnats, see G. P. Makarova, *Narodnyi kommissariat po delam natsional'nostei RSFSR, 1917-1923* (Moscow, 1987). See also Pipes, op. cit., pp. 34-46.

15. For a monographic work on Sultangaliev and his theories, see A. Bennigsen and E. Wimbush, *Muslim National Communism in the Soviet Union. A Revolutionary Strategy for the Colonial World* (Chicago, 1979).

16. Stalin, op. cit., vol. 2, p. 286.

17. See Bennigsen and Lemercier-Quelquejay, op. cit., pp. 123-9.

18. On the formation of the Uzbek nation, "the masterpiece of realpolitik," see B. Fragner, "Probleme der Nationalwerdung der Usbeken and Tadschiken" in Kappeler, Simon, Brunner, op. cit., pp. 19-34. Consult also G. Wheeler, *The Modern History of Soviet Central Asia* (New York, 1964), pp. 117-37; S. Becker, *Russia's Protectorates in Central Asia: Bukhara and Khiva, 1865-1924* (Cambridge, Mass., 1968).

19. G. Liber, "*Korenizatsiia*: Hopes and Contradictions in Soviet Nationality Policy in the 1920s," paper delivered at the Conference on

National Identity in the Soviet Union and Eastern Europe, London, March 1989.

20. On the periodization of Soviet Muslim policies, see H. Braker, "Die sowjetische Politik gegenüber dem Islam" in Kappeler, Simon, Brunner, op. cit., pp. 131–54.

Chapter 13

Soviet Emigration Policies toward Germans and Armenians[1]

Sidney Heitman

Among the dramatic results of Mikhail Gorbachev's policies of *glasnost'* and *perestroika* has been a sharp increase in emigration from the USSR to the West. When recent figures are added to the total exodus since its inception at the end of World War II, more than half a million Soviet citizens have now resettled abroad in a unique movement today called the "Third Soviet Emigration." In contrast to two earlier flights of refugees from revolution and war, the Third Emigration has been a voluntary, organized and legally sanctioned process involving three national minorities—318,500 Jews, 168,100 ethnic Germans and 66,500 Armenians by the end of 1988. Jews have resettled chiefly in Israel and the United States, Germans in West Germany and Armenians in the United States.

Though the origins of this movement go back to the early postwar years, the vast majority of emigrants have left since 1971, when the Soviet government relaxed its historic antipathy to emigration for a time. After a decade the exodus was sharply restricted, but since 1987 it has revived and in 1988 attained a record level of departures surpassing the previous peak year of 1979.

The rise, decline and revival of the Third Emigration is of wide interest today because of its profound significance for the emigrants and its political importance for the USSR and the West. Notwithstanding its interest and importance, however, the movement is not well known or understood because it has not been systematically or thoroughly studied until now. Despite the existence of a growing body of literature dealing with various aspects of the subject, many questions concerning it have inadequate answers or none at all. Based on research for a full-scale study of the Third Emigration now in progress, this chapter is concerned with a limited dimension of the movement, namely, Soviet policies toward German and Armenian emigration.[2] Jewish emigration is dealt with separately elsewhere in this volume.

Soviet policies toward German and Armenian emigration will be examined by addressing three of the many questions arising from the Third Emigration, namely, the origin and evolution of the movement until now; its causes and dynamics; and its present status and future prospects under the current Soviet leaders. Though the discussion will concentrate on German and Armenian emigration, it will for the sake of clarity cover other aspects of the subject, including Jewish emigration, but only insofar as needed to provide proper background and perspective.

Before turning to the first question, the origin and evolution of the Third Emigration, it is necessary to clarify several points that are not generally understood today. These relate to the distinctive character of the exodus and its place in Soviet history.

Background and Character of the Third Emigration

In the first place, it should be noted that the very designation "Third Soviet Emigration" is a misnomer, for it is not the *third* such outmigration from the USSR but the *first*. This distinction is not simply a matter of semantics but one of substance.

Since the founding of the Soviet regime in 1917, there have been many external population movements from the USSR by more than 15 million persons, ranging from the flight of refugees from revolution and war, to the transfer or repatriation of citizens of other countries resulting from geopolitical changes, to voluntary emigration *per se*. The term "emigration" is used here to mean the movement of self-selected persons from one country to another by choice for the purpose of establishing new homes, lives and identities. A classic example of this is the emigration of millions of eastern and southern Europeans and Asians to the New World in the late nineteenth and early twentieth centuries, or the earlier emigration of Western Europeans to North America. In this sense of the term, emigration differs from the involuntary displacement of refugees by man-made or natural disasters or the forced exile of political or religious dissidents, for example.

In the strict, or classic, sense of the term, there has been only *one* emigration movement from the USSR—the so-called Third Emigration of Jews, Germans and Armenians since World War II. Two earlier outmigrations have come to be called the "first" and "second" emigrations" in the literature on Soviet history, but these designations are inaccurate. The first of these was the flight of one and a half million Russian refugees from war and revolution between 1918 and 1922, the second the exodus of two million displaced persons from the

USSR during and after World War II. Why these two movements have been called "emigrations," though they do not fit the classic pattern, and why they have been given consecutive numerical designations, though they were separated by many years and many other outmigrations, is not clear. Nor is it clear why they have been linked consecutively to the so-called Third Emigration, for there is no relationship among them. If the Third Emigration has an affinity with an earlier comparable movement, it is with the mass emigration of Jews and Germans from the Russian Empire in the years preceding and following the turn of the century, but not with the two preceding flights of refugees and displaced persons from the USSR. This distinction is important because the voluntary character of the Third Emigration raises questions concerning the motives of the emigrants for leaving and Soviet policy toward them that are not relevant to the other two movements, questions that will be discussed in this chapter. Notwithstanding the inaccuracy of the designation Third Soviet Emigration, it will be used here rather than coin a new term and risk confusing the issue further, but with the stated provisos.

Secondly, it should be noted that although the Third Emigration has proceeded for more than 40 years now, there is no legal right for citizens of the USSR to emigrate at will. Despite the fact that the Soviet Union has signed a number of international agreements providing for free movement across national boundaries, this has never been a right of Soviet citizens. Egress from the country has generally been treated as a special privilege dispensed to selected individuals in accordance with specific requirements and in the interests of the state as determined by the authorities. Until now, emigration has been permitted solely for the purpose of reuniting Soviet citizens with families living abroad, not as a basic right or discretionary act.[3]

Moreover, this privilege has been accorded only to certain categories of citizens based on their nationality, namely Jews, Germans and Armenians. Though other ethnic groups (such as Ukrainians, Koreans and Baltic peoples) have also expressed a desire to leave, they have not been permitted to until now. Furthermore, those who are eligible to emigrate undertake much personal risk in seeking to do so, for emigration is viewed by the Soviet authorities as a hostile or unpatriotic political act, and applicants to leave have often been punished with social ostracism, dismissal from jobs, eviction from living quarters, denial of social services and official harassment. Some persistent "refusniks" have also been imprisoned, exiled, and confined to psychiatric "hospitals." Finally, it should be noted that the determination of who may leave and who may not has been highly arbitrary and unpredictable and has undergone wide swings of permissiveness and restrictiveness until now.

These characteristics of the Soviet emigration process raise two sets of questions concerning (1) the motives of the emigrants for undertaking the hazards and hardships of seeking to leave, and (2) Soviet emigration policy and its determinants over time. These are the questions with which this chapter is concerned and to which it may now turn, beginning with the evolution of the movement from its inception to the present, focusing on German and Armenian emigration viewed from the perspective of the exodus as a whole.

Evolution of the Third Emigration[4]

This section is based on the data in Tables 13.1–3, which cover the period from 1948, when the movement began, to the end of 1988, when this chapter was written. These tables show the changes in the numbers, composition and destinations of the emigrants during the four stages through which the exodus has passed since its inception. These stages consist of an initial period from 1948 through 1970; a second period from 1971 through 1980; a third stage from 1981 through 1986; and a fourth stage that began in 1987 and continues today.

The first stage was one of relatively low and irregular levels of emigration, during which a total of 59,600 persons left the USSR, or only 10.8 per cent of the entire movement until now, an annual average exodus of 2,600 persons (see Table 13.1). The second stage was marked by a sharp increase in numbers of emigrants, during which 347,100 persons left the Soviet Union, comprising 62.8 per cent of the total movement, or an annual average rate of 34,700 person during the ten-year period, more than a tenfold increase over the preceding stage. The third stage was one of sharply reduced emigration, during which only 42,600 persons were permitted to leave, or 7.7 per cent of the total emigrants since 1948, or an annual average rate of 7,100 individuals, far below the preceding period. The fourth and current stage is one of greatly expanded emigration, in which 103,700 persons left, or 18.7 per cent of the total movement for an annual average number of 51,800 persons, higher than at any other time. This stage is also noteworthy because during 1988, a total of 77,800 emigrants left the USSR, more than in the previous record year of 1979, when 67,000 Jews, Germans and Armenians emigrated to the West.

Not only the numbers of emigrants, but also their ethnic mix has changed over the four stages, reflecting changes in their motives for

Table 13.1 Emigration by periods, 1948–1988

Nationality	1948–70 Number	%	1971–80 Number	%	1981–86 Number	%	1987–88 Number	%	Totals
Jews	25,200	42.3	248,900	71.7	16,900	39.7	27,500	26.5	318,500
Germans	22,400	37.6	64,200	18.5	19,300	45.3	62,100	59.9	168,100
Armenians	12,000	20.1	34,000	9.8	6,400	15.0	14,100	13.6	66,500
Total for period	59,600	100.0	347,100	100.0	42,600	100.0	103,700	100.0	553,100
Period total as percentage of all emigration	10.8%		62.8%		7.7%		18.7%		100.0
Annual average emigration	2,600		34,700		7,100		51,800		—

Source: Compiled from data provided by the Israeli Embassy, Washington, D. C.; the Israel Ministry of Immigrant Absorption; the Hebrew Immigrant Aid Society (HIAS); the West German Foreign Office, Ministry of Interior, and emigrant reception center at Friedland; the Landsmannschaft der Deutschen aus Russland; the Internationale Gesellschaft für Menschenrechte; the U.S. Department of State; and Armenian informants.

Note: Figures may not add up to totals due to rounding.

leaving and in Soviet policy toward their exodus, as will be shown. Overall, Jews have far exceeded the number of Germans, who have surpassed the number of Armenians since 1948, accounting, respectively, for 318,500 (57.6 per cent), 168,100 (30.4 per cent), and 66,500 (12 per cent) of the total emigrants until now (see Table 13.2).

During the first stage, the relative numbers and percentages of Jews, Germans and Armenians did not vary greatly, compared to the second stage, when the flow of Jewish emigrants far exceeded that of both Germans and Armenians. During the third stage, when overall numbers declined, there was again a more nearly even proportion among the three groups, but significantly, for the first time the number of Germans exceeded the number of Jews. The fourth stage has continued and indeed intensified this disproportion to the point that in 1988, whereas 19,365 Jews left the USSR, 47,572 Germans—by far the largest number of Germans in any single year—and a record 10,864 Armenians emigrated to the West.

Table 13.3 charts the changes of destinations of the emigrants over the 40 years of the movement, resulting from their changing motives for leaving and sociodemographic composition, as it will be seen. During the first stage, all Jewish emigrants went to Israel, whereas during the three successive stages increasing proportions of Jews "dropped out" at the Vienna way-station to Israel and chose to resettle elsewhere—chiefly the United States, but also various countries in Europe, and Canada, Australia and New Zealand. By contrast, except for 11,000 Germans who opted for the German Democratic Republic, all other German emigrants have gone to the Federal Republic, where they are provided with generous assistance

Table 13.2
Emigration by Nationalities, 1948–1988

Period	Jews		Germans		Armenians		Totals
	Number	%	Number	%	Number	%	
1948–70	25,200	7.9	22,400	13.3	12,000	18.0	59,600
1971–80	248,900	78.1	64,200	38.2	34,000	51.1	347,100
1981–86	16,900	5.3	19,300	11.5	6,400	9.6	42,600
1987–88	27,500	8.6	62,100	36.9	14,100	21.2	103,700
Totals	318,500	100.0	168,100	100.0	66,500	100.0	553,100
Proportion of total	57.6%		30.4%		12.0%		—

Source: Compiled from sources listed in Table 13.1.
Note: Figures may not add up to totals owing to rounding.

Table 13.3 Destinations of Emigrants, 1948-1988

Period	Jews						Germans					Armenians			
	Israel	%	U.S.	%	Other	%	FRG	%	GDR	%	France	%	U.S.	%
1948-70	11,200	44.4	—	—	14,000[a]	55.6	22,400	100.0	—	—	12,000	100.0	—	—
1971-80	156,300	62.8	83,400	33.5	9,200	3.7	63,200	98.4	1,000	1.6	—	—	34,000	100.0
1981-86	8,200	48.5	7,800	46.2	900	5.3	9,300	48.4	10,000	51.6	—	—	6,400	100.0
1987-88	4,200	15.3	21,800[b]	79.3	1,500	5.4	62,100	100.0	—	—	—	—	14,100	100.0
Subtotals	179,900	56.5	113,000	35.5	25,500	8.0	157,100	93.5	11,000	6.5	12,000	18.0	54,500	82.0
TOTALS	318,500						168,100				66,500			

Source: Compiled from sources listed in Table 13.1.
Note: Figures may not add up to totals owing to rounding.
[a]These 14,000 Jewish emigrants first went to Poland and later re-emigrated to Israel, but they are not counted in the figure under the heading "Israel."
[b]This figure includes 400 Soviet Jews who emigrated directly to the United States instead of passing first through the Vienna way station to Israel and were either admitted as refugees or granted parole status.

to resettle and adjust. Those who went to the GDR did so presumably because they had relatives there or believed they could more easily leave the Soviet Union for an Eastern-bloc state and later re-emigrate to West Germany, but only little is known about them. In the mid-1980s the government of the GDR closed off immigration to them (and to other Eastern-bloc ethnic Germans), and since then all Soviet German emigrants have resettled in West Germany.

With the exception of 12,000 Armenians who returned to France in the late 1950s from where they had emigrated to the USSR a few years earlier, all Armenian emigrants have resettled in the United States. Most have gone to the Los Angeles area, but some have resettled in Armenian-American communities in the northeastern and midwestern parts of the country.

Causes of Emigration

It is now possible to turn to the question of the causes of the Third Emigration, or the motives of the emigrants for leaving and the precipitants that initiated their exodus and sustained it. That is, why did these three groups risk the hazards of seeking to leave the USSR and undertake the hardships of resettling in new and strange lands, and how have their motives changed over time? Though the focus of this chapter is on German and Armenian emigration, it is necessary to view them comparatively from the perspective of the movement as a whole and to begin, therefore, with a brief consideration of the causes of Jewish emigration, which preceded that of the other two groups in time and influenced them in important ways.

Causes of Jewish Emigration[5]

In the postwar years approximately two million Soviet Jews formed a diverse and geographically dispersed minority, without a territorial base, and composed of three communities distinguished by history, culture and traditions—namely, Asiatic Jews, Western Jews and so-called core, or heartland, Jews. Asiatic Jews had lived for centuries in Central Asiatic Russia and were ethnocentric, religiously observant, and traditional in culture. Western Jews lived in territories annexed by the Soviet Union during World War II (Poland, the Baltic states and Bessarabia) and were also observant, as well as strongly Zionist. The majority of Soviet Jews were the core, or heartland, Jews, who had lived in European Russia since 1917 and had become largely Russified and secularized by 1970. Regardless of type, Soviet Jews were preponderantly urban, well educated and disproportionately represented in professional, scientific and creative fields, which made them of value to the Soviet regime.

Nonetheless, they experienced endemic discrimination and periodic persecution under Stalin and his successors, but they had no recourse other than to survive by their wits. There could be no thought of flight or emigration and nowhere to go even if they could have left. To be sure, several thousand former Polish Jews had been repatriated to Poland after the war, and in the 1950s a number of elderly and infirm Jews had been permitted to join relatives in Israel as part of the postwar population settlements (see Tables 13.1-3), but these transfers were considered by the Soviet government to be special cases that in no way violated the historic proscriptions against emigration or constituted a precedent for others to follow.

This situation lasted until the late 1960s, when three new developments changed the status of the Soviet Jews. One was the rise of a particularly virulent wave of Soviet antisemitism, which caused widespread international protest. The second was the stunning Israeli victory in the 1967 Six-Day War, which stirred Jewish pride and nationalism around the world, including in the USSR, and revived dormant Soviet Jewish national consciousness. The third development was the advent of détente. The new interest in Israel, fear of a return of persecution, and the mobilization of world opinion on behalf of the Soviet Jews prompted some of them to apply to emigrate on the grounds of family reunification, as had occurred during the 1950s, as seen. Surprisingly, the Soviet government assented, and in the new atmosphere of international détente and relaxed internal political controls after 1970, increasing numbers of Jews were permitted to leave for Israel on the nominal grounds of reuniting families, which circumvented the official proscriptions against voluntary emigration *per se*. Most Jewish emigrants did not in fact have relatives in Israel, but invitations to them (*vízovs*) were readily arranged in the Jewish state, and the Soviet authorities found it expedient to wink at the subterfuge so as to accommodate the exodus and yet not compromise the prohibition against voluntary emigration as such.

Between 1971 and 1979 Jewish emigration swelled to a flood, cresting in the latter year with more than 51,500 persons. Thereafter, the tide of emigration of all three nationalities ebbed for several years, as shown, but rose again in 1987, attaining a new peak in 1988. In the first half of the 1970s, mainly Asiatic and Western Jews left the USSR, seeking an opportunity to observe their religions and cultures freely, and they settled chiefly in Israel. From the second half of the decade onward, however, core Jews joined the exodus, not out of religious motives but to seek better personal, economic and professional opportunities in the West, and they increasingly chose to resettle not in Israel, but in the United States and other countries, as shown. When emigration levels revived again after a period of decline in the 1980s, this pattern of emigration continued. Proportionately larger numbers of Soviet Jews applied to leave on Israeli visas issued by the Dutch Embassy acting as a proxy for Israel, which does not have diplomatic relations with the USSR, ostensibly for family reunification, and then "dropped out" at the Vienna way-station to Israel to resettle elsewhere. The Soviet authorities permitted the subterfuge to go on, for it was in the government's interest to permit Jewish emigration, while the ruse prevented compromising the official restrictions against voluntary emigration *per se*.

Today, estimates of how many more Jews would leave the USSR if permitted to range from a few tens of thousands to half a million or more, but no one knows the actual number.

Causes of German Emigration[6]

The motives and precipitants of German emigration have interesting parallels to Jewish emigration, but also important differences. Two million ethnic Germans in the USSR in 1970 were, like the Jews, an unassimilated, dispersed and alienated national minority with a legacy of discrimination and persecution under both the tsars and the Soviets. Their history and status in the USSR was different than that of the Jews, however. They were descendants of German colonists invited to Russia by Catherine the Great and Alexander I in the late eighteenth and early nineteenth centuries to settle and develop newly acquired lands along the Volga River and the northern littoral of the Black Sea, from which the two main groups took their names—the Volga Germans and Black Sea Germans. Each group had different origins in Germany and different experiences in Russia, and they lived apart from one another as they did from the Russian peasants among whom they settled.

For a century after their arrival, the German colonists flourished and multiplied as a result of their diligence and skills and of special privileges from the government, including economic favors, cultural and religious autonomy, and exemption from military service. In the last quarter of the nineteenth century their fortunes turned, however, when they suffered economic reverses and lost their privileged status, forcing many of them to emigrate to the New World. Those who remained experienced successive tragedies in World War I, the Revolutions of 1917, the civil war that followed, and the collectivization drives of the 1930s, when the well-to-do German *kulaks* suffered especially harsh treatment.

There was a brief respite in the 1920s under the New Economic Policy, when an autonomous Volga German republic and several autonomous districts were formed, in which a vigorous German cultural and religious life flourished for a time. Ethnic Germans also participated actively in Soviet politics and held important posts in both the Soviet government and the Communist Party.

World War II ended all organized German life in the USSR. When the Nazis invaded the Soviet Union in 1941, Stalin suspected the Germans of treason and ordered them deported to the east. Six hundred thousand Volga Germans were brutally uprooted and shipped to Siberia and Central Asia, where they were confined in forced labor camps under inhuman conditions. Their autonomous governments were dissolved, their cultural and religious institutions were closed, and their property was confiscated. Before they were released in 1955, more than 300,000 of them perished from the brutal treatment and primitive conditions of the camps.

The Black Sea Germans were overrun by the invading Nazis before they too could be deported to the east, and 350,000 of them were evacuated to Poland and incorporated into the Third Reich. After the war, all but 100,000 of them were forcibly repatriated to the USSR, and they too were interned in camps in Siberia.

Though the end of the war ended the pretext for their imprisonment, the Germans were confined to the camps for another decade before they were released in 1955 when Konrad Adenauer, chancellor of the new West German government, interceded on their behalf. They were permitted to leave the camps and resettle in Siberia and Central Asiatic Russia, where the majority of Soviet Germans live today, but they were prohibited from returning to their former homes or seeking restitution for lost lives and property. In 1964 the Germans were granted an amnesty absolving them of wartime charges of treason, but these restrictions remained in place. Thereafter, conditions generally improved, particularly their economic status, for their productive labor was highly valued and well rewarded by the Soviet state. But they resented their continuing disabilities, periodic discrimination and persecution, and the prohibition against restoring their prewar status.

Consequently, Germans responded in one of three ways. Some sought to rid themselves of the disadvantages of their German identity by assimilating into Russian society. Others resisted by joining various dissident movements. A third group, however, inspired by the success of the Jews in emigrating from the USSR in the 1970s, sought to emulate them by leaving the Soviet Union and returning to their own historic homeland in West Germany. Their efforts to emigrate were more complex than those of the Jews, however, for reasons rooted in the early postwar years.

At the end of World War II, there were in the USSR besides the Soviet Germans many German prisoners-of-war and 160,000 other ethnic Germans in the annexed territories of the Baltic states, Poland and Bessarabia. Most of the prisoners-of-war and ethnic Germans were transferred to West Germany between 1945 and 1955. No Soviet Germans were involved in these transfers, for most of them were still in the special labor camps in the east.

Upon their release from internment in 1955, thousands of Black Sea Germans asked to be transferred to West Germany, where many of them had relatives from whom they had been separated when they had been forcibly repatriated to the USSR after the war. Their requests were rejected by the Soviet government, but under pressure from Bonn, Moscow permitted 16,500 selected elderly and infirm Germans to emigrate to the Federal Republic between 1955 and 1964, the same time that some Jews were also being allowed to leave for Israel. The rehabilitation decree of 1964, intended to normalize conditions within the USSR and improve relations with West Germany, opened the way for a reconsideration of the status of the Soviet Germans. Representatives of the West German and Soviet Red Cross organizations met in Vienna in 1965 to consider special hardship cases of separated families, and it was agreed to permit 40,000 selected individuals to emigrate. Actually, only a few thousand were eventually permitted to leave—again, mainly elderly and infirm persons—and in 1968, when relations with the West deteriorated over the Soviet invasion of Czechoslovakia, the USSR declared the reunification program arranged in Vienna "completed" and reduced the flow of emigrants to a mere trickle.

Two sets of events shortly afterward revived the issue of German emigration, however. One was the adoption of a new *Ostpolitik* by Willy Brandt, who became chancellor of West Germany in 1969. Brandt used the improved relations with the USSR to induce Moscow to increase German emigration. The other was the rejection by the Soviet government of requests in 1964 and 1965 by a group of Volga Germans to restore their prewar status. Rebuffed in this effort, they turned instead to emigration in emulation of the Black Sea Germans and the Jews.

The decision of the Volga Germans to emigrate posed a problem, however, for unlike the Black Sea Germans, they had no claim to family reunification, the only grounds on which the Soviet government permitted emigration, for the Volga Germans had all been deported to the east early in the war. Circumstances played into their hands, however, for West Germany's new *Ostpolitik* began an era of détente, and, anxious to improve relations with the Federal Republic and the West, the Soviet government opened the gates of emigration for the Volga Germans, notwithstanding their ineligibility to leave. Between 1971 and 1980, when the exodus was restricted again, 64,000 Germans, most of them Volga Germans, left the USSR, a tenfold increase over the preceding decade. Like the Jews during the same years, they left on false claims of family reunification and *vizovs* arranged by confederates in West Germany, which the Soviet government tolerated because it was in its interest to do so. During the same period, an additional 1,000 Germans resettled in East Germany for reasons noted above.

After 1980 the erosion of détente and *Ostpolitik* led to a sharp reduction in not only German but also Jewish and Armenian emigration, as it has been seen, but in 1987 the exodus revived, and German levels of emigration surpassed those of the 1970s, exceeding also the number of Jews permitted to leave. By the end of 1988 a total of 168,100 Germans had left the USSR since the beginning of the Third Emigration in 1948, the vast majority of them resettling in West Germany. It is estimated that from 100,000 to one million more Germans would leave today if permitted to, but there is no way of knowing how many would do so in fact, for many Germans have now made an accommodation with conditions in the USSR, and in recent years the Soviet government has made efforts to improve their circumstances, as it will be seen below.

Causes of Armenian Emigration[7]

The causes of Armenian emigration are different from (though not unrelated to) those of the Jewish and German exodus because the status of the Armenians in the USSR is unique. Since 1920, when a short-lived independent Armenian republic was annexed by the Soviet Union, there has been a nominally autonomous Armenia in the eastern part of what was once an extensive Armenian empire. In 1979, 4.15 million of the world's five million Armenians lived in the USSR, 70 per cent of them in the Armenian SSR, the rest elsewhere in the Soviet Union. Within the Armenian republic, Armenians comprised 90 per cent of the population, used their native language rather than Russian, and observed their historic cultural, religious and national customs with a high degree of freedom compared with other ethnic minorities in the USSR. They also governed themselves, albeit under the guidance of the Communist Party, in which Armenians held high positions, and the Armenian SSR has been and is today one of the most prosperous republics in the Soviet Union. Armenians are, moreover, generally well educated, boast a rich cultural legacy, and rank high in scientific, creative and intellectual achievements. Until the devastating earthquake in December 1988, their conditions of life have been uncommonly abundant and free by Soviet standards.

Why then have thousands of Armenians left the USSR and do many more still seek to do so? The answer is that the initial impetus for emigration came not from native Armenians, but from immigrants to the Armenian SSR during the postwar years, who responded to a call by the Soviet government to former nationals and others to return and help rebuild the country. Among those who came between 1946 and 1960 were an estimated 250,000 diaspora Armenians living in the Middle East, Europe, North Africa and the Americas. Though they had never lived in the USSR, they considered Soviet Armenia their historic homeland and religious center, and they were attracted by promises of generous aid made by Soviet agents sent abroad to recruit them. Instead of housing, jobs and assistance, however, they found a backward, undeveloped country, peopled by an uneducated and impoverished peasantry who spoke a different dialect from theirs and resented the newcomers. They were forcibly billeted in the homes of the natives or housed in makeshift shelters; the money and valuables they brought were confiscated; they were barred from desirable positions in the economy and administration by jealous local officials; and thousands were arrested and deported to Siberia when they complained or resisted. As a result of their treatment, they remained apart from the local inhabitants, nursed their grievances, and looked for an opportunity to return to the West. Though they contributed importantly to and benefited from the postwar economic development that transformed the sleepy Caucasian republic into a modern, productive region, they knew they could fare better in the West.

In the late 1950s an unexpected opportunity arose for 12,000 Armenians who had emigrated to the USSR from France to return to France when the French government intervened on their behalf. Anxious at the time to accommodate Paris, the Soviet government arranged for the "repatriation" of the Armenians to their country of origin, thus circumventing the legal inhibition against voluntary emigration. By 1960 this exodus had ended, but the remaining Armenians awaited an opportunity also to leave.

Such an occasion occurred when the Soviet government eased emigration for Jews and Germans on the grounds of family reunification in the 1970s. Many Armenians had extended families abroad, and beginning in 1972, they also applied to join their relatives in the West. Surprisingly, the Soviet authorities approved, and between 1972 and 1980, 34,000 Armenians left the USSR, more than half the total Armenian exodus to date. This flow peaked in 1980 with 14,000 persons, after which it declined along with the decrease in Jewish and German emigration, but in 1987 the movement revived, and in 1988 more than 10,800 Armenians left for the West. Except for the initial group that returned to France, all other Armenians have gone to the United States rather than return to their troubled former homelands in the Middle East and North Africa, most of them resettling in the Los Angeles area.

Until the mid-1980s Armenian emigrants were almost entirely members of the original immigrant community or their descendants. Since 1985, however, growing numbers of native Armenians have joined the exodus. Some are spouses or children of the immigrants, but others are Soviet Armenians who have become increasingly dissatisfied with conditions in the Caucasian republic. Reasons for their disaffection include disgust with endemic corruption and venality in public life; environmental degradation; overcrowding in urban centers where most Armenians live; a general decline in the quality of life; political insecurity; and the constriction of economic opportunities. These conditions have always existed in varying degrees, but since the mid-1980s they have become more oppressive. Improved opportunities for travel by Armenians to and from the Armenian SSR have magnified these shortcomings when they are contrasted with the free and opulent West, and they have also been exacerbated by the rising tide of expectations resulting from the policies of *glasnost'* and *perestroika*, which have promised much but not yet produced tangible benefits. It should be noted that the destructive earthquake in December 1988 may impel some Armenians to leave the country, but so far this has not occurred. Similarly, emigration has not yet been directly affected by the controversy over Nagorno-Karabakh, which may have been resolved by placing it under central state administration early in 1989.

Estimates of how many more Armenians would leave the USSR if permitted to vary from tens to hundreds of thousands, but, as with Jewish and German estimates, there is no way of knowing with certainty. Interestingly, the large influx of Armenian emigrant applications in 1988 has created a problem not only for the Soviet government, which discourages emigration from the USSR generally, and for the international Armenian diaspora, which deplores the depopulation or weakening of the Armenian national homeland, but also for the government of the United States. In the summer of 1988 US refugee quotas were filled and funds for the resettlment of refugees were exhausted, causing the American embassy in Moscow to suspend the issuing of visas for a time. This created much hardship for many Armenians who had left their jobs, sold their property and converged on Moscow in preparation for traveling to the United States. The crisis was resolved, but it left open the question of future US policy toward Soviet emigration to the United States and divided both the State Department and the Immigration and Naturalization Service into two camps. One advocates unlimited sanctuary in the United States for all emigrants from the USSR and other Eastern-bloc states. The other contends that Soviet Armenians and Jews today do not meet the definition of political refugees according to the current (1980) immigration statute, and are coming to the United States for personal gain and should be required to enter as immigrants. Moreover, it is held, Soviet Jews and Armenians fill limited refugee quotas and consume limited funds, denying sanctuary to genuine political refugees from Southeast Asia and Latin America.

At the time of writing in early 1989 the issue remains unresolved and was compromised away for another year by the outgoing Reagan Administration. It is of interest to note here that such questions have not arisen in West Germany, where by law all ethnic Germans outside the Federal Republic may immigrate and claim German citizenship at will. There is apprehension over the capacity of the country to absorb and pay for the already increased numbers of emigrants from the USSR and other socialist countries over the past two years—let alone a massive influx of immigrants in the event that the gates of emigration from the East are thrown wide open, which is possible, though not likely, in the near future.

Soviet Emigration Policy[8]

The discussion now examines more closely the question of Soviet emigration policy and its determinants. How has this policy evolved since 1948, and what accounts for its changes over time? Before considering this issue, however, it is necessary to clarify three aspects of Soviet emigration policy that have been touched on only lightly until now. These are the disparity between Soviet principle and practice concerning emigration from the USSR; the status of emigration in Soviet law; and the official rationale underlying Jewish, German and Armenian emigration since World War II.

It has been seen that in principle the Soviet government opposes voluntary emigration from the USSR *per se*. Reasons for this antipathy have never been publicly explained, but they may be inferred from the historical record. One observer has written, for example:

> Soviet opposition to emigration ... grows out of historical traditions of isolation and immobility and basic aspects of Marxism in the Russian setting: the focus on state power and the collective interest, the call for mobilization of the entire public, the sense of being besieged by a hostile world, the belief that departure is an act of betrayal, the instinctive closure of communication with the outside, and the reservation of foreign travel—as in the time of Catherine the Great—as an elite privilege. As elsewhere in post-World War II Eastern Europe, it was reinforced by war losses, a declining birth rate, labor shortages and ethnic considerations.[9]

Another reason is that according to Communist doctrine, emigration is caused by the defects of capitalist society, which cannot provide regular employment for all its members and forces some to emigrate in order to survive. This is not supposed to happen in a socialist society, which has theoretically resolved these defects, and therefore there can be no economic basis and no need for emigration from the USSR. In fact, thousands of Jews, Germans and Armenians have left, a fact which embarrasses the Soviet leaders not only because it conflicts with Communist doctrine, but also because it exposes shortcomings of Soviet society and belies the claim that the nationality problem has been resolved in the USSR "for all time." Finally, there is opposition to emigration because it drains away skilled labor at a time of economic crisis and declining population growth.

For these and other reasons the Soviet government has consistently opposed emigration in principle, even while honoring its antipathy in the breach as well as the observance by permitting thousands of emigrants to leave nonetheless. This is all the more paradoxical because the government is not obliged to do so, since there is no legal right to emigrate in the USSR as there is in other modern countries. Though emigration is possible and has occurred, it is not guaranteed by law.

To clarify the legal status of emigration in the Soviet Union, it is useful to quote at length from an explanation of it by a leading Western authority on the subject, Dr George Ginsburgs, who wrote in 1973:

> To appreciate the problem properly, one must bear in mind that, in Soviet law, a citizen does not possess a right to emigrate at will. To be sure, the concept of emigration is not unfamiliar to Soviet authorities. Thus, the Regulations on Entry into the USSR and Exit from the USSR ratified by Resolution of the USSR Council of

Ministers of 19 June 1959, no. 660, specify that exit from the USSR of Soviet citizens is permitted on the strength of passports for travel abroad or substitute documents accompanied by an exit visa furnished by the Union or Republican Ministries of Foreign Affairs, diplomatic missions of the USSR Ministry of Foreign Affairs, the Ministries of Internal Affairs of the USSR, the Union and Autonomous Republics, and their organs, depending on the official position of the interested citizen, his passport category, and location at the time of issuance of the visa. In cases not involving diplomatic or service passports, Soviet citizens going abroad temporarily or for permanent residence receive a *permis de séjour*. Foreign documents and exit visas are issued in accordance with the established procedure on the basis of a written petition from the individual citizen desiring to go abroad on private business. Special instructions for the application of these Regulations, with respect to the issuance of documents and visas by the USSR Ministry of Foreign Affairs and its subordinate agencies, were to be issued by the USSR Ministry of Foreign Affairs in consultation with the USSR Ministry of Internal Affairs and the Committee on State Security (KGB) of the USSR Council of Ministers; the method of issuance of documents and visas by the USSR Ministry of Internal Affairs and its affiliates in the Republics and Autonomous Republics was to depend on rules laid down by the USSR Ministry of Internal Affairs in conjunction with the USSR Ministry of Foreign Affairs, the Committee on State Security and the USSR Ministry of Defence.

The obvious implication of the directive is that exit from the USSR, even for permanent residence, is both possible and legitimate—whenever the competent institutions approve a personal request to that effect. The last word, however, rests with the administrative authorities and, without their consent, the application must fall. What is more, the Regulations do not indicate what criteria govern the whole process, presumably leaving these to be defined by the aforementioned, supplementary departmental instructions, but meanwhile furnishing the average citizen wanting to depart from the USSR no clue as to how the system is supposed to operate, what type of official treatment his bid might encounter and what results he can expect.

Hence, where, on a number of occasions, an opportunity to leave the USSR has been granted to specific categories of Soviet nationals, the episodes have duly been viewed as unique concessions and not symptomatic of any public recognition of the inherent freedom of the individual to emigrate. Inasmuch, then, as Soviet law has sanctioned the emigration of various people over the years, the phenomenon represents, and locally has always been perceived as, an incidence of political dispensation constituting a special privilege conferred on the interested party by the organs of the state and not something that a person can claim unilaterally independently of or in opposition to the regime's express wishes.[10]

The 1959 regulations were revised in 1970 and 1986, but their main provisions were not changed and are still in force (though new, more liberal rules are reportedly under consideration today). Permission to leave the USSR still requires a petition by the emigrant and approval by the proper authorities at their discretion and in the interests of the state as they see it. On what basis, then, is emigration approved or disapproved?

Until now, there has been only one legitimate reason for emigrating from the USSR—to be reunited with families living abroad. This is the sole basis for granting permission to leave the Soviet Union (apart from special cases of binational spouses, persons needing medical care in the West, or prominent dissidents). Until now, as it has been seen, only three groups of Soviet citizens have been permitted to avail themselves of this privilege—Jews, Germans and Armenians.

It is well known, however, that family reunification has become a cover for emigration by many persons who have no relatives in the West, as in the case of the Volga Germans or of Jews resettling in the United States, for example. Why has the Soviet government violated its own principles by permitting thousands of persons to emigrate under false pretenses? Clearly because it served the interests of the leaders to use the cover of family reunification to achieve other objectives without setting precedents that would open up uncontrolled emigration by others. What then has determined Soviet emigration policy until now?

Going back to the first stage of the Third Emigration (1948–1970), it has been seen that several thousand Jews, Germans and Armenians were permitted to emigrate because of intervention on their behalf by the governments of Israel, West Germany and France, respectively, at a time when the Soviet Union was anxious to accommodate them. Undoubtedly in their favor was the fact that these years were a time of massive population movement resulting from the dislocations of the recent war, which overshadowed the emigration of a few thousand non-Russians. Moreover, since most of the Jews and Germans were elderly or infirm individuals of no value to the Soviet state and, indeed, liabilities as pensioners, there was no resistance to their leaving.

During the second stage of the movement (1971–1980), three main factors influenced Soviet emigration policy, at least toward the Jews and Germans. Other considerations underlay policy toward the Armenians, as it will shortly be seen. The three determinants affecting Jewish and German emigration were certain internal developments in the USSR; the actions of Western governments on behalf of the Jews and Germans; and the impact of international public opinion on the Soviet leaders. One of the internal developments was the general relaxation of political controls in the USSR that paralleled détente with the West and resulted in, among other things, more liberal emigration requirements for Jews and Germans. Another was the rise of an unprecedented political activism by prospective Jewish and German emigrants, who staged public demonstrations, held unauthorized meetings with foreign journalists and visitors, and sent petitions to Soviet and Western leaders demanding the right to leave. Surprisingly, the authorities reacted to these unaccustomed activities with moderation and gradually increased emigration quotas over the decade of the 1970s.

At the same time, the American and West German governments sought to influence Soviet policy by linking East-West trade and exchanges, nuclear arms control agreements, and the resolution of regional conflicts to Soviet conduct on human rights generally and emigration in particular. Another source of pressure was the impact of Western public opinion on the Soviet leaders, expressed by prominent political figures, the press and concerned groups. By means of parliamentary declarations, massive publicity, demonstrations before Soviet embassies in foreign capitals, and other forms of activism, supporters of the emigrants succeeded in persuading the Soviet leaders to liberalize emigration for a time, for they were sensitive to their "image" in the West in those years.

When relations between the Soviet Union and the West deteriorated after 1980, the government of the USSR no longer had an incentive to accommodate the United States and West Germany or international public opinion, and it sharply reduced emigration along with enacting other restrictive political measures. The revival of détente and the initiation of *glasnost'* and *perestroika* in 1987 began the fourth stage of the Third Emigration, and the improved relations with the West and internal reforms were accompanied by a sharp increase in emigration, as it has been seen.[11]

While the correlation between Soviet internal policy and foreign relations, on the one hand, and Jewish and German emigration, on the other, is clear, the determinants of Soviet policy toward the Armenians are not. In contrast to the Jews and Germans, Soviet Armenians have no foreign government championing their cause and no supporting pressure groups in the West. On the contrary, the leaders of the international Armenian diaspora deplore the flight from Soviet Armenia because they claim it weakens and discredits their national homeland and religious center and the core of what they hope will become a future restored independent Armenian state.

In the absence of the incentives underlying Soviet emigration policy toward the Jews and Germans, why has the government of the USSR permitted thousands of Armenians to leave? The most honest and direct answer is that no one really knows. The Soviet authorities have never explained it, and even Armenian emigrants cannot account for it. Possible reasons have been suggested, but they cannot be substantiated. One suggestion is that the Soviet government desires Armenian goodwill at home and abroad in order to encourage tourism and foreign investment in the Armenian SSR, which yields needed hard currency. Another is the desire of the leaders in Moscow and Erevan to be rid of disaffected elements, who might spread discontent to others. It has also been suggested that a general lassitude by the central authorities toward Soviet Armenia until recently, particularly during the Brezhnev years, accounts for the liberal emigration policy. Other suggested reasons for the benign policy toward Armenians involve the strategic importance of the Armenian SSR in case of a dispute with neighboring Turkey or trouble in the turbulent Middle East, when access to the republic and the support of its population would be critical. The disturbances over Nagorno-Karabakh and the disastrous earthquake in 1988 have not yet (at the time of writing) measurably affected Armenian emigration or Soviet policy toward it.

Present Status and Future Prospects of the Movement

The preceding discussion has dealt with Soviet emigration until now. What is the present status of the movement (as of January 1989), and what are its prospects for the future? Though predicting Soviet actions is even more difficult than accounting for past behavior, some things can be said.

At present, the Soviet government is following an ambivalent policy toward Jewish, German and Armenian emigration alike. On the one hand, in the spirit of détente, *glasnost'* and *perestroika*, emigration requirements have been liberalized and emigrant quotas increased since 1987, as shown. On the other hand, emigration is still being discouraged in two main ways. One is the continuation of limited numerical quotas and the usual bureaucratic obstructions. The other is an effort to remove the sources of discontent underlying the desire to leave. Thus, apart from the promised benefits of *glasnost'* and *perestroika*, Jews and Germans have recently been given greater cultural, linguistic and religious freedom, and some of the main causes of dissatisfaction in the Armenian SSR are presently being reformed. These two conflicting policies probably reflect the larger political divisions in the Soviet hierarchy that have not yet been resolved.

The future of the Third Emigration hinges, then, on the fate of the entire spectrum of internal and international forces that have impinged upon it until now and of which it is a function—indeed, a hostage. Over the long term, its outcome depends upon the ultimate resolution of the current struggle in the Soviet Union over the soul and destiny of the Russian Revolution. In the short term, it will be determined by one of two things—whether and how long Gorbachev remains in power and continues his present policies, and whether he will either be forced to change them or be replaced by other leaders with policies that cannot be foreseen.

Notes

1. The research for this chapter was assisted by many individuals and organizations, to whom proper acknowledgment will be made in another place. Special thanks are expressed for support provided by the American Philosophical Society, the American Association for the Advancement of Slavic Studies, Colorado State University, the U.S. Department of State and the Deutscher Akademischer Austauschdienst. Appreciation is also expressed to the editors of *Soviet Jewish Affairs* for permission to use material.

2. Sources for the larger study on which this chapter is based consist of materials located in libraries, archives and private collections in the United States, Europe and Israel and information provided by many specialists, government officials and Soviet emigrants. Specific sources for this chapter are noted below. For an extensive list of materials relating to the Third Emigration, see Sidney Heitman, *The Third Soviet Emigration: Jewish, German and Armenian Emigration from the USSR Since World War II* (Cologne, West Germany: Bundesinstitut für ostwissenschaftliche und internationale Studien, 1987).

3. For a discussion of the legal status of emigration in the USSR, see pp. 12-19 in the study cited in note 2.

4. Besides the data in Tables 13.1-3, see also the extended account of Soviet emigration in Chapter 2 of the study cited in note 2.

5. This section is based on various published accounts, including the following: A. Alexander, *Immigration to Israel from the USSR* (Tel Aviv: Faculty of Law, Tel Aviv University, 1977); Joel Cang, *The Silent Millions: A History of the Jews in the Soviet Union* (New York: Taplinger Publishing Co., 1969); Robert O. Freedman (ed.), *Soviet Jewry in the Decisive Decade, 1971-80* (Durham, N.C.: Duke University Press, 1984); George Ginsburgs, "Soviet Law and the Emigration of Soviet Jews,"

Soviet Jewish Affairs, vol. 3, no. 1 (1973); Zvi Gitelman, *Antisemitism in the USSR: Sources, Types, Consequences* (New York: Institute for Jewish Policy Planning and Research of the Synagogue of America, 1974), "Moscow and the Soviet Jews: A Parting of the Ways," *Problems of Communism*, vol. 39, January-February 1980, and "Soviet Jewish Emigrants: Why Are They Choosing America?" *Soviet Jewish Affairs*, vol. 7, no. 1 (1977); Ben Zion Goldberg, *The Jewish Problem in the Soviet Union: Analysis and Solution* (New York: Crown Publishers, 1961); Dan N. Jacobs and Ellen Frankel Paul, *Studies of the Third Wave: Recent Migration of the Soviet Jews to the United States* (Boulder, Colo.: Westview Press, 1981); William Korey, *The Soviet Cage: Antisemitism in Russia* (New York: Viking Press, 1973); Thomas E. Sawyer, *The Jewish Minority in the Soviet Union* (Boulder, Colo.: Westview Press, 1979); and Victor Zaslavsky and Robert J. Brym, *Soviet-Jewish Emigration and Soviet Nationality Policy* (New York: St. Martin's Press, 1983).

6. This section is based on various sources, including C. C. Aronsfeld, "German Emigration from the Soviet Union," *Research Report* (London: Institute of Jewish Affairs, no. 2, September 1982); *30 Jahre Lager Friedland* (Hannover, West Germany: Herausgegaben vom Niedersächisischen Minister für Bundesgelegenheiten, 1975); CDU/CSU Group in the German Bundestag, *White Paper on the Human Rights Situation in Germany and of the Germans in Eastern Europe* (Bonn: CDU/CSU Group in the German Bundestag, 1977); Ingeborg Fleischhauer, *Die Deutschen im Zarenreich: 200 Jahre deutsch-russischer Kulturgemeinschaft* (Stuttgart, West Germany: Deutscher Verlag Anstalt, 1986); Ingeborg Fleischhauer and Benjamin Pinkus, *The Soviet Germans; Past and Present* (New York: St. Martin's Press, 1986); Adam Giesinger, *From Catherine to Khrushchev: The Story of Russia's Germans* (Saskatchewan, Canada: Marian Press, 1974); Sidney Heitman, *The Soviet Germans in the USSR Today* (Cologne, West Germany: Bundesinstitut für ostwissenschaftliche und internationale Studien, 1980), and "Soviet German Population Change, 1970-1979," *Soviet Geography: Review and Translation*, vol. 22, no. 9 November 1981; James W. Long, *From Privileged to Dispossessed; The Volga Germans, 1860-1917* (Lincoln: University of Nebraska Press, 1988); *Re Patria; Sbornik materialov posviashchennyh istorii, kul'ture i problemam nemtsev Sovetskogo Soiuza* (Moscow: Samizdat, 1974); and *Untersuchung über die Aussiedler in der Bundesrepublik Deutschland—Anpassung, Umstellung, Eingliederung* (Bad Homburg v.d. Höhe, West Germany: AWR-Forschungsgesellschaft für das Weltflüchtlingsproblem, deutsche Sektion e.V., 1982).

7. Information concerning Armenian emigration is scarce, for the subject has been intentionally obscured until now by the Soviet government and the international Armenian diaspora, for both of whom it is a politically sensitive issue. This section is based on information provided by various informants and the following written sources: Esther Agabian, "In the Shadow of Ararat, Armenia Revisited," *Christian Science Monitor*, March 5, 1979; Akademiia Nauk Armianskoi SSR, *Atlas Armianskoi Sovetskoi Sotsialisticheskoi Respubliki* (Erevan and Moscow: Glavnoe upravlenie

geodezii i kartografii, 1961); Ellie Andrassian, "Immigrants from Soviet Armenia Today" (unpublished paper, 1985); Michael J. Arlen, *Passage to Ararat* (New York: Farrar, Straus & Giroux, 1975); Elizabeth Fuller and Ann Sheehy, "Armenia and Armenians in the USSR," *The All-Union Census of 1979 in the USSR; Radio Liberty Research Bulletin* (Munich, West Germany: Radio Free Europe-Radio Liberty, 1980); "Armenians," *Great Soviet Encyclopedia*, vol. 2 (English trans. of 3rd Russian ed.; New York: Macmillan, 1973); Robert Mirak, "Armenians," *Harvard Encyclopedia of American Ethnic Groups* (Cambridge, Mass., and London: Harvard University Press, 1980), and *Torn Between Two Lands: Armenians in America 1890 to World War I* (Cambridge, Mass.: Harvard University Press, 1983); Richard G. Hovannisian, *Armenia on the Road to Independence, 1918* (Berkeley: University of California Press, 1967), and *The Republic of Armenia*, vols. 1 and 2 (Berkeley: University of California Press, 1971 and 1982); Mary K. Matossian, "Armenia and the Armenians," in *Handbook of Major Soviet Nationalities* (New York: The Free Press, 1975), and *The Impact of Soviet Policies in Armenia* (Leiden, The Netherlands: E. J. Brill, 1962; and Westpoint, Conn.: Hyperion, 1981); Claire Mouradian, "L'immigration des Arméniens de la diaspora vers la Rus d'Arménie, 1946-1962," *Cahiers du monde russe et sovietique* no. 1 (1979); and Ronald Grigor Suny, *Armenia in the Twentieth Century* (Chico, Calif.: Scholars Press, 1983).

8. Except as otherwise noted, this section is based on the following sources: Robert O. Freedman, "Soviet Jewry and Soviet-American Relations: A Historical Analysis," in *Soviet Jewry in the Decisive Decade*, cited in note 5; Georg Brunner et al., *Minderheitenschutz in Europa* (Heidelberg, West Germany: C. F. Müller Juristischer Verlag, 1985); Rupert S. Dirnecker, "Between Helsinki and Belgrade; A Balance Sheet of CSCE," *Strategic Review*, vol. 5, no. 4 (1977); Robin Edmonds, *Soviet Foreign Policy; The Brezhnev Years* (Oxford and New York: Oxford University Press, 1983); William E. Griffith, *The Ostpolitik of the Federal Republic of Germany* (Cambridge, Mass.: MIT Press, 1978); Wolfram F. Hanreider (ed.), *West German Foreign Policy: 1949-1979* (Boulder, Colo.: Westview Press, 1980); John P. Hardt and Donna L. Gold, *Emigration: Soviet Compliance with the Helsinki Accords* (Washington, D.C.: Congressional Research Service, Library of Congress, 1984); William Korey, *Human Rights and the Helsinki Accord; Focus on U.S. Policy* (Headline Series No. 59; New York: Foreign Policy Association, 1983); Benjamin Pinkus, "The Emigration of National Minorities from the USSR in the Post-Stalin Era," *Soviet Jewish Affairs*, vol. 13, no. 1 (February 1983); Donna L. Gold, *Soviet Jewry: U.S. Policy Considerations* (Washington, D.C.: Congressional Research Service, Library of Congress, 1985); and Victor Zaslavsky and Robert J. Brym, *Soviet-Jewish Emigration*, cited in note 5.

9. Alan Dowty, "The New Serfdom: Contemporary Control of Emigration and Expulsion," chapter 6 of his unpublished study "The Contemporary Challenge to Free Movement," p. 36.

10. George Ginsburgs, "Soviet Law and the Emigration of Soviet Jews," cited in note 5.

11. It should be noted that the publication by Zaslavsky and Brym cited in note 5 and a related article by John L. Scherer, "Soviet Emigration Policy: Internal Determinants; A Note on Soviet Jewish Emigration, 1971–1984," *Soviet Jewish Affairs* vol. 15, no. 2 (1985) question the linkage between Soviet emigration policy and Western foreign relations with the USSR. The authors propose other internal determinants of Soviet emigration policy, but their thesis is not convincing.

Postscript

The rush of events since this chapter was written (in early 1989) has overtaken its findings. Recent developments include:

1. A new record number of emigrants was set in 1989 when 72,550 Jews, 98,000 Germans, 14,000 Armenians, and 22,200 others were permitted to leave, a total of 206,550 persons for the year.

2. At the very time the USSR was easing emigration requirements, the United States government imposed limits on the number of immigrants from the Soviet Union (50,000 annually), forcing Jews to resettle primarily in Israel and creating problems there of handling and financing their resettlement and dealing with protests from the Arab states and the Soviet Union against the resettlement of some of the newcomers in disputed West Bank housing.

3. The immigration of 840,000 East Germans, ethnic Germans from Eastern Europe, and Soviet Germans to West Germany in 1989 created similar problems of resettling them and triggered a political backlash that may force limits on the number of Soviet Germans permitted to settle in the Federal Republic in the future. In the long run this may reduce emigration of Germans from the USSR; in the short run it may cause a flood of emigration while it is still possible, exacerbating the problem of accommodating refugees in West Germany.

4. Within the USSR two new developments in 1989 have impinged on the Third Emigration. One is the rise of a virulent wave of antisemitism that is driving many Jews who might otherwise have remained to emigrate from the country. The other is the preliminary approval of a new draft law on foreign travel that will probably be adopted in 1990 and will remove many of the obstacles to free emigration. The result will be an enormous increase in emigration, provided emigrants can find countries willing to accept them for resettlement.

Chapter 14

Soviet-Jewish Emigration Policy: Anti-Zionism and Philo-Semitism

Zachary Irwin

In the autumn of 1988 Robert Cullen, an American journalist, proposed that the United States begin admitting Soviet-Jewish emigrants within the overall quota set for all emigrants. Supposedly such an arrangement would signal satisfaction with the Soviet decision to permit a relatively high level of Jewish emigration and deny permission to relatively few. In October more than 2,000 Jews had obtained exit permits, and of all applicants, only about 5 per cent were considered "refusniks," i.e. those denied permits.[1] Supposedly, if the United States ceased to admit an unlimited number of Jewish émigrés, General Secretary Mikhail Gorbachev's concern about a "brain drain" would be allayed; the most politically and religiously qualified individuals would win exit visas; and the United States could let lapse the Jackson–Vanik amendment restricting Soviet–American trade. Within days of Cullen's proposal the Department of State acknowledged that for several months at least 175 Soviet Jews had been denied refugee status apparently because they "could not demonstrate a well-founded fear of persecution," according to terms of the 1980 Refugee Act.[2] The implications of American policy for overall Soviet-Jewish emigration to the United States or Israel are not yet clear, and I do not wish to judge them or Cullen's suggestion. At present, the limitations affect a small percentage of the more than 13,000 Soviet-Jewish emigrants in 1988, but the change in American policy signals a new stage in the Soviet-Jewish question. For nearly 20 years Jewish emigration has been a central issue in Soviet–American relations. I wish to examine certain questions of Soviet policy on Jewish emigration whose answers remain uncertain or controversial. One could plausibly argue that few such questions remain.

Soviet Jewish policy has attracted a high level of scholarly interest for good reasons. Soviet-Jewish émigrés have provided an excellent source of information about daily life in the Soviet Union. Accurate data on the number of emigrants between 1968 and the 1980s allow informed speculation about the motives and variables affecting policy. Also, emigration policy intersects problems of human rights, and foreign and nationality policy. Good communications between Soviet-Jewish dissidents and interested Western groups have guaranteed the attention of government officials and scholars alike. Of course, while a great deal is known about Soviet Jewry, somewhat less is known about Soviet policy. While it is probably true that the decision to permit large-scale emigration was made in response to Jewish militancy and in pursuit of better commercial relations with the United States, it is uncertain why the level of emigrants peaked at 50,000 in 1979 at a time when neither factor was especially relevant. The intense Soviet press campaigns against "Zionism" between 1967 and 1984 indicate more than a casual deterrent to would-be emigrants. There may be indirect evidence that anti-Zionism expressed a permitted opposition to emigration policy, but there is no satisfactory explanation about emigration and anti-Zionism as concurrent policies. We don't know with certainty which individuals or groups in the Soviet leadership supported increased emigration because of the closed nature of Soviet decision-making and because of the uncertain outcomes that might be associated with the policy. Concessions to the United States could be perceived as either a mark of weakness or of serious intent. Emigration could win the political support of nationalities who perceived Jews as professional rivals, or it could create resentment of unjustified Jewish privilege. American Jewish groups could become supporters of détente or remain opponents of any Soviet-American understanding in the Middle East.

Perhaps the best-answered question about Soviet emigration policy concerns the motives of Soviet Jews for emigrating. There are several levels at which the question has been approached. Zvi Gitelman refers to the Soviet failure to create a "secular, Soviet and socialist" Jewish identity. Jews could choose emigration "either external or internal" or seek acculturation, "but in most cases no assimilation." "Since the legitimate expression of Jewish identity has been so narrowed, the assertion of Jewish nationality, especially when coupled with religious commitment, becomes almost actually an oppositionalist statement."[3] Ludmilla Alexeyeva notes how restrictions affect several classes. Jewish professionals confront a "lack of creative freedom, a lack of freedom in general and poor monetary compensation." Workers suffer from "low pay" and "the impossibility of a legal struggle to improve their lot." Those who would "engage in business—an activity considered normal in the free world—are subject to persecution in socialist countries [and] also leave."[4] The existence of *numerus clausus* in Soviet professional life and educational institutions is a general feature of Soviet life inimical to Jewish interests.

John Armstrong's concept of a "mobilized diaspora" allows a systematic framework for broader comparison with other nationalities. Supposedly Jews, overseas Chinese, Armenians and Germans (under Tsarism) share special skills enabling them "to occupy a special functional position in a modernizing society." Armstrong develops five propositions that help explain the rise of anti-Semitism since the Revolution.[5] At first, the mobilized diaspora is "temporarily indispensable for the dominant ethnic [Russian] elite," and "depends for its security" on the dominant group. In support of Armstrong's assertion, one could cite the importance of Jews in the revolutionary movement, their prominence in the Soviet Union before 1928, and, in particular, the role of the Yevsektsia, the Jewish sections of the Communist Party. But within the multiethnic polity a "delicate balance of forces is most apt to be upset by a sharp rise in social mobilization." Mobilization of all non-Russian nationalities was certain to challenge Jewish positions eventually. Meanwhile, "dominant ethnic perceptions of the mobilized diaspora tend to negate the value of the diaspora for external relations." Since the creation of Israel and Polina Molotov's warm reception of Golda Myerson (Meir), Israel's first Ambassador to the USSR, Jews have been distrusted for their potential disloyalty.[6] Armstrong finds that "the most potent source of dominant ethnic suspicion of the mobilized diaspora is the existence of its 'homeland' outside the dominant elite's territorial control." He carefully distinguishes this distrust from the anti-Semitic practice of "scapegoating" which seeks to hold the diaspora responsible for the regime's faults.

The advantages of Armstrong's model as a basis for explaining emigration policy appear compelling. The phases of Soviet-Jewish experience since the Revolution offer support for the sequential propositions of a "mobilized diaspora." By emphasis on the consequences of mobilization and modernization for interethnic relations, the problem of Soviet anti-Semitism can be understood less as a question of atavism and more as a result of development in a multinational society. Emigration emerges as a rational solution to a definable problem. Of course, that the USSR may be particularly susceptible to the problem allows consideration of anti-Semitic precedents in Soviet political culture. American interest in Jewish emigration even promises to turn to advantage the problem of Soviet "suspicion" that Jews are disloyal. Finally, the concept of a mobilized diaspora is not exclusively Jewish and permits comparison of Jewish, German and Armenian diasporas. The question of which interests and individuals could be aggregated on behalf of emigration allows examination of the decision taken in late 1970 or early 1971 to permit large numbers of emigrants.

Certainly the political style of seeking consensus associated with General Secretary Brezhnev is compatible with agreement about emigration among dominant Soviet interests. Brezhnev's "peace policy" sought improved relations with the West. Industrial managers could hope for benefits from imported technology, at least before the Soviet denunciation of American conditions required for an expansion of commercial relations. Non-Jewish professionals could expect increased employment opportunities. Security forces elicited less foreign protest in repressing dissent, while concern for "human rights" centered on emigration. With some dialectic legerdemain, attacks in the press on "Zionist" enemies mollified Russian chauvinists and neo-Stalinists. If these groups were divided, there remains a presumption that Jewish emigration enjoyed considerable political support.

Soviet Jewish Policy in the 1960s

To appreciate the significance of emigration policy during the 1970s, it is important to understand how the Soviet regime's approach had changed from the previous decade. Between 1962 and 1966 the number of Jewish emigrants increased from 184 to 2,047, falling sharply to 229 in 1968 (see Table 14.1).[7] Inasmuch as these data are less well known than that for later years, there is no account of the fluctuation. I wish to suggest that between 1964 and 1966 a trend of relative philo-Semitism existed within certain segments of the Communist Party of the Soviet Union (CPSU), which sought to place

Table 14.1 Soviet Jewish Emigration: 1959–1987

Year	#	Year	#	Year	#	Year	#	Year	#
1959	3	1965	891	1971	13,022	1977	16,736	1983	1,314
1960	60	1966	2,047	1972	13,681	1978	28,865	1984	896
1961	202	1967	1,406	1973	34,733	1979	51,320	1985	1,140
1962	184	1968	229	1974	20,628	1980	21,474	1986	914
1963	305	1969	2,979	1975	13,221	1981	9,448	1987	8,000 (est.)
1964	537	1970	1,027	1976	14,736	1982	2,692		

Sources: Benjamin Pinkus, "The Emigration of National Minorities from the USSR in the Post-Stalin Era," *Soviet Jewish Affairs*, 13(1), 1983, pp. 27, 28, 30; Zvi Nezer, "The Emigration of Soviet Jews," *Soviet Jewish Affairs*, 15(1), 1985, p. 17; *American Jewish Year Book, 1987*, vol. 87 (New York: American Jewish Committee, 1987), p. 266; *The New York Times*, January 7, 1987, p. 18, and November 12, 1988, p. 26.

increased emigration within a larger context of improved relations with Israel and more open Jewish cultural expression within the USSR. The reversal of this tendency following the 23rd CPSU Congress in 1966 required a new basis for policy in the 1970s. Under Mikhail Gorbachev's leadership, anti-Stalinism has again combined increased emigration with more open Jewish cultural expression and a new approach to Israel. With the obvious caveat that any labels demand qualified caution, two distinct policy models exist. The first I wish to call anti-Stalinist philo-Semitism, the second neo-Stalinist anti-Zionism. Recalling that levels of emigration for any year indicate relative rather than absolute significance, the tenfold increase between 1962 and 1966 requires consideration.

In early July 1965 Katriel Katz, Israel's new Ambassador to the Soviet Union, was granted an interview with *Sovetskaya Rossiya*. Katz promised to "find new ways to develop economic and cultural relations" between the two states, adding, "[N]ow relations between our states are constantly improving. We ought to try to improve them more quickly and intensively, to find new areas for common activity."[8] Dimitri Chuvakhin, Katz's Soviet counterpart, expressed his "sincere wish for friendship with Israel."[9] The claim of improved relations was not without substance. The previous year the Soviet Union completed negotiations to transfer to Israel some 68 *dunams* of property in Jerusalem that had formerly belonged to the Russian Orthodox Church, as well as parcels of land in Nazareth, Haifa, Afula and Tiberas.[10] For the first time, a Zionist organization was welcomed in the Soviet Union. Representatives of the Women's Section of the World Zionist Organization toured the Soviet Union, and in July 1964 *Sovetskaya Litva* reported a delegation of the Soviet–Israeli Friendship Society in Vilnius.[11] The next year Peltours, an Israeli organization, announced substantial reductions in the costs of group and individual tours.[12] In the autumn there was a report that several prominent Soviet artists would visit Israel.[13]

These events represented a fundamental change from the state of relations before 1964. The increased level of Soviet–Israeli contacts was perhaps less remarkable than the absence of reported incidents involving Israeli diplomats and Soviet Jews. The extent of clandestine contact between Israeli officials and Soviet Jews cannot be estimated. Leonard Schroeter refers to a special office attached to the Israeli Foreign Ministry that dealt with Soviet-Jewish problems. Schroeter mentions the head of the office, Nechemiah Levanon, but without elaboration.

> Since it had no official name, and its very mention in the media was subject to official censorship, Soviet-Jewish emigrants came to call it

Nechemiah's office, and immigrants who wished contact, material assistance, or other help from Jews in the Diaspora were referred to it.[14]

Schroeter cites a Soviet pamphlet which identifies Levanon by name as responsible for the activity of an "intelligence service code-named Netiva operated under the cover of the Israeli Embassy in Moscow."[15] There is no evidence that Israel was prepared to negotiate its contacts with Soviet Jews in exchange for marginal increases in emigration, but there is little doubt that they were associated with improved diplomatic relations. American foreign policy had not yet taken up the question of emigration.

American involvement in Soviet-Jewish affairs at the time was limited to improving conditions for Jews in the Soviet Union. In April 1964 President Lyndon Johnson and Secretary of State Dean Rusk met with representatives of major American Jewish organizations to discuss Soviet Jewry. The Secretary of State promised to pursue "further steps the United States might take to be helpful in the matter."[16] The following year the President's special counsel, Lee White, acknowledged that Rusk had kept his word.[17] In mid-1965 American Jewish organizations held a rally in Madison Square Garden, New York, attended by 16,000. Senators Robert Kennedy and Jacob Javits appeared on the dais with Governor Nelson Rockefeller, while the President cabled his endorsements, advising Moscow that removing "restrictions" against "Jews would go a long way towards removing a moral and emotional barrier between us and contribute to a relaxation of tension."[18] A concurrent resolution adopted unanimously in the Senate deplored Soviet discrimination against the Jewish minority.[19]

Publicly, the Soviet response was to invite a delegation from the Rabbinical Council of America to meet with the Chief Rabbi in Moscow, the first such invitation in a decade. The American delegation was assured that there would be no impediments to the distribution of Matzoth, that 10,000 Jewish prayer books would be printed, and that more residency permits would be granted to students at the Moscow Yeshiva.[20] Nahum Goldman, President of the World Jewish Congress, acknowledged that in 1965 he was accorded "more understanding than in previous years by Soviet officials."[21] Reportedly, Goldman was involved in negotiations to establish a central body to represent Soviet Jews abroad. The measures had the desired effect. A letter to Senator James Fulbright from the State Department observed, "The Soviet Government appears to have become increasingly sensitive to the unfavorable publicity it has received . . . and may have moderated some of its policies accordingly."[22]

Domestic developments indicated that Soviet Jewish policy was changing rapidly by the autumn of 1964. The French scholar Michael Tatu refers to "marked waverings" in various Soviet policies from the time of Khrushchev's ouster through 1966. Supposedly the vacillation resulted from the activities of different "lobbies" or interest groups which gained influence in the absence of a single dominant leader. "Instead of one person to approach there were eleven, each of whom needed support in the inevitable power struggle . . . thus any group which felt injured by some decision was inclined to regard it as provisional."[23]

In particular, liberal writers, such as Evgenii Yevtushenko, Andrei Voznesensky and Ilya Ehrenburg, felt emboldened to raise the question of anti-Semitism in Soviet life. Under the editorship of Alexander Tvardovsky, *Novy Mir* serialized Ehrenburg's memoirs, *People, Years and Life*, including his "most difficult years," before Stalin's death. The writer warned about lessons to be drawn from the "shameful" campaign against "cosmopolitanism" under Stalin: ". . . all racism, including anti-Semitism, ran counter to the tradition of the Russian intelligentsia, including those lofty ideas of internationalism that were Lenin's behest."[24] Yevtushenko's poem *"Bratsk"* included the character Izzy Kramer, a survivor of the wartime Riga ghetto, who knew "much light will be needed . . . Before Jews will no longer be exposed to someone's jeers. Before the word Yid will vanish forever."[25] Yevtushenko's 1961 poem *"Babi Yar"* had earlier raised the question of anti-Semitism and provoked attack, but in 1965 there was no rejoinder.[26] Jewish authors, including Lev Kvitko and Isaac Babel, victimized by Stalin, now appeared in translation. Soviet politics and literary expression moved in tandem.

On September 5, 1965, *Pravda* carried an editorial consistent with the changes. It cited the authority of Lenin: "He wrathfully assailed any manifestation of nationalism whatsoever, and in particular, he demanded an unceasing struggle against anti-Semitism, that foul fanning of social exclusiveness and national enmity brought about by the exploiting classes."[27] The editorial was not without foundation. Grigory Svirsky, a former member of the Soviet Writers Union who emigrated to Israel in 1972, described a meeting of the Writers Union on October 27. Here Piotr Demichev, a Secretary of the Central Committee responsible for ideology, addressed the meeting.

> He [Demichev] said that we Communists had indeed broken off the struggle against anti-Semitism too early. Anti-Semitism was still with us . . . "[it] should be a reason for expulsion from the Party!" shouted the old Bolshevik Landres. . . . That is correct, confirmed the Central Committee Secretary . . . the penalty for anti-Semitism should be expulsion from the Party.[28]

According to Svirsky, Demichev repeated the speech at Moscow University and elsewhere.

The event may have been part of a reconsideration of the status of Jews and Germans. In December 1964, a Supreme Soviet decree declared earlier charges against the Volga Germans had been "unfounded" and a result of the "arbitrary rule under conditions of the Stalin personality cult." "Help and economic assistance" were promised for resettlement.[29] Early in 1965 a second decree downgraded the Jewish Autonomous *oblast'* (JAO) (region) to the status of a *raion* (district), an important change in territorial administration which would have been consistent with the elevation of Soviet Jewish cultural rights outside of Birobidzhan.[30] The positive association between the demotion of the JAO, the "struggle" against anti-Semitism and increased emigration in 1965 is inferential but plausible. In 1958 and 1959, years of the least emigration, the JAO had been praised. In August 1958 *Sovetskaya Rossiya* touted the *oblast'* as a triumph of Soviet nationality policy.

> Only the country of the Soviets, where the nationality question had been solved on the basis of Marxism-Leninism, gave land to the Jewish working people. This is why contingents of Jewish settlers began pouring in . . . people, who had never worked on the land in the past because they had none, came to Birobidzhan, received land, and became collective farmers . . .[31]

Yiddish culture was to be found everywhere in the JAO, according to the author. "How can one exchange this land for something else?" asked local inhabitants. Nonetheless, instances were revealed of those deceived by "Zionist propaganda," "tragic stories" of those who endured a "miserable existence" and "humiliations" in Israel. The appearance of such testimony in the Soviet press was an obvious rationale for denying exit permits. Jews who had not assimilated could go to the JAO.

Demichev's speech about anti-Semitism and the greater number of emigrants in 1965 created a different set of expectations from those of the more repressive late 1950s. Svirsky reports a confidant's warning shortly after Demichev's speech:

> There are signs. Some Jews want to leave for . . . Israel, making out that things are bad. Then there are the young people, here dancing in the Synagogues . . . and tongues are beginning to wag—people saying that they can't get jobs or university places and so on. The City Committee [of the CPSU] is watching out for it. Your speech was water on the mill wheel of Zionist elements.[32]

Soon after the Six Day War, the full impact of the phrase "Zionist elements" became quite obvious. The full fury of the press campaign against Zionism was released. Indeed, within less than four months the trial of the Soviet dissidents Sinyavsky and Daniel and the 23rd Party Congress marked a conservative reaction against any consideration of anti-Semitism. The trial of the two writers has been considered a "watershed" in the political struggle between liberals and conservatives in that it marked the beginning of a wave of repression against dissent and the decline of liberal influence.[33] Sinyavsky had published abroad under the pseudonym of Abram Tertz, the Jewish "King of Thieves" of the Tsarist Odessa underground. *Izvestia* observed:

> Sinyavsky was trying to create the impression that anti-Semitism exists in our country, that presumably an author with the name of Abram Tertz must look for publishers in the West if he wishes to write "candidly" about Soviet life.[34]

In March 1966, the 23rd Party Congress confirmed the significance of the trial. Brezhnev set the tone of the proceedings by his denunciation of "renegades ... who select as their specialty the denigration of our system and slander against our heroic people."[35] N. G. Yegorychev, First Secretary of the Moscow City Party Committee, spoke of the danger of taking "a tolerant attitude towards alien views and moods."[36] Furtseva, Minister of Culture, recalled the Stalinist cultural policy *Zhdanovschina* in taking the "offensive" in the "sharp ideological struggle between the two worlds."[37] Soviet press vignettes emphatically condemned Israel's role in Western protest against the treatment of Soviet Jews. Israeli tourists and diplomats were harassed for their distribution of "Zionist literature," following a Supreme Soviet decree establishing criminal penalties for foreign tourists who strayed from a prescribed route of travel.[38] In April a Syrian delegation led by Prime Minister Zayen arrived. The two sides reaffirmed "solidarity with the Palestinian Arabs and support for their legitimate rights against Zionism, which is used by the imperialist forces to exacerbate tension in the Near and Middle East."[39] Reference to Zionism had not previously appeared in such communiqués. Syrian instability and the vulnerability of the leftist Ba'ath regime in Syria are believed to have been factors in the events that led to the Six Day War. Suspecting an Israeli strike against Syria, Soviet strategy sought Egypt's redeployment of forces to bolster Syria's position.[40] President Nasser's closure of the Straits of Tiran led to Israel's pre-emptive war rather than the desired relief for Syria.

Despite the harsh line against Jewish expression in the Soviet Union after 1966, the number of emigrants increased in that year from 891 to 2,047. In December, at a Paris news conference, Prime

Minister Kosygin denied that anti-Semitism existed in the Soviet Union: "There is nothing of that kind in our country and cannot be." But he also made a promising statement on family reunification: "As for reuniting families, if some families want to meet or want to leave the Soviet Union, the road is open to them, and no problem exists here."[41] This was the first public statement by a Soviet leader establishing a general criterion for emigration. The comment was significant not only for its originality but because Kosygin had been associated with the line taken by Demichev. In a 1965 speech given in Riga on nationality relations, Kosygin stated that "national vestiges in any form, whether it be a manifestation of nationalism, great power chauvinism, racialism or anti-Semitism, are phenomena absolutely alien and contrary to our worldview."[42]

Those individuals associated with the theme of anti-Zionism are somewhat easier to identify. Party Secretary Mikhail Suslov's involvement is highly probable. Suslov had been a direct beneficiary of the anti-Semitic "Doctors' Plot" of 1953, in which a group of Soviet doctors, mostly Jewish, were alleged to have tried to murder various prominent Soviet personalities. Elected to the "expanded" Party Presidium at the 19th Party Congress in 1952, Suslov was responsible for propaganda as a Central Committee Secretary and managed the deportation of the Caucasian Karachai for alleged pro-Nazi sympathies, suggesting he played a similar role in organizing the Doctors' Plot.[43] Boris Ponomarev had become a Central Committee Secretary in 1961 after six years of work in the International Department. Still a relatively minor official at the time of Stalin's death, Ponomarev is believed to have been responsible for disbanding the wartime Jewish Anti-Fascist Committee, which worked abroad to promote wartime support for the Soviet Union.[44] The relationship between the Doctors' Plot and the anti-Zionism of the 1970s is further indicated by an ally of Suslov, Frol Kozlov, who had been incapacitated by a stroke in 1963. Kozlov emerged in the late 1950s as a critic of détente and a spokesman on Jewish questions.[45] He had written a leading article on "vigilance" in *Kommunist* at the time of the Doctors' Plot.[46] Suslov and Kozlov represented a hard-line faction who opposed concessions to the West, and, according to Mikhail Agursky, a prominent dissident author, both Suslov and Ponomarev had also opposed Soviet support for Israel in 1948 and normal relations between the two states subsequently.[47] Both had also mediated the 1965 split in the Israeli Communist Party between the *Maki* and the pro-Palestinian *Rakah* factions, recognizing *Rakah* as the legitimate party.[48] Agursky notes that Ponomarev's deputy, Vadim Zagladin, became a vocal anti-Zionist in the 1970s.

Did this faction oppose increased emigration? In view of Suslov's influence within the divided leadership of Brezhnev and Kosygin of 1966, his acquiescence to the "reunion of families" policy is virtually certain. Suslov had once remarked to a foreign Communist that "if one but touches a hair on the head of any Jew, all Jews begin to clamor in all four corners of the world."[49] Anti-Zionism and emigration satisfied certain goals of those, particularly Suslov, who opposed a return to the mood of 1965 bequeathed by Khrushchev's de-Stalinization. At the same time, emigration at the 1966 level would discourage foreign protest.

The reunion of families line represented a limited concession to Western opinion which was compatible with greater attention to "alien moods and views" criticized at the 23rd Party Congress. By early 1969, attacks on Zionism as the centerpiece of Israeli imperialism had given way to a more extensive and diffuse campaign against anti-Soviet "international Zionism." The themes and distribution of the press campaign have been carefully studied,[50] but there is no obvious connection between anti-Zionism and Soviet emigration policy. One approach to Soviet policy in general, developed by Alexander Dallin, emphasizes the distinction between "left" and "right" policy commitments, e.g. "monolithism" v. "pluralism," "heavy industry" v. "light industry," "Red" v. "expert."[51] Dallin observes that "shifts in Soviet domestic, foreign and ideological positions have tended to go hand-in-hand."[52] Emigration and anti-Zionism were, of course, derivative of larger policy goals, but together they are suggestive of the right and left priorities that Dallin finds were "descriptive of profoundly divergent attitudes" within the Soviet leadership. For example, the right goal of improved relations with the West attained through emigration could be combined with the left goal of repressing dissent. The concept of the mobilized diaspora mentioned earlier is relevant to the right objective of promoting support among non-Jewish nationalities able to assume professional positions vacated by emigrating Jews. Identifying Zionism with other forms of bourgeois nationalism offered a second defense against nationalist dissent compatible with a left emphasis on ideological militancy.

The compatibility of left and right policies expressed through emigration and anti-Zionism may indicate a source of durability for both policies between 1971 and 1985. There is considerable evidence from different aspects of the two policies throughout the period. Frederick Barghoorn points out the considerable "overlap" of the movement for Jewish emigration and the larger dissenting Democratic Movement.[53] Barghoorn cites Leonard Schroeter's estimate that "60 to 70 per cent of the democrats are Jews or married to

Jews."[54] The Moscow Human Rights Committee supported Jewish goals in its 1971 protest to the Supreme Soviet concerning the "persecution of Jewish repatriates." Emigration or expulsion of dissenting Jews deprived both movements of effective leaders. The removal of Piotr Shelest from the Ukrainian leadership in the spring of 1972 eliminated a vocal opponent of détente, as well as a Communist who had allegedly tolerated Ukrainian bourgeois nationalism.[55] Shelest's successor, V. V. Shcherbitsky, found the theme of anti-Zionism a convenient justification for the arrest of Ukrainian dissenters.

> The alliance of international Zionism with various overt reactionary bourgeois and chauvinistic circles is nowadays consolidated on an anti-Communist base. International Zionism, for example, subsidizes diverse groups of Ukrainian bourgeoisie, supports their espionage and sabotage activities and particularly their anti-Soviet actions.[56]

Discrediting Ukrainian nationalists by associating them with Zionism could be logically, if implausibly, extended to other nationalities (except the Russian), and pre-eminently to Jewish bourgeois nationalists, a line compatible with increased emigration in the 1970s. As Shmuel Ettinger, a Soviet Jewish writer, notes, "Attacks on the 'reactionary Jewish bourgeoisie' can serve as a cover for the rise in the number of emigrants and justify those who call for the expulsion of untrustworthy elements."[57] Of course, implementing a left policy of anti-Zionism and a right policy of emigration was subject to inconsistent levels of emphasis on each.

Fluctuating levels of emigration between 1968 and 1970 were a consequence of American diplomatic involvement, domestic opposition to emigration, and the resumption of fighting in the Middle East. The more than tenfold increase between 1968 and 1969 (229 to 2,979) followed the first American diplomatic approach. Henry Kissinger recalls:

> Early in Nixon's first term we had decided to raise this [Jewish emigration] in the special channel we maintained through Anatoly Dobrynin to the Soviet leadership.... Starting in 1969, I approached Dobrynin with the proposition that we would take note of any voluntary regard for the moral concerns of our people with respect to Soviet emigration practices. The effort was low key but persistent; we sought action, not acclaim.[58]

Kissinger refers to lists of "hardship cases" Dobrynin received without comment; Kissinger claims that the Soviet policy was responsive. The outbreak of the "Canal War" between Egypt and Israel in 1969 and the dramatic increase in Soviet forces stationed in Egypt the following year brought objections to emigration from the Soviet military. In January 1970, at a time when Soviet and Israeli fighter pilots were directly engaged over the Canal, *Krasnaya Zvezda*, the organ of the Soviet armed forces, observed that "the level of production of the Israeli aircraft industry has increased 30 per cent compared with last year and now employs more than 10,000 persons. Among those are a considerable number of specialists and skilled workers who recently emigrated to Israel."[59] No other recent group of emigrants existed besides those who emigrated from the Soviet Union. Plausibly the 50 per cent decline in emigration in 1970 was a response to such concern. By 1970 the demand for emigration from Soviet Jews had reached a high level with literally hundreds of collective petitions addressed to the Soviet leadership.

The sharp decline in emigration permits provoked militant Jewish response, including the abortive Leningrad hijacking attempt by 11 dissidents, nine of whom were Jews. Two Jews were sentenced to death for their part in the episode. According to an acquaintance of the convicted, their attempt to hijack the plane had followed the "despair" of being denied exit.[60] If the sentences were intended to intimidate Soviet Jews, the effect was the opposite. An extensive protest campaign abroad on behalf of the hijacking suspects led to commuted executions, reduced sentences and postponement of an additional trial scheduled for early 1971.[61]

Thus, by 1971 the intensity of the Jewish emigration movement had become an overt challenge to the Soviet leadership. An analysis of Jewish petitions for emigration between 1968 and 1971 reveals that 89.2 per cent of the petitions originated in three republics: Georgia (36.2 per cent), the RSFSR (27.7 per cent) and Latvia (25.3 per cent).[62] Respectively, the three republics accounted for 2.6 per cent, 37.6 per cent and 1.7 per cent of the Soviet Jewish population. The distribution of the petitions supports an important distinction for emigration policy made by Victor Zaslavsky and Robert Brym.[63] The authors note the higher proportion of emigrants from the non-Slavic periphery compared with the Slavic "heartland." Between 1971 and 1975 the heartland accounted for only 17.5 per cent of emigrants arriving in Israel, a period when those emigrating elsewhere were relatively insignificant.[64] The lower level of Jewish emigration in the peripheral areas explains the greater likelihood of national revival and the potentially less-disruptive consequence of emigration.

The case of the ballet dancers Valery and Galina Panov is instructive. The couple emigrated early in 1974 after a protest campaign mounted on their behalf. Shortly after their departure, a letter appeared in *Sovetskaya Kultura* from Mrs Panov's mother, objecting to her daughter's marriage to a "morally unscrupulous person possessed by money-grubbing aims abroad." And more seriously,

> ... as a Jew he [Panov] had received permission to leave for Israel and he wanted to take Ganya with him.... I categorically refused.... I said she was a Russian and ought to serve her people.... I repeat my daughter is a Russian.[65]

Emigration of assimilated Jews potentially threatened to create more divided families than any policy directed at "family reunification." The strident anti-Zionist campaign took an apparently ominous tone in February 1971. *Pravda* warned that anyone espousing Zionist beliefs would "automatically become an agent of international Zionism and hence an enemy of the Soviet people."[66] Enemies were not suitable for Soviet society.

In March 1971 approximately 1,000 Jews were allowed to leave the Soviet Union, a number in excess of all those who emigrated in 1970. By the end of 1971 more than 13,000 had emigrated, and by 1975 more than 90,000. This extraordinary migration took place against the background of a fundamental improvement in Soviet-American relations, an improvement superficially threatened by Jewish militancy. A number of incidents in Washington and New York involving Soviet diplomatic personnel were attributed to the Jewish Defense League. Following the explosion of a bomb near a Soviet building in Washington, Foreign Minister Gromyko delivered a "stern protest," threatening reciprocal harassment of American diplomats in the USSR.[67] In the same month Kissinger and Dobrynin began secret discussions on strategic-arms limitation after a Soviet proposal to limit antiballistic missile systems.[68] The SALT negotiations could be insulated from Jewish agitation, whether its source was inside or outside the USSR. Certainly there was no reason to suppose the appeasement of militant Jewish demands would lead to their diminution, but a Soviet objective for the new emigration policy was aimed at a wider audience: broader circles of American Jewish opinion, and concurrently of the United States Congress. Secretary Brezhnev's address to the 24th Congress of the CPSU in March 1971 made clear that the scope of Soviet-American relations promised new levels of cooperation.

Brezhnev addressed the conference concerning his new "Peace Policy":

> We proceed from the premise that the improvement of relations between the USSR and the USA is possible ... consistently and fully [to] implement in practice the principles of peaceful coexistence, and to develop mutually advantageous ties.[69]

Peter Volten's description of the peace policy finds it a blend of "ideological and internationalist restraint, conventional state diplomacy and a reappraisal of the importance of the West in Soviet foreign policy."[70] Volten's analysis identifies coalitions of Politburo members arrayed in a continuum among three major issue areas of the Peace Policy: multilateral v. unilateral security policy, economic interdependence v. economic independence, and state diplomacy (peaceful coexistence) v. Communist diplomacy (proletarian internationalism).[71] The General Secretary could depend on consistent support in all areas from only a few colleagues, e.g. Andropov, and possibly Ustinov. Most were like Suslov and Gromyko. Suslov was an opponent of initiatives in the areas of economic interdependence and state diplomacy but a supporter of multilateral security. Gromyko supported both state diplomacy and multilateral security, but he opposed economic interdependence.

During the 1970s the Peace Policy would be implemented with considerable inconsistencies because the cross-cutting cleavages were stable and evenly divided. The Four-Power Berlin Agreement signed in 1971 represented an achievement of state diplomacy; and increasing Soviet involvement in East Africa after 1975, a case of Communist diplomacy. Understandably, some who sought to discover a consistent détente policy found such behavior opportunistic or confusing. The policy on Jewish emigration intersected all three major areas at different periods in the decade.

Initially, before 1975, all issues benefited from emigration concessions: congressional support for the SALT, annual summit conferences, and expectations of Soviet most-favored-nation commercial status. During the second half of the decade and in the early 1980s, inconsistent levels of emigration were vulnerable to the vagaries of specific policies. For example, the extraordinary emigration of 1979 (51,320 individuals) occurred during the year of the Brezhnev–Carter summit, but by 1982 the numbers had fallen to less than 3,000 after the sharp deterioration in bilateral relations and the Polish declaration of martial law. Adam Ulam, a leading scholar of Soviet–American relations, finds the volume of emigration followed the "general features of détente."[72]

At different points in the decade, emigration policy was the subject of diplomatic and popular attention. The strains created by large-scale emigration soon became apparent. For example, in August 1972 the Soviet Union announced the so-called education tax, requiring would-be emigrants to reimburse the state for the costs of higher education. In October Senator Henry Jackson and Representative Charles Vanik introduced an amendment to the bill granting the

Soviet Union most-favored-nation status, an amendment requiring unrestricted Soviet emigration. Ambassador Dobrynin presented Kissinger a demarche, warning that emigration policy "fell exclusively within the jurisdiction of the Soviet State"; it complained of the "noisy campaign" on emigration, which it denounced as "artificial and ill meaning."[73] But Kissinger adds that the note also offered the "good news" that the education tax had been suspended, leaving only "usual and insignificant duties which were also being collected before the decree of August 3, 1972." Of course, by his own admission, Kissinger proved to be "wildly off the mark" in assuring Dobrynin that "no outstanding issues stood in the way of implementing the US–Soviet Trade Agreement of 1972."[74]

Ultimately the Soviet Union denounced the Agreement because the "compromise" between Kissinger and Congress to replace the provision for unrestricted emigration with a quota of 60,000 emigrants annually proved unacceptable to the Soviet Union and because of the limitations on export credits offered to the Soviets.[75] This episode with the education tax and the Jackson–Vanik amendment highlighted the problems of perception and asymmetry in the policymaking process of each state. The reason for the education tax is obscure. Kissinger suggests that limiting emigration was a panicked response to the sudden expulsion of Soviet military advisors from Egypt.[76] Regardless of the motives behind the Jackson–Vanik amendment, President Nixon's ability to deal with Congress was impaired by the Watergate Affair. Kissinger's attempt to contain the emigration issue through his own influence had failed.

By the time of the Carter administration, it was difficult to insulate aspects of Soviet policy other than emigration from official concern. During the Nixon and Ford administrations, the repression of Soviet Jewish dissent was a matter for Jewish protest, but, by the the time of the Carter administration, it was difficult to avoid executive involvement. President Carter's own predilection in the matter was a likely factor. For example, American reaction to the "treason" trial of Natan Shcharansky was an impediment to a summit. Demonstration of Soviet good intentions appeared to require a substantial increase in emigration during the following year, 1979. There is indirect evidence that the response to the trial was unanticipated. *Pravda* wrote about the "anti-Sovietism" expressed surrounding the trial, which it claimed was being used as a pretext. "Alas, representatives of some democratic organizations have allowed themselves to be drawn into the anti-Soviet campaign...."[77]

Whether Soviet emigration policy was shaped by foreign or domestic policy considerations is not an either/or question, but a matter of both factors. I believe that the coincidence of changes in Soviet–American relations and the level of emigration is a compelling association, but the composition of emigration and its impact on Soviet society were no less important for the policy's decline. Again, Dallin's model of political linkage is suggestive.

> One may assume that—holding the external environment constant—the stability of a given Soviet policy orientation tends to be greatest when there is reinforcement or cumulation of (a) perceived national interest at the top; (b) self-serving interest on the part of multiple subnational groups and actors; (c) a network of bureaucratic politics that creates a vested interest in the status quo.[78]

By the late 1970s the first two of these conditions were no longer met by emigration policy. It is doubtful if the third had ever been realized. Regarding the second, non-Jewish professionals had little more to gain from additional emigration. Between 1970 and 1975 the number of Jewish full-time postgraduates (*aspiranty*) decreased by 40 per cent, from 4,949 to 2,841, and representation among "scientific workers" from 6.9 per cent to 6.1 per cent.[79] Additional decline over the next decade would be less, particularly among graduate students. While the replacement of Jewish émigrés by non-Jewish nationalities was a promising rationale for emigration in 1971, by 1976 the appeal had diminished, especially for non-Slavic nationalities.

The number of Jewish émigrés from non-Slavic republics continued to fall, and by 1981 emigrants from the RSFSR, the Ukraine and Belorussia accounted for 72.6 per cent of the total number—a virtual reversal of emigration from peripheral republics a decade earlier.[80] Between 1980 and 1984, 69.9 per cent of all émigrés chose some destination besides Israel, an increase from 2.1 per cent between 1968 and 1973.[81] The result of the heartland emigration was a sharp increase in the number of refusniks, i.e. some 4,741 (an increase of 58 per cent) in 1980, and 7,040 (48 per cent) in 1981.[82] Some 70 per cent of refusniks were from the three Slavic republics. The changing composition of émigrés and the "dropouts" from Israel occasioned doubts about whether emigration any longer served the "national interest." The problem mentioned earlier of the Panov's mixed nationality became commonplace. An 1979 report in *Izvestia* claimed that many Jews unsuited to life in capitalist countries now petitioned to return to the USSR. This group was distinctive, as "without any sort of compulsion from the authorities, there began a process of spiritual assimilation with the Russian people. This was conscious for some, unconscious for others. . . ."[83]

Suslov's opposition to emigration of assimilated Jews is virtually certain. At a 1977 conference on ideology, he not only denounced "the whole noisy campaign of slander over human rights" created in the West, but stated that "among the most important theoretical problems [of socialism] are problems involving movement toward homogeneity in the social structure of our society, the increasing strengthening of its unity and the ever drawing together of all the country's nations and nationalities."[84] The Anti-Zionist Committee of the Soviet Public, organized in 1983, pointed to one source of homogeneity. In explaining the decline in emigration, S. L. Zivs pointed to the "smaller and smaller" number of people "who fall for the Zionist bait" and the fact that [family] unification has largely been completed."[85]

A Return to Philo-Semitism: The Altered Basis of Soviet Rule

The interregnum between Brezhnev and Gorbachev witnessed a hardening of anti-Zionism and a consistently low level of emigration, but by 1987 the number of emigrants had increased eightfold to more than 8,000 individuals.[86] Initially, there was little expectation of substantial emigration. Although Gorbachev's address to the January 1987 CPSU plenum had equated both "Zionism" and "anti-Semitism" as unacceptable forms of nationalism, high levels of emigration seemed unlikely.[87] Jewish intellectual skills would be at a premium for *perestroika*. Privately, Soviet officials ridiculed Brezhnev's willingness to tolerate the emigration of 250,000 Jews in exchange for so few political gains.[88] Nevertheless, the Reagan administration and Secretary of State George Shultz persisted in their demand to alter the "bleak and deteriorating situation of Soviet Jewry" and the unresolved problem of emigration.[89] Prior to the Reykjavik summit, Shultz presented Soviet officials with the names of 11,000 Jews seeking to emigrate that had become known to the National Conference on Soviet Jewry. At Reykjavik, Soviet authorities agreed to continue discussion about Soviet Jewry, and in April 1987 Richard Schifter, Assistant Secretary of State for Human Rights and Humanitarian Affairs, completed a week of conversations with Soviet officials. He later explained: "What they [the Soviets] would like to accomplish ... is to get the refusnik group out of here and hope there would be a significant decline in pressure for emigration, so they can put the issue out of the way."[90] The release of such prominent refusniks as Natan Shcharansky, Ida Nudel, Iosef Begun and Vladimir Feltsman confirmed the accuracy of Schifter's comment. In November, before the impending summit, Deputy Secretary of State John Whitehead continued the discussion.[91]

The diplomatic effort produced substantial results in increased emigration overall and of refusniks in particular. The policy included high-level negotiations in March 1987, as well as talks between representatives of American Jewish organizations and the World Jewish Congress on the one hand, and the Ministers of Culture and Foreign Trade, the Procurator General and the Chairman of the State Council for Religious Affairs, on the Soviet side.[92] A communiqué promised resolution of the refusnik issue, "except for legitimate national security cases"; an appeal procedure for refusniks; and a categorical commitment to emigration for "first-degree relatives ... within an established time-frame." Within the Soviet Union, the promises extended to the importation of "all Jewish religious books," the opening of synagogues "in all sites where there is a demonstrated need," and "evaluation" of restrictions on the teaching of Hebrew in synagogues.[93] Not surprisingly, the anti-Zionist Committee for the Soviet Public was scheduled for dissolution later in the year. That so much could be promised, and be in the process of implementation at the time of writing, had required the replacement of most members of the Soviet leadership. With the exception of the Ukrainian Party chief V. V. Shcherbitsky, virtually all high-level Soviet leaders associated with opposition to détente, and by implication anti-Zionism, had been replaced. They included Secretary member Boris Ponomarev, Alexander Yepishev, head of the Main Political Directorate of the Soviet armed forces, and Viktor Grishin and Grigory Romanov, of the Moscow and Leningrad Party organizations, respectively. The only representative of the earlier phase of philo-Semitism in 1964–1965 was Pyotr Demichev, First Vice-President of the Supreme Soviet Presidium. In November 1987 Demichev presented the Order of Peoples Friendship to the Rabbi of the Moscow Choral Synagogue for his "patriotic activity."[94] Soviet–Israeli diplomatic contacts and substantive negotiation completed the symmetry of the philo-Semitic policies of the 1980s with those of the 1960s.[95]

Ultimately the change of Soviet personnel must stand as a guarantor of Gorbachev's philo-Semitism. *Glasnost'* has also occasioned a reaction from the anti-Semitic right in the nationalist organization Pamyat' (memory) and the controversial "letter" of Nina Andreeva opposing *perestroika*.[96] Pamyat' is a self-styled patriotic organization committed to the preservation of Russian architectural monuments and the study of Russian history. The group's assertion of a "Zionist–Freemason" conspiracy against

Russian national values identifies Lazar Kaganovich's reconstruction of Moscow in the 1930s as an early episode in the continuing struggle of "bureaucrats" against things Russian.[97] According to a Soviet press account, Pamyat' meetings assert that allegiance to Communism is consistent with belief in the notorious *Protocols of the Elders of Zion*.[98] The relevance of the group to emigration policy is both immediate and distant. In 1987 Academician Vitalii Goldansky wrote Secretary of State Shultz an open letter expressing concern that foreign emphasis on the emigration issue had the consequence of "whipping up anti-Semitic feelings in the USSR."[99] Presumably, emigration sustains more emigration but creates distrust of Jews who decide to remain. Second, reports that the Moscow membership of Pamyat' numbers 20,000 and extends throughout the RSFSR suggest that the Soviet regime could turn to anti-Semitic nationalism to support faltering legitimacy. Without referring directly to Pamyat', the émigré Alexander Yanov's idea of a "Russian New Right" as a "counter-reform" movement would include the organization.[100] The virulent anti-Semitism of Yanov's New Right in power would extinguish philo-Semitism with unpredictable consequences for emigration.

Mikhail Agursky suggests a more complex interpretation of Pamyat'. Agursky finds Russian nationalism represented in the Soviet leadership since the rise of Stalin's aide Alexander Shcherbakov, the architect of such wartime policies as reconciliation with the Orthodox Church, the Western Alliance, and creation of the Jewish Anti-Fascist Committee.[101] Shcherbakov's prescription for an isolationist postwar Soviet Union was eclipsed by the expansionist "National Bolshevism" of Andre Zhdanov and Suslov. Extreme "Anti-Zionism" was a "tactic" of the latter group to discredit the tradition of Shcherbakov's nationalism, lately identified with the "Russian opposition" of Mikhail Grishin, Ivan Kapitanov and Pyotr Demichev.[102] I have mentioned Demichev's role as an opponent of anti-Semitism. Agursky maintains that opposition to "Zionism" among the nationalists is exclusively domestic opposition to policies of "national integration" pursued by the militant traditions of Zhdanov and Suslov. Curiously, the link of "National Bolshevism" to Pamyat' lies in the anti-Zionist authors, including some Jews, active in the 1970s, who now find refuge in the organization.[103]

Agursky's account is consistent with the variety of positions concerning the Jewish question that Dimitry Pospielovsky finds in nationalist *samizdat*.[104] In my judgment, it is unwise to dismiss all Russian nationalists as anti-Semitic and all nationalists as sympathetic to Pamyat'. At the very least, the association of Pamyat' with a pre-existing tradition within the CPSU helps answer the Soviet critic whose attack on Pamyat' expressed "amazement" at the membership of Moscow Communists among the organization's leadership.[105] The importance of Soviet Jewish cultural expression lies in its symbolic value for anti-Stalinism and less repressive nationalist expression *of all types*. Whether anti-Stalinism can aggregate Soviet political interests will determine the fate of philo-Semitism. At present philo-Semitic attitudes are a more durable basis for continuing emigration than a return to the expedient arrangement devised with the anti-Zionists in the 1970s.

Notes

1. Robert Cullen, "For a Quiet Deal on Soviet Emigrants," *New York Times*, November 30, 1988, p. 25.

2. *The New York Times*, December 3, 1988, pp. 1, 6.

3. Zvi Gitelman, "Jewish Nationality and Religion in the USSR and Eastern Europe" in *Religion and Nationalism in Soviet and East European Politics*, ed. Pedro Ramet (Durham: Duke University Press, 1989), p. 68.

4. Ludmilla Alexeyeva, *Soviet Dissent: Contemporary Movements for National, Religious and Human Rights* (Middletown, CT: Wesleyan University Press, 1985), p. 80.

5. John Armstrong, "Mobilized and Proletarian Diasporas," *American Political Science Review*, 70(2), 1976, pp. 393–408.

6. Polina Molotov (Zhenschzunia) proudly announced to Myerson, "I too am a daughter of the Jewish people." She was exiled to Siberia shortly after. Apparently her husband's position as foreign minister offered no protection. Golda Meir, *My Life* (New York: G. P. Putnam, 1975), p. 250. Khrushchev reports Stalin's distrust of Jews especially when Solomon Lozovsky allegedly proposed that the Crimea be made a "Jewish Soviet Republic." "Stalin saw behind this proposal the hand of American Zionists operating through the Sovinformbureau." N. S. Khrushchev, *Khrushchev Remembers* (Boston: Little Brown, 1970), p. 260.

7. Benjamin Pinkus, "The Emigration of National Minorities from the USSR in the Post-Stalin Era," *Soviet Jewish Affairs*, 13(1), 1983, pp. 27–8.

8. *Sovetskaya Rossia*, September 23, 1965, in *Evrei i evreiski narod* (EEN), 6(3), 1965, Item 343, p. 184.

9. *The Jerusalem Post*, March 7, 1965, p. 6.

10. Ibid., January 24, 1964, p. 1.

11. Ibid., May 27, 1964, p. 2; and *Sovetskaya Litva*, July 2, 1964, in *EEN*, 5(3), 1964, Item 285, p. 199.

12. *The Jerusalem Post*, August 26, 1965, p. 7.
13. Ibid., May 21, 1965, p. 7; and July 29, 1964, p. 4.
14. Leonard Schroeter, *The Last Exodus* (New York: Universe Books, 1974), p. 189.
15. *The Deceived Testify* (Moscow: Novosti, 1971), cited in Ibid., p. 189.
16. *The New York Times*, April 8, 1964, p. 2.
17. In an interview with *The Jerusalem Post*, White stated that "few people know the extent of the President's concern about Russian Jews." Following the 1964 meeting, White stated that the President and Rusk decided "all possible avenues of action would be explored." *The Jerusalem Post*, September 22, 1965, p. 3.
18. *The New York Times*, June 4, 1965, p. 13.
19. Senate Concurrent Resolution 17 (1965), *The Congressional Record*, February 2, 1965, 89th Congress, First Session, vol. III, part 2, p. 1,805.
20. *The New York Times*, April 14, 1965, p. 4.
21. *The Jerusalem Post*, July 18, 1965, p. 2; and *The New York Times*, July 16, 1965, p. 1.
22. *The New York Times*, April 14, 1965, p. 4.
23. Michael Tatu, *Power in the Kremlin: From Khrushchev to Kosygin* (New York: The Viking Publishing Co.), 1969, p. 429.
24. *Novy Mir*, no. 2 (1965), cited in the *Current Digest of the Soviet Press (CDSP)*, 17(23), 1965, p. 5.
25. *The New York Times*, May 15, 1965, p. 7.
26. The entire "*Babi Yar* affairs"—including the original poem, Yevtushenko's defense, A. Markov's "Reply" and D. Starikov's "About a certain poem"—are reprinted in Benjamin Pinkus, *The Soviet Government and the Jews 1948-1967* (Cambridge: Cambridge University Press), 1984, p. 114-23.
27. *Pravda*, September 5, 1979, cited in *EEN*, 6(3) 1979, Item 134, p. 96.
28. Grigory Sversky, *The Hostages* (New York: Alfred A. Knopf, 1976), p. 207.
29. *Vedomosti verkhovnogo soveta SSSR*, no. 52 (1964), cited in *CDSP*, 17(1), 1965, p. 3.
30. *Vedomosti verkhovnogo soveta SSSR*, no. 8 (1965), pp. 108, 111, cited in *EEN*, 6(19), 1965, Item 171, p. 89.
31. *Sovetskaya Rossia*, August 6, 1958, p. 3, as cited in *CDSP* 10(32), 1958, pp. 12-13.
32. Sversky, *The Hostages*.
33. Abraham Rothberg, *The Heirs of Stalin* (Ithaca, NY: Cornell University Press, 1970), p. 145.
34. *Izvestia*, January 13, 1966, in *EEN*, 7(1), 1966, Item 192, p. 110.

35. *Current Soviet Policies*, Vol. V *The Documentary Record of the 23rd Congress of the Communist Party of the Soviet Union*, ed. Leon Gruilow (Columbus, OH: AAASS, 1973), p. 23.

36. Ibid., p. 45.

37. Ibid., p. 120.

38. *Vedomosti verkhovnogo soveta SSSR*, no. 32, August 11, 1966, p. 649.

39. *Izvestia*, April 26, 1966, p. 3, cited in *CDSP*, 18(17) 1966, p. 24.

40. Nadav Safran, *From War to War: The Arab-Israeli Confrontation, 1948-1967* (New York: Pegasus Publishing Co., 1969), p. 274-7.

41. *Pravda*, December 5, 1966, cited in Pinkus, *The Soviet Government and the Jews (supra)*, p 78.

42. *Pravda*, July 19, 1965, cited in Pinkus, *The Soviet Government and the Jews*, p. 77.

43. Christian Schmidt-Hauer, *Gorbachev: The Path to Power* (London: I. B. Tauris, 1986), pp. 45, 76.

44. Shimon Redlich, "Propaganda and Nationalism in Wartime Russia: The Jewish Antifascist Committee in the USSR, 1941-1948." Boulder CO: *East European Quarterly*, 1982, p. 167.

45. Kozlov followed Khrushchev on a trip to the United States in 1959, where he denied closure of synagogues and instead answered, "Just recently I visited Kiev and I saw the Jews there leading a happy life in their usual daily pursuits and bathing in the Dnieper and they looked no worse than you." Such flippancy contrasted sharply with the attitudes of Mikoyan and Khrushchev on the subject. *New York Times*, July 13, 1959, cited in Pinkus, p. 67.

46. F. Kozlov, "Politicheskaya b'ditelnost'-obyazannost' chlena partii," *Kommunist* 29(1), January 1953, p. 49.

47. Mikhail Agursky, "The Knots behind Soviet-Israeli Ties," *Jerusalem Post Magazine*, August 2, 1985, p. 4.

48. Meir Edelstein, "The 1965 Split in the MAKI and the CPSU," *Soviet Jewish Affairs*, 3(1), 1973, pp. 22-36.

49. F. F., "The USSR, the Soviet Jews and Israel," *The World Today*, 14(12), December 1958, p. 523.

50. Jonathan Frankel, *The Soviet Regime and Anti-Zionism: An Analysis*. Research paper no. 55, Jerusalem: The Soviet and East European Research Center, 1984.

51. Alexander Dallin, "Soviet Foreign Policy and Domestic Politics: A Framework for Analysis" in *The Conduct of Soviet Foreign Policy*, ed. Erik P. Hoffmann and Frederic J. Fleron (New York: Aldine Publishing Co.), 1980, p. 45.

52. Ibid., p. 45.

53. Frederick C. Barghoorn, *Detente and the Democratic Movement in the USSR* (New York: The Free Press), p. 106.
54. Schroeter, *The Last Exodus*, p. 377, as cited in ibid., p. 106.
55. Grey Hodnet, "Succession Contingencies in the Soviet Union," *Problems of Communism*, 25(3), April–May 1976, p. 12.
56. L. Yu. Berenshteyn, "Zionism—A Tool of Imperialist Reaction," *Pravda Ukrainy*, no. 3, March 1973, as cited in Israel Klejner, "The Soviet Ukrainian Press on Zionism and Israel," *Soviet Jewish Affairs* 4(2), 1974, p. 47.
57. Shmuel Ettinger, "Historical and Internal Political Factors in Soviet Anti-Semitism" in *Anti-Semitism in the Soviet Union: Its Roots and Consequences*, Theodore Freedman (New York: B'nai B'rith, 1984), p. 178.
58. Henry Kissinger, *Years of Upheaval* (Boston: Little, Brown, 1982), p. 249.
59. *Krasnaya Zvezda*, January 6, 1970, p. 3.
60. Alla Rusinek, *Like a Song, Like a Dream* (New York: Charles Scribner's Sons, 1973), p. 162.
61. *New York Times*, January 1, 1971, pp. 1, 2; and January 5, 1971, p. 2.
62. Shimon Redlich, "Jewish Appeals in the USSR: An Expression of National Revival," *Soviet Jewish Affairs*, 4(2), 1974, p. 33.
63. Victor Zaslavsky and Robert J. Brym, *Soviet-Jewish Emigration and Soviet Nationality Policy* (London: Macmillan, 1983), pp. 31–6.
64. Ibid., p. 39.
65. *Sovetskaya Kultura*, March 22, 1974, p. 6, cited in *CDSP*, 26(12), 1974, p. 18.
66. *Pravda*, February 19, 1971, cited in *The New York Times*, February 20, 1971, p. 1.
67. *The New York Times*, January 6, 1971, p. 1.
68. Henry Kissinger, *White House Years* (Boston: Little, Brown, 1979), p. 544.
69. Peter M. E. Volten, *Brezhnev's Peace Program: A Study of Soviet Domestic Process and Power* (Boulder, CO: Westview, 1982), p. 61.
70. Ibid., p. 62.
71. Ibid., p. 227.
72. Adam Ulam, *Dangerous Relations: The Soviet Union in World Politics, 1970–1982* (New York: Oxford University Press, 1983), p. 81.
73. Kissinger, *Years of Upheaval*, p. 252.
74. Ibid., p. 253.
75. The Stevenson Amendment placed a limit of $300 million on United States credits. Harry Gelman finds of all the "accumulating

disappointments" of the Soviet leadership that that limit was a "decisive defeat" for "the Politburo's hopes for very large economic benefits from the bilateral relationship." Harry Gelman, *The Brezhnev Politburo and the Decline of Detente* (Ithaca, NY: Cornell University Press, 1984), p. 148.

76. Kissinger, *Years of Upheaval*, p. 250.

77. *Pravda*, July 19, 1978, p. 4 in *CDSP*, 30(28), 1978, p. 4.

78. Alexander Dallin, "The Domestic Sources of Soviet Foreign Policy," in Seweryn Bialer, *The Domestic Context of Soviet Foreign Policy* (Boulder, CO: Westview, 1981), p. 347.

79. Thomas E. Sawyer, *The Jewish Minority in the Soviet Union* (Boulder, CO: Westview, 1979), pp. 46, 49.

80. Zvi Nezer, "The Emigration of Soviet Jews," *Soviet Jewish Affairs*, 15(1), 1984, p. 22.

81. Benjamin Pinkus, "National Identity and Emigration Patterns Among Soviet Jews," *Soviet Jewish Affairs*, 15(3), 1985, p. 20.

82. Zvi Nezer, "The Emigration of Soviet Jews," *Soviet Jewish Affairs*, 15(1), 1984, p. 22.

83. *Izvestia*, February 19, 1979, p. 3.

84. *Pravda*, November 11, 1977, p. 1, in *CDSP*, 29(45), 1977, p. 1.

85. *Literaturnaya Gazeta*, June 22, 1985, p. 11, in *CDSP*, 35(26), 1985, p. 10.

86. *The New York Times*, December 12, 1987, p. 1.

87. For an analysis of Gorbachev's speech, see David Floyd, "Perestroika, Glasnost and Soviet Jewry: Gorbachev's Address to the January 1987 CPSU Plenum," *Soviet Jewish Affairs*, 17(1), Spring 1987, pp. 3–8.

88. *The New York Times*, January 2, 1987, p. 5.

89. The phrase is from Shultz's October 30, 1987, address to the Los Angeles World Affairs Council. Ibid., November 1, 1986, p. 1.

90. Ibid., April 18, 1987, p. 3.

91. Ibid., November 10, 1987, p. B20.

92. "Documents: Western Jewish Leaders Receive Reassurances in Moscow," *Soviet Jewish Affairs*, 17(2), 1987, p. 49.

93. Ibid., p. 51–2.

94. *Izvestia*, October 28, 1987, p. 2.

95. Zachary T. Irwin, "The USSR and Israel," *Problems of Communism*, 36(1), January–February 1987, p. 36–45.

96. Howard Spier, "Glasnost and the New Russian Antisemites," *Soviet Jewish Affairs*, 17(2), 1987, p. 53–68; and Kevin Devlin, "*L'Unità* on the 'Secret History' of the Andreeva Letter," *Radio Free Europe Research*, USSR Report, 93, May 27, 1988.

97. *Komsomolskaya Pravada*, May 22, 1987, translated in Spier, "Glasnost and the New Russian Antisemites," p. 54.

98. *Izvestia*, June 3, 1987, translated in Spier, "Glasnost and the New Russian Antisemites," p. 60.

99. *Moscow News*, no. 18 (1987), p. 4.

100. Alexander Yanov, *The Russian Challenge and the Year 2000* (New York: Basil Blackwell, 1987), p. 9.

101. Mikhail Agursky, "The Prospects of National Bolshevism" in *The Lost Empire: Nationality and the Soviet Future*, ed. Robert Conquest (Stanford, CA: Hoover Institution Press, 1986), p. 91.

102. Ibid., p. 100-2.

103. *Sovetskaya Kultura* reported on June 18, 1987, that some of the "favorite" lecturers of the Pamyat' group in Moscow and Novosibirsk were none other than the well-known anti-Zionist authors Evgenii Evseev, Vladimir Begun, Aleksandr Romanenko and Julia Wishnevsky, "*Glasnost* on Anti-Semitism in the Soviet Union," *Radio Liberty Research*, no. 254, July 6, 1987, p. 4.

104. Dimitry V. Pospielovsky, "Russian Nationalist Thought and the Jewish Question," *Soviet Jewish Affairs*, 6(1), 1976, p. 3-17.

105. *Sovetskaya Kultura*, June 18, 1987, translated in Spier, "Glasnost and the New Russian Antisemites," p. 65.

Chapter 15

Conclusion: Towards a Multiethnic Soviet State: Managing a Multinational Society since 1985

Henry R. Huttenbach

Shortly after all the chapters of this book were completed, Mikhail Gorbachev implicitly rejected a key provision of Marxist doctrine towards the nationalities (as many of the authors had already hinted might have to happen), by recognizing that the contradictions between the theory of a single Soviet people and the reality of a pervasive multinationalism had become untenable. Confronted by a rising tide of dissent from the minorities, Gorbachev publicly retreated somewhat from the Soviet state's fixed ideological goal of fusing the peoples of the republics into one meta-national cultural entity. On January 6, 1989, speaking before the representatives of the USSR's cultural and scientific elite, Gorbachev indirectly admitted that *sliianie*, the ideologically motivated policy goal of transforming a multinational population into one cohesive Soviet citizenry, had to be re-examined as practically unrealistic *and*, as presently applied, humanly *wrong*.[1] The dramatic announcement of intended ideological retreat, if acted upon, may have profound influence on Moscow's future policy *vis-à-vis* the national minorities and, equally important, on its response to the demands put on the central authorities in the capital by individual national republics, by ethnic autonomous territories, and by nonterritorially based minorities scattered throughout the republics.

What characterized the first seven decades of Soviet rule of a multinational population has been the colonial style of imperial power relationship between the center and the periphery: in large measure, initiative came from above; resistance, if any, came from below. For more than two generations the Marxist-Leninist assumption prevailed, that local nationalisms (like the state), would eventually evaporate and become superfluous with the onset of a bona fide USSR-wide socialist economy. Instead, the floundering centrally controlled economy has failed to satisfy even the basic expectations of the many peoples of the Soviet Union, leading to the present crisis of a resurgence of ethnic nationalisms fueled by glaring economic disparities among minorities, forcing the leadership in Moscow to respond to agendas, this time largely set by the non-Russian periphery. Whereas the capital traditionally dictated the style and content of nationality policies, it is now the republics who are trying to assert their economic, cultural, territorial and political priorities. From the Baltic republics to Moldavia, from a small Polish minority in Belorussia to tiny ethnic groups in Northern Siberia, a swelling chorus of voices sends a clear message to the Soviet authorities in Moscow and in regional capitals to take ethnic demands seriously. Evidently, a new era of nationalities policy-making is in the offing.

The government has already given way on many fronts: Soviet Jews have been allowed to establish cultural centers in Moscow and Riga; Soviet Germans as well as Tatars may now apply at newly opened offices to regain their properties in the lower Volga and the Crimea, lost due to Stalin's deportation policies during World War II; Moldavians have managed to have their language accepted unquestionably as a variant of Romanian; Armenians in Nagorno-Karabakh in Azerbaijan are now under more direct Moscow rule; and Estonian has become the official language of the Estonian Republic. Meanwhile Abkhazian minorities seek to secede from Georgia; and the Gagauz want territorial separation from Moldavia. None of these pressures from the grass-roots of the multinational Soviet Union can be permanently swept under the rug or imperially resolved by naked force such as poison gas in Georgia, tanks in Armenia, mass arrests in Astrakhan and military intervention in Azerbaijan. Minimal if not maximal concessions will have to be made at the top as recent decisions by Moscow have demonstrated. The extraordinary turn of events in the Baltic republics is a case in point: as of January 1, 1990, economic autonomy for Estonia and Lithuania, including a legalization of market principles, has been officially condoned.

The classic Marxist expectation that improved economic circumstances will lead to a diminution of nationalistic tendencies has been challenged head on. Rising living standards in Estonia, Latvia and Lithuania, designed and promoted by *local* republican governments, will lead inevitably to a greater sense of minority pride and desire for further emancipation from the center. This can only be reinforced by cultural factors (such as designating the native language as the official one, and teaching national minority history with no supervision from Moscow), thereby further isolating the local population from the greater context of the Soviet Union.

Throughout this book, all authors have exercised great caution and restraint *not* to predict, not to turn their chapters into charts projecting the future. Nevertheless, recent events, including those they have had the opportunity to observe, do at least suggest that the new Soviet government as designed by Gorbachev is prepared to govern a multinational populace more realistically according to the dictates of objective circumstances and revised official attitudes. The Soviet center can no longer operate blindly according to the strictures of an inflexible ideology. The rulers of the Soviet Union must, if the whole is to conform to the parts, pay stricter heed to the needs of republican minorities and to other nonterritorial ethnic groups. If a multinational body politic such as the USSR is to survive as a functioning, internally harmonious entity, significant rethinking of nationality policy more in accordance with the wishes of a diverse population will have to be made. Gorbachev's January 1989 partial retreat from fixed ideological doctrine betrays a new pragmatism that could become the basis of a more viable nationalities policy for the Soviet Union. Greater maneuverability for the republics and more open borders for prospective ethnic emigrants may combine to help bring about the preconditions for an overall economic revival of the Soviet Union so its multifarious peoples will freely opt for a future within rather than outside a multinational USSR. However, this goal of providing a tolerable autonomous setting for each national minority will require creative management on the part of Gorbachev and his successors; basically it will mean learning to live with a Soviet Union in which multinationalism is a *permanent* fact of life that cannot be struck from history by the sheer force of ideological cant and insensitive state bureaucratic intervention. The sooner multinational pluralism becomes a permanent guiding principle of Soviet nationalities policy, the greater the chances this giant diverse population under one political roof may enter peacefully and united into the next century. At the heart of the challenge lies the Soviet rulers' ability to switch from a *nationality* policy, based on the doctrine of *transitory* multinationalism aimed at fusion (*sliianie*), to a radically new *nationalities* policy based on the concept of *continual* multinationalism; from a policy of pursuing a doctrine of dismantling multinationalism, to a more moderate and realistic stance of promoting constant harmonious multinational pluralism. Just as Western Europe is evolving away from the limitations of absolute national sovereignty, so will the Soviet empire have to evolve more readily away from unlimited statism towards a modified form of confederation.

Nevertheless, the legacy of empire and the commitment to ideological supranational internationalism remain powerful traditions and inhibiting factors. Writing as recently as 1987, Daniel Matuszewski sensed more potential for confrontation and collision between Moscow and its minority peoples than the likelihood of benign compromise.[2] Till late in 1989, the bulk of Gorbachev's reforming efforts as part of *perestroika* have in fact focused on strengthening central authority, on purging the Party of incompetents, and on encouraging the rise of an efficient corps of technocrats. All three orientations suggest a meta-nationalities, centrist focus. In the last year, however, Gorbachev has been forced to give in to crucial minority requests (some of them definitely in contradiction to his earlier centralizing efforts), in order to preserve the spirit of *glasnost'* and keep domestic peace.

At the same time there is the troubling rise of ethnic Russian nationalism, some of it, like Pamyat', deeply disturbing. A mixed focus on the "glories" of an imperial past, on the "virtues" of an Orthodox Christian heritage, on Russian cultural "primacy," and on xenophobic responses to non-Russians (spiced with an ugly dose of anti-Semitism) has spawned a potentially destabilizing set of ethnic Russian organizations that have allied themselves on occasion with a number of causes, most of them of a reactionary sort that are, generally, opposed to Gorbachev's semi-liberalizing policies and are, specifically, hostile to national minority pluralism.[3]

Given the tragic legacy of Stalinism, it is too early to tell whether its deep roots have been completely extracted from Soviet soil. One of its central sins with respect to the Soviet nationalities was the treacherous turn to a policy of blatant Russification. There is no guarantee yet that in the future there may not be a resurgence of Stalin-like reaction—a marriage between chauvinistic ethnic Russians, Party conservatives and anxious technocrats afraid of the disintegration of the Soviet Union under the pressure of minority nationalisms whose pent-up energies were unleashed by Gorbachev's "liberalism."

Nor should one expect the decentralizing forces generated by minority nationalisms to prevail *per se*. Given the unusual multinational diversity in the Soviet Union, there is little overall coordination yet among the minorities to assure a fusion of many nationalisms acting in tandem against the center. Interethnic rivalries, long lingering mutual animosities, bitter territorial disputes, fervid religious antagonisms, and conflicting economic ambitions serve to weaken any concerted anti-Soviet multinationalism. In most cases of minority discord, Moscow's role as referee and protector is essential, as was the case, for example, with the evacuation of the Meskhetians from Kazakhstan and the placing of Soviet troops in Sumgait and, more recently, in Baku in Azerbaijan to prevent further massacres.

No one is more sensitive to the negative implications of rampant multinationalism than Gorbachev, who has staked his career on reviving an economically moribund system by reawakening the enthusiasm of a dispirited Soviet labor force. Nothing would be more fatal to his reforms than a myriad of major disruptions to the economy caused by ethnic unrests and demands for autonomy that would put into question the Soviet center's authority. His January 1989 statements must be balanced off by an earlier speech given in January 1987 to the plenum of the Central Committee.[4] On that occasion Gorbachev warned against the "negative phenomena" of multinationalism that cannot be tolerated, such as "ethnic arrogance," "ethnic isolationism," "nationalist deformation" and "parochialism." To counter these attitudes, Gorbachev called for greater efforts to inculcate into the younger generation a sense of meta-ethnic identity by means of intense internationalist education. In other words, the goal of a Soviet people, a *homo sovieticus*, must not be abandoned if a strong Soviet future is to be achieved.

To understand Gorbachev's January 1989 speech (tempered by the caution he expressed in January 1987) one must also turn to one of his predecessors and mentor, Iu. V. Andropov. Speaking in 1982 on the occasion of the 60th anniversary of the USSR, Andropov stressed that "national differences will continue considerably longer than class differences."[5] There is, therefore, as much reason to believe in ideological continuity as in ideological evolution in the thinking of the highest echelons of the Soviet leadership. As with Lenin's reply to Bullitt in 1919, Gorbachev may, *in extremis*, be ready to settle for far less; but, as a visionary, he has no more abandoned the preservation of the integrity of the Soviet Union's Eurasian territorium than Lenin had given up the dream of reassembling the entire empire of the tsars in the name of the Soviet Revolution. Multinationalism, therefore, will continue to be a central ideological and managerial challenge and concern to those who govern the USSR.

The present politicization of the many minorities in the USSR should be seen as an on-going dynamic in the context of not only the Soviet-dominated twentieth century but also in historic terms of hundreds of years of Tsarist governance. Each generation of rulers will have to come to terms with the validity of multinationalism in the Eurasian heartland and the problems it poses. Inasmuch as the Soviet center succeeds, it will be a test of its imagination, its will and its institutions to decide whether to rule the multinational landscape of the Soviet Union by hammer-like ukase or by more subtle persuasion, whether to give in to the temptations of unbending centrism or to risk the path of limited polynationalism as the wiser course.

Much depends on demographic evolution, on the quantitative

differential growth and decline of the birth rates of each national minority and their relative balances to one another. Much depends on the expansion of the Muslim, non-European populations, especially in Central Asia, the "soft underbelly" of both the Tsarist and Soviet Empires. Similarly, much depends on the future of self-assertion in the Ukraine, geopolitically the most important republic in the European Soviet Union. Just as much depends on continued social peace in Eastern Europe as it devolves out of the post-World War II Soviet satellite system. No less so does the precarious balance between center and periphery in the Soviet Union depend on peace and tranquility in regions of the world more distant from the USSR.

There are, therefore, too many internal variants and external unknowns to permit any kind of even speculative projection of the future of multinationalism in the Soviet Union. Soviet rulers will have no choice but to remain alert to ever-shifting circumstances that may affect the equilibrium of their multinational society, the most lasting heritage they received from the surprising Bolshevik "colonial" victories in 1917-1921 and the Stalinist imperialistic acquisitions in 1939-1941. Policy toward the nationalities, whether primarily fine-tuned as "nationality policy" or as "nationalities policy," will be a constant high priority whatever the future brings. The immediate challenge is to navigate Soviet multinationalism out of the uncertainties of the last decade of the twentieth century into the even murkier waters leading to the unknowns of the *terra incognita* of the twenty-first century.

Notes

1. *Report on the USSR* (formerly *Radio Liberty Research Bulletin*), vol. 1 no. 5 (1989): see "Gorbachev Disavows Merging of Nations" by Bohdan Nahaylo.

2. Daniel Matuszewski, "Nationalities in the Soviet Future: Trends under Gorbachev" in Lawrence W. Lerner and Donald W. Treadgold (eds.), *Gorbachev and the Soviet Future* (Boulder, Co., 1988), pp. 90-113.

3. On the rise of ethnic Russian nationalism and its very conservative (antimultinational pluralism) stance, see Robert Conquest (ed.), *The Last Empire: Nationality and the Soviet Future* (Stanford, 1986).

4. *Pravda*, January 28, 1987.

5. See Iu. V. Bromlei, "Etnograficheskoe izuchenie sovremennykh natsional'nykh protsessov v USSR," *Sovetskaia etnografiia*, No. 2 (March-April 1983), p. 5.

Index

Abkhaz ASSR 145, 146, 148–9
Adenauer, Konrad 245
Afghanistan 75
Agursky, Mikhail 269, 279
Akulov, Ivan 183
Aleksandr III, Emperor 100
Alexander I, Tsar 244
Alexeyeva, Ludmilla 261
All-Union Commissariats 52, 53
All-Union Soviet (Council) of Nationalities 126
Allworth, Edward 164
Alma-Ata riots (1987) 89
Ambrazas, Vytautas 216
Andreeva, Nina 278
Andropov, Yuri 274, 290
 and the cadres policy 65
 nationality policies 16, 20, 30, 31, 57–8, 68
Anthropological studies and new Soviet rituals 96–7, 104
AOs (autonomous oblasts) 121, 122, 126–7, 127–8, 165–6
 establishing boundaries of 129–41
 population changes in 142–51, 154
Arab states 232
Armenia 51, 71, 73
 changes in border districts 141
 demonstrations (1988) 89–90
 earthquake (1988) 248, 249, 255
 and Nagorno-Karabakh 90, 171–3, 287
 participation in patriotic activities 86
 population changes 133
 Soviet identity in 87
Armenian emigration 235, 237, 239, 240, 241, 242, 253, 254–5, 255
 causes of 247–50
Armenians 65, 66

Armstrong, John 262
Arutjunjan, Yu. V. 115
Assimilation of ethnic groups 36, 37, 40
ASSRs (Autonomous Soviet Socialist Republics) 29, 121, 122, 126, 127–9, 165
 establishing boundaries of 129–41
 population changes in 142–51, 154
Azerbaidzhan (Azerbaijan) 51, 71, 73, 165, 289
 changes in border districts 141
 conflict in Nagorno-Karabakh 90, 171–3, 287
 interethnic tensions in 90
 Muslims in 221, 222, 226, 227, 229
 participation in patriotic activities 86
 population changes 133
 Soviet identity in 87

Babel, Isaac 266
Bagramov, Eduard 10, 20
Balkars 42
Baltic states 4, 13, 49, 71, 73
 ethnic assertiveness in 170, 173–5, 287
 ethnic Russians in 29, 217, 219
 and nationalism 85
 participation in patriotic activities 86
 religious practices 96
 and the Russian language 67
 and Soviet emigration policies 237
 and Soviet language policy 206–20
 see also Estonia; Latvia; Lithuania

Barghoorn, Frederick 270
Barth, Fredrik 123–4
Bashkir ASSR 128, 131, 135, 136, 145, 146
Bashkirs 52, 54, 57, 66
Basmachi movement (Turkestan) 227
Bear Holiday 111–12
Begun, Iosef 277
Belorussia 2, 30, 35, 49, 50, 54, 67, 287
  changes in border districts 141
  and Jewish emigration 276
  nomenklatura 72
  pageants 84
  patriotic education 84, 86
  population changes 132
  and the Russian Federation 50, 51
  and Soviet language policies 213
  UN delegates 165
  and World War II 169
Belorussians 68
Belyk, N. A. 95
Beria liberalization 207
Bilingualism in the Baltic republics 206
Birch Tree holiday 95, 99, 110, 116
Birobidzan (Jewish Autonomous *oblast*) 267
Black, Cyril E. 3
Black Sea Germans and Soviet emigration policies 244, 245, 246
Bogdanov, Aleksandr 77
Boggs, S. W. 139
Bolsheviks 291
  nationality policies 11
  and non-Russian territories 3–4, 11, 13, 163–4
Borderlands
  and economic decentralization 16
  incorporation into Soviet Union 13
  rights of secession 48–9, 54, 57
  Stalinist policy towards 14–15
Brandt, Willy 246
Brezhnev, Leonid 91
  and the 1977 Constitution 57
  and Jewish emigration 277
  and language policy in the Baltic republics 208
  nationality policies 16, 20, 29, 32, 42–3, 69
  and new Soviet rituals 96
  "Peace Policy" 273–4
  and Soviet-Jewish emigration policies 263
  and the trial of Sinyavsky 268
Brezhnev era, patriotic and internationalist education 73–89
Bromlei, Yu. V. 113, 152
Brunashev, Aziz 80
Brym, Robert 272
Bullitt, William C. 2, 3, 4, 290
Bureaucracy and nationality policy 11, 17–19
Buryat-Mongolian ASSR 137, 139

Cadres policy 63, 64–6, 71, 72
  in the Baltic republics 207, 208
Carter, Jimmy 275
Catherine the Great 244, 251
Caucasus *see* Armenia; Georgia; North Caucasus
Central Asia 13, 15, 291
  autonomous subunits of 128
  Basmachi Wars 81–2
  cadres in 72
  constituent republics 53–4
  deportations to 143
  and interethnic cooperation 83–4
  Navruz holiday 103–6
  participation in patriotic activities 86
  war heroes 81
Chamber of Nationalities 52, 54
Checheno-Ingush ASSR/AO 169
Chechens 42
Chernenko, K. 17, 20
Chuvakhin, Dimitri 264
Chuvash ASSR 131, 136, 139, 145, 146, 150
Circassian AO 132, 137, 139
Civil War 2, 3, 4, 6, 170
Class and nationalism 123

Classification of nationality
  groups 39–40
Clem, Ralph 144
Codification of Soviet nationality
  policies 47–61
Communist Manifesto 12, 48, 49,
  54, 56, 163
Communist Party *see* CPSU
Congress of Soviets 51, 54
Constituent republics 53–4, 55,
  122, 126, 130
Constitution
  1924 64, 126
  1936 53, 55, 56, 142, 167–8
  1977 57, 168
Constitutional rights of union
  republics 63, 66
Cooperation, interethnic 82–4
Cossack nationalism 192–3
CPSU (Communist Party of
  the Soviet Union) 30, 31,
  50
  and ethnic assertiveness 174–5
  and ethnic groups 31
  and nationality policies 9–10,
    15, 16, 26–7
  nationality policy 26–7
  and Pamyat' 279–80
  Program
    1919 50, 56
    1961 56, 58
    1985 69
    1986 58–9
  and the Soviet administrative-
    territorial system 166
  and the Soviet federal
    system 168
  and Soviet-Jewish emigration
    policies 263–4
  on Soviet values 74
Crimean Tatar ASSR 131, 166
  wartime territorial changes 169
Crimean Tatars 29, 35, 37, 44, 64,
  67, 106, 173, 175, 287
  deportation of 143
  and ethnic assertiveness 170,
    171
Cullen, Robert 260
Cultural unification 56, 58–9
Culture, national versus all-
  union 63, 66–8

Dallin, Alexander 270, 276
Declaration of the Rights of the
  Peoples of Russia
  (1917) 66, 70
Demichev, Piotr 266–7, 269, 278,
  279
Denikin, A. I. 192
Détente and Soviet-Jewish
  emigration policies 243,
  273–4
Deutsch, Karl 124
Dobrynin, Anatoly 271, 273, 275
"Doctors' Plot" (1953) 269
Drobizheva, Leokadija 105
Dzyuba, Ivan 43

East Germany and Soviet-German
  emigrants 240, 241, 242,
  247
Economic decentralization 16
Education
  patriotic 73–93
  and Russian-language teaching
    in the Baltic
    republics 208–10
Education tax 274, 275
Egypt and Soviet-Jewish
  emigration policies 268,
  271–2, 275
Ehrenburg, Ilya 266
Elder brother, Soviet Union as 70
Emigration policies
  Armenians 235, 237, 239, 240,
    241, 242, 247–50, 253,
    254–5, 255
  causes of emigration 242–50
  and family reunification 269,
    270, 273
  Germans 235, 237, 239, 240,
    241, 242, 244–7, 250,
    253–4, 255
  Jews 235, 237, 239, 240, 241,
    242–4, 253, 254, 255,
    260–80
  legal status of emigration 251–3
  numbers of emigrants 236–7,
    238–42, 263, 268, 273, 274
  refusniks 237, 260, 276, 277
Encouragement of ethnic
  groups 35–6, 40

Engels, F. 75
  on ethnic oppression 31
  on nationalism 11-12, 47, 48
Enloe, Cynthia 152
Estonia 49, 70, 71, 128, 170, 173, 287
  Estonian language 206, 219, 287
  participation in patriotic activities 86
  Slavic population in 174
  and Soviet language policies 207, 208, 209, 210-12, 215-16, 217, 219
Estonians 29, 43
Ethnic assertiveness 88-9, 90, 287
  in the Baltic republics 170, 173-5, 287
  and Soviet federalism 163, 167, 170-5
Ethnic groups
  convergence of 30-1
  interethnic relations 27, 28
  punitive measures against 29
Ethnocide 35, 36, 40
Ettinger, Shmuel 271
Exile
  ethnic group 37-8, 40
  from Kuban to the North 195
Expulsion of ethnic groups 35, 36

Famine (1932-3) and Soviet nationality policy 177-205
Federal Republic of Germany *see* West Germany
Federalism, Soviet 48-55, 164-7
Federated Commissariats 52, 53
Feltsman, Vladimir 277
Fesenko, Dmytro 196
Finland 2, 48, 54-5, 128
Fisherman's Day, Latvia 102
Folk festivals 97-117
Foundations of Leninism (Stalin) 67
Four-Power Berlin Agreement 274
France, patriotic education in 76
French Revolution 95
Fulbright, Senator James 265
Furtseva, Ekaterina (Soviet Minister of Culture) 268

Gasprinskii, Ismail bey 223-4
Genoa Conference (1922) 49
Genocide of ethnic groups 35, 36
Georgia 51, 287
  changes in border districts 141
  ethnic assertiveness in 170
  and Jewish emigration 272
  nationalist feelings in 71-2
  participation in patriotic activities 86
  population changes 133
  Soviet identity in 87
Georgians 65, 66
German Democratic Republic *see* East Germany
German emigration 235, 237, 239, 240, 241, 242, 250, 253-4, 255
  causes of 244-7
  see also Black Sea Germans; Volga Germans
Ginsburgs, Dr George 251-2
Gitelman, Zia 261
Gogol, Nikolai 100
Goldansky, Vitalii 279
Goldman, Nahum 265
Gorbachev, Mikhail
  and Armenian claims to Nagorno-Karabakh 173
  on Black problems in the United States 64
  and the cadres policy 65
  and ethnic disturbances 89-91
  and multinationalism 286, 288, 289-90
  and nationality policies 10, 19, 20, 26-7, 68, 69, 71
  and new Soviet rituals 113, 117
  and Soviet emigration policies 235, 256
  and Soviet-Jewish emigration policies 260, 264, 277
  and Soviet multinationalism 6
Gorbunovs, Anatolijs 213
Gosplan 167
Great Patriotic War *see* Wars: World War II
Grechkina, Elsa 209
Grishin, Mikhail 279
Grishin, Viktor 278
Gromyko, Andrei 171, 273, 274

Guboglo, M. 211, 212
Guidance system on nationality policy 31-5, 38
Gypsies 29

Heroes and patriotic education 77, 79-82, 83, 85
Hint, Mati 217
Holidays and new Soviet rituals 96, 97-117
Homelands *see* National homelands
House, Colonel Edward 2
Hryn'ko, Hryhorii (Grigorii Grin'ko) 178
Hungary 15
Huseynzade, Ali bey 225

Iavors'kyi, Matvii 180, 191
Indigenization policies (*korenizatsiia*) 177
  in Ukraine 178, 192, 197
Integrationists, Soviet 9
Intelligentsia
  in Estonia 211
  Stalinization of 181
  in Ukraine 180
Internationalism and patriotic education 74, 75, 77, 78-9, 82-4
Israel
  Six-Day War (1967) 243
  and Soviet-Jewish emigration 235, 241, 243, 244, 253, 260, 262, 264-5, 267-8, 272
Ivan Kupala holiday 100-1
Ivan the Terrible 221, 222

Javits, Jacob 265
Jewish Autonomous *oblast* (JAO) 166, 267
Jewish emigration 235, 237, 239, 240, 241, 254, 255, 260-80
  causes of 242-4
  and philo-Semitism 263-4, 277-80

Jews 29, 38, 44, 64, 67, 70, 287
Johnson, Lyndon B. 265

Kabardino-Balkar ASSR/AO 169
Kaganovich, Lazar 179, 182, 194, 279
Kalmyk ASSR/AO 169
Kalnyn, Dzidra 102
Kampars, P. P. 112
Kapitanov, Ivan 279
Karachai-Cherkess AO 169
Karakalpak AO 137, 139
Karakalpak ASSR 146, 149
Karelian ASSR 131, 136, 139, 145, 146, 147, 150
Karelian SSR 130
Karelo-Finnish Republic 55, 62
Karklins, Mirdza 209
Karklins, Rasma 18, 19
Katz, Katriel 264
Kazakhstan 38, 73, 83, 166, 170-1, 289
  changes in border districts 141
  deportations to 143
  famine in 182, 198
  participation in patriotic activities 86
  population changes 132
Kazan Tatars, Sabantui holiday 106-7
Kelley, Donald R. 3
Kennedy, Robert 265
KGB (Committee of State Security) 29, 65
Khataevich, M. 183-4, 187
Khrushchev, Nikita 266
  and language policy in the Baltic republics 207-8
  nationality policy 15, 20, 42, 43, 56-7, 62
  and new Soviet rituals 96
  and patriotic education 77
  restoration of territories 64
  secret speech 169
  and Soviet-Jewish emigration policies 270
Khvylia, Andrii 190
Khvyl'ovyi, Mykola 180
Kirgiz ASSR, changes in border districts 141

Index

Kissinger, Henry 271, 273, 275
Kolbin, G. 65, 171
(Komi-) Permyak Okrug 145, 150
  creating optimum
      boundaries 160-1
Kopelev, Lev 102
Koreans 35, 37, 237
Kossior, Stanislav 188-9
Kostiuk, Hryhory 187
Kosygin, A. 269, 270
Kotov affair 195
Kozlov, Frol 269
Kuban, nationality policy under
    Stalin 184, 192-7
Kunaev, Dinmkukhed 171
Kurbatskij, G.N. 111
Kurochkin, A.V. 101, 108, 109
Kurochkin, P.K. 97
Kvitko, Lev 266

Language policies 56, 58, 59, 67,
    67-8
  in the Baltic republics 206-20
  in Georgia 170
Lapidus, Gail Warshofsky 17
Latvia 49, 71, 128, 170, 173, 287
  holidays 101-3
  and Jewish emigration 272
  participation in patriotic
    activities 86
  population by ethnic
    Russians 29
  religious practices 96
  Slavic population in 174
  Soviet language policy in 207,
    208, 210, 212-13, 214-15,
    216, 217, 218, 219
Lenin, V. I. 167, 290
  on nationalism 12-13, 32, 47-8,
    123, 164, 266
  nationality policies 5-6
  and non-Russian territories 2, 3,
    48-9
  and the Russian Federation
    49-50, 125-6
  see also Leninist nationality
    policy
Leningrad, Russian Winter
    Holiday in 98-9
Leninist nationality policy 9-23
  evolution of 14-17
  style of 17-19, 20
Levanon, Nechemiah 264-5
Ligachev, Yegor 65-6, 90-1
Ligo (Yanov's Day) holiday 101-3
Lithuania 44, 49, 71, 128, 170,
    173, 287
  participation in patriotic
    activities 86
  Slavic population 174
  Soviet language policy 207,
    209-10, 215, 216-17,
    217-18, 219
Lloyd George, David 49
Lobacheva, N. P. 104

Magdeev, Professor M. 107
Makhnovists 190-1, 192
Malanka holiday 108-9
Marx, Karl 75
  on ethnic oppression 31
  on nationalism 11-12, 47, 48
Marxism
  on inequality of ethnic
    groups 40
  and nationalism 5, 32, 123, 286
  and the Soviet federal
    system 167-8
"Marxism and the National and
    Colonial Question''
    (Lenin) 48
Maslenitsa (Shrovetide)
    holiday 100, 115
Matrosov, Aleksandr 82
Matuszewski, Daniel 288-9
Mel'nikov, M. N. 115
Midsummer Night holiday 100-1
Mirrakhimov, Dr M. 105
Moldavia 287
  holidays 101, 108-10
  Ivan Kupala holiday 101
  language 287
  participation in patriotic
    activities 86
  population changes 132
  religious practices 96
  Soviet identity in 87
Moldavian ASSR 140, 141
Molotov, Polina 262
Molotov, Viacheslav 181, 182
Mordvinian ASSR 144, 145, 146,
    147-8, 150

hypothetical formation
  of 158-60
Moroz, Valentin 114
Multinationalism, management of
  1917-1985 1-7
  since 1985 286-91
Muslim national Communism 228
Muslim republics
  cadres policy in 64, 66, 71
  participation in patriotic
    activities 86-7
  traditional customs 113
Muslims, Soviet 128, 221-32, 291
  numbers of 221
MVD (Minister of the Interior) 29

Naadum Holiday of Independence,
  Tuva 110-11
Nagorno-Karabakh AO 90, 163,
  171-3, 287
  population changes 133
Nasser, G. 268
National homelands and regional
  population redistribution
  121-61
National security and the Soviet
  federal system 167, 168-70
National-territorial
  autonomy 13-14
Navruz holiday (Central
  Asia) 103-6
New Year holidays 110
Nixon, Richard M. 275
Nizhni Tagil, Sabantui
  holiday 107
NKVD (People's Commissariat for
  Internal Affairs) 29
North Caucasus 128
  autonomous subunits of 144,
    145, 146, 148, 149, 150, 151
  famine of 1932-3 182, 185, 189,
    192-7
  Muslims in 226-7
Nudel, Ida 277
Nullification of ethnic groups 36,
  38, 40

OGPU (United State Political
  Administration) 29

Orthodox Church
  holidays 108
  Ukrainian 180
Ostpolitik and Soviet-German
  emigration 246, 247

Pamyat' (nationalist
  organization) 278-80, 289
Pan-Turkism 223-4, 226, 231
Panov, Valery and Galina 272-3,
  276
"Paper Flowers"
  (Petrukhov) 114-15
Patriotic education and Soviet
  state identity 73-93
Patriotism, definition of
  Soviet 74-5
Pelkaus, E. 213
People's Commissariat of
  Nationalities 49-50
Perestroika
  and nationality policy 19, 20,
    70-2, 289
  and patriotic education 91
Permyak Okrug *see* (Komi-)
  Permyak Okrug
Peters, Janis 214-15
Petliura, Semen 193, 194
Petliurists 190-1, 192
Petrovs'kyi, Hryhorii 178
Petrukhov, A. 114-15
Plato 76
Plesovskikh, V. N. 111
Pokrovskii, M. N. 177
Poland 4, 15, 57, 128
  and Soviet Germans 245, 246
Polish Jews 242, 243
Poltev, A. 218
Ponomarev, Boris 269, 278
Population redistribution,
  regional, and national
  homelands 121-61
Pospielovsky, Dimitry 279
Postyshev, Pavel 187-8, 190-2,
  195, 197
Prescription of ethnic
  groups 40-1, 42
Preservation of national groups 37
Publication policy in the Baltic
  republics 210-12, 214, 216

Index

Pugo, Boris 216
Punished nations/people 29, 35, 64, 143, 169
Pushkin, Alexander 231

Rakhimov, A. M. 104
Rashidov, Sharif 209
Rasulzade, Mammed Emin 225, 226
Reindeer Holiday 112
Religion and Muslim republics 86–7
Remizov, I. S. 97
Republic Commissariats 52, 53
Resettlement of ethnic groups 36, 37
Reykjavik summit 277
Rigby, T. H. 17
Rituals
  new 94–120
  patriotic 77–8
Rockefeller, Nelson 265
Romania 4, 57
Romanov, Grigory 278
Roses, Holiday of 102
RSFSR (Russian Soviet Federal Socialist Republic) 6
  changes in border districts 141
  and Jewish emigration 272, 276
  and patriotic education 85–6
  population redistribution 131, 143, 149–51
  Soviet identity in 87
Rudnev, V. A. 98
Rusk, Dean 265
Russian Federation 5, 49, 50, 51
Russian language 42, 58, 59, 67–8, 125, 174
  in the Baltic republics 206–20
Russian nationalists 71
  Pamyat' 278–80, 289
  "Russian New Right" movement 279
Russians
  in autonomous subunits 130
  dispersal to non-Russian territories 143
Russification policies 51, 289
  and Brezhnev-style Soviet patriotism 79
  linguistic 67–8
  and new Soviet rituals 116
  and Soviet patriotism 79
  under Lenin 5–6

Sabantui holiday 106–7
Sakharov, Andrei 43
SALT (Strategic Arms Limitation Talks) 273, 274
Sblizhenie (rapprochement) of nations 5, 13, 16, 19, 69, 70, 71, 231
Schifter, Richard 277–8
Schroeter, Leonard 264–5, 270
Secession, rights of 54, 57, 66
Security *see* National security
Segregationists, Soviet 9
Semenov, P. G. 168
Shagaa holiday 110
Shcharansky, Natan 275, 277
Shcherbakov, Alexander 279
Shcherbitsky, V. V. 271, 278
Sheboldaev, Boris 195, 196
Shelest, Piotr 271
Shrovetide (Maslenitsa) holiday 100, 115
Shultz, George 277, 279
Shums'kyi, Oleksander 180
Siberia 287
  autonomous subunits of 145, 146, 147, 149
  holidays 111–12, 115
Simis, Konstantin 57
Sinyavsky ("Abram Tertz") 268
Skrypnyk, Mykola 178, 190, 191
Sliianie (fusion) of nations 5, 13, 15, 153, 286, 288
Smirnov, Savvati 211–12
Smith, Gordon 2–3
Snesarev, G. P. 104
Sociological studies in ethnic expression 87–9
Solzhenitsyn, Alexander 170
Spanish Civil War 95
Spataru, G. I. 109
Stalin, Joseph 59
  and anti-Semitism 266
  and the federal structure 50–1, 127
  and Finland 48, 54–5

Georgian and Armenian
  policies 63, 65, 66
 invasion of non-Russian
  territories 4
 and Leninist nationality
  policy 14–15, 20
 on national culture 66, 67
 and national-territorial
  autonomy 13
 nationality policies 14–15, 32,
  48, 50, 62, 68–9, 71
 religious policies 96
 on rights to secede 52, 54
 Russification policy 5
 and the Soviet federal
  system 167–8, 168–9
 and Soviet Germans 245
 and Soviet-Jewish emigration
  policy 243
 and Soviet Muslims 225, 227–8
 Ukrainian policies 177–94, 196,
  197–8
Sudrabkaln, Jan 103
Sukhareva, O. A. 104
Sultangaliev, Mir Said 228–9, 231
Susanin, Ivan 82
Suslov, Mikhail 269–70, 274,
  276–7, 279
Svirsky, Grigory 266–7
Syria and Soviet anti-Zionism 268

Tadzhikistan 83
 changes in border districts 141
 Navruz holiday 103, 104, 105
 population changes 133
Tarrow, Sidney 18
Tartu 3
Tatar ASSR 131, 136, 146, 150
Tatars 52, 54, 57, 66, 287; *see also*
  Crimean/Kazan/Volga
  Tatars
Tatu, Michael 266
Territorial autonomy, principle
  of 62, 63–4
Territorial bureaucracy and
  nationality policy 18
Territorial units as nationality
  policy 163–76
Theory of Soviet nationality
  policies 24–46

Tokarev, S. A. 112
Toporov, V. 217–18
Transcaucasia 2, 13, 20, 28, 71
 autonomous subunits of 145,
  146, 148–9
 Kurds of 37
 Muslims in 222, 226, 229
 and the Russian Federation 51
Transcaucasian Federated Soviet
  Socialist Republic 51, 53,
  132
Treaty of Union (1922) 53
Trotsky, Leon 94, 96
Tsarist Russia
 German colonists in 244
 Muslims in 221–5
Tsuba, Ivan 80
Turdyev, Saidkul 83
Turkey 232
Turkic languages 221, 223–4, 226,
  230, 231, 232
Turkism 223–4
Turkmen SSR
 changes in border districts 141
 population changes 133
Tuva 35
 holidays 110–11
Tvardovsky, Alexander 266

Udmurt ASSR 145, 146, 150
Ukraine 2, 13, 49, 50, 54, 291
 administrative subunits 139–40,
  141
 holidays 100–1, 108–10, 113
 and Jewish emigration 276
 nationality policies under
  Stalin 177–94, 196, 197–8
 nomenklatura 72
 participation in patriotic
  activities 86
 population changes 132
 religious practices 96
 and the Russian Federation 50,
  51
 and Soviet language policies 213
 UN delegates 165
 and World War II 169
Ukrainian nationalism 271
Ukrainians 67–8, 237
Ulam, Adam 274

United Nations 66
United States
  Gorbachev on Black problems 64
  Jackson–Vanik amendment 260, 274–5
  and Soviet emigration policies 235, 240, 241, 242, 244, 249–50, 254
  and Soviet-Jewish emigrants 260, 265, 271, 273, 274–6, 277–8
Urazmanova, R. K. 113
Ustaev, Sh. U. 104
Uzbekistan (Uzbek SSR) 28, 65, 73, 83, 84
  changes in border districts 141
  holidays 113
  Navruz holiday 104
  participation in patriotic activities 86
  and patriotism 81, 82
  population changes 133
  Soviet identity in 87

Veresaev, Vikentii 94, 96
Verkovich, V. 218
Volga-German ASSR 131, 136
  wartime territorial changes 169
Volga Germans 29, 37, 43, 170–1, 287
  deportation of 143
  reconsideration of status of 267
  and Soviet emigration policies 244, 245, 246–7, 253
Volga Tatars 221, 222, 224, 226, 229, 287
Volga-Urals 128, 145, 146, 147–8, 151
Volobuiev, Mykhailo 180
Voznesensky, Andrei 266

War games 84
Wars
  Basmachi Wars (Central Asia) 81–2
  Civil War 2, 3, 4, 6, 170
  World War I 41–2
  World War II 6, 42, 55, 64, 65, 82–4, 287
    heroes 80–1, 82
    and population redistribution 142, 143, 147, 151, 169
    and territorial changes 169
West Germany and Soviet-German emigrants 235, 240–2, 246, 250, 253, 254
White, Lee 265
Whitehead, John 278
Wilson, Woodrow 2, 48
Winter Holiday, Russian 98–9, 115, 116

Yakovlev, Alexandr 175
Yanov, Alexander 279
Yegorychev, N. G. 268
Yepishev, A. 75, 278
Yevtushenko, Evgenii 266
Youth programmes, patriotic and internationalist education 73–93
Yvarova, Irina 108

Zagladin, Vadim 269
Zaikov, Lev N. 173
Zakovich, H. M. 112
Zaslavsky, Victor 272
Zatons'kyi, Volodymyr 190
Zayen (Syrian prime minister) 268
Zhdanov, Andre 279
Zhukovskaia, N. 218
Ziedonis, Imants 213
Zimmerwald plotters 47–8
Zinoviev, G. 70
Zionism, Soviet anti- 261, 264, 267–8, 269–70, 277, 280
Zivs, S. L. 277
Zlatkovskaia, Tat'iana 108